Assignments in Exposition

8th EDITION

Louise E. Rorabacher

Georgia Dunbar

1817

HARPER & ROW, PUBLISHERS, New York
Cambridge, Philadelphia, San Francisco,
London, Mexico City, São Paulo, Singapore, Sydney

Sponsoring Editor: Phillip Leininger
Project Editor: Brigitte Pelner
Text and Cover Design: Frances Tilley
Photo Research: Mira Schachne
Production: Marion A. Palen
Compositor: ComCom Division of Haddon Craftsmen, Inc.
Printer and Binder: R. R. Donnelley & Sons Company

Assignments in Exposition, Eighth Edition

Copyright © 1985 by Louise E. Rorabacher and Georgia Dunbar

Library of Congress Cataloging in Publication Data

Rorabacher, Louise Elizabeth, 1906–
  Assignments in exposition.

  Includes indexes.
  1. Exposition (Rhetoric) 2. English language—
Rhetoric. 3. College readers. I. Dunbar, Georgia
Dolfield Sherwood, 1919–   . II. Title.
PE1429.R5 1985   808'.042   84-12924
ISBN 0-06-045577-2

84 85 86 87 88 9 8 7 6 5 4 3 2 1

Contents

---

*Examples marked with an asterisk have marginal notes on structure.

iii

Unit 3:   Narration   39

Unit 4:   Exemplification   57

Unit 14: Definition 265

Acknowledgments

Mortimer J. Adler, "Book Owners"—from "How to Mark a Book," first published in *Saturday Review,* July 6, 1940. Reprinted by permission of Saturday Review-World.

Americana Encyclopedia, "Hellbender"—from the *Encyclopedia Americana,* 1969 edition.

Robert Ardrey, "Light from an Ape's Jaw"—Excerpt from *African Genesis* by Robert Ardrey. Copyright © 1961 by Literat S. A. Reprinted by permission of Atheneum Publishers.

Arthur Ashe, "An Open Letter to Black Parents"—© 1977 by The New York Times Company. Reprinted by permission.

Isaac Asimov, "Male Humor"—Copyright © 1983 by The New York Times Company. Reprinted by permission.

Russell Baker, "The Boy Who Came to Supper"—Copyright © 1980 by The New York Times Company. Reprinted by permission.

Donald Bell, "Conflicting Interests"—Copyright © 1983 by The New York Times Company. Reprinted by permission.

Lerone Bennett, Jr., "Benjamin Banneker"—from Lerone Bennett, Jr., *Before the Mayflower: A History of the Negro in America 1619–1964* (revised edition). Copyright © 1961, 1962, 1964 by Johnson Publishing Company, Inc.

Dwight Bolinger, "We Reduced the Size Because We Didn't Want to Increase the Price"—from Dwight Bolinger, *Language the Loaded Weapon.* Copyright © 1980 by Longman.

Jane Brody, "Mental Depression"—Copyright © 1977 The New York Times Company. Reprinted by permission.

Jacob Bronowski, "A Metaphor Used Twice"—from Jacob Bronowski, *Science and Human Values.* Copyright © 1956, 1965, J. Bronowski. Reprinted by permission of Julian Messner, a division of Simon & Schuster.

Anthony Burgess, "Splitting the Word"—from Anthony Burgess, *Language Made Plain,* The English Universities Press. 1964. Copyright © by Anthony Burgess.

Tom Carson, "David Bowie Looks Back in Horror"—in the *Village Voice,* 8–14 October 1980. Reprinted by permission.

John Cohen, "The Language of Uncertainty"—from John Cohen, "Subjective Probability," copyright © 1957 by Scientific American, Inc. All rights reserved.

Dorothy Collier, "Where Is My Child?"—from the *Sunday Times,* London, 13 November 1977.

Pat Conroy, "Death of an Island" and "Yamacraw"—from *The Water Is Wide* by Pat Conroy. Copyright © 1972 by Pat Conroy. Reprinted by permission of Houghton Mifflin Company.

Guy Davenport, "Trees"—*Excerpted from: The Geography of the Imagination,* Forty Essays by Guy Davenport, © 1981 by Guy Davenport. Published by North Point Press. All rights reserved. Reprinted by permission.

Howard Gardner, "Are Television's Effects Due to Television?"—from Howard Gardner, *Art, Mind, and Brain.* Copyright © 1982 by Howard Gardner. Reprinted by permission of Basic Books, Inc.

Martin Gardner, "The Holes in Black Holes"—Reprinted with permission from *The New York Review of Books.* Copyright © 1977 Nyrev, Inc.

Georgie Anne Geyer, "Living on the Altiplano"—from Georgia Anne Geyer, "Peru's Inca Renaissance," in "Reports: Washington, Hong Kong, Peru," *The Atlantic Monthly,* November 1967. Copyright © 1967 by the Atlantic Monthly Company, Boston, Mass. Reprinted with permission.

Acknowledgments are continued on page 388.

Preface

An effective essay, like a well-built house, has a firm structural foundation. *Assignments in Exposition* emphasizes the basic structural patterns of organization that are fundamental to effective writing and logical thinking. These patterns do not limit our creative ability. Instead, like the foundations and framework of a house, they act as a support, liberating our imaginations to discover new approaches and fresh insights.

Assignments in Exposition, Eighth Edition, offers these major features:

a full unit on each basic structural pattern

111 selections of writing in which one or more patterns may be examined

31 new in this edition

85 by a wide variety of published writers

26 by good student writers—a special feature of this book, all either complete essays or self-contained excerpts

each short enough to be seen as a structural whole and to be analyzed in a class period

many topics likely to spark class discussion

a new unit on exemplification

a new unit on quoting, paraphrasing, and summarizing

a largely new unit on inductive and deductive reasoning, combining two units from earlier editions for easier comprehension

a new unit with seven "classic" essays showing various combinations of patterns—

four, originally delivered as speeches, providing material for comparison and contrast of the structures and methods of persuasive argument

rough drafts of President Kennedy's inaugural address, giving valuable insights into the composing process

Each unit offers these features:

an introduction (newly revised to stimulate readers' curiosity)
a definition of the pattern
step-by-step directions on how—and how not—to use the pattern
examples of the pattern in published writing and good student writing
an introduction (new in this edition) to the examples, giving cross-references to selections elsewhere in the book in which the pattern appears in combination with one or more other patterns
headnotes for the examples with information on the writers, often with cross-references to selections in which the writers present a different view on the same topic or use a different pattern
marginal notes for one example indicating the writer's use of the pattern under discussion
questions to direct attention to specific points in the example and to encourage close reading and class discussion
writing assignments for which the particular pattern would be appropriate, designed to encourage peer evaluation, collaborative criticism, and awareness of audience

The book also offers these features:

eight photographs with questions (new in this edition) to test the readers' accuracy of observation and with topics for discussion and for writing assignments
an opening unit with a thorough discussion of the composing process, from prewriting through revision
a descriptive table of contents (new in this edition)
a thematic table of contents (revised and developed in this edition)
an author and subject index with special marking (new in this edition) to indicate rhetorical terms
easy reference to each example by an identifying letter as well as the unit number; numbered lines in all examples to make precise references easy
a flexible sequence of units adaptable to the needs and interests of different classes and courses
information (revised to accord with the new policy of 1982) on the MLA system of documenting research and also information on the APA system
an instructor's manual with further information and suggestions for using the book

*   *   *   *   *   *   *   *   *

Dr. Rorabacher ended her preface to the fifth edition by thanking her former students at the University of Illinois, Purdue University, and Western Carolina University, the *Green Cauldron,* a magazine of freshman writing at the University of Illinois, Professor Janet McNary of South Carolina State College at Orangeburg, Dr. Mildred Martin of Bucknell University, Mrs. John Karling of West Lafayette, Indiana, and Miss Carol Lawrence of Cullowhee, North Carolina. As the reviser of the sixth and seventh editions and now of the eighth, all direct descendants of the fifth, I too thank all those named, for I have been their beneficiary.

Many people have generously given advice to guide us in preparing this edition, and I would particularly like to thank the following (listed alphabetically): Professors Evan Antone of the University of Texas at El Paso, D. A. Bartlett of the University of Alaska, Elizabeth S. Byers of Virginia Polytechnic Institute, Kathy A. De Ste Croix of Angelo State University, Herbert S. Donow of Southern Illinois University at Carbondale, Sister Mary Ely of Rosary College, Mary Ann Emery of the University of Wisconsin, Sylvia H. Gamboa of the College of Charleston, Alan J. Glossner of Monroe Community College, L. D. Groski of La Roche College, Ken Hammes of Cisco Junior College, James Hines of Saddleback College, Joseph Keller of Iowa Central Community College, Russell Long of Tarleton State University, Helen Maloney of Tidewater Community College, Debra Munn of Northwest Community College, Patsy B. Perry of North Carolina Central University, Monty Pitner of Montgomery College, Rockville, Maryland, Martin Ranft of Harcum Junior College, Manuel Schonhorn of Southern Illinois University at Carbondale, R. Baird Shuman of the University of Illinois at Urbana, Caroline Smith of Independence Community College, William R. Thurman, Jr., of Georgia Southwestern College, James Tichenor of Emory University, Edward L. Tucker of Virginia Polytechnic Institute, Arthur Wagner of Macomb College, and Terry S. Wallace of Harrisburg Area Community College.

In addition, I thank all my own students at Hofstra University, Borough of Manhattan Community College (CUNY), and the Hofstra–District 65 Institute of Labor Studies; the many colleagues and friends at Hofstra and Adelphi Universities who gave invaluable help in finding appropriate student papers, particularly Professors Donald Wolf, Gloria Beckerman, Robert Sargent, Hyman Enzer, Sandra Enzer, and Robert Keane; the many members of the Harper & Row staff who have been unfailingly helpful and encouraging throughout the many complexities of producing this edition, most notably Phillip Leininger and Brigitte Pelner; and last but most important, Dr. Rorabacher herself, who so generously gave me a free hand and a fine book—any flaws in this edition are mine, but the virtues are hers.

GEORGIA DUNBAR

UNIT 1

The Fundamentals of Writing

What makes one of the following student papers more effective than the other?

The two writers have the same purpose and use the same kinds of material. They have corrected all their errors in spelling, grammar, and punctuation. Nevertheless, one paper is clearly more effective than the other. Why?

The three essentials for effective writing are **mechanical correctness** (standard grammar, spelling, punctuation, and general form), **content** (something to say), and **organization** (a structure for presenting the content). Of these, organization is the most important. We can write grammatically correct sentences and present fascinating material, but if our remarks are disorganized, seem unrelated to each other, and do not contribute to our main point, our readers will be confused and will misunderstand us.

What makes the organization of Y's paper more effective than X's?

Note: These papers were written as homework after the first class meeting of the fall term, in which the students interviewed each other in small groups. Each then wrote a paper about someone in his or her group and at the next class meeting read it aloud to introduce that student to the rest of the class.

My Interview with Michael

Student X

I would like to introduce Michael. I really enjoyed interviewing him. He is a great guy. He played a lot of basketball in high school and hopes to go out for the team, and he likes dramatics a lot, too. He played the lead in *Death of a Salesman* in his senior year in high school. We read that play in my senior English class, and it's very sad. Michael 5

comes from Texas and agrees with me that living in the dorms is great.
Last summer he and a friend backpacked in Colorado. The scenery in
the Rockies must be great. I would like to go there sometime, especially
for the skiing. Right now, Michael thinks he will probably major in
accounting because that field offers the best chances for a career these 10
days, but maybe he will change his mind when he has had more time
to look over the possibilities.

He wants to get a job on campus because that would be convenient.
He hopes to save up enough to get a car. A car is practically a necessity
when you're living in the dorms here. At home I can borrow my 15
mother's car a lot, but here I have to hitch rides with friends, and
because I'm only a freshman I don't know a lot of people here yet.
Michael is taking the same psych course I am. It's a great course to take
because knowing something about people is always helpful, whatever
you do in later life. Michael's family lives in Texas, and Michael grew 20
up there, but he was born in New Jersey. He has two sisters and a
brother.

If he can't get a job on campus, Michael will try to get one at
McDonald's because it's nearby. He worked at a McDonald's in Texas
for a month last summer. He knows a lot about music and plays a guitar. 25
He also knows a lot about rocks. While he was in Colorado he collected
a lot of different ones. I said I thought he might major in geology.

Michael's brother graduated from a college in California last year
and is now working in Los Angeles. If Michael ever visits him he
should go to see Disneyland. It's a great place for grown-ups as well as 30
children. He likes to read science fiction and histories and biographies
about the Civil War. At the end of the interview I said I would like to
learn the basic fingering for the guitar, and maybe I'll ask Michael to
teach me.

Jane

Student Y

I would like to introduce Jane, a commuting student, whose biggest
interest is science. In her senior year in high school she organized the
Chemistry Club and was elected president. She also set up a small lab
of her own in a corner of her family's garage. She plans to major in
chemistry and become a research scientist, and so she foresees many 5
years of study ahead of her.

Her other interests include sports, popular music, and travel. In
high school she played on the girls' basketball team, but she does not
think that she will have time to go out for the team here. She has a large
collection of albums, particularly of British rock groups. Last summer 10
she combined her interests in music and travel and went to England for

two weeks where she was able to see some of her favorite groups perform.

Jane, like most students these days, needs money for college expenses, and she is looking for a part-time job. She has had some experience already, having worked as a counselor at a day camp last summer and in the post office during the Christmas rush last winter.

Jane lives with her family about ten miles from the campus, and she grew up in this part of the state. She has an older sister and a younger brother. Her sister shares Jane's interest in science and is now in medical school, but her twelve-year-old brother, David, has so far shown no interest in anything but baseball and his stamp collection. Jane hopes to convert him before too long. With a sister who is such a dedicated scientist, young David will probably soon be trading his stamp collection for a microscope.

* * *

In organization, the two essays differ sharply. X seems to have had no plan in mind and hops from one topic to another and back again, probably in the way the conversation hopped around. In the first third we are told about Michael's extracurricular activities in high school, his family home, his summer vacation trip, and then his probable choice of major, with no suggestion that these are in any way related to each other. This chaotic jumble continues throughout the paper, and the ending is the author's purely personal wish to learn to play the guitar. Although at first glance X's paper seems to have conventional paragraphs, a closer look shows that the paragraph divisions have no connection with the content. Apparently, X started a new paragraph when enough paper had been covered to *look* like a paragraph. Properly organized, with important points emphasized and less important ones subordinated in a logical order, the information on Michael could have made an interesting picture of someone with a variety of experiences and activities. The poor organization has spoiled it.

The paper by Y is only two-thirds as long but says much more because the information is grouped logically. Each of Y's paragraphs begins with a clear indication of its general topic, and the rest of the paragraph develops that topic. Y begins with Jane's main interest in college—the one that will take the greatest part of her time and effort —goes on to her other interests, then to her need to find a job, and finally to her family background. At the end of the paper, Y makes information on Jane's brother and sister seem relevant by connecting it to Jane's interest in science. The ending therefore helps to unify the paper by reminding readers of the point established.

The handling of the content also differs in the two papers. X has plenty of information on Michael but seems almost as much interested in telling about X. For this assignment, to introduce Michael to the class, much of X's paper is irrelevant. Another weakness that suggests carelessness is X's frequent use of vague words, such as "a lot" and "great," which are almost meaningless here. Y, on the other hand, concentrates entirely on Jane, mentioning Jane's brother and sister only in order to relate them to Jane's interest in science.

To sum up, X and Y had exactly the same assignment and the same kinds of information for their material. By selecting and organizing the information and sticking to the subject, Y produced a satisfactory paper that fulfilled the assignment, but X did not.

With even the most specific assignment, you have many choices for words and for the structures of your sentences and paragraphs. An overall plan will guide you to make the best choices. Moreover, as you jot down notes for a plan with your material at hand, the sight of your notes will suggest new insights into the material—new connections and interpretations that may strengthen and enrich your paper.

Whenever you write, make what you have to say effective by planning how to present it.

*   *   *   *   *   *   *   *   *

COMPOSING: GATHERING AND SELECTING MATERIAL

Given a writing assignment, what do you do first? Whatever the success of your past procedures, the best way to begin to write is by not writing.

For the sake of discussion, imagine that you are a freshman and have two days to write an essay of about 500 words on a typical day in your first week as a college student. Imagine, also, that your instructor plans to give copies of the essays written by your class to the guidance counselors of several high schools where the juniors and seniors will read them to get up-to-date, firsthand information on what to expect in college.

1. **Determining constraints.** First think over the assignment and the exact nature of the constraints that are part of it—the limitations placed on you not only by the deadline and required length but, more important, by your subject, general purpose, and intended readers. Make sure that you understand precisely what and who these are. If you have any doubts, ask your instructor for clarification. (For this imaginary assignment, the constraints have been spelled out.)

2. **Gathering material.** For many assignments, gathering material may include research in the library, laboratory experiments, interviews, or a survey of opinion. For this imaginary assignment, your memories are your material, but whatever the sources, the general purpose is the same—to gather as much as possible in the time available. For this assignment, think over what your experience at college has been like so far, and, at the same time, jot down notes. Do not be selective or critical. What seems trivial now may seem significant later. Give yourself ample opportunity for two very different kinds of think-

ing—logical analysis and the free-wheeling association of brainstorming. Because our minds are wonderfully complex, we can switch back and forth between the two many times in a few moments, with each kind contributing to the other. In the first, we concentrate on the subject and systematically examine all its parts and purposes. In the second, we let our minds range freely over and around the subject, even off it, and ideas seem to pop up without our conscious search. Never be in such a hurry that you limit yourself to the logic of the first kind of thinking; always take advantage of the imaginative insights of the second.

With both kinds of thinking, be sure to take short notes on scratch paper—the shorter the better, perhaps only a word or two for each or a symbol of some kind, just enough to serve as a reminder later. The notes will free you of the burden of remembering, and, even more important, seeing several together may suggest new associations that in turn may suggest new thoughts and interpretations. This is why your notes should be short enough for you to read several at a glance. Sight can give us insight.

If your mind goes blank, as it will sometimes, try to see your subject from your readers' point of view. Jog your imagination with questions:

What do your readers probably already know about your subject?
What do they probably not know about it?
What opinions may they now have about it?
What do you think will be most valuable or interesting in it for them and why?

Don't stop when you think you have enough for the assignment. The more material you have to choose from, the more you can make your paper a selection of the very best. Continue until you have exhausted the possibilities.

3. Grouping your material. Next, look over your jottings and consider the same questions again, but this time keep your specific purpose in mind. In our imagined case, your purpose is to inform your readers. Make a fresh list of everything in your notes that could possibly be of any help in accomplishing your purpose, particularly your answers to the fourth question. Then consider these questions:

What is the exact nature of each item?
To which items, if any, is each related and how?
Under what headings can the items be grouped? (For this imagined assignment, some headings might indicate the nature of your activities, such as "recreation" and "classes"; others might indicate the time of day, the location, the number of people involved, and so on.)
What combinations of headings can you think of? ("Morning classes" or "dorm room late night snacks" might be appropriate for this assignment.)
What subdivisions and sub-subdivisions can you think of? (For example, under "morning classes" you might list their size, academic level, location, and type, such as discussion, laboratory, or lecture.)

As you make notes on all these groupings, additional memories and ideas may occur to you. Be sure to jot these down, too, and sort them under headings.

4. Choosing and defining your main point. To hold your readers' attention, your essay must have a main point, a controlling idea—the fact, opinion, or emotion that you most want your readers to recognize in your material and to understand and remember. When you have thought of as many groupings as you can, begin to narrow your subject by considering these questions in relation to your purpose. In this imaginary assignment, since your purpose is to inform your readers, use these questions to find the information you think they will consider most useful and interesting:

What general parts of your material do you want your readers to notice most? what specific parts?
What opinions do you want them to form?
What interests you most in your material? (You are more likely to be able to interest your readers in something you find interesting.)

Whatever you most want your readers to see in your material will be your main point. For example, for this imaginary assignment, you might want them to see that college level work is more difficult than work in high school or that your program is more demanding than is suggested by the number of hours you spend in class.

When you have chosen a main point, sharpen your thinking by assuming that your readers will be difficult to convince so that your main point must be presented clearly and supported with solid evidence. To make it definite in your own mind, try on scratch paper to express it in as few words as you can, preferably in a single sentence. This will be the rough draft of the **thesis statement** for your paper. A thesis is a proposition, the main point that a writer not only presents and explains but defends throughout a piece of writing. In the thesis statement, the writer is, in effect, saying, "I believe this is true and hope to make my readers agree or at least give it serious consideration."

In most expository writing, you will find the thesis directly stated, but sometimes it is only implied. (There are examples of both methods in this book.) Whichever way you present it, your thesis will determine what material you use in your essay and how you organize it.

Do not, however, close your mind to making changes in your thesis. At every stage in composing your essay, test the validity of your thesis in relation to the particular part of the material you are considering. You may decide to modify it or even reject it entirely and start again. Keep your mind open to new ideas and new interpretations.

Note: With many writing assignments, particularly essay examinations, you will be given a thesis and expected to find material to support it, but the procedures for gathering and sorting the material are the same, as are those for organizing it.

5. Organizing the main body. With your readers and thesis in mind, consider three more questions:

What general background information will your readers need to understand your thesis?
What specific information will they need to understand it?
What information, general or specific, will they need to become convinced that your thesis is valid or at least deserves serious consideration?

For our imaginary assignment, you would need to write little or nothing about a typical day in high school because your readers are familiar with that, but you would have to explain such things as the lists of readings some of your instructors have given you and the frequency and nature of your writing assignments. Mark in your notes all the items that directly explain and support your thesis. If you find many, make a fresh list so that you can see them more easily. These items will form the main body of your paper.

When you believe that you have found every usable item, ask yourself how you can best organize them to make your thesis clear, interesting, and convincing for your readers. On more scratch paper, try out as many patterns of organization as you can imagine. If you see any items that duplicate others or seem weak or not very relevant, eliminate them. You may find it helpful, if time permits, to express your thoughts in rough sentences, as well as in notes. Constructing sentences may sharpen your thinking, but do not let them freeze your ideas into a permanent form. Keep your mind open to new insights and interpretations. Such changes are all part of the two kinds of thinking required for writing. Nothing is final until you hand in your paper.

Important: If at this stage you fear that you will not have enough material for a paper of the required length, go over all your notes in close detail, rethink them from every angle, discuss your thesis with friends, and ask for their suggestions. You may think of material you overlooked before or have new insights into what you have already gathered. Whatever you find, add it to your notes. Achieve the required length by going more deeply into material that contributes to your thesis, **not** merely by adding words.

5-a. The chronological pattern. This is the simplest pattern. With it, a list of points to cover for the imaginary assignment might look like this:

(1) Getting up
(2) Washing and dressing
(3) Eating breakfast
(4) Attending English class
(5) Studying in the library
(6) Having coffee with friends
(7) Attending economics class
(8) Eating lunch
(9) Working in chemistry lab
(10) Having soda with friends
(11) Working at a part-time job
(12) Eating dinner
(13) Studying in room
(14) Telephoning a friend
(15) Watching TV
(16) Having a snack
(17) Undressing and washing
(18) Going to bed

This covers your day, but the small details seem rather pointless when set down one after another. If you group them into larger units of related items, they will be more manageable. Your plan may now look like this:

I. Early morning activities
  A. Getting up
  B. Washing and dressing
  C. Eating breakfast
  D. Attending English class
II. Late morning activities
  A. Studying in library
  B. Having coffee with friends
  C. Attending economics class
  D. Eating lunch

III. Afternoon activities
  A. Working in chemistry lab
  B. Having soda with friends
IV. Early evening activities
  A. Eating dinner
  B. Studying in room
V. Late evening activities
  A. Telephoning a friend
  B. Watching TV
  C. Having a snack
  D. Undressing and washing
  E. Going to bed

The items and their order have been left unchanged, but now, instead of handling eighteen small items, you are planning in terms of four large sections made up of varying numbers of subpoints. This new perspective shows the relative importance of the parts of your material and will help your readers in following your train of thought and you in composing the main body.

5-b. Other patterns of overall organization. The use of other patterns depends on the nature and relative importance of the material. Items such as getting up, going to bed, and eating, which are routine in everyone's life, may be handled together briefly or even omitted. Others, such as your classes and study periods, are more important and are special characteristics of academic life. Still others are the social contacts that enliven college routine. If you follow this line of thought, your main headings might be:

I. Routine Activities
II. Academic Activities
III. Recreation

(You can supply the appropriate subpoints under each from the original list.)

5-c. Patterns for main headings. A glance at this new list reveals that there is no built-in sequence, as there was with the chronological pattern. Depending on your material, your main point, and your readers' needs and interests, you may choose among many basic patterns:

(1) from the known to the unknown
(2) from the simple to the complex
(3) from the specific to the general (see Unit 13)
(4) from the general to the specific (see Unit 13)
(5) from the less important to the more important

For this imaginary assignment, you might choose the first pattern and start by describing the routine activities briefly to get them out of the way since your readers already have a general knowledge of them. Which of the two remaining topics to take next depends on what you want to emphasize. If you think that academic activities are more important to your readers, emphasize them by writing last and longest on your classes and assignments. If you think that the chances for socializing in college are more important to your readers, discuss these last. With anything you write, always arrange your main points, no matter how many you have, in an ascending order of difficulty or importance. Your readers will expect that order and will feel let down if you anti-climactically fire your smaller guns after your larger ones.

5-d. Patterns for subpoints. Good preliminary organization involves not only determining the main points and their logical arrangement but also discriminating carefully among them. What is really of first importance? What is second? and so on. In the plan to make the main headings for this imaginary assignment "routine activities," "academic activities," and "recreation," an outline of the first division might have these subheadings:

I Routine Activities
   A. Preparations for the day
      1. Getting up
      2. Washing and dressing
      3. Straightening room
   B. Eating and drinking
      1. Regular meals
      2. Snacks
   C. Preparations for the night
      1. Undressing and washing
      2. Listening to the late news
      3. Going to bed

(For many of these you will think of sub-points and even sub-sub-sub-points.)

For a short paper with uncomplicated subject matter you may not need a formal outline, but a list showing the relative importance of your material will help you keep a sense of proportion as you write, and then you will not give too much space to a minor point or too little to a major one.

COMPOSING: WRITING AND REVISING ROUGH DRAFTS

When you have chosen what appears to be the best arrangement for your material, you are ready to write a rough draft of the whole paper. Everything that you have listed should lead your readers to conclude that your thesis is valid or that, at the very least, it deserves their serious consideration. To make sure of this, you must compose a beginning that will catch their attention and start them on the right track and an ending that will be as convincing as you can make it.

1. The ending is what readers are likely to remember best, simply because it comes at the end—your last words with nothing following to overshadow them or alter their meaning. You will be wise, therefore, to plan now what you want to say at the end of the paper—not the precise words and sentences, but the main thought, the essence. (Of course, when you have completed a rough draft and can see it as a whole, you may decide to change your first version of the ending, perhaps drastically.)

2. The beginning must give your readers essential guidance for reaching the main point at the end. If you decided, for our imaginary assignment, to end with the opinion that the typical day of a college freshman is long and hectic but worth the struggle, you should begin by mentioning your general subject (a typical day) and what you want your readers to notice most in the main body (the hectic quality of the day). **Caution:** Do **not** spend time and energy now on composing the perfect beginning. You can do that best when you have finished a rough draft that seems fairly satisfactory and can therefore see your work as a whole.

3. The main body is the real substance of your paper. Armed with the essence of the beginning and ending, with all the notes on your material handy to refresh your memory, and with your thesis statement and notes on organization in an eye-catching position as reminders, you should now forge ahead and write a rough draft of the main body as rapidly as you can. Postpone any questions on small points of spelling, grammar, and punctuation. You can correct these in your final version. Also postpone any questions on choosing the precisely right word or constructing a forceful sentence, even questions on where to divide your paragraphs. Remember that this is a rough draft and that you may write several more before you are satisfied. You can polish it more effectively when you can see it as a whole.

As you write and see your thoughts take shape in sentences, other ideas may occur to you, other interpretations of your material, even other material that you had overlooked. Make notes on everything so that you can use it later if you wish and so that you will not find yourself wondering what that forgotten flash of inspiration was. If you think of a better way to arrange your material and decide to start a new draft for any section, be sure to keep the old version—you may decide later that your first choice was the best after all, or you may want to salvage part of it. By planning at the start, you will probably not make big revisions as you go along, but after seeing the draft as a whole, you may want to perform major surgery. Such changes are all part of composing.

4. Make revisions with your readers in mind. When you have finished what you think is a satisfactory rough draft, set it aside for at least an hour or two, preferably overnight, while you do something else quite different. Then, refreshed mentally, read it quickly. Remember that a revision, as the root of the word shows us, is a *reseeing,* not a mere hunt for mistakes. In planning and writing the rough draft, you probably had many moments of reseeing what you wrote and made changes accordingly. Now you can resee everything as parts of a whole. Imagine as strongly as you can that you are seeing the paper through your readers' eyes. What would be their answers to these questions which you asked yourself earlier?

(1) Does the main line of thought develop clearly?
(2) Do the examples and details give good support to the thesis?
(3) Are there parts that are not necessary?
(4) Are there parts that need strengthening?
(5) Would any part be more effective in another position?

COMPOSING: COMPLETING THE ROUGH DRAFT

When you think that the rough draft as a whole is satisfactory, it is time to polish your writing—to make the beginning and ending as effective as you can, to rethink your word choice and sentence structure, to give your readers clues that something is important or that it has a special connection to something else.

1. **The beginning** may not stick in your readers' minds—the effectiveness of the main body and the force of the ending may make them forget it—but it is as essential as any other part of your paper. Your readers' first impression and their understanding of your purpose and general thesis depend on the beginning. But it must do more than help them to understand what you have written. It must also catch their interest. Otherwise, you will have no readers.

The length of the beginning should depend on the length and complexity of what you are writing. Most books need a chapter, but shorter works may begin with a few paragraphs, a single paragraph, even a single sentence, or—very rarely—a single word. A fairly brief beginning is usually most effective—roughly one-seventh or less of the whole. For our imaginary paper any of the most frequently used forms could be appropriate.

a. An **explicit statement** of your topic and purpose or of your thesis is preferred for more technical types of writing, such as reports, and for anything based on material that will be difficult or unfamiliar for the readers:

> A typical day in the life of a college student is likely to be long and full of varied activities—academic study, a part-time job, extracurricular affairs, social gatherings, and the routine duties of daily living.

Caution: Avoid, however, flatfooted turns of phrase such as:
In this paper I intend to show that a typical day in the life of a college student is. . . .

b. The **history** or **background** of a subject is often helpful to give the context and suggest why it is important:

> The number of high school graduates who go on to college has steadily increased over recent years, but many of these students have no idea beforehand what a typical day in the life of a college student is like.

c. A **definition** of your subject or of the key terms you used to discuss it can also help readers to follow an argument easily:

> A "typical day" is probably one that never occurs in reality because no two days are ever exactly the same. A typical day for me as a college freshman would be a composite picture, an average, formed from several quite different days.

Caution: Definitions quoted from dictionaries make boring beginnings because they are of necessity so general. Use one only when you must define something both complicated and unknown to your readers. Even then, you should reword the definition to make it fit smoothly into your own writing.

d. An indication of your **qualifications** to discuss the subject, if it is unusual or specialized, may be needed at the beginning, and, in any case, should appear early in the paper so that the readers will have confidence in your accuracy:

> As an entering freshman in college, I have been on campus only a week, but I have met a great many other freshmen and think that my experiences have been fairly typical.

These forms are very clear and widely used, but, unless the subject is unusual or very timely, they will attract only readers who already have a wish to be informed on it. To attract other readers, consider using a rhetorical device.

e. A **rhetorical question** may arouse readers' curiosity:

> With only a few hours a week spent in class, how can a typical college freshman claim to be busy?

f. A **startling statement** or exclamation may also arouse curiosity:

(1) On a typical day, most college freshmen have had about four hours sleep, missed breakfast, slept through most of their classes, and have been thinking about nothing but drugs and the opposite sex—or so some magazine writers suggest.

(2) Work! Work! Work! Nobody warned me that I'd have my nose in a book ten hours a day.

g. A bit of **narrative**, especially if humorous or dramatic, that illustrates your main point, appeals to almost anyone:

> My alarm rings—7:15. I leap from my bed and dash to the bathroom in hopes of a vacant shower stall. No luck. Back to my own room and a quick wash in the basin. I pull on underwear, tee shirt, and blue jeans, and

by 7:35 I'm in the cafeteria line for breakfast. At 7:59 I slide into my seat in English class, ten seconds before the professor arrives. Another typical day has begun.

h. Quoted remarks can draw the reader into the situation being described:

> "Read at least the first forty pages before Thursday," the instructor announced at the end of our first class meeting. "Take full, careful notes. 300 It's a vital section of the book." In all my other classes the instructors had made much the same announcement.

i. An appropriate quotation, preferably from a well-known source, is an old device that works well:

> "Of making many books there is no end, and much study is a weariness of the flesh"—the Book of Ecclesiastes in the Bible was written many centuries ago, but the message is truer than ever, especially for college freshmen.

j. A description of something familiar that is comparable to your subject in important ways can help your readers picture it:

> Ants seem to lead frantically busy lives. Around an ant hill we can watch lines of creatures rush in different directions, intent on reaching their destinations as quickly as possible, but sometimes pausing to greet each other with a wave. Between classes the campus resembles a busy ant hill.

k. A direct appeal to your readers' concerns or a reminder of a current problem or issue may make readers identify with your subject:

> If you are like most high school students who plan to go to college, you are concentrating now on your grades, thinking that once you are accepted by the college of your choice your problems will be over and you will relax.

Caution: Do not overdo your use of rhetorical devices. The more natural interest your readers are likely to have in your material, the less you need to make a "hard sell." Like hot spices in food, a little rhetoric can go a long way. Practice composing different beginnings for each assignment to try out their effect. Also, practice composing different beginnings for some of the examples in this book.

2. The ending, like the beginning, should be relatively brief, preferably not more than one-seventh of the whole paper. Most devices suggested for beginnings are appropriate for endings. The shorter you make your ending, the more forceful it will seem and the more easily your readers will remember it.

a. A brief restatement of the thesis after a capsule summary of the main body will not be dramatic, but the brevity can give it force; it may be the best ending if your readers are unfamiliar with your subject or likely to be hard to convince.

b. Saving the only **complete statement of your thesis** for the end can have great dramatic force if your readers can follow the logic of everything leading up to it. This inductive pattern of organization (see Unit 13) may be difficult to handle but is worth trying.

c. A **redefinition** of the meaning of a key term in the light of what you have said in the main body of your paper may pinpoint your meaning for your readers.

d. Suggesting a **result** or finding a **significance** that goes beyond the immediate scope of the paper can show your readers the wider importance of your thesis and material.

e. A specific **reference to the beginning** or to the title may round off the whole by "framing" it—as Y did at the end of the paper on Jane.

f, g, h. A **rhetorical question,** an **exclamation,** a **challenging statement,** or a **direct appeal** to your readers for action can make them rethink your thesis and the whole paper.

i, j, k. An appropriate bit of **narrative,** a **quoted remark,** or a **quotation** from a well-known source that sums up or illustrates your main point may be easily remembered.

COMPOSING: POLISHING THE ROUGH DRAFT AND MAKING THE FINAL COPY

1. The paragraph structure should guide your readers throughout your paper. A paragraph is one or more sentences that develop one main thought. It helps readers to see, in every sense of the word, that it forms a subdivision of the whole, to see it both as a unit in itself and as part of a larger unit, the whole essay. That is why the beginning is indented and the line is left blank after the last word.

A paragraph may be any length, from one sentence to hundreds, just as a sentence may have from one word to hundreds, or a book from a few pages to thousands. The length of a paragraph depends on the subject matter, the intended reader, and the form in which the reader will read it. Newspaper paragraphs are usually brief, often only one sentence each, because the narrow columns cause most sentences to occupy several lines and therefore to appear longer than they are. In most other forms of writing, however, paragraphs are longer, and the one-sentence paragraph is rare, reserved to emphasize a dramatic or significant remark. A series of short paragraphs makes a piece of writing look choppy, even more than a series of short sentences does. Conversely, a series of paragraphs each a page or more long will discourage readers even from starting. In most writing, paragraphs average between 75 and 175 words, or roughly one-third to two-thirds of a double-spaced, typed page.

Whatever its length, a paragraph should contain only one main thought, but it may have many related thoughts to make the main one clear. It may be organized in any of the patterns used to organize an essay, and many paragraphs can be read alone as if they were miniature essays. All the patterns of organization discussed in this book apply to paragraphs as well as to essays. Choose the structure for each paragraph just as you choose the organization for the whole paper, according to your thesis, content, and readers' needs.

Check the structure of each paragraph by considering these questions:

a. Does this paragraph have one main point? Could it be given a heading, like the headings for points in an outline, that would cover everything in it? Are all its less important points clearly related to the main one? If you answer "no" to any of these questions, make one or more of these revisions:

(1) Remove any parts that are not clearly related to the main point and put them elsewhere in the paper or leave them out altogether.

(2) Rearrange the order of the parts so that they fit together more clearly.

(3) Add one or more of the transitional devices described in answer to question **e,** page 16 that follows.

b. Is the paragraph roughly between 75 and 175 words long?

(1) If it is much shorter, ask yourself whether it is more important than the paragraphs before and after it. If it is more important, keep it short. If it is not, combine it with another paragraph, revising both as necessary to fit them together.

(2) If it is much more than 175 words, **is everything in it not only related to your main point but essential?** If everything is essential, try to find a way to divide the paragraph logically in two (you will then probably need to revise some of your sentences to form the beginnings and endings of the two paragraphs that result from the division).

c. Do the paragraph and sentence structures emphasize your important points?

(1) Is there variety in the length and structure of this paragraph in relation to those near it? Is there variety in the sentences in this paragraph? Avoid the monotony of using the same pattern again and again, especially in paragraphs or sentences of about the same length, unless you want to emphasize similarities in their content (see 3 and 4 in this section).

(2) Does the paragraph build up to the important point? If you lead to that point with sentences of average length and complexity and then present the point in a short, uncomplicated sentence, it will stand out by contrast and catch your readers' eyes. Similarly, a very short paragraph coming after several moderately long ones will be eye-catching.

(3) Have you taken advantage of "end focus" in your paragraphs and sentences to emphasize important points? We tend to notice the end of something simply because it is the end. If you construct a sentence or a paragraph that presents a particularly important point so that the most significant words are at the end, they will

stand out as a climax. Note how Red Smith ends his narrative (page 22).

(4) Have you taken advantage of parallelism to emphasize a comparison, contrast, or list of any kind? To compare, contrast, or list two or more opinions or pieces of information, present them in parallel structures—ones that are as nearly the same as possible. The repetition will emphasize what is similar, and the differences will stand out by contrast. Note Smith's use of parallelism in the second and third sentences in his first paragraph (page 21) to emphasize Reggie Jackson's calm behavior.

d. Are pronouns, verb tenses, and terminology clear and logically consistent within the paragraph and between it and the rest of the paper?

(1) Switch pronouns (*I, you, it, he, she, they,* and so on) only to indicate a different person or thing. If you write "People want peace," don't switch later to "You want peace" or "We want peace," unless you mean to make a distinction between "people" and "you" or "we."

(2) Make sure that each pronoun's references are clear and that there is no word nearby that a reader could possibly mistake for its reference. In "The students took their coats off because they were wet," does "they" refer to "students" or to "coats"?

(3) In narrating events, change from one verb tense to another only to indicate a difference in time.

(4) Stick to the same names whenever possible for what you are discussing. If you have referred to a "residence hall," don't later call the same building a "dormitory"—your readers may think that you mean a different building. If the result is monotonously repetitious, try to recast your sentences so that you can use a pronoun instead of repeating the word. If using a synonym seems essential, be sure that the reference is clear.

e. Is the paragraph's relationship to what precedes it clear? Is the relationship directly stated or strongly implied by the content? Are the relationships among the points within the paragraph similarly clear? If not, add transitional words or phrases to indicate relationships. Usually, the best position for a transition is at or very near the beginning of the paragraph or sentence that you wish to link to what has gone before, but sometimes you may want to put it at the end to lead to what follows. Transitional words and phrases are most commonly used to indicate these kinds of relationships:

(1) a **sequence** according to space or time or relative importance, as with *next, in the meantime, later, behind, above all, most* or *least of all, first, second, finally*

(2) an **addition** to the preceding material, as with *and, also, furthermore, moreover, in addition to, incidentally, similarly*

(3) a **contrast,** as with *but, however, on the other hand, yet, nevertheless, in contrast*

(4) **results or conclusions** drawn from preceding material, as with *so, therefore, consequently, as a result, thus, hence.*

Not every paragraph, by any means, needs a transitional device, but in the examples in this book you will see how often such devices help to guide the reader and unify the thought. Notice, for instance, the way a student writer, William Nilsson, begins the five successive paragraphs of the main body of his essay (pages 224–226): "A good starting point. . . . Another source. . . . Still another reason. . . . Economic factors, too, may. . . . The question that may follow from this. . . ."

Note: You may have been warned when you were younger never to start a sentence with "and" or "but." In general, this is good advice to follow. Strings of "ands" make all your points seem equal; nothing stands out. Strings of "buts" will make you seem to go round in self-contradicting circles. But an occasional "but" or "and" can make an effective start for a sentence whose connection with what precedes it deserves emphasis. You may also have been told never to start a sentence with "because"; the danger is that you might forget to complete the sentence with a main clause, but a modifying clause such as "Because these actions were dangerous" can make a useful link between the sentence it begins and the information in the preceding sentence.

2. Word choice is such an important part of writing that a whole unit (5) is devoted to it, with detailed suggestions. Read, also, Theodore Sorensen's account of John F. Kennedy's search for the most appropriate words to use in his inaugural address (Unit 20). Before making the final copy of your paper, reread it slowly with these questions in mind:

a. Have you used words accurately and in their generally accepted meanings?

(1) If you have any doubts about accuracy, look up the word immediately in a good desk-size or unabridged dictionary.

(2) If you want your readers to give a special interpretation to a word, make sure that you include an explanation.

b. Is the level of word choice appropriate for this assignment—for this subject and these readers?

For most writing assignments, aim for a level somewhere between the very literary or very technical and the very informal. Some of the examples in this book are more formal than others and some less formal, but none goes to an extreme. All are meant for the "general reader," someone who is not a specialist in the subject being discussed but who is educated and intelligent. Probably, most of what you write, now and later, will be for the general reader.

c. Do your words express your meaning forcefully?

(1) Whenever possible, choose words with specific, concrete associations. For example, Red Smith writes "The crowd was still *bawling* for him" (page 22), not merely *shouting* or *calling,* and "the ball *streaked*" (page 22), not merely *went.*

Caution: Like many other devices and practices recommended here, this can easily be overdone. If you make every remark colorful, nothing stands out.

(2) Avoid clichés—expressions used so often that they have become colorless, as in "It rained cats and dogs," or "Their hearts were as big as all outdoors."

(3) Such words as "really," "very," "terribly," and "awfully" add little or nothing. "They were really terribly happy" would be better as "They were delighted" or "They were overjoyed."

d. Do your words express your meaning compactly?

(1) "Brevity is the soul of wit" is a cliché but also a valuable truth. For example, "The subject that was discussed in Green's essay was that of the next election" would be better as "Green's essay was on the next election."

(2) Deliberate repetition of an important word or phrase can give it effective emphasis. Note Red Smith's repetition of "again" in "there was a runner on base again, and again he hit the first pitch. Again it reached the seats in right" (page 22). Careless repetition, however, is boring. Don't, for example, repeat "college program" five times in six lines if "program" or, better still, "it" would be clear.

3. The title will, of course, stand first in your paper. Nevertheless, it will often be one of your last considerations. You have known your general topic all along, of course, and it has determined your choice of plan and treatment, but only now, with the last rough draft before you, can you decide definitely what to call it.

A title should be brief, a word or phrase, not a complete sentence, and should indicate not only the specific content of the paper but its purpose. For matter-of-fact, informative writing, such as reports, a descriptive title stating the actual content of the paper as clearly as possible in a few words is best, as in a recent magazine article called "Alcohol, Marijuana, and Memory." This kind of title is also good when you are sure that your subject will interest your readers. For less utilitarian writing, you may prefer an imaginative title to catch a reader's attention, such as *Life for Death,* a book on the effects of the verdict in a murder trial. Often, writers add a subtitle to explain an imaginative title, as in the magazine article called "Matter over Mind: The Big Issues Raised by Newly Discovered Chemicals."

4. The final copy of your paper should follow the conventional format unless your instructor has given you specific instructions to do otherwise.

a. Use white, standard-size paper (8½″ × 11″). Do *not* use pages torn from a spiral binder.

b. Write or type on only one side of each page.

c-1. If you are writing, choose wide-lined paper (about ⅜″ between lines) or skip a line after each line of writing. Leave a left-hand margin at least 1½ inches wide. Use ink, either blue or black, not any other color. Never use pencil.

c-2. If you are typing, double space (skip a line after each typed line). Leave margins at least 1½ inches wide at the left side and the top and bottom of the page; leave at least a 1-inch margin on the right. Skip one space after each comma and semicolon and two after all other forms of punctuation except dashes. Indicate a dash by typing two hyphens with *no* space before, after, or between them. Add in ink any symbols that are not on the typewriter.

d. Try to avoid splitting a word to fill up the end of a line. Instead, leave the extra space blank and put the whole word on the next line— your readers will be grateful.

e. Indent the beginning of each paragraph the equivalent of a five-letter word.

f. Spell out all numbers below ten unless you are using several in a small space (many authorities recommend spelling out all numbers below a hundred). Spell out any number, large or small, that begins a sentence. If the result seems awkward, as it will in a sentence with other numbers that are not spelled out, try to revise the sentence so that you can begin it with a word instead.

g. Proofread your final copy with the greatest possible care, paying close attention to mechanics—your spelling, punctuation, grammar, and usage. Accuracy in mechanics will not guarantee you a good grade, but it is essential. The best subjects and plans will not impress readers who are constantly distracted or confused by mechanical errors. Solve difficulties with mechanics by careful drill with a good handbook. (If your instructor has not already told you which to buy, ask for a recommendation.)

Also, beware of the careless mistakes that slip in because your mind travels ahead of your hand. You may know the difference between *to* and *too,* but just "didn't think." You must try to develop the eagle eye of the professional proofreader, who is responsible for the almost flawless pages of the better books and magazines. Careful correction is an essential last step for anything you write outside of class; but remember that it is equally important in letters, in-class themes, and examinations written under pressure. Write less, if necessary, to save time for proofreading. It is a good rule never to give anything you have written to a reader until you have checked it carefully, *letter by letter,* for possible slips.

Correct any slips of your pen or typewriter by firmly crossing out the error and writing the correct version neatly above it. Erasures are usually messy. If you find several errors on a page, or if you have a large one, recopy the page.

* * *   * * *   * * *

Examples

To begin our discussion of various patterns of logical organization, let us look at two examples of the simplest one—the chronological pattern. The first covers about three consecutive hours, the second much less than that. Both writers have the same general purpose—simply to share an enjoyable experience with their readers. You will 5 notice that their paragraphs have topics but no topic sentences and that the complete essay, "Sunday Morning in Haiti," has no thesis statement, but in each essay the thesis is implied throughout.

1-A   Sunday Morning in Haiti

Anaica Lodescar (student)

OUTLINE
I. First time division
A. Sounds of activity
B. Purpose of activity

Three o'clock on Sunday morning. I have been sound asleep. I hear only the end of the carillon for the first call to go to mass. Three-thirty. The sound of steps breaks the silence of the dark street outside my window and tells me that I am already almost late. Dogs are bark- 5 ing everywhere. Alarm clocks are ringing in other houses. People from a distance are arriving, rushing toward the cathedral. Even people in the neighborhood are hurrying because the seats will soon be filled with churchgoers. 10

At a time like this, so early in a Sunday morning, a stranger would not believe that there are so many people going to mass. He would think that there must be some very unusual event—a fire or some other disaster, perhaps, to bring so many people out into the streets when it is still 15 dark.

II. Second time division
A. Sounds
B. Sights
C. Other Sounds

By the time I reach the stairs of the big cathedral, the carillon wakes me up. My ears ring with the ringing bells. The churchyard is full of cars and of early vendors of fruit, vegetables, milk, patés, candles. Inside, the cathedral is 20 crowded. There are no more seats. Some people would rather stand up so that they won't fall asleep during the service, and others have brought their own chairs. The priest is wide awake in his white robe. He moves quickly to and fro as he conducts the mass. The attendance of the 25 choir is excellent, and all through the service the singing is loud, clear, very alive. Outside, the streets are calm again and the latecomers move quietly, trying to slip in unobserved.

III. Third
time
division
A. Sights
B. Sounds
C. Smells

The service is long, but at last it reaches the end. It's five-thirty, still dark, and almost time to go back home. I must choose what to do: go back to bed, or study my many lessons for Monday, or go to the market or to the baker. The streets are full of people now, and there are many more food vendors. From each corner they're calling "Paté, paté." Oh, how I love those patés! Other vendors are selling candles to people coming for the next service.

About five or six blocks away from the cathedral are the vendors of "café" and bread. They are not calling anybody. They don't have to. The smell of their merchandise is call enough. They're sitting calmly in front of their big pots, an oil lamp standing behind each vendor on a small table. For some grown-ups a good cup of black coffee is a delight, but the "café au lait" I'll have at home will be even better.

IV. Fourth
time
division
A. Sounds
B. Color

A new carillon in the air is announcing the next service. The roosters everywhere are calling "co-co-ri-co." The dogs sound louder—they are competing with each other. From the radios in the houses comes soft music or hymns. A new group of churchgoers streams toward the cathedral. I hear many greetings—"Bonjour," "Bonjour!"

The sky in the east has turned a golden pink. Soon a beautiful sun will show its round face in a beautiful blue sky. In Haiti it seems that the weather is always lovely on Sunday.

1. Why does the writer tell us so much about the sounds?
2. What transitional devices do you find?
3. Why are almost all the verbs in the present tense?
4. How does the writer indicate the passing of time?
5. What seems to be the basis for the paragraph divisions?

1-B   One-Man Show

Red Smith

The writer was for many years a columnist for the *New York Times* and one of the most popular sportswriters in the country. The selection that follows forms the second half of a column on Reggie Jackson's historic performance on October 18, 1977, when he hit three home runs in a row so that the Yankees won the World Series. In the first half of the column Smith gave the highlights of the games leading up to Jackson's special triumph.

The stage was set when he [Reggie Jackson] went to the plate in last night's second inning with the Dodgers leading, 2–0. Sedately, he led off with a walk. Serenely, he circled the bases on a home run by Chris Chambliss. The score was tied.

Los Angeles had moved out front, 3–2, when the man reappeared 5
in the fourth inning with Thurman Munson on base. He hit the first
pitch on a line into the seats beyond right field. Circling the bases for
the second time, he went into his home-run glide—head high, chest out.
The Yankees led, 4–3. In the dugout, Yankees fell upon him. Billy
Martin, the manager, who tried to slug him last June, patted his cheek 10
lovingly. The dugout phone rang and Reggie accepted the call gra-
ciously.

His first home run knocked the Dodgers' starting pitcher, Burt
Hooton, out of the game. His second disposed of Elias Sosa, Hooton's
successor. Before Sosa's first pitch in the fifth inning, Reggie had strolled 15
the length of the dugout to pluck a bat from the rack, even though three
men would precede him to the plate. He was confident he would get
his turn. When he did, there was a runner on base again, and again he
hit the first pitch. Again it reached the seats in right.

When the last jubilant playmate had been peeled off his neck, 20
Reggie took a seat near the first-base end of the bench. The crowd was
still bawling for him and comrades urged him to take a curtain call, but
he replied with a gesture that said, "Aw, fellows, cut it out!" He did
unbend enough to hold up two fingers for photographers in a V-for-
victory sign.   25

Jackson was the leadoff batter in the eighth. By that time, Martin
would have replaced him in an ordinary game, sending Paul Blair to
right field to help protect the Yankees' lead. But did they ever bench
Edwin Booth in the last act?

For the third time, Reggie hit the first pitch but this one didn't take 30
the shortest distance between two points. Straight out from the plate
the ball streaked, not toward the neighborly stands in right but on a
soaring arc toward the unoccupied bleachers in dead center, where the
seats are blacked out to give batters a background. Up the white speck
climbed, dwindling, diminishing, until it settled at last halfway up those 35
empty stands, probably 450 feet away.

This time he could not disappoint his public. He stepped out of the
dugout and faced the multitude, two fists and one cap uplifted. Not only
the customers applauded.

"I must admit," said Steve Garvey, the Dodgers' first baseman, 40
"when Reggie Jackson hit his third home run and I was sure nobody was
listening, I applauded into my glove."

1. Where has the writer used the end of a paragraph or sentence to emphasize
   an important or dramatic point?
2. What is the effect of starting the second and third sentences in the same way?
   of repeating "again" three times at the end of the third paragraph?
3. What specific details help us to picture the event and the emotions of all
   concerned?

*   *   *   *   *   *   *   *   *

Assignments

1. For each of the following general subjects, make a list of five or six specific topics on which you feel you could write, *from your own experience,* 250- to 500-word papers of interest to the nonspecialist reader: chemistry, religion, education, cars, music, agriculture, sports, literature, television programs, nature, social change, art.

   Example: General subject—Education

   Specific topics—My First Day of College Classes
   Taking Examinations
   My Interview for Admission to College
   My Worst Teacher
   My Favorite Extracurricular Activity
   Graduation Day

2. For any one of the topics you listed in answer to the preceding question, write five different openings, a sentence to a paragraph in length, each suitable for a different purpose or directed to a different type of reader. Explain what you hope the effects of each will be and why.

3. Prepare a plan for a paper on several hours spent at a fair, in a city, on a job, at a beach, at a family picnic, or in some other specific environment.

   a. Set down in chronological sequence the dozen or so items you wish to discuss.
   b. Group them under appropriate headings into a few manageable units.
   c. Regroup them according to some order other than time sequence.
   d. Arrange your groupings in c into what you consider the most effective order and explain why you chose it.

4. Look over the photographs on pages 37, 55, 81, 179. In what groups can you arrange them, according to subject matter, the number of people involved, the types of people, and so on? List them in as many combinations as you can imagine.

5. Go through a unit of this book (both text and examples), a chapter of another textbook, or a current magazine article, as assigned, pointing out transitional devices, both between paragraphs and within them.

6. a. For six of the theme subjects you listed in assignment 1, compose titles to stimulate interest as well as to inform; for example, Graduation Day— Start or Finish?
   b. Choose one of the groups in which you arranged the photographs for assignment 4; compose a title for the group and a separate title for each photograph in it. Compose titles that will catch your readers' attention.
   c. For class discussion, bring in a list of ten titles of nonfiction books or magazine articles that have especially caught your attention, listing after each the subject with which it deals.

7. Having noted the divisions of the *chronological* patterns used in the examples in this section, try your hand at other *logical* arrangements of their material. (See the illustration of the two types in section 5, "Organizing the Main Body" on pages 7–9.) What are the advantages and disadvantages of these differing patterns?

8. Using as material some job you have had or some particular kind of life you have lived (at school or camp, for instance), write an essay in which you present your experience chronologically, as a typical "day in the life of—." Limit your material by excluding all irrelevant details, as the authors of the examples have done; include only experiences appropriate to your limited subject and to the particular attitude you decide to take.

UNIT 2

Description

Which way of expressing a thought are you more likely to notice and remember—"There was a dishonest financial transaction" *or* "That check for fifty dollars signed 'George Henderson' bounced and is stamped 'Account closed' "? "Natural scenes are beautiful" *or* "In the sunlight, the yellow trumpets of the honeysuckle sparkled with drops of dew"? "Humanity is interesting" *or* "Her brown eyes shining and her cheeks puffed, the little girl leaned forward to blow out the three candles on her birthday cake"?

We must often deal with abstract concepts such as dishonesty, nature, or humanity, but the concrete catches our attention more easily —a bad check, a flower, a child. Yet even these are general, and our imaginations respond most to details like those in the examples above. With specific, concrete details you can make a vivid and memorable point of something that your readers might otherwise forget or never notice.

For this unit you will write short pieces of almost unmixed description to practice accurate observation and word choice. But remember that description is best used only to assist you in informing or persuading your readers. In most exposition, give only the descriptive details that will make your main point clear and memorable. Spread them through your essay so that they will not slow down your readers.

* * *　* * *　* * *

Description may be informative or evocative, depending on your purpose. You may wish simply to give your readers facts, or you may wish to give them pleasure as well. Both types aid exposition—the first is a necessity, the second an enjoyable luxury.

1. Use informative description to explain a mechanism or a process. Be practical, not poetic. Give the essential facts in the briefest and

clearest terms you can find. If these are not sufficient, use comparisons with more familiar objects: "The shovel handle is D-shaped"; "Sand the wood until smooth as glass"; "The mixture gave off the odor of rotten eggs." Drawings may supplement or replace words in such descriptions. Be as brief as you can without losing clarity and completeness. Your goal is information, only information. Such description is required in technical reports and all writings calling only for facts.

2. **Use evocative description** to appeal to your readers' senses and emotions and to add vividness to facts. In "Your dollar will help to feed this haggard mother and her crippled child," what might have been bare fact becomes a plea because of the emotional power of specific details that *suggest* as well as *mean.* A general idea—your money is needed—comes alive in the particulars. *Money* is your tangible dollar; *need* is the hunger of a definitely pictured woman and child.

* * *   * * *   * * *

Your **selection of descriptive details** must fit your purpose. From a mass of sense impressions, take the few that are relevant, the ones your readers must have to understand your point, and omit the rest. In describing a machine in terms of its function, you need not mention its odor; in creating a mood of gloom, you should omit any details that might suggest cheerfulness. Moreover, your physical point of view will limit you to the sensations you would actually have at the time and place you describe. You cannot see the back jeans pocket of your host as he opens the door or smell the flowers on a distant hillside. If you are walking around a building or across a field, your description must take into consideration the changes in your viewpoint.

* * *   * * *   * * *

The **organization of descriptive details** is usually easy because in most expository essays you will need only one or two details to illuminate any one point, but when you must describe something at greater length, the arrangement of the details becomes an important choice.

1. **The chronological pattern** is the simplest—the arrangement of details according to the time sequence in which they were observed. The examples in Unit 1 are organized chronologically, as are the first three in this unit.

2. **The spatial pattern** is next in simplicity—the arrangement of details according to physical shape and position. In describing a room, you might start at one side and walk around it, naming the objects you see as you move. Similarly, you might describe a person from head to foot or from foot to head, or a landscape from near to far or far to near.

3. **The most noticeable feature** can be the basis for a more selective arrangement. In describing the room, you might first mention a piano

or a fireplace, for the person perhaps a big nose, and for the landscape a large tree; then you would give the rest of the details in relation to the outstanding feature.

4. Relative importance can be the basis for a still more selective arrangement. This centers on the detail you want your readers to notice most—an unmade bed, a shy smile, the honeysuckle on a fence—including other details only to reinforce the impression of the important one.

* * *   * * *   * * *

Word choice is by far the most important element in creating an effective description. Our awareness of the physical world comes to us primarily through our senses, and well-chosen words can stimulate readers' imaginations to recreate physical sensations.

1. Use concrete, specific words. Avoid the abstract and general whenever you can. Saying that a room is clean or a girl is beautiful gives your opinion but creates no picture for the reader. A mention of a freshly waxed floor, however, or of large brown eyes with long lashes will stimulate your readers' imaginations.

2. Appeal to all the senses. Most often, we think of description in terms of what we see. But the sensations of sound and scent, touch and flavor, can be essential in description. Imagine trying to tell foreigners about the fun of an American county fair. If you described only what you saw, they would miss much of the experience—the shouts of the barkers at the amusement concessions and the clatter of the machinery for the various rides; the odor from the food stands, the barns, and the crowd; the spicy flavor of the hot dogs and the intense sweetness of the cotton candy; and everywhere the grittiness of the dust stirred up by hundreds of feet.

3. Use a comparison or contrast with something familiar. English has many words describing size, shape, and color but few for sound, flavor, odor, or texture. After classifying a taste sensation as sweet or sour, bitter or salty, you have used almost all our appropriate adjectives, but you have not recreated that sensation for the reader. A description such as "Venison tastes like beef but has a more intense flavor," however, will help your reader imagine the taste of the less familiar meat. The comparison does not have to be literal; it may only suggest a point of similarity as in "The bad news was like a slap in the face," or, more forcefully, "The bad news was a slap in the face."

4. Consider using personification—describing animals, inanimate objects, or abstractions as if they have human characteristics can also help the reader to imagine them more vividly, as in "The engine coughed and sneezed before it died," or "The neighborhood dogs held a committee meeting behind the garage."

5. Consider using onomatopoetic words—these are words whose sound imitate the sound they name, for example, *crash, murmur, buzz, whir, sigh,* or *shuffle.*

See Unit 5 for a more detailed discussion of word choice and of figures of speech.

Examples

In each of the following selections, the writer's main point is to make a description, but all the other writers in this book also use description to some degree. Look again at Lodescar's "Sunday Morning in Haiti" (1-A) and Smith's "One-Man Show" (1-B). Notable examples of description in later selections are in Ward's "Yumbo" (3-A), Kru- 5 lish's "The Start of a Long Day" (4-G), all the selections in Units 5 and 9, Lanning's "The Ones Left Behind" (10-B), Hall's "The Pervasive Set" (10-F), Nemy's "Business Status" (10-H), *The New Yorker's* "The Bad and Worse Sides of Thanksgiving" (11-H), Conza's "Christmas Eve" (11-I), Satriale's "Dix Hills" (12-D), Keremes's "The Passing of 10 Little Gibbs Road" (13-E), Hillary's "Epitaph to the Elusive Abominable Snowman" (13-J), Ardrey's "Light from an Ape's Jaw" (13-K), Twain's "Lagniappe" (14-C), Myers's "No Sweat" (14-D), and Carson's "David Bowie" (16-G).

2-A   Cold Orange Juice

Wayne Smith (student)

This description was written as a fifteen-minute exercise in class. The students were asked to describe in detail the sensations of drinking something very cold.

I was so thirsty that I could already taste the orange and feel the cold go down my throat. My mouth started to water when I picked up the glass. As the cold numbed my fingers I felt the frost melt under them. I took my first gulp. It was so cold that I had to squint my eyes. My teeth tingled. The tiny fruit cells popped against my tongue and 5 filled my mouth with acid sweetness. A piece of ice slid down, leaving my mouth numb and my throat aching. I sucked in air to make my throat warm again and licked my teeth to warm them, too.

How does each of these words chosen by the writer differ from the near synonym paired with it: *gulp* and *swallow; squint* and *narrow; tingled* and *felt cold; popped* and *broke open; sucked* and *breathed in?*

2-B   The Great Blue

Lucian K. Truscott IV

This is the second half of an informal essay published in the *Saturday Review*. In the first half, the writer described an uneventful afternoon fishing alone in Maine as background to emphasize the drama of his sudden view of the rare bird.

I had just fished the pool and was rounding a gradual bend upstream, wading slowly so as not to disturb the slow-moving clear water, when up ahead I noticed a gigantic bird atop a tiny, demure beaver dam, a creature almost too large to be real. He had his back to me and seemed to be peering intently into the pool on the other side of the 5 dam. I froze, stood perfectly still as I watched him preside magnificently over the pond. I was only about fifteen or twenty feet away, and he was an elegant sight—a great blue heron.

The beaver pool was twenty or thirty yards in length and pear-shaped; it was shallow at the near end, deep at the far. Over to one side 10 I could see a beaver lodge—still lived in, it appeared; in good repair at any rate—and at the far end a brief falls, where water rushed into the pond with a white giggle, audible even from where I stood. The woods were that quiet.

The heron had the hue of a blue-point Siamese cat, a dusky gray- 15 ness, bluish only on the edges, the high points in the fading, late-afternoon sun. Maybe three feet tall, he towered greatly over the beaver pond. I wondered: Do the beavers know he is here, and if so, does his great size cause them to slap the water and crash-dive, heading for the womb of their upside-down coffee-cup lodge?   20

Then, suddenly, he whooossshhhed his wings upward once, then down, stretched to their full four or five feet—it seemed like six—and took off from the dam, glided over the beaver pond for a few yards, and rose slowly, his wings beating the air slowly like a rug strung over a clothes line in the backyard, his great neck doubled back arrogantly 25 against his chest, then thrust forward almost wantonly as he passed above the trees, heading north.

I watched his low and easy disappearance against the sky until he was as blue as it was.

1. Which words and groups of words give you the most precise impressions of what the writer saw and heard?
2. Why does he describe the bird's color twice in one sentence: "the hue of a blue-point Siamese cat" and "a dusky grayness, bluish only on the edges"?
3. What is gained by the spelling "whooossshhhed"?
4. What may have been his reason for comparing the bird's wings to a rug on a clothesline instead of to something graceful?

5. Check all the definitions for these words in a large dictionary: *demure, wantonly.*

2-C   More Power to You

Time

This description was written in 1948, when jet engines were new, but the thrill for an observer can be much the same today. Vivid description is as possible with a mechanical subject as with a natural one.

DESCRIPTIVE
DEVICES
Negatives
(3)
Contrast

Bolted motionless on a test stand, the little monster is not impressive. It has no coolly symmetrical propeller, no phalanx of cylinderheads, none of the hard geometrical grace of the conventional aircraft engine. Yet the un-prepossessing turbojet engine has thrown the air design- 5 ers into ecstatic confusion: nobody yet knows how fast the jet will enable man to fly, but the old speed ceilings are off. In their less guarded moments, sober designers talk of speeds so high that aircraft will glow like meteors.

Comparison
Animation

To watch a jet engine spring into life is to feel that 10 power. (Only when the engine is set up with a pipe to catch its gases is it safe to watch the fires kindle.) Dimly

Comparison
Sound
Smell

visible inside is the turbine, like a small windmill with close-set vanes. When the starting motor whines, the turbine spins. A tainted breeze blows through the exhaust 15 vent in the tail, followed by a thin grey fog of atomized

Onomato-
poeia
Sight
Onomato-
poeia
Comparison

kerosene. Deep in the engine a single spark plug buzzes. A spot of fire dances in a circle behind the turbine. Next moment, with a hollow *whoom,* a great yellow flame leaps out. It cuts back to a faint blue cone, a cone that roars like 20 a giant blowtorch. The roar increases to thunder as the turbine gathers speed. Then it diminishes slightly, masked by a strange, high snarl that is felt rather than heard. This is "ultrasonic" sound (a frequency too high for the ear to hear). It tickles the deep brain, punches the heart, makes 25

Feeling

the viscera tremble. Few men like to stay in a test room when a jet is up to speed.

The engine now has the fierce beauty of power. Its massive rotor, the principal moving part, is spinning some

Informative
comparisons

13,000 times per minute (though with only the faintest 30 vibration). The fire raging in its heart would heat 1,000 five-room houses in zero weather (though much of the engine's exterior is cool). From the air intake in its snout,

Animation   invisible hooks reach out; their suction will clasp a man who comes too close and break his body. The blast roaring 35 out the tail will knock a man down at 150 feet. The reac-

Informative   tion of the speeding jet of gas pushes against the test stand

comparisons   with a two-ton thrust. If the engine were pointing upward and left unshackled, it would take off like a rocket, each pound of its weight overbalanced by more than two 40 pounds of thrust.

1. Point out in this section any effective choices of concrete, specific words.
2. What is the cumulative effect of the words *life, tail, snarl* (¶2), *heart, snout* (¶3)?
3. Check all the definitions for these words in a large dictionary: *unprepossessing, ecstatic, meteor, turbine, tainted, cone, viscera, snout, unshackled.*

2-D   The Hellbender

The Encyclopedia Americana

This paragraph from an encyclopedia is intended to give facts. It is typically informative description in which essential details are listed in such an objective manner that only one word, "repulsive," expresses an opinion. Scientists in all fields use objective description as an aid in explaining all kinds of natural phenomena.

Hellbender, *Cryptobranchus alleganiensis,* most robust and second largest of North American salamanders. It attains a length of slightly more than two feet. Despite a somewhat repulsive appearance, and the presence of teeth in both upper and lower jaws, the hellbender is quite harmless. The small eyes are set in a massive head. 5 Both head and body are much depressed, and the outlines of the body are disguised by a fleshy fold of wrinkled skin along either side and the posterior aspects of each limb. Though relatively short, the limbs are functional, the front pair being provided with four toes, the hind limbs with five. A crest is present along the upper side of the strongly 10 compressed tail. Hellbenders are entirely aquatic, yet the adults are without gills and have only a single pair of inconspicuous gill slits, which are more or less concealed by skin folds. Their coloration varies considerably, ranging from yellowish brown through dull brick red to near black.   15

The organization of Examples A, B, and C was determined by the chronology of the experiences. What principle of organization is used here? What reason may the writer have had to use it?

2-E   The House

Anne Moody

This is the first paragraph of a book, *Coming of Age in Mississippi*. It is the autobiography, starting with her childhood, of a young black woman who was active in the Civil Rights movement of the 1960s when she was a college student.

I'm still haunted by dreams of the time we lived on Mr. Carter's plantation. Lots of Negroes lived on his place. Like Mama and Daddy they were all farmers. We all lived in rotten wood two-room shacks. But ours stood out from the others because it was up on the hill with Mr. Carter's big white house, overlooking the farms and the other shacks 5 below. It looked just like the Carters' barn with a chimney and a porch, but Mama and Daddy did what they could to make it livable. Since we had only one big room and a kitchen, we all slept in the same room. It was like three rooms in one. Mama [and the rest of] them slept in one corner and I had my little bed in another corner next to one of the big 10 wooden windows. Around the fireplace a rocking chair and a couple of straight chairs formed a sitting area. This big room had a plain, dull-colored wallpaper tacked loosely to the walls with large thumbtacks. Under each tack was a piece of cardboard which had been taken from shoeboxes and cut into little squares to hold the paper and keep the 15 tacks from tearing through. Because there were not enough tacks, the paper bulged in places. The kitchen didn't have any wallpaper and the only furniture in it was a wood stove, an old table and a safe.

1. How has the writer used a spatial order to organize details?
2. What details support her point that her parents tried to make the shack livable?
3. Why does she devote one-fifth of the paragraph to the wallpaper?

2-F   Yamacraw

Pat Conroy

This excerpt comes from *The Water Is Wide* (1972), in which the writer describes a year he spent as a teacher on Yamacraw. The book has been made into a movie, *Conrack*.

Yamacraw is an island off the South Carolina mainland not far from Savannah, Georgia. The island is fringed with the green, undulating marshes of the southern coast; shrimp boats ply the waters around her and fishermen cast their lines along her bountiful shores. Deer cut through her forests in small silent herds. The great southern oaks stand 5 broodingly on her banks. The island and the waters around her teem with life. There is something eternal and indestructible about the tide-eroded shores and the dark, threatening silences of the swamps in the heart of the island. Yamacraw is beautiful because man has not yet had time to destroy this beauty.   10

The twentieth century has basically ignored the presence of Yamacraw. The island is populated with black people who depend on the sea and their small farms for a living. . . . Thus far, no bridge connects Yamacraw with the mainland, and anyone who sets foot on the island comes by water. The roads of the island are unpaved and rutted 15 by the passage of ox carts, still a major form of transportation. The hand pump serves up questionable water to the black residents who live in their small familiar houses. Sears, Roebuck catalogues perform their classic function in the crudely built privies, which sit, half-hidden, in the tall grasses behind the shacks. Electricity came to the island several 20 years ago. There is something unquestionably moving about the line of utility poles coming across the marsh, moving perhaps because electricity is a bringer of miracles and the journey of the faceless utility poles is such a long one—and such a humane one. But there are no telephones (electricity is enough of a miracle for one century). To call the island you 25 must go to the Beaufort Sheriff's Office and talk to the man who works the radio. Otherwise, Yamacraw remains aloof and apart from the world beyond the river.

1. What characteristics of the island does Conroy emphasize?
2. What pattern of arrangement does he use for the details?

2-G   My Son Jonah

Cecilia Cardeli (student)

Green eyes, speckled with gold, rust colored baby-fine hair bluntly cut in a Buster Brown, jeans worn out at the knees, unlaced pro-Keds on feet forever moving—that is my son Jonah.

From Jonah's lips laughter flows uncensored by propriety. He sees humor in the bra advertisements of the *Ladies Home Journal,* stout 5 people bending over, and the gait of intoxicated gentlemen. He idolizes Robin Williams, and Orkian is his favorite language. But nothing is funnier than his mom trying to do the steps of the latest dance craze.

A male chauvinist with nine years of experience in male/female relationships, Jonah has deduced that boys are smarter than girls and 10 mothers shouldn't work. He is a firm believer in girls with long hair down to the waist and boys with hair going no further than the neck. Against all current psychological theories, Jonah is convinced that dolls, washing dishes, anything pink, and pants without flies are sissy. In fact, he won't wear an off-white Aran sweater I bought on sale because the 15 label reads "Mimi, Ltd."

My son—what a curious mixture of humanity he is. Jonah can spell "Khomeini," collects Billy Joel records, is an avid Yankee fan, and beats me at chess. On the other hand, he still makes knots of his shoelaces, forgets to brush his teeth, does not believe in undershirts, loses one 20 mitten a week, and needs a nightlight to sleep.

1. How has the writer organized her description?
2. Why does she emphasize the information on Jonah's childishness by giving it last? How does this information affect our understanding of everything preceding it?

2-H   Benjamin Banneker: Room to Dream and Dare

Lerone Bennett, Jr.

This description comes from *Before the Mayflower: A History of the Negro in America* (1964) and gives the kind of factual information we expect from histories and encyclopedias. The brief references to Wheatley are transitional devices, connecting this section of the book to the preceding section.

Benjamin Banneker, like Phillis Wheatley, was a child of an age of birth pains. He was born in Maryland, the grandson of an Englishwoman and an African native. The Englishwoman, Molly Welsh, came to America as an indentured servant, worked her time out and bought a farm and two slaves. She freed the slaves and married one of them. 5 Banneker's mother, Mary, was one of four children born to this union. Banneker's father was an African native.

Banneker attended a local school with Negro and white children. Like Phillis Wheatley, he hungered and thirsted after books. His forte, however, was science—mathematics and astronomy. He became so 10 proficient in these subjects that he was named to the commission which surveyed the territory which became Washington, D.C. The Georgetown *Weekly Ledger* of March 12, 1791, noted the arrival of the commission. Banneker, the paper said, was "an Ethiopian whose abilities as surveyor and astronomer already prove that Mr. [Thomas] Jefferson's 15 concluding that that race of men were void of endowment was without foundation."

Beginning in 1791, Banneker issued an annual almanac which has been compared with Benjamin Franklin's *Poor Richard's Almanac.* He also continued the study of astronomy and other scientific subjects.   20

His was an idyllic life. He lived on a farm, about ten miles outside Baltimore. A confirmed bachelor, he studied all night, slept in the morning and worked in the afternoon. He washed his own clothes, cooked his own meals and cultivated gardens around his log cabin. He had an early fondness for "strong drinks," but later became a teetotaler. 25

His habits of study were odd, to say the least. Of a night, he would wrap himself in a great cloak and lie under a pear tree and meditate on the revolutions of the heavenly bodies. He would remain there throughout the night and take to his bed at dawn.

A contemporary has left a portrait of the stargazer. "His head was 30 covered with a thick suit of white hair, which gave him a very dignified and venerable appearance. . . . His dress was uniformly of superfine broadcloth, made in the old style of a plain coat, with straight collar and long waistcoat, and broad-brimmed hat. His color was not jet-black, but

decidedly Negro. In size and personal appearance, the statue of Frank- 35
lin at the Library of Philadelphia, as seen from the street, is a perfect
likeness. Go to his house when you would, either by day or night, there
was constantly standing in the middle of the floor a large table covered
with books and papers. As he was an eminent mathematician, he was
constantly in correspondence with other mathematicians in this coun- 40
try, with whom there was an interchange of questions of difficult solution."

Banneker, unlike Wheatley, boldly lashed out at the injustices of the
age. In a famous letter of 1791, he reminded Thomas Jefferson that words
were one thing and slavery was another. "Suffer me to recall to your 45
mind that time, in which the arms of the British crown were exerted,
with every powerful effort, in order to reduce you to a state of servitude;
look back, I entreat you . . . you were then impressed with proper ideas of
the great violation of liberty, and the free possession of those blessings, to
which you were entitled by nature; but, sir, how pitiable is it to reflect, 50
that although you were so fully convinced of the benevolence of the
Father of Mankind, and of his equal and impartial distribution of these
rights and privileges which he hath conferred upon them, that you
should at the same time counteract his mercies, in detaining by fraud
and violence, so numerous a part of my brethren under groaning captiv- 55
ity and cruel oppression, that you should at the same time be found guilty
of that most criminal act, which you professedly detested in others."

Banneker and Wheatley demonstrated, in their own ways, latent
possibilities in the burgeoning American Dream. To be sure, things
were not rosy in this period. But some men, a very few men, had room 60
to dream and dare and hope.

1. What information does the author give to support the claim made in his first
   sentence? How has he organized it?
2. Where and how does the author use specific detail, quotations, and historical
   data to develop his portrait? Why does he give the letter to Jefferson last?

Assignments

1. Make the following bare statements vivid through descriptive details, using
   concrete, specific words to evoke a particular situation and mood. Then
   rewrite each in different words so that you present an entirely different
   picture.
   Example: A child was looking out of a window.
   > A chubby girl of six with a tangle of brown curls pivoted on her
   > stomach across the window ledge as she surveyed the empty
   > street with a bored stare.
   > A skinny, undersized girl of six, her matted brown hair hanging to
   > her shoulders and her smudged cheeks streaked by tears, shiv-
   > ered fearfully in a corner of the window as she peered through
   > the slats in the Venetian blind at the angry, shouting mob in the
   > street below.

    a. A car went by.

    b. The rain fell.

    c. The music began.

    d. The man started to speak.

    e. The woman stood still.

    f. The crowd began to move.

2. Replace the following trite descriptions with fresher ones.

    Example: My feet felt as cold as ice.

              My feet felt like gravestones in a lonely cemetery.

    a. You look as fresh as a daisy.

    b. He turned as white as a sheet.

    c. The price of steak has gone sky-high.

    d. We laughed our heads off.

    e. The flowers danced in the breeze.

3. a. Imagine yourself somewhere alone in the dark, obliged to rely on senses other than sight, and write a paragraph describing your sensations.

    b. Then imagine yourself in the same place in daylight with a blind person, and write another paragraph describing it to that person.

4. Choose one of the photographs on pages 37 or 81. What in it first catches your attention? Why? Compose a paragraph of about 150 words explaining your answers to these questions. Imagine that your readers will be from one of the following groups, and indicate which you have chosen: (a) people living and working in small towns; (b) people living and working in large cities; (c) elderly people; (d) students in your college; (e) tourists from foreign countries who want to learn about American life.

5. Choose one of the photographs on pages 37 or 55 and compose a detailed description of it in about 250 words. Imagine that you will read your description to another student who is suffering from temporary eye trouble and who wants to be able to follow class discussion of the photograph.

6. a. Using strictly informative words, describe your room at home or at college so factually and accurately that the reader could readily draw a floor plan, complete with furnishings.

    b. Then write an evocative description of the same place, determining before you start exactly how you wish your reader to react and choosing your details carefully to evoke that reaction.

7. Write an exposition of some personal experience, enlivening it by the generous use of whatever descriptive devices you find suitable, particularly those that will evoke for the reader the sensations you yourself experienced. Look through the examples of descriptive writing in this unit for suggestions. Other possible subjects (which may remind you of still better ones) are getting up on a cold morning, attending a football game, participating in a swimming meet, riding on a roller coaster or an iceboat or in a racing car or a small plane, eating at a quick-lunch counter, visiting a fair or a stockyard, attending a religious service or a wedding reception.

8. Study the use of description as an aid to exposition in other selections, particularly those mentioned in the introductory note for the examples in this unit.

PHOTOGRAPHS FOR UNIT 2

How good an eyewitness are you? Test yourself by answering the questions on the next page. Be honest with yourself and do not turn back to look at the photographs until you have finished the test.

Photograph A   Wide World Photos

Photograph B   Rudy L. Klaiss, NYT/Pictures

Photograph A
1. How many people are pushing the car?
2. How many other people are in the picture?
3. What are the other people doing?
4. How many people are wearing black-belted coats?
5. On which person has the dog placed a paw?
6. One other car is visible—where is it?

Photograph B
1. What word is printed on the glider?
2. Do we see only one of the person's feet or both?
3. In what position are his or her elbows?

If you have more than half the right answers, you have done very well.

WRITING ASSIGNMENTS BASED ON THE PHOTOGRAPHS

1. Assume that these photographs are to be published in a newspaper in a northern city in the winter and compose a title and a statement of about 50 words for each to attract the reader's attention.
2. Assume that these photographs are to be published in a newspaper in a city in the Sunbelt and compose a title and a statement of about 50 words for each to attract the reader's attention. In what ways would your approach be different from the one you used for the first question?
3. Choose one of the photographs and write a detailed description of it for a reader who has not seen it. Assume that you are *not* able to send a copy of the photograph along with your description.

UNIT 3

Narration

What happened when Mary told her boss she wanted a raise? Did you hear about Dr. Brown and the rattlesnake in Arizona last summer? When Jim Drake was mayor, what were the main events in the city's history? What's the story behind your company's merger? Have you heard the one about the guy who bought a kayak to impress his girl friend, but. . . .

Our curiosity about other people, real or imaginary, seems endless. We all enjoy a good story, not only in a novel, a play, or a movie, but in almost anything we read. Narration, like description, particularizes rather than generalizes; it deals with the concrete rather than the abstract. An appropriate narrative, whether short or long, can strengthen and enliven almost anything you write. With it, you not only inform your readers but stimulate their imaginations so that they feel as if they themselves are experiencing the events you present, not merely hearing about them.

* * *   * * *   * * *

A narrative may be any length, from an anecdote to a long, complex story. You may use it to make your expository point explicit or only to imply it.

1. The brief narrative. An anecdote can catch your readers' attention *at the beginning* of a serious discussion. You may wish to make it humorous or provocative, but it should be related to your main idea and lead your readers into the main body of your essay. For example, the story of the three blind men who each formed a different idea of what an elephant was like could begin a discussion of a serious problem that you think is the result of misunderstanding. *Throughout the main body* of your essay, you may use brief narratives to make difficult points in your thought clear and vivid.

2. A long narrative as the main body. Over half your essay may be narrative, ending with an expository discussion of the point made. For example, in the parables of Jesus, a story is told and then interpreted as a moral lesson. *Aesop's Fables* are almost entirely narrative, with only the final line stating the expository purpose, the "moral."

3. A long narrative as the entire essay. Any account that lists consecutive actions or events is essentially a narrative; yet it is intended, of course, to explain, and is therefore basically informative rather than entertaining. An allegory, such as Bunyan's *Pilgrim's Progress,* and a satire, such as Swift's *Gulliver's Travels,* may at first seem to be only story-telling, but they are really narrative presentations of deeper moral meanings and social criticism. The "social purpose" novel concentrates on some problem that the story illustrates. In Steinbeck's *Grapes of Wrath,* for instance, the experiences of the Joad family are particular examples of the general problems farmers faced in the severe drought of the 1930s. These works are completely narrative in presentation but completely expository in purpose.

*   *   *   *   *   *   *   *   *

Catching and holding your reader's interest is essential to the success of any narrative. You do not have to write of dramatic adventures to make a good story. Indeed, some of the best stories tell of everyday experiences. Whether you describe a plane crash or a sandlot baseball game, a trip into space or a backyard picnic, the purpose of your essay will determine your choice of narrative material. What matters is how you handle it.

1. Subject matter. Choose an event that has *significance* for you—an emotional force or an intellectual meaning that you can pass on to your readers. If your only point about a trip is that "We went to Key West" or about a ball game that "Our side won," your narrative will not interest your readers. The more strongly you care about an event, whether real or imaginary, the more likely you are to make it interesting for your readers, and your point of view, whether humorous, whimsical, or serious, will give it unity.

2. Suspense. All narratives should have suspense. They should make readers want to know what happened next, who won, what was the final outcome. Suspense is based primarily on conflict—whether mild or intense—between characters, between a character and circumstances, between conflicting desires in a single character's mind. Two students struggling for the same prize, a woman battling against alcoholism, a teenager torn between duty to parents and the desire to leave home—all these conflicts and similar ones create suspense.

3. Climax. Narrative incidents should build up progressively to the climax, the highest point of interest. Some narratives stop short when they reach that point, as O. Henry did with his "surprise endings," and others unwind more slowly after it, but the ending should always be brief. Any material after the climax may seem anticlimactic and dull.

4. Time. Description deals primarily with spatial patterns, but narrative deals primarily with chronological patterns.

a. Sequence. For a short incident, the normal sequence of start to finish may work well; for a longer one, it is often more effective to begin at an exciting point anywhere in the action to catch your readers' interest, returning to it later to fill in briefly any necessary background. Compare these two ways of handling the same material:

(1) One fine April afternoon three of us sixth-grade boys decided to skip school. We wandered indecisively for an hour or two through the outskirts of the town and finally landed at the ball park, where we began a game of old cat, doubly delightful because illicitly enjoyed. Bill finally hit the ball over the fence, where it went through the window of the caretaker's cottage.

(2) "Home run!" yelled Bill triumphantly, leaning on his bat while he watched the ball he had just struck sail over the park fence. But his triumph was short—a shattering of glass from the caretaker's cottage struck us all numb. A broken window on top of our earlier sin! For we three sixth-grade boys had skipped school that fine April afternoon, and after an hour or so of indecisive wandering through the outskirts of town had wound up at the ball park for a game of old cat—doubly delightful because illicitly enjoyed.

b. Compression and expansion. In narration, you may compress or expand the time element to suit your purpose, summarizing ten unimportant years in less than a sentence but spending pages to recount the events of ten shattering seconds. Skillfully handled, variations in time can help you to emphasize incidents important to your purpose and to ignore unimportant ones.

* * *   * * *   * * *

Creating the illusion of reality is the special strength of narrative, and your effectiveness will depend on it. Consider these devices to help you.

1. Present tense verbs can make past events come to life, as in "Then I start to run, and he throws to first, but Mac fumbles the ball." Remember, however, not to change tenses within a single part of your narrative unless you wish to indicate a change in time.

2. Concrete and **specific diction** is as important to narrative as it is to description. Help your readers to see and hear the events you narrate (and to smell, taste, and feel them if they involve other sensations). In dialogue, for instance, if the speakers reveal their emotions by their tone of voice, choose verbs that suggest the tone, such as *mutter, sigh,* or *yell.*

Caution: Do not overdo this. Vigorous words call attention to themselves. If what is said is important but not the manner of speaking, a simple *said* will be better.

3. Dialogue, directly transcribed, is more lifelike and often more compact than indirect reporting of what was said. For example, compare the directly reported dialogue in "Yumbo" (page 44) with this indirectly reported version:

> The eruptive girl at the counter asked what the man wanted. He repeated that he wished to order a ham and cheese sandwich. The girl said that she was sorry but that they did not carry ham and cheese sandwiches. All that they had was what was on the menu board above her.

If you must make up the dialogue, take care that the content and the manner of speaking are both appropriate to the speakers. For the conventional methods of punctuating dialogue, consult a handbook and note the examples in this unit.

4. Characters, setting, and details should be as real and vivid as the events of the narrative. Action does not occur in a vacuum. Give specific, concrete descriptions to show your readers when, where, and how it takes place. Also show briefly the kinds of people involved by giving speech, actions, and specific details of appearance, not by making long explanations. Readers cannot have much interest in "us" or "them" if they are never told who "we" and "they" are. Compare these two versions of the same incident:

> (a) We had been working for an hour to get our truck jacked up so that my companion could change a tire that had gone flat on our way to town. Once more the jack slipped, and he started to try yet again.
> (b) The slab of wood on which the jack was resting tilted gently into the roadside ooze and let the rear of the heavy truck down for the third time in that hour of mud and sweat.
> "Dang it! Er—pardon me, miss" was the only reaction of the patient, elderly "hired hand" who was helping me to deliver my load of sheep. Without another word he gave his suspenders a hitch and crawled doggedly under the truck to try again.

5. Personal experience is always the best source of narrative material. A student once tried to write dramatically of a parachute jump; but factual errors revealed what she later confessed—that she had never even been in an airplane. Some professional writers of fiction can produce the illusion of reality without having known the people, visited the scenes, or experienced the events they describe. As a beginning writer, however, you will be wise to base your narratives entirely on your own experiences. Then you will have a large fund of accurate, specific details and can select the best to give your narrative reality.

❋   *Examples*

In the following selections, the writers support their main points primarily by narration; you will find that nearly half the writers of the other selections in this book also use narratives, sometimes only a few sentences long, sometimes several paragraphs. Look particularly at Smith's "One-Man Show" (1-B), White's "Farewell, My Lovely" (5-C), Davenport's " 'Trees' " (7-A), Baker's "The Boy Who Came to Supper" (9-D), Panzeca's "Outer Limits" (10-E), Nemy's "Business Status—How Do You Rate" (10H), Ivins's "Why They Mourned for Elvis Presley" (11-F), King's "The Decisive Arrest" (12-C), Huxley's "The Method of Scientific Investigation (12-B), Zinsser's "Letter from Home" (13-C), Huttmann's "A Crime of Compassion" (15-D), and Hoggart's "The Prestige of PRAL" (16-H).

3-A   Yumbo

Andrew Ward

This short essay appeared in the *Atlantic Monthly* (1977). The writer narrates two experiences to explain his dislike of the way some restaurants treat their customers.

NARRATIVE
DEVICES
Setting,
character

Generaliza-
tion

Details

Generaliza-
tion
Details

Generaliza-
tion

Details

I was sitting at an inn with Kelly Susan, my ten-year-old niece, when she was handed the children's menu. It was printed in gay pastels on construction paper and gave her a choice of a Ferdinand Burger, a Freddie the Fish Stick, or a Porky Pig Sandwich. Like most children's menus, it first anthropomorphized the ingredients and then killed them off. As Kelly read it her eyes grew large, and in them I could see gentle Ferdinand being led away to the stockyard, Freddie gasping at the end of a hook, Porky stuttering his entreaties as the ax descended. Kelly Susan, alone in her family, is a resolute vegetarian and has already faced up to the dread that whispers to us as we slice our steaks. She wound up ordering a cheese sandwich, but the children's menu had ruined her appetite, and she spent the meal picking at her food.

Restaurants have always treated children badly. When I was small, my family used to travel a lot, and waitresses were forever calling me "Butch" and pinching my cheeks and making me wear paper bibs with slogans on them. Restaurants still treat children badly; the difference is that restaurants have lately taken to treating us all as if we were children. We are obliged to order an Egg McMuffin when we want breakfast, a Fishamajig

when we want a fish sandwich, a Fribble when we want
a milkshake, a Whopper when we want a hamburger with 25
all the fixings. Some of these names serve a certain purpose. By calling a milkshake a Fribble, for instance, the
management need make no promise that it contains milk,
or even that it was shaken.

Generaliza-
tion

But the primary purpose is to convert an essentially 30
bleak industry, mass-marketed fast foods, into something
festive. The burger used to be a culinary last resort; now
resorts are being built around it. The patrons in the com-

Details

mercials for burger franchises are all bug-eyed and goofy,
be they priests or grandmothers or crane operators, and 35
behave as if it were their patriotic duty, their God-given
right, to consume waxy buns, translucent patties, chewy
fries, and industrial strength Coca-Cola.

Setting,
character

Happily, the patrons who actually slump into these
places are an entirely different matter. I remember with 40
fond admiration a tidy little man at the local Burger King
whom I overheard order a ham and cheese sandwich.

"A wha'?" the eruptive girl at the counter asked, pencil poised over her computer card.

"I wish to order a ham and cheese sandwich," the man 45
repeated.

Dialogue

"I'm sorry, sir," the girl said, "but we don't carry ham
and cheese. All we got is what's on the board up there."

"Yes, I know," the man politely persisted, "but I believe it is up there. See? The ham and cheese?" 50

The girl gaped at the menu board behind her. "Oh,"
she finally exclaimed. "You mean a *Yumbo.* You want a
Yumbo."

"The ham and cheese. Yes."

Conflict

"It's called a *Yumbo,* sir," the girl said. "Now, do you 55
want a Yumbo or not?"

Suspense

The man stiffened. "Yes, thank you," he said through
his teeth, "the *ham* and *cheese.*"

"Look," the girl shouted, "I've got to have an order
here. You're holding up the line. You want a *Yumbo,* don't 60
you? You want a *Yumbo?*"

But the tidy man was not going to say it, and thus were
they locked for a few more moments, until at last he stood
very straight, put on his hat, and departed intact.

1. Where does the writer first state his thesis?
2. How are the generalizations placed in relation to the specific details?

3. In the second illustration how does the writer indicate the stages of increasing tension between the counter girl and the man?
4. The first illustration contains no dialogue. Why is it unnecessary here?
5. Check all the definitions for these words in a large dictionary: *anthropomorphized, resolute.*

3-B   A Loaf of Bread and the Stars

Richard Wright

Wright narrates this experience in his autobiography, *Black Boy* (1937), in which a major point is his struggle growing up black in a white-dominated society.

One day I went to the optical counter of a department store to deliver a pair of eyeglasses. The counter was empty of customers and a tall, florid-faced white man looked at me curiously. He was unmistakably a Yankee, for his physical build differed sharply from that of the lanky Southerner.   5

"Will you please sign for this, sir?" I asked, presenting the account book and the eyeglasses.

He picked up the book and the glasses, but his eyes were still upon me.

"Say, boy, I'm from the North," he said quietly.   10

I held very still. Was this a trap? He had mentioned a tabooed subject and I wanted to wait until I knew what he meant. Among the topics that southern white men do not like to discuss with Negroes were the following: American white women; the Ku Klux Klan; France, and how Negro soldiers fared while there; Frenchwomen; Jack Johnson; the   15 entire northern part of the United States; the Civil War; Abraham Lincoln; U. S. Grant; General Sherman; Catholics; the Pope; Jews; the Republican party; slavery; social equality; Communism; Socialism; the 13th, 14th, and 15th Amendments to the Constitution or any topic calling for positive knowledge or manly self-assertion on the part of the   20 Negro. The most accepted topics were sex and religion. I did not look at the man or answer. With one sentence he had lifted out of the silent dark the race question and I stood on the edge of a precipice.

"Don't be afraid of me," he went on. "I just want to ask you one question."   25

"Yes, sir," I said in a waiting, neutral tone.

"Tell me, boy, are you hungry?" he asked seriously.

I stared at him. He had spoken one word that touched the very soul of me, but I could not talk to him, could not let him know that I was starving myself to save money to go north. I did not trust him. But my   30 face did not change its expression.

"Oh, no, sir," I said, managing a smile.

I was hungry and he knew it; but he was a white man and I felt that if I told him I was hungry I would have been revealing something shameful.   35

"Boy, I can see hunger in your face and eyes," he said.

"I get enough to eat," I lied.

"Then why do you keep so thin?" he asked me.

"Well, I suppose I'm just that way, naturally," I lied.

"You're just scared, boy," he said.   40

"Oh, no, sir," I lied again.

I could not look at him. I wanted to leave the counter, yet he was a white man and I had learned not to walk abruptly away from a white man when he was talking to me. I stood, my eyes looking away. He ran his hand into his pocket and pulled out a dollar bill.   45

"Here, take this dollar and buy yourself some food," he said.

"No, sir," I said.

"Don't be a fool," he said. "You're ashamed to take it. God, boy, don't let a thing like that stop you from taking a dollar and eating."

The more he talked the more it became impossible for me to take   50 the dollar. I wanted it, but I could not look at it. I wanted to speak, but I could not move my tongue. I wanted him to leave me alone. He frightened me.

"Say something," he said.

All about us in the store were piles of goods; white men and women 55 went from counter to counter. It was summer and from a high ceiling was suspended a huge electric fan that whirred. I stood waiting for the white man to give me the signal that would let me go.

"I don't understand it," he said through his teeth. "How far did you go in school?"   60

"Through the ninth grade, but it was really the eighth," I told him. "You see, our studies in the ninth grade were more or less a review of what we had in the eighth grade."

Silence. He had not asked me for this long explanation, but I had spoken at length to fill up the yawning, shameful gap that loomed 65 between us; I had spoken to try to drag the unreal nature of the conversation back to safe and sound southern ground. Of course, the conversation was real; it dealt with my welfare, but it had brought to the surface of day all the dark fears I had known all my life. The Yankee white man did not know how dangerous his words were.   70

(There are some elusive, profound, recondite things that men find hard to say to other men; but with the Negro it is the little things of life that become hard to say, for these tiny items shape his destiny. A man will seek to express his relation to the stars; but when a man's consciousness has been riveted upon obtaining a loaf of bread, that loaf of bread 75 is as important as the stars.)

Another white man walked up to the counter and I sighed with relief.

"Do you want the dollar?" the man asked.

"No, sir," I whispered.   80

"All right," he said. "Just forget it."

He signed the account book and took the eyeglasses. I stuffed the book into my bag and turned from the counter and walked down the aisle, feeling a physical tingling along my spine, knowing that the white man knew I was really hungry. I avoided him after that. Whenever I 85 saw him I felt in a queer way that he was my enemy, for he knew how I felt and the safety of my life in the South depended upon how well I concealed from all whites what I felt.

1. Where does Wright place his chief expository remarks?
2. How is this placement different from that in the first example of narrative used for an expository purpose?
3. What would have been the effect if Wright had placed all of them at the very end? at the beginning?
4. Check all the definitions for these words in a large dictionary: *elusive, profound, recondite.*

3-C

A New Life

Carl Granville (student)

It was 9:26 P.M. on December 11th, 1974. I had awaited this moment nine months. I had left work early to be by her side. She was always adamant that I should be there when it happened.

She had been in the labor room for almost ten hours. The endless screams from the woman in the next room made my wife become more 5 and more frightened. As gently as possible, I tried to calm her, but I myself had been having doubts. What if something went wrong? What if their lives were in danger? My fears were forgotten as the baby's head began to emerge. I felt a sparkling tingle throughout my body. What a moment! The birth of my child!   10

"Mr. Granville, you'll have to leave now." Pause.

"Sir, you'll have to leave now." The voice was firm, official.

It was like being rudely interrupted in the middle of a wonderful dream, and a full minute elapsed before I realized what was happening. I started to speak, but seeing the futility of a protest, I dejectedly left 15 the room. At 9:35 P.M. they whisked her off to the delivery room.

Here I am in the waiting room. There are three more expectant fathers present. One is anxiously wearing out the carpet, pacing up and down. Another seems nervously impatient. The third one, seated in a corner away from the rest, seems to be in a daze. I sit and try to read 20 a book.

"This is your first?" asks the impatient one.

"Uhh?"

"This your first?"

"Oh, yes . . . yes." 25

"This is my third. I got two girls already. Man, girls cost too much, but with my old lady always wrapped around me, what else can I do?"

My sudden laughter disrupts the pacer and breaks the trance of the man in the corner.

"Oh, man," the talkative one goes on, "she's been in there for about 30 a half-hour already. What the hell's keeping them this long?"

My analysis was right. He is impatient. Five minutes later the nurse announces that he has girl number three. He shakes my hand gloomily and wishes me luck as he leaves. Immediately after, a very broad smile runs across the face of the man in the corner. He has just heard that his 35 wife has given birth to an eight-pound boy.

I put down the book. "I hope I get a boy, too," I think. I start to imagine all the fun we will have together. Why, when he's six, I'll only be twenty-six myself. He will be "wicked" but obedient. He will be just like his daddy. We will have such fun. Please, please, let it be a 40 boy.

The pacer leaves to purchase a soda. We have exchanged only a few words so far. In his absence the nurse appears to announce that his wife gave birth to a ten-pound boy. I find that his wife is the woman who was screaming. I greet him with the news as he returns, and his face lights 45 up like a Christmas tree. He startles me with a tremendous shout of glee. I cannot help feeling happy for him. The joy in his face is overwhelming. Now more than ever I want a boy.

The nurse appears again. "Mr. Granville, your wife gave birth to a girl. She weighs six pounds, eleven ounces." 50

The time is 10:11 P.M. For the second time tonight I feel throbs of depression. My wife is aware of this as I stand by her bed. She reminds me that I should be thankful that she and the baby came through in good health. I feel ashamed at my show of depression. Oh, but I so wanted a boy. How can I have much fun with a girl? Try as I do, it's hard 55 to shake off the depression that engulfs me. After half-heartedly joking with my wife for a while, I leave for home.

I buy myself a tall can of beer to celebrate my parenthood and I telephone my best friend to let him know the news. While I am chatting with him, a new thought dawns. What important difference, other than 60 sexual, is there between a boy and a girl? I mean, why can't I have as much fun with a girl as I think I will have with a boy? Why try to put people into pigeonholes? Why don't I give her a chance to prove her-self?

The next day at 8:40 A.M. I present myself at the Kings County 65 Hospital, maternity section. I am joyful with a vibrant new perspective, evident in my bounce and spirit. I kiss my baby and look upon her not as a girl or boy, but as a living, capable, human being. I ask my wife's forgiveness for my behavior last night and tell her how much I love her for bringing us closer together through our baby.   70

Now, two years later, I could not be happier as a father. I have kept my resolution to treat my daughter as a human being, which in turn has made me more appreciative of my wife. The fun that I have with my daughter goes way beyond my expectations; the joy she has brought into my life can never be described in mere words. She surely has had 75 a positive effect in changing my attitude towards others, sex notwith-standing. As a matter of fact, I could not care less whether my next baby is a boy or a girl.

I'll always treasure my daughter for this change in me, but right now all I can do is reflect on the beauty, the mystery, the sweetness, the 80 power of life and love. Thank you, Chère, and you, too, Pauline.

1. Why does the author begin with verbs in the past tense and then shift to verbs in the present tense?
2. What do the references to the specific times and the descriptions of the other expectant fathers contribute? Why is the nurse only a voice?

3-D   The Logical Cab Driver

David Schoenbrun

This anecdote appears in *As France Goes* (1957), which presents the writer's views on France and the French, gained from his long experience living there as a political corre-spondent for the *New York Times*.

The "intellectualism" of the French is found at every level of soci-ety. The café waiter, the taxicab driver, the restaurateur, the so-called "little people" of France are the most stimulating, if frequently exas-perating, conversationalists in the world. Of them all, the most anarchis-tic and voluble is the taxicab driver. I deliberately provoke arguments 5 with them—an easy thing to do—to see what they will say next. Of the hundreds of discussions in cabs one remains in my memory as uniquely, superbly French. It could not have occurred in any other country, except possibly in Brooklyn, where there exists a species of man akin in spirit if not in actual form to the French.   10

It was midnight in Paris and we were rolling along the Quai d'Or-
say toward the Avenue Bosquet, where I live, on the left bank of the
river Seine. As we came to the Pont Alexandre III the cab slowed down,
for the traffic light was red against us, and then, without stopping, we
sailed through the red light in a sudden burst of speed. The same 15
performance was repeated at the Alma Bridge. As I paid the driver I
asked him why he had driven through two red lights.

"You ought to be ashamed of yourself, a veteran like you, breaking
the law and endangering your life that way," I protested.

He looked at me astonished. "Ashamed of myself? Why, I'm proud 20
of myself. I am a law-abiding citizen and have no desire to get killed
either." He cut me off before I could protest.

"No, just listen to me before you complain. What did I do? Went
through a red light. Well, did you ever stop to consider what a red light
is, what it means?" 25

"Certainly," I replied. "It's a stop signal and means that traffic is
rolling in the opposite direction."

"Half-right," said the driver, "but incomplete. It is only an automatic stop signal. And it does not mean that there is cross traffic. Did
you see any cross traffic during our trip? Of course not. I slowed down 30
at the light, looked carefully to the right and to the left. Not another
car on the streets at this hour. Well, then! What would you have me do?
Should I stop like a dumb animal because an automatic, brainless machine turns red every forty seconds? No, monsieur," he thundered,
hitting the door jamb with a huge fist. "I am a man, not a machine. I 35
have eyes and a brain and judgment, given me by God. It would be a
sin against nature to surrender them to the dictates of a machine.
Ashamed of myself, you say? I would only be ashamed of myself if I let
those blinking lamps do my thinking for me. Good night, monsieur."

Is this bad, is this good? Frankly I no longer am sure. The intellec- 40
tual originality of the French is a corrupting influence if you are subjected to it for long. I never doubted that it was wrong to drive through
a red light. After more than a decade of life in Paris, however, I find my
old Anglo-Saxon standards somewhat shaken. I still think it is wrong to
drive through a stop signal, except possibly very late at night, after 45
having carefully checked to make sure there is no cross traffic. After all,
I am a man, not a machine.

1. The writer wants us to see his experience as an illustration of his generalization that the French have great intellectual originality. What narrative devices does he use to try to make us share his experience and hear and see
   the cab driver?
2. The writer could have told the anecdote in far fewer words if he had summa-
   rized much of what he and the driver said instead of reporting it in full. What
   would be lost in a shorter version?

3. Although the writer quotes five statements, he uses "said" only once (line 25). How does he indicate elsewhere the speaker and tone of voice?
4. Check all the definitions of these words in a large dictionary: *anarchistic, voluble.*

3-E   On a Commuter Train

Willie Morris

This anecdote appears in *North Towards Home* (1967), Willie Morris's autobiographical account of his experiences growing up in a small Mississippi town and then working in New York. Throughout the book, he emphasizes the respect, or lack of it, shown by Americans toward each other. Although no thesis statement appears in this excerpt, Morris implies his dismay at the impersonality of life in a big city.

One afternoon in late August, as the summer's sun streamed into the car and made little jumping shadows on the windows, I sat gazing out at the tenement-dwellers, who were themselves looking out of their windows from the gray crumbling buildings along the tracks of upper Manhattan. As we crossed into the Bronx, the train unexpectedly 5 slowed down for a few miles. Suddenly from out of my window I saw a large crowd near the tracks, held back by two policemen. Then, on the other side from my window, I saw a sight I would never be able to forget: a little boy almost severed in halves, lying at an incredible angle near the track. The ground was covered with blood, and the boy's eyes 10 were opened wide, strained and disbelieving in his sudden oblivion. A policeman stood next to him, his arms folded, staring straight ahead at the windows of our train. In the orange glow of late afternoon the policemen, the crowd, the corpse of the boy were for a brief moment immobile, motionless, a small tableau to violence and death in the city. 15 Behind me, in the next row of seats, there was a game of bridge. I heard one of the four men say as he looked out at the sight, "God, that's horrible." Another said, in a whisper, "Terrible, terrible." There was a momentary silence, punctuated only by the clicking of the wheels on the track. Then, after the pause, I heard the first man say: "Two hearts." 20

1. Is Morris necessarily condemning the man who resumes the bidding?
2. Why does Morris repeat three times in one phrase that the scene was still, saying that everything was "immobile, motionless, a small tableau"?
3. An incident that presents such a dramatic contrast in behavior in such a short space may seem like a writer's attempt to find an easy way to impress readers. What of Morris's own role in this narrative and the fact that, like the card players, he is shut in a moving train and cannot be more than a spectator?
4. Check all the definitions of these words in a large dictionary: *incredible* (how does it differ from "incredulous"?), *tableau.*

3-F   Conflict

Roger A. Painter (student)

The writer begins by narrating three incidents to illustrate his point and lead to his
expository discussion. Note how the ending unifies the essay and emphasizes the conflict.

He came into the house quietly and made sure the door was locked.
He walked silently to his bedroom and turned the lamp on low-beam.
"Where have you been?"
"Mother, I've been out."
"What were you doing?"   5
"Mother, I was out."
"Who were you with?"
"Mother, please go to sleep. I was out."
"But what were you doing this late?"
"Mother, if you didn't live here and I went to school here you 10
wouldn't know I was out and it wouldn't bother you."
"But I'm worried."
"I know, Mother. It is late. Good night."
                    . . .
"Where were you?"   15
"Hello."
His bicycle had jangled as he put the kickstand down and the sound
brought her to the door.
"I was studying."
"Have you had supper?"   20
"Yes."
"Where?"
"At the Union."
"I had supper for you."
"I'm sorry. I tried to call."   25
                    . . .
"You can't go to class in that outfit."
"Why not?"
"You have better shoes than that. Those things look like your par-
ents don't give you any money."   30
"This is what I feel like wearing today."
"You had better not leave with those shoes on."
"I'm almost late now—good-bye."
"Change them."
"Good-bye."   35
                    . . .
With these sketches I hope to illustrate the sometimes trivial, but
nevertheless real conflict from which I draw certain conclusions. Resid-
ing under the wings of the hen in the postadolescent years may cause

problems that, while seemingly only trivial at the time, collectively 40
produce an amount of friction that makes smoke.

Living at home has advantages for the college student: automobile, cheap room and board, and a vast number of other benefits easily enumerated by most parents. These things tend to build dependence on parents that is hard to break later on. At school, attendance is not 45 taken in most classes, daily assignments are not collected, and students are, to a large extent, on their own. The campus students, in most cases, must keep a watch on their money supply, their time, and their actions, and in general must learn to get along without their parents. This is a part of education that I miss.   50

I am rebellious, as is natural at my age, and, whereas the campus students take this feeling out in actions and bull-sessions with their friends, I take it out on my parents. This isolation and lack of communication with campus life is one of the greatest problems the "townies" have to cope with. The effort to fit in socially is hampered by the fact 55 that many campus organizations and activities are organized on the housing-unit basis: intramurals, dances, programs, and a large number of lesser things. But it is hard to justify a separate residence and its expense for these activities alone.

The questions and conflicts are many, and I think that the conflict 60 of interest will inevitably cause a break. If the break is hastened by prolonged and forced confrontation, it is less likely to be friendly. The on-campus student does not have the burden of forcing such a break, and I think this is much better. It is a real problem that I face, and it is not an easy one.   65

· · ·

"What are you writing?"
"A rhetoric theme, Mother."

Assignments

1. Think back to your earliest memories of school. What incident stands out most? Why? Compose a narrative about it in which you give your readers the details they need to be able to picture the experience and relive it with you.
2. Choose a personal experience for which an old proverb such as "He who hesitates is lost," "A stitch in time saves nine," "A friend in need is a friend indeed," "Man proposes, God disposes," or "Penny-wise but pound-foolish" would make an appropriate title. Then narrate the experience briefly in such a way that your readers will see your point with little or no direct explanation from you.
3. Imagine that the editor of a magazine that tries to appeal to the "general reader" plans to use one of the photographs on page 55 or 81 and has asked you to write a narrative of about 300 to 500 words for which the photograph would be an appropriate illustration. You may draw on your own experience, actual events, your imagination, or any combination of these.

4. Most well-known children's stories have strong moral points. Choose a familiar one such as "Little Red Ridinghood," "Cinderella," or "Jack and the Beanstalk" and retell it with specific descriptive detail and as much suspense as you can create, building up to the moral point. Imagine that you will read your version to an intelligent, appreciative child about 7 or 8 years old.
5. Use the plot of the same story or a similar one, but this time give it a modern setting and logical explanations for any fantastic elements. Imagine that your readers will be people of your age and general interests.
6. Choose any fairly short television drama or comedy that you have enjoyed and that made a strong point. Retell it as a story, with full background detail.
7. Choose an editorial with which you agree and compose a short anecdote that illustrates its point in some way and that could therefore be used to introduce it.
8. Study the contribution that narrative makes to exposition in examples in other units, particularly those mentioned in the introductory note for the examples in this unit.

PHOTOGRAPHS FOR UNIT 3

How good an eyewitness are you? Test yourself by answering the questions on the next page. Be honest with yourself and do not turn back to look at the photographs again until you have finished the test. If you answer six of the twelve questions correctly, you are more observant than the average person.

Photograph A   Hoops, de Wys

Photograph B   Hoops, de Wys

QUESTIONS ON THE PHOTOGRAPHS FOR UNIT 3

Photograph A
1. Which of the woman's hands is the man holding?
2. How far across his body does her other hand reach?
3. How many of her fingers can you see?
4. In which of his hands is the man holding the woman's hand?
5. What clothing can you see on the man?
6. What jewelry of any kind can you see?

Photograph B
1. On which child can we see part of a shirt?
2. Do the children's jackets seem to be the same style?
3. What kind of shirt can we see on one child?
4. Is there a knife or a fork in the picture?
5. How many plates can you see in the picture?
6. What is the design of the plates?

WRITING ASSIGNMENTS BASED ON THE PHOTOGRAPHS

1. Assume that these photographs are to be published together in a small-town newspaper as examples of "human interest" photography. For each one, compose a title and a statement of about 50 words to attract the readers' attention.
2. Choose one of the two photographs and compose a short narrative for which it could be an illustration.

UNIT 4

Exemplification

"A picture is worth a thousand words," the familiar saying tells us. A single example—a picture in words—can help to explain, support, and bring to life a theory or opinion more effectively than a thousand generalizations can. Of all the ways to make theories and opinions understandable, examples are by far the most widely used and helpful.

The writer of "More Power to You" (2-C) does not merely claim that "To watch a jet engine spring to life is to feel that power." He goes on to give us the sight, sound, smell, and throbbing feeling of the engine. Andrew Ward does not merely claim that "Restaurants have always treated children badly" (3-A). He immediately tells us that when he was small "waitresses were forever calling me 'Butch' and pinching my cheek and making me wear paper bibs with slogans on them." You may have noticed that all the pieces of writing in this book are presented as "examples" of exposition and are further labeled as examples of description, narration, and so on, because they are chosen to help explain what those generalized terms mean.

Choosing what examples to use and deciding where and how to use them in any piece of writing will depend on your answers to these closely related questions:

1. **What is your precise subject?**
2. **Who are your intended readers**—what are they likely to know of your subject, what are they likely not to know of it, and what opinions on it are they likely to have formed?
3. **What is your main purpose** in writing on this particular subject for these particular readers?
4. **What should you most emphasize** to achieve your purpose?

The less your readers know about the subject, the more they will need examples to help them understand it and the more detailed and basic those examples must be. Even knowledgeable readers need examples when the subject is complex or controversial. If your main purpose is to do more than simply inform them, choose examples that are lively and colorful as well as understandable.

This advice will be clearer if we take it ourselves and illustrate it with examples. Imagine that two recent graduates of your college who now live far away and who are ardent soccer fans have asked you to write them about a recent game. You know that they will be happy to learn that the home team played well. In your narrative of who did what and when during the game, you will therefore choose examples of the players' skill to support your claim that the team played well. Since your intended readers are soccer fans and familiar with the team and the college, you can freely use technical terms and local references. To give your readers the feeling that they are actually watching the game, you will include as many examples of the play in as much detail as you have the time and strength to write, arranging them in chronological order.

Now, imagine instead that your intended readers are recent graduates who have little interest in soccer but who love the college and will be pleased to learn that the team has won a major victory. For them you will select the most dramatic moment of the game as your main example of the team's skill and describe it in some detail but with few technical terms. To increase the dramatic effect, you will lead up to it with short descriptions of three or four exciting moments as examples of the team's skill, starting with the least dramatic so that your sequence will build up to the most important moment.

Next, imagine that your intended readers are friends who live too far away for you to see them often and who have never visited your college. You suspect that they have asked you to describe a soccer game only out of politeness because they know of your interest in the sport. For them you will choose examples—two or three at the most—with a general appeal, those primarily of human interest and, if possible, with humorous overtones. You will present these briefly with just enough specific detail to make them colorful, saving the best for last to serve as a climax and using technical terms only when you also define them.

You may draw examples from your subject matter, as in the case of the soccer game, or from any source that you think will help your readers to understand your point. For instance, in a discussion of political leaders you might use George Washington as an example of a generally admired president, thus drawing on your historical knowledge and reminding your readers of their own study of history. You might use Romeo and Juliet as examples of young lovers, drawing on your own and your readers memories of a well-known literary work. Using your imagination, you might suggest that a child who shares his favorite toy with a playmate and who does not complain when the playmate accidentally breaks it illustrates the meaning of unselfishness.

In using examples, always use the questions listed earlier as a guide, and on the basis of your answers do the following:

1. Choose examples that your readers will understand readily; explain any details that might puzzle them.
2. Develop each example with only as much detail as is essential for your readers' understanding—remember that the example is meant to be an assistance, not the whole subject.
3. Draw on the descriptive and narrative skills discussed in Units 2 and 3, and be concrete and specific.

 Examples

The writers of the following selections rely primarily on exemplification to support their main points; you will find exemplification in some degree in almost every selection in this book. Look again at Cardeli's "My Son Jonah" (2-G), Ward's "Yumbo" (3-A), Wright's "A Loaf of Bread and the Stars" (3-B), and Schoenbrun's "The Logical Cab 5 Driver" (3-D). In later units notice the exemplification in Thomas's "On Societies as Organisms" (5-B), White's "Farewell, My Lovely" (5-C), Zinsser's "Clutter" (6-D), Sybul's "Taking Care of Contacts" (8-C), *New Society*'s "Social Control" (9-F), Gould's "Left Holding the Bat" (12-F), Ashe's "An Open Letter to Black Parents" (13-F), Trippett's "A Red 10 Light for Scofflaws" (13-H), Ketchum's "The Farmer—an Endangered Species?" (15-E), and Hoggart's "The Prestige of PRAL" (16-H).

4-A   The Greatest Welterweight in the World

Mark Manganiello (student)

This was written in a fifty-minute class period in the last week of the term. The assignment was to choose a particularly admirable athlete, or performer in the arts, or political leader, and to write a paper defending the choice as forcefully as possible.

Boxer Sugar Ray Leonard is the world's greatest fighter in the welterweight (up to 147 pounds) and junior middleweight (up to 165 pounds) categories. I can back up my seemingly exaggerated opinion with facts.

Sugar Ray won four gold medals as an amateur in the 1976 Olympic 5 Games. He went on to win his first championship crown by defeating welterweight champion, Pipino Cuevas. Then, after twenty-four successive victories, he lost his title in a disputed bout to Roberto Duran, who was known as the best fighter, pound for pound, in the welterweight division. But four months later, in October of 1980, Leonard 10 defeated Duran. He then beat Thomas "Hit Man" Hearns, the hardest puncher in the welterweight division, who also held the World Boxing

Association version of the welterweight crown. This victory unified the welterweight title for the first time in fifteen years. Sugar Ray won his third title by knocking out previously undefeated junior middleweight 15 champion Ayub Haluk. This gave him special prestige because he moved *up* in weight to win a title, whereas most of the other champions moved down in weight to gain a title. Also, only twelve fighters in the entire history of boxing have held three world championship titles and only four of these have held the titles simultaneously, but Sugar Ray 20 Leonard has done both.

Now Sugar Ray has retired with grace and dignity and with a 40-1-0 record and three world championships under his belt at only twenty-eight years of age. I do not know of anyone who has completed half as much as he has in such a short time. I rest my case.   25

1. What kinds of examples does the writer use to illustrate Sugar Ray's success?
2. In what order has the writer arranged the examples? What are the advantages and disadvantages of using this order?

4-B   Le Contrat Social

H. L. Mencken

Henry Louis Mencken (1880–1956), an American journalist, editor, and critic, was respected for his intelligence and feared for his satiric wit. His book *The American Language*, first published in 1918 and revised several times, remains a classic on the subject. Mencken delighted in taking an adversary position on most issues and attacking widely held beliefs of all kinds. This essay, here complete, appears in his *Prejudices: Third Series* (1922).

ANALYSIS
General
assumption
Conclusions
#1 and #2
based on
assumption

Conclusion
#3, based
on #1 and
#2

Conclusion
#4

Conclusion
#5

All government, in its essence, is a conspiracy against the superior man: its one permanent object is to police him and cripple him. If it be aristocratic in organization, then it seeks to protect the man who is superior only in law against the man who is superior in fact; if it be democratic, 5 then it seeks to protect the man who is inferior in every way against both. Thus one of its primary functions is to regiment men by force, to make them as much alike as possible and as dependent upon one another as possible, to search out and combat originality among them. All it 10 can see in an original idea is potential change, and hence an invasion of its prerogatives.

The most dangerous man, to any government, is the man who is able to think things out for himself, without regard to the prevailing superstitions and taboos. Almost 15 inevitably he comes to the conclusion that the government he lives under is dishonest, insane and intolerable, and so, if he is romantic, he tries to change it. And even if he is not romantic personally he is very apt to spread discontent among those who are. Ludwig van Beethoven 20 was certainly no politician. Nor was he a patriot. Nor had he any democratic illusions in him: he held the Viennese in even more contempt than he held the Hapsburgs. Nevertheless, I am convinced that the sharp criticism of the Hapsburg government that he used to loose in the 25 cafés of Vienna had its effects—that some of his ideas of 1818, after a century of germination, got themselves translated into acts in 1918. Beethoven, like all other first-rate men, greatly disliked the government he lived under. I add the names of Goethe, Heine, Wagner and Nietzsche, to keep among Germans. That of Bismarck might follow: 30 he admired the Hohenzollern idea, as Carlyle did, not the German people or the German administration. In his "Errinerungen," whenever he discusses the government that he was a part of, he has difficulty keeping his contempt within the bounds of decorum.   35

Nine times out of ten, it seems to me, the man who proposes a change in the government he lives under, no matter how defective it may be, is romantic to the verge of sentimentality. There is seldom, if ever, any evidence that the kind of government he is unlawfully inclined to 40 would be any better than the government he proposes to supplant. Political revolutions, in truth, do not often accomplish anything of genuine value; their one undoubted effect is simply to throw out one gang of thieves and put in another. After a revolution, of course, the successful 45 revolutionists always try to convince doubters that they have achieved great things, and usually they hang any man who denies it. But that surely doesn't prove their case. In Russia, for many years, the plain people were taught that getting rid of the Czar would make them all 50 rich and happy, but now that they have got rid of him they are poorer and unhappier than ever before. The Germans, with the Kaiser in exile, have discovered that a shoemaker turned statesman is ten times as bad as a Hohenzollern. 55 The Alsatians, having become Frenchmen again after forty-eight years anxious wait, have responded to the boon by becoming extravagant Germanomaniacs. The Tyrolese, though they hated the Austrians, now hate the Italians enormously more. The Irish, having rid themselves of 60 the English after 700 years of struggle, instantly discovered that government by Englishmen, compared to government by Irishmen, was almost paradisiacal. Even the American colonies gained little by their revolt in 1776. For

Margin notes:

Example #1 of conclusion #4

Five more examples

Assumption #2

Example of assumption #2

Example #2

Example #3

Example #4

Example #5

Example #6   twenty-five years after the Revolution they were in far 65
(extended)   worse condition as free states than they would have been
as colonies. Their government was more expensive, more
inefficient, more dishonest, and more tyrannical. It was
only the gradual material progress of the country that
saved them from starvation and collapse, and that material 70
progress was due, not to the virtues of their new government, but to the lavishness of nature. Under the British
hoof they would have got on just as well, and probably a
great deal better.

Summing up   The ideal government of all reflective men, from Aris- 75
totle to Herbert Spencer, is one which lets the individual
alone—one which barely escapes being no government at
all. This ideal, I believe, will be realized in the world
twenty or thirty centuries after I have passed from these
scenes and taken up my home in Hell.   80

1. To what extent is the last paragraph a repetition of the first three sentences?
   What is the effect of the repetition?
2. Why has Mencken placed America as the last of the examples?
3. Check all the definitions of these words in a large dictionary: *prerogative,*
   supplant.

4-C   When Is a Joke Not a Joke?

Edwin McDowell

This newspaper article, here complete, first appeared in the *New York Times* in July 1983.
The writer gives many examples of the widely varied reactions to ethnic jokebooks.

Racial and ethnic jokes have landed in force on the nation's book-
shelves under the imprint of such major paperback publishers as Ballantine Books, Bantam Books and Pocket Books. But even as the once-
taboo volumes have begun to scale the best-seller lists, social historians
are deploring them as a reflection of declining standards.   5
   "All these terribly tasteless, disgusting books and films represent a
breakdown of decency and of standards of taste," said Barbara W. Tuchman, a Pulitzer Prize-winning historian. Publishers, by contrast, think
that critics are taking the books too seriously. "We're not interested in
making any grand statements about American culture, but the books 10
seem to have struck a chord because they are selling, and we haven't
gotten any letters of protest," said Sandy Bodner, a spokesman for
Ballantine Books, publisher of two best-selling collections.
   Both *Truly Tasteless Jokes,* published last year by Ballantine, and
Truly Tasteless Jokes Two, published recently, include chapters 15
about blacks, Jews, Poles and white Protestants, as well as jokes about

homosexuals, the handicapped and the blind. The jokes are typically a
paragraph or two in length. They use slang and often are filled with
sexual references. They frequently employ ethnic and racial epithets.
And the punch lines commonly depict members of minority groups as 20
shiftless or stupid, or as connivers or drunkards.

Both collections are currently on the mass-market best-seller lists
of *The New York Times, Publishers Weekly* and the *Washington Post.
Truly Tasteless Jokes* has been on the *Times*'s list for twenty weeks.
"Any books that sell this well have to appeal to everyone," said Sally 25
Neal, the mass paperback humor buyer at B. Dalton, the nationwide
book chain. They also inevitably spawn imitators. Already out or about
to be published are such books as *Gross Jokes, Outrageously Offensive
Jokes* and *The Complete Book of Ethnic Humor.* Most authors of the
books use pseudonyms. Both volumes of *Truly Tasteless Jokes,* for exam- 30
ple, are attributed to Blanche Knott, a made-up name. The author of
Outrageously Offensive Jokes is listed as Maude Thickett.

Critics have reacted for a variety of reasons. "There is a lot to make
fun of, but not the foibles of human beings who have already suffered
a lot," said John Hope Franklin, who is the James B. Duke Professor of 35
History at Duke University. "We should be coming to grips with the
dignity of the human spirit, not embarrassing or shaming whole groups
of people. The success of these so-called joke books is a sad testament
to the taste of this country." Jacqueline G. Wexler, president of the
National Conference of Christians and Jews, said: "I think it's the most 40
wholesome thing in the world when ethnic groups laugh at themselves.
But it's dangerous when someone else does it to you, because almost
always there's an element of denigration."

The authors have a different interpretation. "When I published my
first collection of Polish jokes ten years ago," Larry Wilde said, "a Polish- 45
American newspaper warned its readers in headlines not to buy the
book; they said it was sick." Mr. Wilde has since turned out twenty-eight
other jokebooks, including individual volumes on Italians, Jews and the
Irish. He has written several volumes of Polish jokes, including the
recently published *The Absolutely Last Official Polish Joke Book,* and 50
he said that he has rarely encountered a word of criticism about any but
the first one. "There have always been ethnic jokes or dirty jokes but
nobody ever wrote about it until the last ten years, when people began
to recognize you can't stop people from telling them," said Mr. Wilde
who is president of the Los Angeles chapter of PEN, the international 55
writers' organization. When *All in the Family* first appeared on television, Mr. Wilde said, there were debates in churches and in the press
about the propriety of racial epithets. "It's salutary to laugh at ourselves," he said. Mr. Wilde, who described himself as a Polish Jew who
grew up in an Irish neighborhood, said that the only people who ever 60
objected to ethnic jokes were "older people, who are less secure in their
roots."

Jack Romanos, publisher of Bantam Books, said he also believed that the ethnic joke had become a respectable form of American humor. "We've come as a culture from one basically segregated to one 65 that is beginning to accept all groups, and humor has followed the same pattern," he said. "It's all intended in good fun." Nevertheless, Bantam delayed the publication of Mr. Wilde's latest jokebook, he said, because it was originally scheduled for publication during the height of the Solidarity strike in Poland. "That's the one time we might have gotten 70 a reaction," he said, "so we made a conscious decision not to publish until a year later."

Aloysius Mazewski, president of the Polish-American Congress, which represents about 3,000 Polish-American organizations, disagreed with Mr. Wilde's thesis. "The purpose of the jokes is to subject people 75 to ridicule," he said. "They may not be harmful to adults, but I've seen children coming home crying, 'Are we really that dumb?' These jokes create an inferiority complex, even among children who laugh at them because they think it's sophisticated."

Dr. Michael Winston, a historian and the vice president for aca- 80 demic affairs at Howard University, also regards such jokes as harmful to young people, as well as to blacks and to second- and third-generation European immigrants. "They are in some ways a measure of how people are regarded by others," he said. But Ashley Montagu, an anthropologist and social biologist, viewed the trend as constructive provided that the 85 jokes were told in the right spirit. "Frequently these jokes are funny even if tasteless," he said. "And on the whole, human beings are health- ier for taking the view that nothing human is alien to them."

So far critics have been reluctant to do more than denounce the books. Nathan Perlmutter, national director of the Anti-Defamation 90 League of B'nai B'rith, said: "Part of it has to do with the self-conscious- ness that some have about seeming to stifle freedom of speech. I'm conscious as director of this agency of my responsibility to be protective of the dignity of the minority group while simultaneously protecting the freedom of speech that is sometimes loud and vulgar. Frequently 95 these are close calls." Mr. Mazewski of the Polish-American Congress said: "I frankly think banning books is not right, that the answer lies in education, so that they'll die from lack of sales. On the other hand, maybe they should change the laws so that groups as well as individuals can sue for defamation, then authors won't be so free with their words." 100

Mrs. Tuchman said she recognized that the popularity of such jokes probably stemmed more from a desire to shock than from an increase in bigotry. But others said that bigotry could well be lurking just below the surface. "Everybody else makes jokes about other people," said Dr. Martin Grotjahn, professor emeritus of psychiatry at the University of 105 Southern California and the author of *Beyond Laughter,* a book on the symbolism of jokes. "But in all jokes there is a disguised aggression, and racial jokes could be an invitation to racial hatred."

Dr. Grotjahn said that he would particularly advise against a non-Jew telling a joke about Jews or a white telling a joke about blacks. And 110 one publisher said that he would issue a volume of black jokes only if the author were Richard Pryor, Bill Cosby, Eddie Murphy or another well-known black. But Professor Franklin of Duke disagreed. "I wouldn't accept jokes swept up from the gutter by Richard Pryor any more than from Blanche Knott," he said. 115

1. The writer quotes twelve people; which ones object to the jokebooks and which do not?
2. What difficulty does Nathan Perlmutter point out? How important do you think it is?
3. This newspaper article is a report on the opinions of others, not an editorial, and so the writer does not state his opinions. Do his choices of people to interview and his arrangement of the quotations suggest that he is in favor of the jokebooks, is opposed to them, or is neutral?
4. Check all the definitions of these words in a large dictionary: *ethnic, connivers, pseudonyms, foibles, denigration, salutary, defamation.*

4-D Conflicting Interests

Donald H. Bell

This essay, here complete, first appeared in the *New York Times Magazine* in 1983. The author, a member of the Harvard faculty, has also written *Being a Man: The Paradox of Masculinity.* Notice his use of several brief examples to develop his point and a major one as the climax.

Change is not easy, and many men have come to feel a good deal of anger and resentment in their lives. There is a sense that somehow we have been deprived of the chance to become the sort of men we expected to be as we grew up—men who, like those of earlier generations, possess a sure-footed sense of what is expected and of how to meet 5 those expectations.

Contradictions increasingly rule our lives. On the one hand, a majority of people now believe that both sexes should enjoy equal employment opportunities. On the other, most also believe that children may be harmed psychologically if their mothers work outside the home. Says 10 Dr. Joseph Pleck, a prominent researcher in this field: "One fundamental American value is that family and parenthood are important, and this belief is now being extended to include men to a much greater degree. This contradicts the traditional belief, however, that a man should be mainly the breadwinner." 15

The result can be considerable strain and tension. "It's really hard to balance my career against my role as a father and also to have some time left over for myself," says Fred Sherman, a Chicago-area lawyer. "I really resent those evenings when I have to stay late at the office and

when I can't get home to see my wife and daughter, or when I have to 20
get out early in the morning. I sometimes have to work six or seven days
a week, and while I enjoy my job, I'm often upset that it pulls me away
from my family. It only takes two or three nights of working late and
having to kiss my daughter after she's asleep to feel that I've really
missed something important." 25

One colleague of mine, a history professor, seems successfully to
combine career aspirations with a family of three children. His wife,
too, enjoys a highly productive academic career with the same rank and
obligations. But the ability to pursue work and personal life comes at
the price of time. "Occasionally, my wife and I both feel a sense of 30
resentment about balancing two busy schedules," he says, "and sometimes we'll let each other know that we feel victimized by the requirements of the other partner. In order to make a go of this sort of life, we
have had to cut out almost everything that does not pertain to family
or career, and we often feel that we are up against the ropes in regard 35
to the time available. Finally, it's the amenities of life in terms of friends,
entertainment and general leisure that get put aside in order to focus
on the everyday essentials."

Dick Young, an Atlanta attorney, speaks of similar conflict. "Although I am a pretty traditional person," he says, "my wife has her own 40
career as a lawyer, and I've had to give up some of my traditional
expectations. When I arrive home from a tough day, all I want to do is
to put my feet up and have a drink—the sort of thing that a man has
always expected. Instead, I have to help with the household or attend
to my children. As a consequence, I sometimes feel that I can't be fair 45
both to my own needs and to those of my family."

I, too, am often beset by such anxieties. My wife now works more
than forty hours a week, mostly in the afternoon and evening. As a
result, I frequently must cut short my own workday in order to pick up
our 18-month-old son from day care or to spend time with my older 50
child. Often, I am also the one who is on call in case of illness, who
prepares many of the meals and who keeps the house clean.

I have many fewer hours available for work than I wish, and sometimes I am too exhausted at the end of a day to resume my work when
the children have gone to bed. I cannot pretend to feel comfortable 55
about this, and at times I explode with rage or I withdraw into sarcasm
and moodiness. There is no question that the rewards of sharing career
achievement and child rearing with one's spouse are great, but the
price paid can be high. It is a price, finally, that many of us never
imagined we would have to pay, and therein lies much of the trouble. 60

"I guess that in terms of work and family," says Nick Taylor, an
Atlanta journalist whose spouse is a television reporter, "we are faced
with having to become supermen in response to today's superwomen."

Maybe some of us might be able to do this. Maybe we might learn
—in the words of my departmental colleague—to give up the amenities 65

of life in order to concentrate on the essentials, adhering not only to precise daily schedules but working late into the night (a major ingredient in the success of many men who seem able to combine the demands of work and family). We might, in addition, learn to exult in the career attainments of our wives, even if we must sacrifice some of our own 70 professional ambitions. We might find the time, as well, to be with our children and to be involved as a matter of course in the necessary household chores. We even might learn to give up the anger and resentment that is often engendered by the need to do all of these things, and to do them well.   75

We might. But most of us, as yet, cannot hope to follow such a program, nor should we berate ourselves if we do not live up to the "superman" image. Despite the things we did learn from our own fathers, we usually did not find out how to balance full participation in work and in family. Now we are exploring uncharted territory, with all 80 of the missteps and false starts that such exploration requires.

Still, if we think about it, we might ultimately come to gain from the new requirements in our lives. On the morning I was to begin writing this column, my 18-month-old son woke up with a low-grade fever. My wife had a full schedule at the office, and this sick child clearly 85 could not go to his baby sitter. The only solution was for me to alter my plans and to stay home, where I diapered, played with, worried over and comforted a still-energetic but cranky baby. I could feel my bitterness and resentment boiling—for lost hours at work, for missed deadlines, for unprepared classes. "Men today," I found myself thinking, 90 "really have a raw deal."

Then I discovered that my son had learned something new. For the first time, he was able to give a proper kiss, puckering up his lips and enfolding my face in his arms. "Kees Dada," he said as he bussed me on the nose and cheeks. No amount of gratification at work could have 95 compensated for that moment. I found out another thing that morning, a discovery that came as a bit of poetic justice. I suddenly realized that in sacrificing my workday, I had learned a lot about how fathers might care for their sons. And I found that I had learned something further about what it means to be a man, something that goes beyond simply 100 bringing home a paycheck.

1. Up to the last two paragraphs, which does Bell emphasize most—the satisfactions or the problems in a two-career marriage?
2. In line 82, Bell says, "We might ultimately come to gain from the new requirements." Would a more positive statement such as "We have much to gain" or even "We are sure to gain" have been a more effective introduction to his last example?
3. Make an opinion survey of the students in your class. What do they—and you—think a husband's role should be in a two-career marriage?
4. Check all the definitions of these words in a large dictionary: *amenities, exult, engendered, bussed* (from "buss," not "bus").

4-E   In Praise of Serious Hats

Lance Morrow

This essay, here complete, first appeared in *Time* in 1983. The writer combines humor and psychology in his discussion of examples of men's hats.

A hat has the effect of making the human head a kind of residence. It gives the brain a dome and porch roof, and a strange little portable sense of place. It is a wonderful spot to look out from under, a sort of individual estate. A man feels at home in a hat, established. But wearing a hat is also like having the FBI set you up with a new identity in a 5 different city. It changes you.

The subject here is the serious hat. Not the "fun" hat. Not the Greek fisherman's hat. The writer Roy Blunt, Jr., has correctly remarked that no man should ever wear a Greek fisherman's hat who is not (1) Greek and (2) a fisherman. In the same spirit, it is probably true 10 that no man should wear a cowboy hat who is not (1) a cowboy or (2) President of the United States. The serious hat is not a masquerade, not a goof and not an announcement that while a man may look like a middle-aged New York City account executive, he harbors a West Texan in his soul, the real interior galoot made manifest in the feath- 15 ered Stetson that sits on the bar. The serious hat is the opposite of a disguise. It is a working piece of clothes and an adjunct of character.

Freud implied that a man putting on a hat was performing a phallic gesture. One historian of costume, James Laver, remarked that "epochs of extreme male domination have coincided with high hats for men." 20 What does that tell us about Abraham Lincoln? Well, Freud is also said to have conceded that a cigar is sometimes merely a cigar.

But a hat does have psychological power. A man places the thing just on top of his brain, and the one takes emanations from the other. The ancient Egyptians would go to parties in an ornamental cone of 25 perfumed wax. The wax would melt down onto the wearer as the party heated up. The hat responded to the brain's temperature. A hat can be revealing, intimate. It can also be dangerous: no other article of clothing has the potential to make a man look so ridiculous. There is the terror of the whisper: *Why does he wear that silly little hat?* 30

The first problem that serious hats and hatters face is that most men tend to think they look idiotic wearing one. That is often true, but need not be. Fred Astaire may be God's best human design for a serious hat (or for something more problematic, like the straw boater). But even short fat men, who think that serious hats turn them into Nikita Khru- 35 shchev, can usually find one that makes them look better than they deserve. Oddly, women often wear men's hats more handsomely than men do.

The second problem facing hatters is that, except in a metaphysical sense, the hat is far less necessary than it once was. Men confront the 40 elements only briefly, as they walk through the parking lot. So hats and hatters live at the mercy of fashion, the whimsical Red Queen. ("Off with their hats!")

The serious hat dies out regularly, like a rare bird. Then it is sighted only occasionally, resting, say, on Tom Wolfe's head, or disappearing down the street on the pate of a doddering banker. But it usually somehow struggles back. Fashion makes great lazy circles in time.

John Kennedy did the most serious recent damage to hats. After all the earnest geriatric hats of the Eisenhower years (John Foster Dulles peering over the Brink in his gray homburg), Kennedy went around tousled and hatless, displaying the thick hair of which he was proud. Hatlessness became a mark of youth. A stretch of profound hatlessness set in.

That may be ending. A period of modestly ripe hattedness could be coming on. It began with the Western hat fad a few years ago. The demand for Western hats has fallen off sharply now, of course. "Nothing dropped dead so fast," says Burton Berinsky, president of New York City's Jay Lord Hatters. "It was like the Nehru jacket." But, fortunately for hatters, a sense of what is called "retro" elegance has taken hold with many men in their 20s and 30s. Movies have made the difference: *Raiders of the Lost Ark* (with Harrison Ford), *Chariots of Fire* and *Brideshead Revisited.* The hats were period costumes, but close enough to be plausibly wearable now. Serious hats skipped the generation of the '60s. Now men are buying trilbies and fedoras and, with spring, panamas and boaters.

The serious hat remains a sort of minority item of clothing. The most popular hats are still the adjustable baseball-type caps, often with the logo of some tractor manufacturer on them. Such hats are entirely serious to farmers and truckers. So are cowboy hats to ranchers. Otherwise they degenerate to the status of costume: rube chic.

Although some men are returning to the serious hat, most find that the point of the thing still eludes them. The hat is a strange, noble, faintly absurd object to put on the top of one's head. Separated by the interval of face from the rest of the body's clothing, it has a certain singularity, resting just above the eyes, the countenance, the character. The hat's ancient (pre-urban, pre-car) purposes were (1) to keep off sun or rain or snow; (2) to protect the soldier's head; (3) to delineate profession and status (the king's crown, the bishop's miter, the academic's mortarboard); (4) to express some religious significance; (5) to provide ornament; and (6) to conceal baldness.

The hat still performs Function 6 well enough. What otherwise is the point? Serious hats can still be useful as signals of social class, and even, vaguely, of profession. The awful old narrow-brimmed Madison Avenue crash helmet of the '50s (what Tom Wolfe calls "the stingy-brim") still walks around Wall Street in numbers. Ornament, certainly. A hat makes a wonderful prop. A man can pose endlessly in it, and scowl

like Bogart. He can display weird vestigial courtesies, like removing it
from his head when a woman gets onto the elevator; the gesture will
inevitably make her think of Rhett Butler. A hat can italicize an attitude
or bring an interesting, enigmatic shade across the upper face.   90

Men for centuries have worn much more bizarre things on their
heads. Disgusting powdered wigs, like great greasy rugs of flour, for
example. In the 16th century, some European men wore a red rose or
a carnation behind the ear. It is probably just as well that that is no
longer the custom among, say, business executives.   95

Some of today's hats are splendidly elegant. They can give a man
a certain jaunty completeness, if he is careful in the way he chooses. The
first rule should probably be: Never try to wear a hat that has more
character than you do.

Note: Tom Wolfe, mentioned in lines 45 and 84, is the author of *Radical Chic,* and his
essays on fashions of the moment appear frequently in magazines.

1. In your opinion, how successful is Morrow in supporting his thesis that a
   "serious" hat is "a working piece of clothes, an adjunct of character?"
2. What examples does Morrow give of "serious" hats? Are they convincing to
   you? Do you think that more men are wearing hats than were five years ago?
3. What is the basis for Morrow's claim that "A period of modestly ripe hattedness could be coming on"?
4. Check all the definitions of these words in a large dictionary: *galoot, phallic,
   emanations, boaters, metaphysical, confront, pate, homburg, trilbies, fedoras, panamas, degenerate, eludes, delineate, miter, vestigial, italicize, enigmatic, bizarre.*

4-F   Do You Inherit Your Personality?

Maryon Tysoe

The following essay, here complete, first appeared in *New Society* in 1983. Notice how
the writer uses a variety of examples of opinions and interpretations by experts to arrive
at her conclusion.

How often have you heard parents say things like "Our little Florence is *so* unlike her brother. She's good-tempered and easy-going, but
he *frets* all the time. And they were like that," they add darkly, "from
the very beginning."

For those of us who are predisposed to believe that our genes have 5
only a small part to play in the development of our personalities, this
looks like bad news. But parents' expectations—wherever they come
from—do, of course, influence their offspring. Psychologists have, for
example, shown that parents treat boy and girl, ugly and attractive
babies, differently from birth.   10

The idea that genes have much to do with anything but our physical condition has, for obvious reasons, been very unpopular since the
second world war. It smacks of evil massacres and breeding pro-

grammes. And the work on intelligence and heredity became linked
with racism in the furore over Arthur Jensen's and Hans Eysenck's 15
writings over a decade ago.

But there are signs that "behavior genetics"—the study of the
genetic influences on individual differences in behavior—is beginning
to come out of the closet. Last week, London saw the thirteenth annual
meeting of the Behavior Genetics Association, held for the first time 20
outside the United States. There were 172 delegates (including 29 from
Britain) from a total of 14 countries. The majority were Americans, who
the previous week had been attending the Fourth International Congress on Twin Studies. They say that interest in their research *is* growing. (When asked about its ethical implications, they reply that their 25
endeavours are scientific and do not have any inherent ideological
connotations.)

The study of twins has been the most popular method of investigating the role of genes in behaviour. This is because identical twins
("monozygotics") come from the same egg and so they share exactly the 30
same genes. But fraternal twins ("dizygotics") come from two eggs, and
therefore they have only 50 per cent of their genes in common. So if
you assume that both types of twins share their environments to the
same extent (are treated equally alike and so on) then, they argue, you
can calculate the influence of genes on any particular behaviour you 35
want to measure. If there *is* any influence, identical twins should be
more similar than fraternal twins.

It has been estimated that there are about 100 million twins in the
world. The Institute of Psychiatry at London University has a register
of British twins, some 2,500 pairs of adults and 2,000 pairs of children. 40
The results produced by research on twins seem, on the face of it, quite
remarkable.

To take one example, Phil Rushton, associate professor of psychology at the University of Western Ontario, on sabbatical at the Institute,
presented a paper at the twins conference, outlining his recent findings 45
on "altruism and genetics." He sent questionnaires measuring kindness,
empathy and concern for others to all the adult twins. Analysing the
responses from 297 identical and 179 fraternal twins, he found that
"virtually half the individual difference variance in altruism is inherited." 50

He says this is in line with other studies: "Variations between people on all kinds of personality and cognitive scales—like aggression,
anxiety, criminality, dominance, intelligence, locus of control, neuroti-
cism, political attitudes like conservatism, sexuality, sociability, shyness
—all seem to be about the same, which is 50 per cent due to genetic 55
differences and 50 per cent attributable to environmental factors."

These percentages are, of course, averages only and so could *not*
be taken to apply to any particular individual. Behaviour geneticists
also say the proportions are likely to vary between times and cultures.

But—hold everything. The main criticism of twins studies has 60 probably already occurred to you. The assumption that identical and fraternal twins share their environments to the same extent seems unlikely. After all, most identical twins *do* look like two peas in a pod, hence the favourite literary ploy of having them mistaken for each other in all sorts of embarrassing circumstances. They do seem likely 65 to be treated as more similar—and to see themselves as more similar —than fraternal twins, who are no more "close" genetically or physically than normal siblings. And certainly identical twins have been found to spend more time together, to be more likely to share the same bedroom, friends, teacher and so on. So this could account for 70 their greater similarity.

What do behaviour geneticists have to say to this? David Fulker has just been elected the first British president of the Behaviour Genetics Association, is senior lecturer in psychology at the Institute of Psychiatry and director of their twins register. He says, "The counter to this 75 argument is, first, are the ways they are treated more alike relevant to the trait in question? It seems to me very unlikely that their great similarity in, say, intelligence is all due to, for example, dressing alike or sharing the same room. Second, there are some studies where people asked parents if they treated their twins alike. Testing if this influences 80 the trait in question, the evidence is that being treated more alike makes no difference to their similarity." But one wonders how accurate parents are when they're asked how similarly they treat their children —and being treated alike is more than likely to affect how you think and behave.   85

And perhaps identical twins *see* themselves as more alike, as well as being treated more alike? But Phil Rushton says, "One of the most compelling arguments is the case where the parents misclassify their twins, and think that identicals are fraternal when in fact they are identical, and vice-versa. And the twins themselves go through life 90 believing they are identical or fraternal when they are the opposite. If you then establish their true zygosity by, for example, bloodtyping and fingerprint analysis, you have a lovely test of the environmentalists' argument. What will predict the degree of similarity the most, the social labelling or the true biological zygosity? And the answer appears to be, 95 true zygosity."

To this the critics reply that there have only been a few of these kinds of studies, and that the number of twin pairs examined has been too small to warrant confidence in the results.

But the behaviour geneticists then say, "Well, what about identical 100 twins reared apart?" Three major studies have been done. But when psychologists such as Leon Kamin, professor of psychology at Princeton University, started rooting around in the detailed case studies, it emerged that "apart" was a bit of a misnomer. It turned out that they were, as someone said to me, "mainly reared in auntie's house." Many 105 of the twins had been raised by different branches of the same family, or at least in the same neighbourhood—and some even attended the same school.

There is a study that is still going on, called the Minnesota Study of Twins Reared Apart. It was publicised in Britain in Peter Watson's 110 book, *Twins* (Hutchinson, 1981). The researchers, headed by Thomas Bouchard, professor of psychology at Minnesota University, have now tested thirty-four pairs of identical twins, many of them British. Most were separated within the first year of life (usually by six months) and never saw each other again until Bouchard brought them together 115 when they were in their late teens at the earliest, some being in their forties.

In his book, Watson chose to concentrate on what seemed to be incredible coincidences in the twins' lives. Probably the most famous pair are the "Jim twins," James Lewis and James Springer. Watson lists 120 a large number of coincidences, including: both had married a woman called Linda, divorced her, then married someone called Betty; one twin named his first son James Alan, the other called his James Allan; both had had a dog they named Toy; both spent their holidays at the same small beach in Florida; both drove a Chevrolet; both bite their 125 fingernails to the quick; both built white benches round the trunk of a tree in their gardens; both have had vasectomies.

But some of these activities, at least, are not so unusual and, as Watson points out, what are the chances that any two people—particularly if asked the thousands of questions that these twins were—would 130 come up with large numbers of coincidences and similarities? This research just hasn't yet been done, and Bouchard himself is cautious about drawing any conclusions until some base rates for these kinds of coincidences can be estimated.

But Bouchard has also administered to the twins a number of per- 135 sonality questionnaires and measures of intelligence and "vocational interests" (such as: preferring to be an accountant rather than an engineer; liking to make things or not). Very few of the results have been published yet; only presented at conferences. But the twins are apparently turning out to be very similar—more similar (according to the 140 standard twin studies) than fraternal twins reared together.

Bouchard says, "It appears there is a greater influence by heredity than we thought in the past. Our findings on personality and intelligence continue to be true as new cases are added. The general picture is very consistent. But our data are barely scratched." And, no doubt, 145 as his findings find their way into print the attention of critics will soon beam in upon them. Bouchard himself points out that many of the twins *were* raised in similar households.

When pressed on the quality of twin studies, behaviour geneticists tend to say, "But we don't need to rely on twin studies. We have 150 adoption studies, and studies of family members with different degrees of relatedness, and these are consistent with the findings of the twin studies." Critics tend to say the family studies can be criticised on the same sorts of grounds as the twin studies, it being more likely that very close relatives share a similar (or even the same) environment than less close relatives. So you'd expect people to be more alike the more they were genetically similar.

But what about the adoption studies? Professor Steven Rose of the Open University, who is a neuro-biologist and the staunchest British critic of behaviour genetics, says, "The adoption studies look quite convincing. When children are taken from their parents at or near birth to an adoptive family, you can compare their behaviour with that of the biological parents and of the adoptive parents. The trouble is, when you look at the studies in detail—the best study was Danish, of schizophrenia—you find there is selective placement for adoption. Adoption agencies go to considerable lengths to find families similar in social class and environment."

David Fulker says, "This has happened in some studies, not all, and not to a sufficient extent to explain the findings [that around 50 per cent of the variance in measured traits is due to heredity]. In the most recent one, the Colorado Adoption Study, there is no evidence of selective placements for social class, abilities, or any measures of personality." But this study undoubtedly won't go unscathed either.

The argument about genes and environment does look like it's hotting up. As behaviour genetics pokes its head round the door, Leon Kamin and Steven Rose are waiting with a club. With a colleague, Richard Lewontin, they have written a book called *Not in Our Genes*, to be published by Penguin, probably later this year.

Rose is vehement that behaviour genetics is totally misconceived, and that it is impossible to separate out the effects of genes and the environment. "Genes and environment interact during development to produce something that is not reducible to *x* per cent genes and *y* per cent environment. To make a cake, you mix sugar, flour, butter, spices and so on. You bake the cake, and when you taste it you can't say 5 per cent of the taste is due to the butter, 10 per cent is due to the flour, and so on. It is qualitatively different from the ingredients you started with."

Social psychologists would probably agree. It's been argued that genes may set some general limits on the way that, say, our personality is likely to develop. For example, extraversion is thought to have something to do with our chronic levels of physiological arousal. But if you're extraverted, they point out, that says *nothing* about how that extraversion will be expressed—whether you'll spend all your time at noisy parties, take up politics, or jump your motorbike over a row of London buses.

We have plenty of scope to become the person we want. Whatever the role of genetics finally turns out to be, no one is suggesting that we are the puppets of our genes.

1. Tysoe alternates between two opposing views on the extent to which personality may be inherited. What transitional devices indicate the shifts from one
view to the other? Look particularly at the first and last sentences of each
paragraph.
2. In presenting the views of the behavior geneticists, how and where does
Tysoe suggest the possibility of flaws in their logic?
3. Check all the definitions of these words in a large dictionary: *predisposed,
sabbatical, altruism, cognitive, locus, ploy, staunchest, extraversion.*

4-G   The Start of a Long Day

William Krulish (student)

In this essay, here complete, the writer gives a colorful extended example of the extra
work at round-up time on a ranch. Notice his use of concrete, specific detail to make clear
an experience that few of his readers are likely to know firsthand.

A new day dawned bright and early, greeting the earth beneath it
with life-giving light and warmth. It was round-up time again and the
normal workday of sunup to sundown was extended to cover the extra
work that had to be done, a schedule designed to sap the strength of
even the strongest ranch hands.   5

The man, having worked late the night before, had fallen asleep on
his bunk fully clothed and now faced the consequences of his act. His
feet, confined in shoes all night long, were the first to complain as they
were swung over the side of the bunk and slammed onto the floor. He
winced at this action, his nose recoiling as the grimace freed the stale 10
odors that had been trapped in his mouth all night long. His head ached,
as with leaden arms he went through the motions of the morning
wash-up.

Clothes were another matter. After little consideration, a reasonably clean shirt was pressed into service to replace the malodorous one 15
he now wore. Blue jeans that had seen better days would do, and the
stickiness of his undergarments was overlooked as he heeded the grum-
blings of a chronically complaining stomach.

Stumbling half-asleep towards the cook house, he exchanged greetings of a sort with others—cowboys, farriers [blacksmiths who shoe 20
horses] and the like—who shared his life and who at this time felt and
smelt the same as he did, moving woodenly through a brand new
sunshiny morning. A thrush was stunned into silence by the many dark
looks sent its way.

The man finished his breakfast and pushed himself away from the 25
table, his stomach quiet for the moment. Stretching, stomping and
scratching, he made his way to the tool shed where the tools he had
dropped unceremoniously the night before awaited him.

A cowboy by choice, he had been pressed into service as a farrier
for the round-up and, while shoeing horses might seem romantic on 30

television, he had his druthers. That is to say, if he had a choice he would rather be doing something else.

The corral that he and another farrier had been assigned to was simply a hard-packed, sun-baked square of dirt surrounded by old plumbing pipe loosely laid between posts, with a snubbing post set in 35 the middle of it. Two horses were already in command of this space and as they had spent a quiet, restful night looked forward to the coming activity with more spirit than did the men.

Sometimes a man can walk up to a horse, put a rope on him and settle down to work. This was not about to be one of those times.   40

The first horse approached by the man was a misnamed, lop-eared, slot-sided son of a bitch who was prone to acrobatics that would have made a gymnast proud. Even when he managed to get one front leg through the railing, a hind leg somehow lashed out and got caught in the farrier's shirt sleeve, ventilating it for all time. The man grunted as 45 the force of the action pushed him to one side. A halter was quickly slipped on and the horse made fast to a length of pipe.

The man turned to help the other farrier.

The second horse must have served an apprenticeship on a merry-go-round, judging by the way he ran around and around the corral. A 50 corral is built square so that you can trap a horse in a corner, but a smart horse will get round this by hugging the snubbing post. The dust raised was enough to choke a horse, but the one in question simply held his head above it, letting the men have it all. To show his dexterity a hoof would slice through the dust, just missing the men, although the harsh 55 words permeating the atmosphere seemed to indicate otherwise. Not to be outdone, the other horse at the rail sent a hoof into the foray from time to time.

Finally tiring of the game, the horse slowed down. As a last show of camaraderie he squeezed the men against the rails, causing them to 60 inhale more dust.

But the farriers quickly recovered and bent to their tasks. Their curses resounded as the horses kicked over tool boxes and yanked their hooves capriciously through work-worn hands. Sweat and flies were troubling men and horses alike, causing the men to swear even more. 65 The horses helped to fend off the flies by flicking their tails across the men and themselves.

Suddenly it was game time again as both horses realized that they were tied to the same length of pipe and it was lying loose in the posts. They shifted and took off at a run, leaving the men gaping at each other. 70 But the horses, still joined by their tethers at each end of the length of pipe, couldn't really run because of their shackles. They simply swept the pipe around the corral, circling the snubbing post, forcing the farriers into an unexpected game of jump-rope in which they leapt higher than they ever had as children.   75

Some spoil sport from a crowd that had gathered to see this brief return to childhood stepped in and stopped the horses before they exhausted themselves, and things slowly eased back to normal.

The horses settled down, the men settled back to their work, and the dust settled over everything as the first hour of the workday passed 80 without further incident.

It was about this time, when the flies had cut their way through all the dust and heat and homed in on the freshly warmed, live meat at the railing, that the man's stomach started again to rumble.

1. Although most of his word choices are formal, Krulish occasionally uses slang and colloquial expressions, such as "stomping" (line 26) and "druthers" (line 31) for local color. What other examples can you find?
2. Krulish concentrates almost exclusively on the man's physical sensations instead of describing his thoughts and opinions. Also, he refers to him only as "the man." What is the effect of this lack of information about the man's personality and background?

4-H   We Reduced the Size Because
       We Didn't Want to Increase the Price

Dwight Bolinger

This essay is part of a chapter in *Language, the Loaded Weapon* (1980). The author shows that names can sometimes take the place of reality, especially when a company is promoting a product.

"By habit," wrote Jeremy Bentham in 1815, "wherever a man sees a NAME, he is led to figure to himself a corresponding object, of the reality of which the NAME is accepted by him, as it were of course, in the character of a CERTIFICATE. From this delusion, endless is the confusion, the error, the dissension, the hostility, that has been 5 derived."

We call this REIFICATION, the materializing of abstractions. It rests, like everything else in language, on the child's experiences while learning. First come words that are visibly and tangibly attached to objects. Then words with pictures or figurines, with verification later— 10 the first soldier is a toy soldier, the first giraffe an illustration in a storybook. Finally words with no immediate counterpart, but by then so much has already been confirmed—real soldiers in a parade, real giraffes in a zoo—that confirmation is expected in all serious discourse, and words are accepted with suspended judgment. As long as there are 15 no indications to the contrary, a word is a ticket to a meaning. . . .

Nouns are the hotbed of pseudonymy. This is to be expected, given their function, which is to lay hold of some portion of reality and hold

it up to view. Hold it up, that is, AS IF it were a portion of reality. It
may embody a slew of things. What is a *vitamin?* To define this word 20
the Merriam *Third* requires a sentence containing a main clause and
ten subordinate clauses, not counting a couple of dozen qualifying adjectives, adverbs, and prepositional phrases. Our confidence in the
name emboldens us to talk about vitamins as if we knew what they
were, and yet the disputes about them—is laetrile a vitamin or a drug? 25
is ascorbic acid a vitamin or a metabolite?—prove that the chief claim
to reality of this conglomeration of things is the name itself.

   . . . The enterprise of concocting goods and promotional ideas is one
vast exercise in pseudo-reification. Each fabricated pseudo-thing comes
neatly wrapped in its noun—a nice grammatical analogy, because pack- 30
aging is the typical result in the real world and the noun is a typical
verbal package.

   The packages contain SOMETHING, of course—the magician
needs props for his illusions. But the entities are potentially random and
limitless—a modern supermarket requires yards of shelf space just for 35
its prepared cereal fantasies; the important thing is to make them AP-
PEAR to have the same reality as an object of nature. A couple of
generations ago, before the pseudo-entity explosion, all "staples" were
sold "in bulk"—pickles came in barrels and flour in bins, and the merchant dipped or ladled out the buyer's portion; the product still took 40
priority over the package.

   The acceptance of packaging leads to the acceptance of the packaged object, promoted as having an existence of its own—capable of
change in size, price, and quality. Milk chocolate sold in bulk could only
vary in price and quality. A reified chocolate bar can also vary in quan- 45
tity. So when the "giant bar" shrank from eight to six ounces, and from
six to five, the manufacturer reassured the public with impeccable logic:
"We reduced the size because we didn't want to increase the price."

   Fabricated reality has its visual and material illusions as well as its
verbal ones. Pink toilet paper says, "I am delicate," and when packed 50
in a loose roll it says, "I am soft" and "I am larger than I really am." The
wasp-waisted bottle of salad oil says, "I am not fattening." Television
newsman Daniel Schorr had this to say about the visual barrage: "For
many who have grown up in the media generation, the television reality is the only reality they have ever known. It may be the only reality 55
that exists."

   The chocolate bar is at least a real dollop of real chocolate. With
many commercial pseudo-entities the contents are chiefly the evoca-
tions of scientific jargon or pure trademarked imagination—the mystery ingredients such as *irium,* the curatives such as *hexylresorcinol,* 60
and the unadulterated hydromancy of *the water* in certain brands of
beer. When the Shell Oil Company advertised that Shell gasoline with
Platformate gave more mileage than any rival brand without that in-

gredient, it made an empty claim, because "Platformate or its equivalent is present in virtually every gasoline refined." 65

The importance of the word in this scheme of things—even when
the entity makes good on its implied claim of intrinsic value—can be
seen in the litigation over trademarks and the vigilance that their owners keep to warn off poachers. Some names—*aspirin and linoleum* are
the classic examples—have been captured for the public domain by 70
individuals exercising squatters' rights, speakers who simply disregard
the proprietary claim; in the long run the courts condone this, for they
do not encourage private ownership of words of the English language.
In 1978 the United States Supreme Court rejected the pretension of the
Miller Brewing Company to exclusive use of *Lite* or *Light* for its low- 75
calorie beer. *Aspirin* and *linoleum* became common nouns by sheer
weight of usage. But *Kodak* has been jealously guarded since 1888.
Xerox holds its own. *Mimeograph* has probably lost the battle. . . .

Some names for concocted entities perform a kind of service. It is
easier to remember and ask for *Clorox* than for 5.25 *per cent solution* 80
of sodium hypochlorite. The mixers and namers count on that. But the
house brand comes cheaper.

. . .

Our reality is a product of ourselves, in large part a reflection of the
categories, moods, and juxtapositions that our language provides us 85
with or makes possible. The legacy of Babel can be drawn as a double
arrow: meanings demand forms to represent them, but forms equally
reach out to meanings. In large degree, we find in the world outside us
what our language leads us to expect to find. . . .

Our brains are terribly efficient mixers and combiners. One who 90
would probably never murder a friend can nevertheless bring "murder" and "friend" together in his mind—the act becomes THINK-
ABLE. Two and two in the head adds up to four in what we buy, sell,
build, and carry. Or it may add up to three—the absurd is just as
thinkable as the rational: it is language, according to Robert Ardrey, 95
that "made inordinately irrational beliefs possible." In children we call
the product imagination. In adults it is sometimes called invention: the
inner map is changed and the reality changes to match. Human
creativity and human destructiveness alike depend on this.

1. Bolinger claims that "we find in the world outside us what our language leads
   us to expect to find." What examples does he give of words used in advertising to suggest that a product has a special quality?
2. Find at least three other examples in current radio or TV commercials or
   newspaper or magazine advertisements of words used to suggest that the
   products advertised are "special" and analyze the way the words are used.
3. Check all the definitions of the following words in a large dictionary: *pseudonymy, entities, impeccable, hydromancy, juxtapositions, inordinately.*

Assignments

1. Choose a public figure you particularly admire, such as a TV or movie performer, an athlete, or a singer, and write an essay explaining the basis for your admiration. Assume your readers know little about the person. Support your claims with several examples.
2. What place do you particularly like to visit on a vacation? Write an essay explaining your choice by giving examples of whatever makes the place attractive. Assume your readers are friends who have asked your advice on where to go.
3. What kinds of drivers do you find most annoying and/or dangerous? Assume that your readers come from another part of the country where driving practices are very different from the ones familiar to you and that they have asked your advice. Support your claims with several examples.
4. Choose a familiar saying such as "Absence makes the heart grow fonder" or "Haste makes waste" and write an essay with examples to show that it is *not* always true.

PHOTOGRAPHS FOR UNIT 4

How good an eyewitness are you? Test yourself by answering the questions on the next page. Be honest with yourself and do not turn back to look at the photographs again until you have finished the test. If you can answer a total of eight questions correctly, you are a good eyewitness.

Photograph A Dorothea Hahn (student)

Photograph B Courtesy Ken Tiemeyer, *Hutchinson News,* Kansas—1983 Kodak International Newspaper Shapshot Awards

Photograph A

1. How many people can be seen, at least partly?
2. What is written on a wall behind the people?
3. What is printed on the bag held by the man in front?
4. How many people are wearing neckties?
5. What is printed on the sign attached to the woman's bag?
6. Is the man in front wearing a light-colored shirt?
7. Can you see if anyone is wearing a wristwatch?

Photograph B

1. How many figures are painted on the wall?
2. How many of the painted figures have hats? rolled-up sleeves?
3. Which of the two seated people is looking up?
4. What are the positions of the arms and hands of the seated figure on your left? of the seated figure on your right?
5. How many steps down would someone leaving the building have to take to reach the ground?
6. What words are painted above the entrance to the building?

WRITING ASSIGNMENTS BASED ON THE PHOTOGRAPHS

1. Assume that these photographs are to be published together in a newspaper or magazine as examples of contrasting moods. Compose a title and a statement of about 50 words for each, emphasizing how they can be seen as examples.
2. Compose an essay of about 300 words in which you describe the behavior of people watching a parade. Use the people in Photograph A as examples and include some description of the personalities that their appearance suggests.
3. What do you think is the mood and the relationship of the two people in Photograph B? Compose an essay of about 300 words describing that mood and using the people in the photograph as an extended example. Imagine personalities and a situation appropriate to what can be seen in the photograph.

UNIT 5

Words

"Open, Sesame!" said Ali Baba, and the door of the robbers' cave obeyed. Folk and fairy tales throughout the world give similar examples of the power of words. "Spell," meaning to say the letters of a word, comes from "spell," a magic formula. The accurate use of words will not give you magical powers, but it is essential for your primary purpose—communicating your meaning. A forceful use of words is essential for your secondary purpose—catching and holding your reader's attention.

The earlier units on composing in general, description, narration, and exemplification, included recommendations to choose appropriate words. This unit will concentrate on them.

The level of the language in any piece of writing determines how formal—or informal—it will seem to readers. English has a large number of words that are **synonyms** or near-synonyms of each other. But synonyms are hardly ever truly interchangeable. The **denotations**—the dictionary definitions—of two words may be exactly the same; but their **connotations**—the associated meanings they have acquired through use—are rarely the same. For example, *female* is one of the dictionary definitions for *woman* and *woman* for *female,* but someone who says "Two females sat in the car" probably has a very different opinion of them from someone who says "Two women sat in the car." Similarly, both *noted* and *notorious* can be defined as *well-known,* and they even come from the same Latin root, but they connote two very different kinds of reputation.

Our many synonyms and varying connotations give us a choice of levels on which to write, from the very formal to the very informal. **Colloquial English** is informal—the level most of us use when writing and speaking to friends. The vocabulary and the sentence structure are relatively simple and may include many contractions, some slang, and some regional and dialect words. A college or unabridged dictionary will tell you if a word is colloquial, dialectal, or slang—and therefore perhaps not appropriate in a formal paper.

Scholarly and technical English includes whatever specialized words and phrases are appropriate to the particular subject. The sentences have standard English structures but are often relatively long with many subdivisions.

Standard English (or "standard edited English") is somewhere between colloquial and scholarly English. It has the kinds of words and sentence structures used by writers for the more serious publications meant for the general reader—big city newspapers, national circulation magazines, and textbooks like this one.

Consider these versions of a single request:

> Leave us go (ungrammatical/dialectal)
> Let's split (slang)
> Let's go (informal)
> Let us go (formal)

Each will be appropriate at some time, including the ungrammatical version if you are quoting a speaker who used it. Whatever level you choose, be consistent. A sudden shift will startle your readers and make them wonder if you have changed your purpose. Good English is appropriate English—appropriate to the occasion, to the subject, and especially to the intended reader.

*   *   *   *   *   *   *   *   *

A good dictionary is as essential for a writer as ink and paper. The more words you know well, the more you will choose those that precisely fit your needs. Keep a dictionary beside you when you write. A pocket-sized edition can help with spellings when you write in class, and an unabridged edition—every library has at least one—will help you with complicated problems. But the college edition is the one you should have on your desk—small enough to be picked up with one hand but detailed enough to answer most of your questions about words.

There are three widely respected American dictionaries. In alphabetical order they are:

American Heritage, published by Houghton Mifflin
Webster's New Collegiate, published by G. & C. Merriam
Webster's New World, published by New World Dictionaries/Simon & Schuster

Each has over 150,000 entries, gives much the same kind of information on each word, and has much the same kind of additional material on punctuation, the history of the language, and so on. Also, they are nearly the same in size, weight, and price. Examine all three carefully before you choose. Decide which seems to have the most readable type, the most understandable abbreviations, and the clearest diagrams and illustrations. A comparison of their entires for "infer" and "irregardless" will give you a good indication of their differences in presentation and degree of conservatism.

Ask for them by the names of their publishers as well as by their titles, particularly the two "Webster's." There are many dictionaries, some relatively worthless, that use Noah Webster's name, so that "Webster's" in the title guarantees nothing. Remember also to check the copyright date on the back of the title page so that you can be sure of getting the latest edition.

Whichever dictionary you buy, study its opening pages carefully for directions on using it. Each has its own system for presenting information and its own methods of abbreviation. Here is the entry for *pleasure* in *Webster's New World Dictionary:*

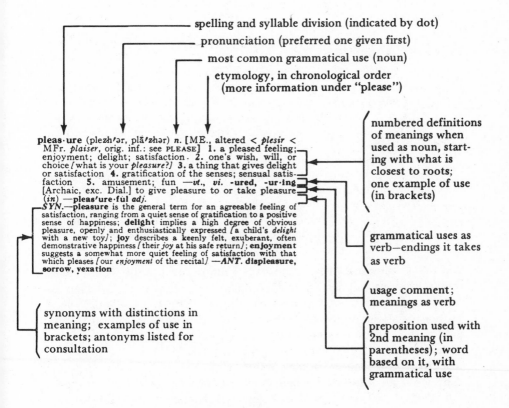

spelling and syllable division (indicated by dot)

pronunciation (preferred one given first)

most common grammatical use (noun)

etymology, in chronological order (more information under "please")

pleas·ure (plezh′ər, plā′zhər) n. [ME., altered < *plesir* < MFr. *plaiser*, orig. inf.: see PLEASE] 1. a pleased feeling; enjoyment; delight; satisfaction. 2. one's wish, will, or choice [what is your *pleasure?*] 3. a thing that gives delight or satisfaction 4. gratification of the senses; sensual satisfaction 5. amusement; fun —*vt.*, *vi.* -ured, -ur·ing [Archaic, exc. Dial.] to give pleasure to or take pleasure (in) —pleas′ure·ful *adj.*
SYN.—pleasure is the general term for an agreeable feeling of satisfaction, ranging from a quiet sense of gratification to a positive sense of happiness; delight implies a high degree of obvious pleasure, openly and enthusiastically expressed [a child's *delight* with a new toy]; joy describes a keenly felt, exuberant, often demonstrative happiness [their *joy* at his safe return]; enjoyment suggests a somewhat more quiet feeling of satisfaction with that which pleases [our *enjoyment* of the recital] —ANT. displeasure, sorrow, vexation

numbered definitions of meanings when used as noun, starting with what is closest to roots; one example of use (in brackets)

grammatical uses as verb—endings it takes as verb

usage comment; meanings as verb

preposition used with 2nd meaning (in parentheses); word based on it, with grammatical use

synonyms with distinctions in meaning; examples of use in brackets; antonyms listed for consultation

To find more synonyms for a word than your dictionary includes, consult a *thesaurus,* or "treasury" of synonyms. The best known, *Roget's Thesaurus,* is published in a variety of editions. When you choose a word from a thesaurus, always check your dictionary as well to be sure that the word has the connotations you want. For example, you may find *fluent, voluble, glib,* and *flippant* listed together, but although speakers will thank you for calling them fluent, they will not be much pleased to be called voluble and will certainly take offense at being called glib or flippant.

*   *   *   *   *   *   *   *   *

Choose specific, concrete words. In most of your nonspecialized writing, in college and later, "standard English" will be appropriate. But this does not mean that you must limit yourself to "safe," dull words. The more precise and economical your word choice is, the more your writing is likely to be clear and forceful. As mentioned in the section on word choice in Unit 2, a specific word like *shuffle* or *trudge* or *saunter* is not only briefer than *walk slowly* but is also more precise and therefore more effective. Notice how Shana Alexander piles up specific words for a dramatic and humorous effect in this paragraph:

> Instead of harrying, chivying, threatening with travel taxes and otherwise cramping the tourist's style, I think we ought to coddle, cosset, encourage, advise, underwrite and indemnify him in every possible way. Huge herds of vigorous, curious, open-eyed Americans freely roaming the world are, it seems to me, quite possibly a vital national resource today as at no other time in our history. . . . I am for tourists of any and all kinds: sneakered and sport-shirted and funny-hatted, pants-suited and pajamaed and jetsetted, knapsacked and bearded, festooned with Instamatics and phrase books and goofy sunglasses, traveling scientists and schoolteachers and schoolchildren and trade missions, Peace Corpsmen, ballet corps, opera companies and symphony players, tennis players, footballers, junketeering congressmen and highballers—all of them to be set wandering and peering and snooping and migrating and exploring and studying and just mooching all over the face of the globe. (Shana Alexander, "The Real Tourist Trap," *Life*.)

Short, simple words in standard English are usually best. Choose longer, more complicated, or technical ones only when they are absolutely necessary to make your meaning clear. More and more often, critics are complaining of the pompousness of much modern writing and of the confusions that result. Some branches of the federal government and some businesses are trying to simplify the language of their reports and contracts, but we still have a long way to go. Theodore Bernstein, an editor of the *New York Times* and author of several books on writing, calls such pompousness "windyfoggery" and illustrates it with this anecdote:

> Dr. William B. Bean, who in the *Archives of Internal Medicine* often tilted a lancet at the writing operations of his fellow healers, has passed on the story of a New York plumber who had cleaned out some drains with hydrochloric acid and then wrote to a chemical research bureau, inquiring, "Was there any possibility of harm?" As told by Dr. Bean, the story continues:

"The first answer was, 'The efficacy of hydrochloric acid is indisputably established but the corrosive residue is incompatible with metallic permanence.' The plumber was proud to get this and thanked the people for approving of his method. The dismayed research bureau rushed another letter to him saying, 'We cannot assume responsibility for the production of a toxic and noxious residue with hydrochloric acid. We beg leave to suggest to you the employment of an alternative procedure.' The plumber was more delighted than ever and wrote to thank them for reiterating their approval. By this time the bureau got worried about what might be happening to New York's sewers and called in a third man, an older scientist, who wrote simply, 'Don't use hydrochloric acid. It eats hell out of pipes." (Theodore M. Bernstein, *The Careful Writer*, 1973.)

Bernstein goes on to say that specialized terminology is, of course, appropriate in technical writing, but "windyfoggery, which often is technical jargon gone wrong and blanketed in blurriness, is not useful to any purpose."

Be concise. Use only as many words as you need to convey your meaning effectively. Omit any that are not necessary, even simple ones. Why, for example, write "It is my opinion that the team won the game due to the fact that they tried really hard" when you can write "I think that the team won because they tried hard"? When you are afraid that your essay is not long enough, do not stretch it with extra words. Find more material—more examples, more details. These will strengthen what you say; extra words will only dilute it.

Be sure to read "Clutter" (Unit 6-D), which gives more advice on how to strengthen your writing by leaving out words you don't need, and President Kennedy's rough drafts, which show how he and his assistants worked to shorten and simplify his inaugural address (Unit 20-F).

* * *   * * *   * * *

Figures of speech are a special use of words, most of them involving a comparison of some kind. Comparisons can help to make the unfamiliar seem familiar to your readers. They bring the abstract and general to life by relating it to the concrete and specific. To show a reader how hot a room was, you could simply state the fact, "The room was 98° Fahrenheit," but a straightforward comparison would help the reader to see that you wanted to emphasize the heat: "The room was almost as hot as an oven."

A figure of speech might be more memorable, because instead of making a logical, literal comparison, it is imaginative. There are several kinds; among the most common and useful are the following:

1. Simile. "The room was like an oven." The room and the oven are compared, but the writer takes for granted that the reader thinks of an oven as hot, whereas in "The room was as hot as an oven" this point is included.

2. Metaphor. "The room was an oven." The room and the oven are presented as one thing, but the writer assumes that the reader knows they are not.

3. Implied metaphor. "The room baked us." Ovens are enclosed spaces used for baking, but they are not mentioned. The writer assumes that the reader will make the connection.

4. Extended metaphor. "The room was an oven that baked our conversation dry, and the soufflé of fantastic ideas on which we had hoped to feast was now only a burnt crust." The association of heat and an oven is carried through several related applications to describe the psychological effect of heat.

5. Personification. "Like a fevered invalid, the room enclosed us in a smothering embrace." The room is described as though it had the characteristics of a human being.

*   *   *   *   *   *   *   *   *

Two other figures of speech use comparison less directly:

6. Hyperbole. "The temperature of the room felt like 1000°." The extreme exaggeration emphasizes the point.

7. Understatement. "With the thermometer at 98°, we can safely describe the room as warm." Understatement is the opposite of hyperbole, but the reader is expected in both cases to realize that the statement should not be taken literally. A variation on understatement, called *litotes,* uses a negative for the same effect, as in "With the thermometer at 98°, the room was not underheated."

Use figurative language cautiously. It can stimulate your reader's imagination and make your writing more memorable, but, to borrow an old simile, it is like seasoning on food—a little goes a long way.

Avoid the mixed metaphor, a combination of comparisons that do not fit together. A political speaker recently claimed, "My ace in the hole is that I'm not a bull in a china shop swinging a meat axe." *Avoid comparisons that may call up inappropriate associations,* as in "With a good manager, the business sprouted like potatoes in a damp cellar." This is partly appropriate because potatoes do indeed sprout quickly in a damp cellar, but most readers will think of damp cellars as unpleasant and will probably go on to imagine the potatoes as rotting. *Avoid clichés,* comparisons that have grown stale through overuse, such as "green as grass," "busy as a bee," or "old as the hills," unless you can breathe new life into them as in "He seemed as busy as a bee, but we never saw any honey."

Euphemisms are related to figurative language. They are words or phrases that let us soften a harsh or unpleasant or embarrassing fact. We have a variety of expressions to describe physical acts we would rather not name directly. For example, rather than say we are going to the toilet, we may say we are going to the bathroom or the john or the rest room, but "toilet" itself is an old euphemism—check its etymology. Many people are reluctant to say that someone has died and prefer saying that he has passed away. Old people are now called senior citizens, and garbage collectors are sanitary engineers. Use such expressions when you think your readers would be offended by more accurate words, but also be on guard against words that conceal the truth. Someone who steals information from our government for a foreign one is a spy, but we call someone who steals information for us an intelligence agent. Is being terminated from your job really easier than being fired? Is an experienced car in better condition than a used car? Don't be afraid to call a spade a spade, or even, sometimes, a shovel.

 ## Examples

In the following selections the writers use precise, concrete words and economical phrases, but they nevertheless differ sharply from each other in style. Notice the discussion of word choice in selections in other units, notably in Mencken's *"Le Contrat Social"* (4-B), Bolinger's "We Reduced the Size" (4-H), Zinsser's "Clutter" (6-D), Cohen's "The Language of Uncertainty" (13-B), Twain's "Lagniappe" (14-C), Hankins's "Clues to Meaning" (16-B), Mahood's "Puns and Other Wordplay" (16-C), Hoggart's "The Prestige of PRAL" (16-H), and Williamson's "How to Write like a Social Scientist" (16-J).

5-A   The Flight of Refugees

Ernest Hemingway

Hemingway has had more influence on contemporary prose than any other modern writer. Sometimes he went to extremes in simplifying word choice and sentence structure and in using understatements, but his news reporting provides excellent examples of forceful simplicity. In the following, a complete news dispatch headed "Barcelona: 3 April 1938," he describes several hours in the Spanish Civil War. Notice his concentration on facts, his choice of details, and the rare indications of his emotions.

It was a lovely false spring day when we started for the front this morning. Last night, coming into Barcelona, it had been grey, foggy, dirty and sad, but today it was bright and warm, and pink almond blossoms coloured the grey hills and brightened the dusty green rows of olive trees.

Then, outside of Reus, on a straight smooth highway with olive orchards on each side, the chauffeur from the rumble seat shouted, "Planes, planes!" and, rubber screeching, we stopped the car under a tree.

"They're right over us," the chauffeur said, and, as this correspond- 10
ent dived head-forward into a ditch, he looked up sideways, watching
a monoplane come down and wing over and then evidently decide a
single car was not worth turning his eight machine-guns loose on.

But, as we watched, came a sudden egg-dropping explosion of
bombs, and, ahead, Reus, silhouetted against hills a half mile away, 15
disappeared in a brick-dust-coloured cloud of smoke. We made our way
through the town, the main street blocked by broken houses and a
smashed water main, and, stopping, tried to get a policeman to shoot
a wounded horse, but the owner thought it was still possibly worth
saving and we went on up toward the mountain pass that leads to the 20
little Catalan city of Falset.

That was how the day started, but no one yet alive can say how it
will end. For soon we began passing carts loaded with refugees. An old
woman was driving one, crying and sobbing while she swung a whip.
She was the only woman I saw crying all day. There were eight children 25
following another cart and one little boy pushed on a wheel as they
came up a difficult grade. Bedding, sewing-machines, blankets, cooking
utensils and mattresses wrapped in mats, sacks of grain for the horses
and mules were piled in the carts and goats and sheep were tethered
to the tailboards. There was no panic, they were just plodding along. 30

On a mule piled high with bedding rode a woman holding a still
freshly red-faced baby that could not have been two days old. The
mother's head swung steadily up and down with the motion of the beast
she rode, and the baby's jet-black hair was drifted grey with the dust.
A man led the mule forward, looking back over his shoulder and then 35
looking forward at the road.

"When was the baby born?" I asked him, as our car swung alongside. "Yesterday," he said proudly, and the car was past. But all these
people, no matter where else they looked as they walked or rode, all
looked up to watch the sky.   40

Then we began to see soldiers straggling along. Some carried their
rifles by the muzzles, some had no arms. At first there were only a few
troops, then finally there was a steady stream, with whole units intact.
Then there were troops in trucks, troops marching, trucks with guns,
with tanks, with anti-tank guns and anti-aircraft guns, and always a line 45
of people walking.

As we went on, the road choked and swelled with this migration,
until, finally, it was not just the road, but streaming alongside the road
by all the old paths for driving cattle came the civilian population and
the troops. There was no panic at all, only a steady movement, and 50
many of the people seemed cheerful. But perhaps it was the day. The
day was so lovely that it seemed ridiculous that anyone should ever die.

Then we began seeing people that we knew, officers we had met
before, soldiers from New York and Chicago who told how the enemy
had broken through and taken Gandesa, that the Americans were 55

fighting and holding the bridge at Mora across the Ebro River and that they were covering this retreat and holding the bridgehead across the river and still holding the town.

Suddenly, the stream of troops thinned and then there was a big influx again, and the road was so choked that the car could not move 60 ahead. You could see them shelling Mora on the river and hear the pounding thud of the guns. Then there came a flock of sheep to clog the roads, with shepherds trying to drive them out of the way of the trucks and tanks. Still the planes did not come.

Somewhere ahead, the bridge was still being held, but it was impos- 65 sible to go any farther with the car against that moving dust-swamped tide. So we turned the car back toward Tarragona and Barcelona and rode through it all again. The woman with the newborn baby had it wrapped in a shawl and held tight against her now. You could not see the dusty head because she held it tight under the shawl as she swung 70 with the walking gait of the mule. Her husband led the mule, but he looked at the road now and did not answer when we waved. People still looked up at the sky as they retreated. But they were very weary now. The planes had not yet come, but there was still time for them and they were overdue.   75

1. What words describe how crowded the road was? How specific are they? What words describe other actions of any kind? colors? sounds?
2. What reaction from the reader does the writer seem to want?
3. In paragraph 5 why list the kinds of things piled on the carts instead of saving space by calling them "household effects" or "portable possessions"? What distinction may be drawn between "crying" and "sobbing"?
4. Are there any words that you could remove without changing the meaning and effect of the description?

5-B   On Societies as Organisms .

Lewis Thomas

This essay, here almost complete, was first published in the *New England Journal of Medicine* and then in *The Lives of a Cell* (1974), a collection of Dr. Thomas's essays. The writer, a noted research scientist, is fascinated by the behavior of living things of all kinds, from the parts of a single cell to human beings. He begins the essay by pointing out that although we often compare the behavior of humans to that of insects, scientists object to any interpretation of insect behavior in human terms.

The writers of books on insect behavior generally take pains, in their prefaces, to caution that insects are like creatures from another planet, that their behavior is absolutely foreign, totally unhuman, unearthly, almost unbiological. They are more like perfectly tooled but crazy little machines, and we violate science when we try to read 5 human meanings in their arrangements.

It is hard for a bystander not to do so. Ants are so much like human beings as to be an embarrassment. They farm fungi, raise aphids as livestock, launch armies into wars, use chemical sprays to alarm and confuse enemies, capture slaves. The families of weaver ants engage in child labor, holding their larvae like shuttles to spin out the thread that sews the leaves together for their fungus gardens. They exchange information ceaselessly. They do everything but watch television.

What makes us most uncomfortable is that they, and the bees and termites and social wasps, seem to live two kinds of lives: they are individuals, going about the day's business without much evidence of thought for tomorrow, and they are at the same time component parts, cellular elements, in the huge, writhing, ruminating organism of the Hill, the nest, the hive. It is because of this aspect, I think, that we most wish for them to be something foreign. We do not like the notion that there can be collective societies with the capacity to behave like organisms. If such things exist, they can have nothing to do with us.

Still, there it is. A solitary ant, afield, cannot be considered to have much of anything on his mind; indeed, with only a few neurons strung together by fibers, he can't be imagined to have a mind at all, much less a thought. He is more like a ganglion on legs. Four ants together, or ten, encircling a dead moth on a path, begin to look more like an idea. They fumble and shove, gradually moving the food toward the Hill, but as though by blind chance. It is only when you watch the dense mass of thousands of ants, crowded together around the Hill, blackening the ground, that you begin to see the whole beast, and now you observe it thinking, planning, calculating. It is an intelligence, a kind of live computer, with crawling bits for its wits.

At a stage in the construction, twigs of a certain size are needed, and all the members forage obsessively for twigs of just this size. Later, when outer walls are to be finished, thatched, the size must change, and as though given new orders by telephone, all the workers shift the search to the new twigs. If you disturb the arrangement of a part of the Hill, hundreds of ants will set it vibrating, shifting, until it is put right again. Distant sources of food are somehow sensed, and long lines, like tentacles, reach out over the ground, up over walls, behind boulders, to fetch it in.

Termites are even more extraordinary in the way they seem to accumulate intelligence as they gather together. Two or three termites in a chamber will begin to pick up pellets and move from place to place, but nothing comes of it; nothing is built. As more join in, they seem to reach a critical mass, a quorum, and the thinking begins. They place pellets atop pellets, then throw up columns and beautiful, curving, symmetrical arches, and the crystalline architecture of vaulted chambers is created. It is not known how they communicate with each other, how the chains of termites building one column know when to turn toward the crew on the adjacent column, or how, when the time comes, they manage the flawless joining of the arches. The stimuli that set them off at the outset, building collectively instead of shifting things about, may be pheromones [odors] released when they reach committee size. 55 They react as if alarmed. They become agitated, excited, and then they begin working, like artists. . . .

The phenomenon of separate animals joining up to form an organism is not unique in insects. Slime-mold cells do it all the time, of course, in each life cycle. . . . Herring and other fish in schools are at times so closely integrated, their actions so coordinated, that they seem to be 60 functionally a great multi-fish organism. Flocking birds, especially the seabirds nesting on the slopes of offshore islands in Newfoundland, are similarly attached, connected, synchronized.

Although we are by all odds the most social of all social animals— more interdependent, more attached to each other, more inseparable 65 in our behavior than bees—we do not often feel our conjoined intelligence. Perhaps, however, we are linked in circuits for the storage, processing, and retrieval of information, since this appears to be the most basic and universal of all human enterprises. It may be our biological function to build a certain kind of Hill. We have access to all the 70 information of the biosphere, arriving as elementary units in the stream of solar photons. When we have learned how these are rearranged against randomness, to make, say, springtails, quantum mechanics, and the late quartets, we may have a clearer notion how to proceed. The circuitry seems to be there, even if the current is not always on. 75

The system of communications used in science should provide a neat, workable model for studying mechanisms of information-building in human society. Ziman, in a recent *Nature* essay, points out, "the invention of a mechanism for the systematic publication of *fragments* of scientific work may well have been the key event in the history of 80 modern science." He continues:

> A regular journal carries from one research worker to another the various . . . observations which are of common interest. . . . A typical scientific paper has never pretended to be more than another little piece in a larger jigsaw—not significant in itself but as an element in a grander 85 scheme. *This technique, of soliciting many modest contributions to the store of human knowledge, has been the secret of Western science since the seventeenth century, for it achieves a corporate, collective power that is far greater than one individual can exert* [italics mine].

With some alteration of terms, some toning down, the passage 90 could describe the building of a termite nest.

It is fascinating that the word "explore" does not apply to the searching aspect of the activity, but has its origins in the sounds we make while engaged in it. We like to think of exploring in science as a lonely, meditative business, and so it is in the first stages, but always, 95 sooner or later, before the enterprise reaches completion, as we explore, we call to each other, communicate, publish, send letters to the editor, present papers, cry out on finding.

1. What specific, concrete words describe actions? living things?
2. Where does Thomas use figurative language? What seems to be the purpose?
3. What distinctions does Thomas make among words in a kind of list at the end of his first sentence, in the sentence beginning in line 8, and in the sentence beginning in line 65?
4. Can you shorten any of Thomas's sentences by changing or omitting words without at the same time changing the meaning and effect?
5. The sentences vary in length from short (under 10 words) to long (over 30 words). Where and how does this variation emphasize Thomas's main points?
6. Check the etymology, denotation, and connotation of these words: *launch, ruminating, neuron, ganglion, forage, tentacle, termites, pellets, quorum, explore.*

5-C   Farewell, My Lovely

E. B. White

This essay, here almost complete, was first published in *The New Yorker* (1936) with which White was connected for many years. Richard L. Strout suggested the idea, and so White signed the essay "Lee Strout White." In it, he pays tribute to the car most responsible for starting the "age of the automobile." Writing nine years after the last Model T was built, he had to assume that few of his readers still drove a Model T. Note how he combines factual information with warm emotion, and formal word choice with colloquialisms.

WORD
CHOICE

Metaphor

Metaphor

Personifi-
cation

Simile

Precise
verbs

The Model T was distinguished from all other makes of cars by the fact that its transmission was of a type known as planetary—which was half metaphysics, half sheer fiction. Engineers accepted the word "planetary" in its epicyclic sense, but I was always conscious that it also 5 meant "wandering," "erratic." Because of the peculiar nature of this planetary element, there was always, in Model T, a certain dull rapport between engine and wheels, and even when the car was in a state known as neutral, it trembled with a deep imperative and tended to 10 inch forward. There was never a moment when the bands were not faintly egging the machine on. In this respect it was like a horse, rolling the bit on its tongue, and country people brought to it the same technique they used with draft animals. 15

Its most remarkable quality was its rate of accelera- tion. In its palmy days the Model T could take off faster than anything on the road. The reason was simple. To get under way, you simply hooked the third finger of the right hand around a lever on the steering column, pulled down 20 hard, and shoved your left foot forcibly against the low- speed pedal. These were simple, positive motions; the car

<table>
<tr><td>Precise
verbal</td><td>responded by lunging forward with a roar. After a few
seconds of this turmoil, you took your toe off the pedal,</td></tr>
</table>

Precise verbal — responded by lunging forward with a roar. After a few seconds of this turmoil, you took your toe off the pedal,

Precise verbs — eased up a mite on the throttle, and the car, possessed of 25 only two forward speeds, catapulted directly into high with a series of ugly jerks and was off on its glorious errand. The abruptness of this departure was never equalled in other cars of the period. The human leg was (and still is) incapable of letting in a clutch with anything like the 30

Metaphor — forthright abandon that used to send Model T on its way. Letting in a clutch is a negative, hesitant motion, depend- ing on delicate nervous control; pushing down the Ford

Metaphor Simile — pedal was a simple, country motion—an expansive act, which came as natural as kicking an old door to make it 35 budge.

Metaphor — The driver of the old Model T was a man enthroned. The car, with top up, stood seven feet high. The driver sat

Metaphor — on top of the gas tank, brooding it with his own body. When he wanted gasoline, he alighted, along with every- 40 thing else in the front seat; the seat was pulled off, the metal cap unscrewed, and a wooden stick thrust down to sound the liquid in the well. There were always a couple

Colloquial- isms — of these sounding sticks kicking around in the ratty sub- cushion regions of a flivver. Refuelling was more of a social 45

Metaphor — function then, because the driver had to unbend, whether he wanted to or not. Directly in front of the driver was the

Metaphor — windshield—high, uncompromisingly erect. Nobody talked about air resistance, and the four cylinders pushed the car through the atmosphere with a simple disregard of 50 physical law.

During my association with Model T's, self-starters were not a prevalent accessory. They were expensive and under suspicion. Your car came equipped with a service- able crank, and the first thing you learned was how to Get 55 Results. It was a special trick, and until you learned it (usually from another Ford owner, but sometimes by a period of appalling experimentation) you might as well

Simile — have been winding up an awning. The trick was to leave

Personifi- cation — the ignition switch off, proceed to the animal's head, pull 60 the choke (which was a little wire protruding through the radiator) and give the crank two or three nonchalant up- ward lifts. Then, whistling as though thinking about some- thing else, you would saunter back to the driver's cabin, turn the ignition on, return to the crank, and this time, 65 catching it on the down stroke, give it a quick spin with plenty of That. If this procedure was followed, the engine

Metaphor

almost always responded—first with a few scattered explosions, then with a tumultuous gunfire, which you checked by racing around to the driver's seat and retarding the throttle. Often, if the emergency brake hadn't been pulled all the way back, the car advanced on you the instant the first explosion occurred and you would hold it back by leaning your weight against it. I can still feel my old Ford nuzzling me at the curb, as though looking for an apple in my pocket. 70

Implied metaphor

old Ford nuzzling me at the curb, as though looking for an apple in my pocket. 75

The lore and legend that governed the Ford were boundless. Owners had their own theories about everything; they discussed mutual problems in that wise, infinitely resourceful way old women discuss rheumatism. Exact knowledge was pretty scarce, and often proved less effective than superstition. Dropping a camphor ball into the gas tank was a popular expedient; it seemed to have a tonic effect on both man and machine. There wasn't much to base exact knowledge on. The Ford driver flew blind. He didn't know the temperature of his engine, the speed of his car, the amount of his fuel, or the pressure of his oil (the old Ford lubricated itself by what was amiably described as the "splash system"). A speedometer cost money and was an extra, like a windshield-wiper. The dashboard of the early models was bare save for an ignition key. . . . Whatever the driver learned of his motor, he learned not through instruments but through sudden developments. . . . 80

Simile

Implied metaphor

85

90

Implied metaphor

Extended metaphor

One reason the Ford anatomy was never reduced to an exact science was that, having "fixed" it, the owner couldn't honestly claim that the treatment had brought about the cure. There were too many authenticated cases of Fords fixing themselves—restored naturally to health after a short rest. Farmers soon discovered this, and it fitted nicely with their draft-horse philosophy: "Let 'er cool off and she'll snap into it again." 95

100

Metaphor

Implied metaphor

Implied metaphor

Implied metaphor

Metaphor

Sprinkled not too liberally among the millions of amateur witch doctors who drove Fords and applied their own abominable cures were the heaven-sent mechanics who could really make the car talk. These professionals turned up in undreamed-of spots. One time, on the banks of the Columbia River in Washington, I heard the rear end go out of my Model T when I was trying to whip it up a steep incline onto the deck of a ferry. Something snapped; the car slid backward into the mud. It seemed to me like the end of the trail. But the captain of the ferry, observing the withered remnant, spoke up. 105

110

"What's got her?" he asked.

"I guess it's the rear end," I replied, listlessly. The 115
captain leaned over the rail and stared. Then I saw that
there was a hunger in his eyes that set him off from other
men.

"Tell you what," he said, carelessly, trying to cover up

Colloquial-
ism
his eagerness, "let's pull the son of a bitch up onto the boat, 120
and I'll help you fix her while we're going back and forth
on the river."

We did just this. All that day I plied between the
towns of Pasco and Kennewick, while the skipper (who

Implied
metaphor
had once worked in a Ford garage) directed the amazing 125
work of resetting the bones of my car.

Springtime in the heyday of the Model T was a deliri-
ous season. Owning a car was still a major excitement,
roads were still wonderful and bad. The Fords were obvi-

Hyperbole
ously conceived in madness: any car which was capable of 130
going from forward into reverse without any perceptible

Colloquial-
ism
mechanical hiatus was bound to be a mighty challenging
thing to the human imagination. Boys used to veer them
off the highway into a level pasture and run wild with

Simile
them, as though they were cutting up with a girl. Most 135
everybody used the reverse pedal quite as much as the
regular foot brake—it distributed the wear over the bands
and wore them all down evenly. That was the big trick, to
wear all the bands down evenly, so that the final chat-

Implied
metaphor
tering would be total and the whole unit scream for 140
renewal.

The days were golden, the nights were dim and
strange. I still recall with trembling those loud, nocturnal
crises when you drew up to a signpost and raced the engine so the lights would be bright enough to read destina- 145

Metaphor
tions by. I have never been really planetary since. I suppose it's time to say goodbye. Farewell, my lovely!

1. What words describe specific actions?
2. What is the effect of White's use of figurative language?
3. Where and how does he explain technical terms?
4. How does the word choice show that White is being both serious and humorous?
5. The sentences vary in length from short (under 10 words) to long (over
   25 words); where and how does White use this variation to emphasize his
   points?
6. Can you shorten any of the sentences by changing or omitting words without
   at the same time changing the meaning and effect?

5-D   Challenge

Jesse Jackson

These paragraphs come from the Reverend Jesse Jackson's speech to an audience composed primarily of black high school students at the 1979 convention of Operation PUSH. Note his use of colloquial language.

The reason I have so much faith in this generation of young people is because down through the years student involvement has made a difference in social change. During the McCarthy Era, students fought the threat of free speech being taken away from us. When Rosa Parks found herself in anguish she went to Dr. King who was a student who 5 led that great struggle somewhere between Selma and Montgomery. Students met a struggle and made a difference. The reason some of us can't make sound decisions is that we've been sidetracked. Some by violence, some by sex, some by lack of opportunity. I tell the story over and over again, how do you measure a man. You can't look at some 10 cowboy definition of a man. You're not a man because you got notches on your belt; you're not a man because you can violate somebody; you're not a man because you can push somebody else down; you're not a man because you can kill somebody.

You're a man because you can heal somebody. You're not a man 15 because you can make a baby; you're a man because you can raise a baby and provide for a baby and produce for a baby. That makes you a man. Young sisters, there's another side to that story. You can't measure yourself by your bosom—you've got to do it by your books. You've got to have something in your mind. There's nothing that's 20 more perverted than to see somebody with a fully developed bottom and a half developed brain. You've got to check out your mind. I got a little message that says—the buses are not leaving now; so just sit down and be cool. The buses are not leaving so just sit down and be cool. We have this situation for many of us do not want to face the 25 reality and the options of our lives. So when we begin to remind you about sex, we're not being unreal. Someone said "Rev., you don't understand about sex—there's a thrill in sex." I understand there's a thrill. I've got five children; I understand thrill, I'm not unaware of that. Except, I also know this; that when people all around you tell 30 you that you can't do something and you can do it, and you do it— that's a thrill. When you graduate from high school, that's a thrill. When you come across that stage and have a Medical Degree or a Law Degree, that's a thrill. When you make a touchdown, that's a thrill. When you do your best against the odds and make it when ev- 35 erybody around you says you couldn't make it, that's a thrill. When you end up going to college instead of to jail, that's also a thrill. And all I'm saying is that we should not have a one-thrill syndrome; all of life can be thrilling if you develop your mind, develop your body and develop your soul. Say amen.   40

1. What specific, concrete words are used?
2. Where is repetition used for emphasis?
3. Can you condense any of the sentences by changing or omitting words or phrases without at the same time changing the meaning and effect?

5-E   A Metaphor Used Twice

Jacob Bronowski

In *Science and Human Values* (rev. 1965), the writer, a scientist and philosopher, argues that creative scientists and creative artists share the same goal, to discover unity in the variety of experience, and both often devote years to uncovering the full significance of a single idea. He illustrates this with two brief quotations from Shakespeare's plays. These paragraphs are given here mainly for the **skilled analysis of Shakespeare's metaphor, but note Bronowski's own word choice.**

What is a poetic image but the seizing and the exploration of a hidden likeness, in holding together two parts of a comparison which are to give depth each to the other? When Romeo finds Juliet in the tomb, and thinks her dead, he uses in his heartbreaking speech the words,

> Death that hath suckt the honey of thy breath.   5

The critic can only haltingly take to pieces the single shock which this image carries. The young Shakespeare admired Marlowe, and Marlowe's Faustus had said of the ghostly kiss of Helen of Troy that it sucked forth his soul. But that is a pale image; what Shakespeare has done is to fire it with the single word honey. Death is a bee at the lips of Juliet, 10 and the bee is an insect that stings; the sting of death was a commonplace phrase when Shakespeare wrote. The sting is there, under the image; Shakespeare has packed it into the word honey; but the very word rides powerfully over its own undertones. Death is a bee that stings other people, but it comes to Juliet as if she were a flower; this 15 is the moving thought under the instant image. The creative mind speaks in such thoughts.

More than ten years later Shakespeare came back to the image and unexpectedly made it concrete, a metaphor turned into a person in the drama. The drama is *Antony and Cleopatra;* the scene is the high 20 tower; and to it death comes in person, as an asp hidden among figs. The image of the asp carries, of course, many undertones; and most moving among these is Cleopatra's fancy, that this death, which should sting, has come to her to suck the sweetness. Cleopatra is speaking, bitterly, tenderly, about the asp: 25

> Peace, peace:
> Dost thou not see my Baby at my breast,
> That suckes the Nurse asleepe.

The man who wrote these words still carried in his ear the echo from Juliet's tomb, and what he added to it was the span of his life's work. 30

1. In the first paragraph, how appropriate are these words to the writer's point: *seizing, shock, fire, packed, rides?*
2. Check the etymology and various meanings of *fancy* and *image;* how is each word used here?

Assignments

1. Write a paper of about 300 words on the word choice and figurative language in the description of the jet engine (Unit 2-C).
2. Revise one of your earlier essays by replacing vague words with precise, concrete ones and by omitting words that you do not need.
3. Read a column by a sports writer or listen to a radio sports announcer who you think makes events exciting; then write an essay discussing how particular words and phrases made the action seem vivid.
4. Compose a three-minute radio commercial for something you like very much, such as a particular product, a performer, a movie, a political leader. Assume that your commercial will be broadcast only on your campus.
5. Rewrite the commercial you composed for assignment 4, but this time assume that it will be broadcast on a regular station. What changes must you make for the different audience?
6. Choose something inanimate, such as a pair of shoes, a bicycle, a stone, or a river, and in 200 to 300 words describe it as if it were a specific kind of animate creature, anything from a single-cell animal to a human being.

UNIT 6

The Outline

An outline lets you see a whole essay or lecture at a glance. It not only records the main ideas—any notes can do that—but it also arranges them on the page to show their relative importance and their connections with each other. An outline can therefore give you essential help in studying and writing. Which of these versions would be more helpful if you were reviewing the information for a test or planning to use it in a report?

1. This version presents the information in a rough summary—

> History is divided into two periods—prehistoric, before writing, and historic, after writing. Prehistoric, known by remaining weapons and utensils, is divided into four stages: Old Stone (rude and primitive), New Stone (more advanced), Copper-Bronze (first use of metals), and Iron. Historic age is much better known through written records.

2. This version presents the same information in a rough outline—

> History is divided into two periods:
>   Prehistoric—before writing—known by weapons and utensils
>   Old Stone (rude and primitive)
>   New Stone (more advanced)
>   Copper-Bronze (first use of metals)
>   Iron
>   Historic—after writing—much better known, through written records

The formal outline is merely a conventional, labeled arrangement of logical indentations like those shown in the second version. It may be more elaborate and precise than you can work out in detail while listening to a lecture, but you can apply the general principles even when in a hurry. Besides helping you to see how the writers and lecturers organized their main ideas, it will help you to organize your own ideas. Every time you plan a paper, you will have occasion to work out a brief outline like that in Unit 1, "The Fundamentals of Writing."

The longer the piece of writing is expected to be, the more detailed your planning should be and the more carefully you should revise to emphasize the logic of your organization.

*   *   *   *   *   *   *   *   *

The **topic outline** and the **sentence outline** are the usual forms of outlining. In both, each heading, subheading, and sub-subheading is based on the relative importance of the parts of the material, without regard to paragraphing. The number of paragraphs in an essay may have no relation to the number of main sections of the thought. Some important points may require several paragraphs, others only one or two, depending on the complexity of the material. But in an outline the material is arranged logically, according to various degrees of importance, through a careful system of designations and indentations.

In the topic outline, a word or phrase indicates an item; in the sentence outline, each item is presented in a complete sentence. The topic outline is easier to write and is usually adequate for small plans for which you need only a reminder of the material and ideas involved. But for complex schemes, for material that you may put aside for some time, and above all for plans that someone else may read and evaluate, the sentence outline is far superior. Moreover, expressing each item in a complete sentence forces you to think through your material more thoroughly and therefore will make writing the paper easier.

*   *   *   *   *   *   *   *   *

The logic of your outline structure—how you choose and arrange items—will determine the value of your outline. You must break down a whole into its main parts and then break each of these coordinate parts into its parts, and so on, with designations and indentations to show the relationships among them.

Designation.   The customary symbols to mark the parts are these:

Roman numerals (I, II, etc.) for main divisions
Capital letters (A, B, etc.) for secondary points
Arabic numerals (1, 2, etc.) for third-degree points
Lower-case letters (a, b, etc.) for fourth-degree points

You will not often need the fifth and sixth degrees, but when you do, indicate the fifth by Arabic numerals and the sixth by lower-case letters, each enclosed in parentheses.

Indentation.   All points of the same rank must be parallel down the page, each one beginning at the same distance from the left-hand margin. Indicate each subordinate rank by indenting it slightly to the right. With this method, all the Roman numerals for the main divisions will be the same distance from the left margin, all the capital letters for the secondary points will be indented slightly farther than the Roman numerals, and so on. If each degree is indented the equivalent of about three letters, you should have enough space left for the subpoints of the fourth degree and even for those of the fifth and sixth degrees, if you have any.

Make sure that the symbols stand out so that the relationships will be clear. The following arrangement is poor because the second line of each of the longer items (I and A) is at the same margin as the symbol for the item:

I. The Aztec Indians had early attained a very remarkable degree of civilization.
    A. Their surviving buildings indicate a considerable knowledge of architecture.
    B. Their ancient weapons are made with great skill.

This next arrangement makes the symbols stand out, and therefore the relationship of the parts is clear:

I. The Aztec Indians had early attained a very remarkable degree of civilization.
    A. Their surviving buildings indicate a considerable knowledge of architecture.
    B. Their ancient weapons are made with great skill.

* * *   * * *   * * *

Making a reading outline is an excellent way to study anything you want to remember, and later the outline will help you to review the reading quickly. Follow these steps:

1. What is the main idea? Read the entire piece through carefully —you would outline a book by chapters or other manageable units, not as a whole. Then reduce its central meaning to a single comprehensive sentence. This is the main idea or thesis, and should always appear at the head of your outline, for it represents the "essay as a whole." This thesis sentence should express content, not purpose, and be long enough to indicate the major divisions of your plan. Omit all unnecessary expressions, such as "the author says."

2. What are the main divisions of the author's thought? These are the major sections into which the lesser points are grouped. If you find eleven, say, or seventeen, reconsider. You are probably "failing to see the forest because of the trees in the way" and are treating small details as important items. A single chapter or essay cannot manage so many main points—probably, in fact, not more than a half-dozen at most. Remember that there will be at least two, however; since outlining is a process of breaking down, a one-point outline is not an outline at all. If at first you think you have only one, it is the main idea, and you must break it down into points I, II, and so on.

3. Make the main points comparable. The material of each should have about the same level of importance as that of the others. If not, that point does not deserve equal rank in the outline. Whenever you can, make such equality clearly evident through parallel wording (see A and B under I in the preceding examples).

4. Break down each main section into its own smaller parts. Thus you arrive at the secondary divisions, which you indicate by capital letters and an indented position.

5. Finish outlining each main section before moving on. It is better not to start on items of the third rank, however, until you have worked out all the second-rank items for that section, or on the fourth until the third is completed, and so on. Otherwise, you may lose perspective and give too much importance to trifling points. Be sure that within every level your points are logically of equal importance, and continue to indicate the fact not only by similar symbols and indentations but, wherever possible, by parallel wording as well.

6. Make your outline follow a deductive order. Proceed from the general to the particular, from the main point to the subpoints beneath it. Even if the author has deliberately reversed the order of the material for emphasis by giving the particulars first and arriving at the main point only through them, your outline must nevertheless present the author's points deductively.

7. Omit everything irrelevant to the main plan. Rhetorical questions, figures of speech, elaborate descriptions, repetitions for effect— reduce them all to the basic points they illustrate or emphasize. The college lecturer who advised students, "Take down the point I am trying to make, not the funny story I tell you in making it," was right —although you might mention such a story in its properly subordinate position as a subpoint under the superior point it illustrates.

8. Use as many levels as you find suitable. The purpose of your outline will determine how much detail you should include. For example, you may or may not choose to list under a point the three subpoints composing it, but if you mention one subpoint you are duty bound to give the others of the same rank.

9. Avoid the meaningless single subpoint. If the information on a point is not divisible into at least two subpoints, it has no subpoint at all. For instance, if the only example that you are going to give under the main heading "A. Trees" is "1. Oak," your main heading should be "A. Oak trees," because you do not have a subpoint. There is only one exception to this rule. If you have information for two or more subpoints under one heading (for example, "A. Dogs, 1. Beagles, 2. Poodles, 3. Boxers") but for only one under a matching heading, you may list that as "1" under "B" (for example, "B. Cats, 1. Siamese") to show that it is parallel with the subpoints under A and not with the more general heading of "A." Otherwise, incorporate the example into your statement of its superior point.

10. Check your work to see that it is entirely logical. Remember that your main-idea sentence must cover, briefly but definitely, the thought contained in the main points of the essay, and point "I" must read so as to include logically its own "A," "B," and "C," and so on.

Similarly, each set of subpoints must add up to the main point under which it appears: "a," "b," and "c" must compose "1"; "1" and "2" must compose "A"; "A" and "B" must compose "I"; and "I," "II," "III" (plus the Introduction and Conclusion) must compose the main idea. (Sometimes a change in wording can correct a flaw in logic. If "a," "b," and "c" fit logically under "2," but "d" does not, you may be able to keep "d" by narrowing its scope or by enlarging the scope of "2" to include it.)

    11. Be consistent. Whichever type of outline you choose for a particular purpose, do not mix it with the other type. Do not use single words or phrases to present any items in a sentence outline. Do not use any sentences in a topic outline.

       * * *   * * *   * * *

Making a writing outline to guide you in your own writing is much like making an outline of your reading. The logical process for both is the same. Just as your reading outline is your version of the framework on which someone else has constructed an orderly essay or report, your writing outline is the framework on which you will construct your essay. But here, instead of a completed work to take apart, you have raw materials to put together: ideas, facts, and opinions drawn from your own experiences, your reading, or the remarks of others. Gathering and organizing material for a preliminary outline for your own writing was discussed in Unit 1 (pages 5–9). All the suggestions given for the reading outline apply to the structure of a writing outline.

    If you will be the only reader of your writing outline, you may, of course, find a rough form adequate, but if others will read it to judge your plans or to clarify your paper, you should follow the formal structure with great care.

Examples

6-A   The Fifth Freedom

Seymour St. John

This essay was first published in the *Saturday Review* in 1955, but the writer's criticism of American education is still widely applicable. Note, for example, William Zinsser's plea in 1977 that students be allowed the "right to fail" (Unit 13-G).

    Important: for your convenience, the paragraphs are numbered. These numbers are repeated in the margin of the sentence and topic outlines to emphasize their relationship with the essay.

[1] More than three centuries ago a handful of pioneers crossed the ocean to Jamestown and Plymouth in search of freedoms they were unable to find in their own countries, the freedoms we still cherish today: freedom from want, freedom from fear, freedom of speech, freedom of religion. Today the descendants of the early settlers, and 5

those who have joined them since, are fighting to protect these free-doms at home and throughout the world.

[2] And yet there is a fifth freedom—basic to those four—that we are in danger of losing: *the freedom to be one's best.* St. Exupery de-scribes a ragged, sensitive-faced Arab child, haunting the streets of a 10 North African town, as a lost Mozart: he would never be trained or developed. Was he free? "No one grasped you by the shoulder while there was still time; and nought will awaken in you the sleeping poet or musician or astronomer that possibly inhabited you from the begin-ning." The freedom to be one's best is the chance for the development 15 of each person to his highest power.

[3] How is it that we in America have begun to lose this freedom, and how can we regain it for our nation's youth? I believe it has started slipping away from us because of three misunderstandings.

[4] First, the misunderstanding of the meaning of democracy. The 20 principal of a great Philadelphia high school is driven to cry for help in combating the notion that it is undemocratic to run a special program of studies for outstanding boys and girls. Again, when a good indepen-dent school in Memphis recently closed, some thoughtful citizens urged that it be taken over by the public-school system and used for boys and 25 girls of high ability, that it have entrance requirements and give an advanced program of studies to superior students who were interested and able to take it. The proposal was rejected because it was undemo-cratic! Out of this misunderstanding comes the middle-muddle. Courses are geared to the middle of the class. The good student is unchallenged, 30 bored. The loafer receives his passing grade. And the lack of an out-standing course for the outstanding student, the lack of a standard which a boy or girl must meet, passes for democracy.

[5] The second misunderstanding concerns what makes for happi-ness. The aims of our present-day culture are avowedly ease and mate- 35 rial well-being: shorter hours; a shorter week; more return for less accomplishment; more soft-soap excuses and fewer honest, realistic demands. In our schools this is reflected by the vanishing hickory stick and the emerging psychiatrist. The hickory stick had its faults, and the psychiatrist has his strengths. But the trend is clear: *Tout comprendre* 40 *c'est tout pardonner* [To understand everything is to excuse every-thing]. Do we really believe that our softening standards bring happi-ness? Is it our sound and considered judgment that the tougher subjects of the classics and mathematics should be thrown aside, as suggested by some educators, for doll-playing? Small wonder that Charles Malik, 45 Lebanese delegate at the U.N., writes: "There is in the West [in the United States] a general weakening of moral fiber. [Our] leadership does not seem to be adequate to the unprecedented challenges of the age."

[6] The last misunderstanding is in the area of values. Here are 50 some of the most influential tenets of teacher education over the past

fifty years: there is no eternal truth; there is no absolute moral law; there is no God. Yet all of history has taught us that the denial of these ultimates, the placement of man or state at the core of the universe, results in a paralyzing mass selfishness; and the first signs of it are 55 already frighteningly evident.

[7] Arnold Toynbee has said that all progress, all development come from challenge and a consequent response. Without challenge there is no response, no development, no freedom. So first we owe to our children the most demanding, challenging curriculum that is within 60 their capabilities. Michelangelo did not learn to paint by spending his time doodling. Mozart was not an accomplished pianist at the age of eight as the result of spending his days in front of a television set. Like Eve Curie, like Helen Keller, they responded to the challenge of their lives by a disciplined training: and they gained a new freedom.   65

[8] The second opportunity we can give our boys and girls is the right to failure. "Freedom is not only a privilege, it is a test," writes De Nöuy. What kind of a test is it, what kind of freedom where no one can fail? The day is past when the United States can afford to give high school diplomas to all who sit through four years of instruction, regard- 70 less of whether any visible results can be discerned. We live in a narrowed world where we must be alert, awake to realism; and realism demands a standard which must either be met or result in failure. These are hard words, but they are brutally true. If we deprive our children of the right to fail we deprive them of their knowledge of the world as 75 it is.

[9] Finally, we can expose our children to the best values we have found. By relating our lives to the evidences of the ages, by judging our philosophy in the light of values that history has proven truest, perhaps we shall be able to produce that "ringing message, full of content and 80 truth, satisfying the mind, appealing to the heart, firing the will, a message on which one can stake his whole life." This is the message that could mean joy and strength and leadership—freedom as opposed to serfdom.

6-B   Sentence Outline of "The Fifth Freedom"

The numbers in brackets near the left margin correspond to the paragraph numbers in the essay. Within the outline, the italicized sentences in brackets are not part of the outline; they give explanations of the outline structure.

Main idea: Besides the four freedoms we cherish, there is a fifth, the freedom to be one's best, which we are in danger of losing through our misunderstandings but which we must preserve and pass on to our children by challenging them.

[1]   I. Today we cherish four freedoms.
           A. The pioneers came to America to find them.
             1. One is freedom from want.
             2. Another is freedom from fear.
             3. Another is freedom of speech.   5
             4. Another is freedom of religion.

               [*These are a common kind of subpoint, a simple enumeration. Here they are written out more fully than in the essay, to satisfy the requirements of the sentence outline.*]   10

           B. Today we fight to protect them.

             [*A and B are parallel subpoints as cause and effect of the introductory statement; note the balanced wording.*]

[2]   II. The fifth freedom is freedom to be one's best. 15
        [*Now the subject of the essay, indicated by the title, begins; the first main section prepared the way for it.*]
           A. It is basic to the other four.
           B. We are in danger of losing it.
             [*The incident of the Arab child, being only an il-* 20 *lustration, may be omitted from a brief outline.*]

[3–6]   III. We are losing this fifth freedom through three misunderstandings.
        [*A question like the one that begins ¶3 is rhetorical and should never appear in the outline in that form.* 25 *Here, moreover, half the answer doesn't appear until the next point, beginning in ¶7.*]

[4]   A. The first misunderstanding is of the meaning of democracy.
             1. We think that democracy in education means 30 gearing all courses to the middle level.
             2. We reject special programs and schools for superior students as undemocratic.
               a. In Philadelphia a special program for superior students was attacked. 35
               b. In Memphis a proposed special school for superior students was rejected.

               [*Here, a and b are examples supporting 2 which in turn supports A and therefore should be included, unlike the illustration in* 40 *II. Notice both the continued reduction of the original wording and the parallel sentence structures for parallel points.*]

[5]   B. The second misunderstanding is of the meaning of happiness and results from our stress on comfort 45 rather than on accomplishment.

           1. Our schools try to excuse children rather than discipline them.

           2. They try to amuse children rather than educate them. 50

[Details such as shorter hours and metaphors such as the hickory stick are omitted, the outline stripping the essay down to its bare ideas.]

[6]   C. The third misunderstanding is of ultimate values.

           1. These values have been denied in recent 55 teacher education.

             a. Eternal truth is denied.

             b. Absolute moral law is denied.

             c. The existence of God is denied.

[Subpoints at this level could be omitted, but 60 if we include one we must include all.]

           2. The inevitable result in mass selfishness is already evident.

[7–9]   IV. To assure our children the freedom to develop, we must challenge their abilities. 65

[Toynbee's statement is a further illustration so that we can omit it from the outline.]

[7]   A. We can give them a demanding curriculum.

           1. Michelangelo did not learn to paint by doodling.

           2. Mozart did not become a pianist by watching 70 television.

           3. They, like Eve Curie and Helen Keller, were challenged by disciplined training.

[1 and 2 are negative examples and 3 is positive, but they are on the same level.] 75

[8]   B. We can give them the right to failure.

[De Nöuy's statements, like Toynbee's, can be omitted.]

           1. We must not give high school diplomas without regard to merit. 80

           2. We must be realistic about failure to meet standards and must teach our children realism.

[Again, 1 is a negative statement and 2 a positive one, but they are parallel points.]

[9]   C. We can give them the best values we know. 85

           1. We can show them what history has taught us to be true.

           2. These truths may inspire us to make a "ringing message" that could mean true freedom for them. 90

[Although 1 is the means and 2 is the end in view, they are parallel points under C.]

Note the following points about the preceding outline:

1. The statement of the main idea makes specific reference to the four main points and is therefore a *one-sentence summary* of the essay; but it does not attempt to jump a level and include any of the supporting points.

2. The four sentences stating the main points, I, II, III and IV, when taken together, form a slightly longer summary of the essay. We can, in turn, expand this by including the sentences for points A, B, and C.

3. These summaries would seem stiff if compared to the summary of the essay on page 122. Sentence designations in the outline have replaced the transitions used in the summary, and the effort to keep parallel points in parallel wording has eliminated sentence variety. As a piece of writing, the summary is obviously better; but as a view of the writer's organization, the outline is better.

4. Starting with the lowest level of subpoints (in this example, designated "a," "b," and so on), check for two things: first, to see that all statements having designations of the same level are actually comparable in importance; second, to see that all subpoints, at every level, are actually logical under the superior point of which they are the divisions.

6-C   Topic Outline of "The Fifth Freedom"

Main idea: Besides the four freedoms we cherish there is a fifth, the freedom to be one's best, which we are in danger of losing through our misunderstandings but which we must preserve and pass on to our children by challenging them.

[1]   I. Four cherished freedoms—from want, from fear, of speech, of religion
          A. Sought by early settlers
          B. Protected by our efforts today
[2]   II. Fifth freedom—to be one's best   5
          A. Basic to other four
          B. In danger of being lost
[3–6]   III. Three misunderstandings of fifth freedom
[4]   A. Democracy
               1. Education geared to middle level   10
               2. Special education for superior students considered undemocratic
[5]   B. Happiness
               1. Children excused, not disciplined
               2. Children amused, not educated   15
[6]   C. Values
               1. Denial of all ultimate values
               2. Mass selfishness as result

[7–9]   IV. Challenge necessary for children's development
[7]   A. Demanding curriculum   20
                    1. Michelangelo
                    2. Mozart
                    3. Eve Curie and Helen Keller
[8]   B. Right to failure
                    1. High school diplomas on merit only   25
                    2. Realistic view of failure
[9]   C. Our best values
                    1. Teachings from history
                    2. Inspiration to be truly free

Compare this topic outline with the sentence outline preceding it. What differences do you see in wording and arrangement? The brevity here results not only from using fewer words in each item but from using fewer low-order subpoints. Although a topic outline can have as many subdivisions as a sentence outline, in practice it usually has fewer.

6-D   Clutter

William Zinsser

Often, what you plan to outline will not have convenient transitional words like "First," "Second," and "Finally" to guide you to the divisions and subdivisions of the material. The third chapter from *On Writing Well* (1980), quoted here in full, lacks such markers, but often the first sentence of a paragraph is a guide to that paragraph's relation to the rest of the discussion. Zinsser develops here the claim he made earlier in his book that "Clutter is the disease of American writing. We are a society strangling in unnecessary words, circular constructions, pompous frills and meaningless jargon."

The numbers and letters in the margin correspond to those of the topic outline that follows.

I.   [1] Fighting clutter is like fighting weeds—the writer is always slightly behind. New varieties sprout overnight, and by noon they are part of American speech. It only takes a John Dean testifying on TV to have everyone in the country saying "at this point in time" instead of "now."   5

II.   [2] Consider all the prepositions that are routinely draped
   A.   onto verbs that don't need any help. Head up. Free up. Face up
      1.   to. We no longer head committees. We head them up. We don't
      2.   face problems anymore. We face up to them when we can free
              up a few minutes. A small detail, you may say—not worth both- 10
              ering about. It *is* worth bothering about. The game is won or
              lost on hundreds of small details. Writing improves in direct
              ratio to the number of things we can keep out of it that
              shouldn't be there. "Up" in "free up" shouldn't be there. Can
              we picture anything being freed *up?* The writer of clean En- 15

glish must examine every word that he puts on paper. He will find a surprising number that don't serve any purpose.

B.

1.   [3] Take the adjective "personal," as in "a personal friend of mine," "his personal feeling" or "her personal physician." It is typical of the words that can be eliminated nine times out of 20 ten. The personal friend has come into the language to distinguish him from the business friend, thereby debasing not only

2.   language but friendship. Someone's feeling *is* his personal feeling—that's what "his" means. As for the personal physician, he is that man so often summoned to the dressing room of a 25 stricken actress so that she won't have to be treated by the impersonal physician assigned to the theater. Someday I'd like to see him identified as "her doctor."

3.   [4] Or take those curious intervals of time like the short minute. "Twenty-two short minutes later she had won the final 30 set." Minutes are minutes, physicians are physicians, friends are friends. The rest is clutter.

C.   [5] Clutter is the laborious phrase which has pushed out the short word that means the same thing. These locutions are a drag on energy and momentum. Even before John Dean gave 35 us "at this point in time," people had stopped saying "now." They were saying "at the present time," or "currently," or "presently" (which means "soon"). Yet the idea can always be expressed by "now" to mean the immediate moment ("Now I can see him"), or by "today" to mean the historical present 40 ("Today prices are high"), or simply by the verb "to be" ("It is raining"). There is no need to say, "At the present time we are experiencing precipitation."

III.

A.   [6] Speaking of which, we are experiencing considerable difficulty getting *that* word out of the language now that it has 45 lumbered in. Even your dentist will ask if you are experiencing any pain. If he were asking one of his own children he would say, "Does it hurt?" He would, in short, be himself. By using a more pompous phrase in his professional role he not only sounds more important; he blunts the painful edge of truth. It 50

B. is the language of the airline stewardess demonstrating the oxygen mask that will drop down if the plane should somehow run out of air. "In the extremely unlikely possibility that the aircraft should experience such an eventuality," she begins—a phrase so oxygen-depriving in itself that we are prepared for 55 any disaster, and even gasping death shall lose its sting. As for those "smoking materials" that she asks us to "kindly extinguish," I often wonder what materials are smoking. Maybe she thinks my coat and tie are on fire.

C.   [7] Clutter is the ponderous euphemism that turns a slum 60 into a depressed socioeconomic area, a salesman into a market-

ing representative, a dumb kid into an underachiever and garbage collectors into waste disposal personnel. In New Canaan,
Conn., the incinerator is now the "volume reduction plant." I
hate to think what they call the town dump.   65

D.   [8] Clutter is the official language used by the American
corporation—in the news release and the annual report—to
hide its mistakes. When a big company recently announced that
it was "decentralizing its organization structure into major
profit-centered businesses" and that "corporate staff services 70
will be aligned under two senior vice-presidents" it meant that
it had had a lousy year.

            [9] Clutter is the language of the interoffice memo ("The
trend to mosaic communication is reducing the meaningfulness
of concern about whether or not demographic segments differ 75
in their tolerance of periodicity") and the language of computers ("We are offering functional digital programming options
that have built-in parallel reciprocal capabilities with compati-
ble third-generation contingencies and hardware").

E.   [10] Clutter is the language of the Pentagon throwing dust 80
in the eyes of the populace by calling an invasion a "reinforced
protective reaction strike" and by justifying its vast budgets on
the need for "credible second-strike capability" and "counter-
force deterrence." How can we grasp such vaporous double-
talk? As George Orwell pointed out in "Politics and the English 85
Language," an essay written in 1946 but cited frequently during the Vietnam years of Johnson and Nixon, "In our time,
political speech and writing are largely the defense of the inde-
fensible. . . . Thus political language has to consist largely of
euphemism, question-begging and sheer cloudy vagueness." 90
Orwell's warning that clutter is not just a nuisance but a deadly
tool did not turn out to be inoperative. By the 1960s his words
had come true in America.

IV.   [11] I could go on quoting examples from various fields—
every profession has its growing arsenal of jargon to fire at the 95
layman and hurl him back from its walls. But the list would be
depressing and the lesson tedious. The point of raising it now
is to serve notice that clutter is the enemy, whatever form it
takes. It slows the reader and robs the writer of his personality,
making him seem pretentious.   100

A.   [12] Beware, then, of the long word that is no better than
the short word: "numerous" (many), "facilitate" (ease), "individual" (man or woman), "remainder" (rest), "initial" (first),
"implement" (do), "sufficient" (enough), "attempt" (try), "referred to as" (called), and hundreds more. Beware, too, of all the 105

B.   slippery new fad words for which the language already has
equivalents: overview and quantify, paradigm and parameter,

input and throughput, peer group and interface, private sector and public sector, optimize and maximize, prioritize and potentialize. They are all weeds that will smother what you write. 110

C.   [13] Nor are all the weeds so obvious. Just as insidious are the little growths of perfectly ordinary words with which we explain how we propose to go about our explaining, or which inflate a simple preposition or conjunction into a whole windy phrase. 115

1.   [14] "I might add," "It should be pointed out," "It is interesting to note that"—how many sentences begin with these dreary clauses announcing what the writer is going to do next? If you might add, add it. If it should be pointed out, point it out. If it is interesting to note, *make* it interesting. Being told that 120 something is interesting is the surest way of tempting the reader to find it dull; are we not all stupefied by what follows when someone says, "This will interest you"? As for the inflated

2. prepositions and conjunctions, they are the innumerable phrases like "with the possible exception of" (except), "for the 125 reason that" (because), "he totally lacked the ability to" (he couldn't), "until such time as" (until), "for the purpose of" (for).

V.   [15] Clutter takes more forms than you can shake twenty sticks at. Prune it ruthlessly. Be grateful for everything that you can throw away. Re-examine each sentence that you put on 130 paper. Is every word doing new and useful work? Can any thought be expressed with more economy? Is anything pompous or pretentious or faddish? Are you hanging on to something useless just because you think it's beautiful?

        [16] Simplify, simplify. 135

6-E   Topic Outline of "Clutter"

Main idea: To write effectively we must reduce clutter in our use of language.

[1]   I. Problem of rapid growth of clutter
           II. Redundancies
[2]   A. Prepositions
                  1. Unnecessary ("head up")
                  2. Illogical ("free up")   5
[3–4]   B. Adjectives
                  1. Unnecessary ("personal friend/feeling/physician")
                  2. Debasing meaning ("personal friendship")
                  3. Illogical ("short minutes")   10
[5]   C. Longer words and phrases

[6] III. Euphemisms and jargon to conceal unpleasant truths
A. Physical pain
B. Danger
[7] C. Social discrimination
[8–9] D. Bad business news
[10] E. Government action
IV. Other redundancies
[11–14] A. Long words and phrases ("numerous" for "many")
B. Fad words ("optimize")
C. Ordinary words
[15] 1. Unnecessary explanations
[16] 2. Inflated prepositions and conjunctions
V. Need for ruthless editing: simplify

1. In "The Fifth Freedom" every paragraph received an outline designation of either the first or second level (I and II, and III. A, B, C, and IV. A, B, and C). How does the relationship between the paragraphs and the outline designations of "Clutter" differ from this?
2. What are the reasons for the differences?
3. Why do paragraphs 4 and 9 have no corresponding designations in the outline?
4. How is paragraph 13 related to the rest of the essay?
5. In the outline II.A and II.B are subdivided, but II.C is not. Why?
6. Make a sentence outline of "Clutter."

Assignments

1. Before you start work on outlining the ideas in an essay, test your knowledge of numbering and arrangement and your sense of logical relationships by putting into proper topical outline form the items in the following unorganized list. Use as many main points and as many degrees of subordination as the material seems to you to require, but limit yourself to these words.

caves	meat	sandals	chicken
clothing	tents	Irish potatoes	fruit
sausage	vegetables	pork	sneakers
potatoes	lemons	boots	shelter
food	suits	oranges	hats
cabins	cottages	hamburger	beans
apples	lima beans	sweet potatoes	houses
sauerkraut	cole slaw	slippers	corn
pineapple	bacon	grapefruit	beef
caps	bungalows	berets	headgear
footwear	navy beans	T-bone steaks	cabbage

a. Assuming common agreement as to the definition of each term, there can be no disagreement as to two aspects of the completed arrangement: the items that will appear in a single group at a given level (such as oranges, lemons, etc.) and the subpoints that will appear under a given main point (such as oranges, lemons, etc., under fruit); for this much is logically inherent in the material.

b. However, the arrangement of the items within a single group at any level will vary according to purpose. Consider, for example, the differing orders of the five items under the larger heading of fruit that may result, depending on whether the issue is size, color, type, price, scarcity, area of production, popularity, or nutritive value. Justify, according to some such purpose, the order within each group in your own arrangement. Will the same purpose determine the order within each?

c. Under what main idea might all these items appear?

2. Choose a magazine article, a book chapter, or an essay from a unit in this book and compose an outline of each type based on it. These should be good for your first efforts: Unit 1-A, Unit 2-G, Unit 4-C and F, Unit 10-B, F, and H. These are more challenging: Unit 2-H; Unit 3-C and D; Unit 4-H; Unit 9-F; Unit 11-D and F; Unit 12-H; Unit 13-I; Unit 14-G; Unit 15-D and E; 16-H; 20-B and C.

3. Check your outlines carefully with the directions given earlier in this unit. Make sure that they are consistent in logic and structure and give a faithful breakdown of the original.

UNIT 7

Quotations, Paraphrases, and Summaries

"According to Webster's. . . ." "In the words of Shakespeare. . . ." "Mary knows the company president, and she says the stock is sure to go up." "Einstein wrote. . . ." "I saw it on the six o'clock news." "I heard it on the radio." "This tip comes straight from the horse's mouth."

In all sorts of situations, we use the opinions and often the words of others to illustrate a point, support an opinion, or show our factual accuracy and firsthand knowledge of a book or speaker. A glance through the examples in this book will show that many of the writers quote, paraphrase, or summarize the writings or sayings of others, often extensively. You can strengthen your own writings by using their methods.

Quote when the original is particularly forceful or colorful in expression or when you think your readers may doubt your accuracy. A quotation is like a *photographic copy* of the original.

Paraphrase when the original may be difficult for your readers to understand because of the word choice, sentence structure, or content of the original. A paraphrase is a *translation* of the original into simpler language.

Summarize when the original is long and your readers will need only the main thought. A summary is a *miniature version* of the original.

QUOTATIONS

There are several conventions to follow when quoting so that your readers will know precisely where each quotation begins and ends. **Enclose short quotations**—ones of not more than about fifty words of prose or a full line of poetry—with a pair of double quotation marks, as in this use of a directly quoted sentence:

> William Zinsser advises his readers, "Re-examine each sentence that you put on paper."

Often, you will not need to quote a complete sentence. Fit the part you consider important into your own sentence:

> William Zinsser advises us to "re-examine each sentence we write."

For an **indirect quotation**—one in which you give the writer's thought but do not use the same words in the same sequence—do not use quotation marks:

> William Zinsser advises us to re-examine every sentence we write.

If the writer you are quoting uses a quotation, enclose it with a pair of single quotation marks to set if off within the quotation containing it:

> "Even before John Dean gave us 'at this point in time,' people had stopped saying 'now,' " Zinsser writes.

Usually, the writer being quoted is named before or after the quotation, as in the preceding examples, but this method can seem monotonous when you have a cluster of quotations. Try occasionally to insert the name in the quotation:

> "Even before John Dean gave us 'at this point in time,' " Zinsser writes, "people had stopped saying 'now.' "

Note: A period or comma at the end of a quotation goes *inside* the concluding quotation mark, whether or not it is part of the original—these two punctuation marks are so small that readers may not see them if they are not close to a word. Place any other punctuation inside the concluding quotation mark if it is part of the original and outside if it is your addition:

> Bill wrote, "I hate spinach!" [**Bill is exclaiming.**]
> Bill wrote, "I hate spinach"! [**You are exclaiming at Bill's remark.**]

Set off **long prose quotations**—ones over about fifty words—by placing them in a block, a separate paragraph conspicuously indented on the left. Otherwise, your readers may forget that you are quoting and think they are reading your own words. Since this method sets the quotation off sharply, do not also use quotation marks around it. If it contains any quotations, set them off in double quotation marks:

> In the third chapter of his book, *On Writing Well,* William Zinsser discusses clutter, which he had earlier called "the disease of American writing":
>
>> Clutter is the laborious phrase which has pushed out the short word that means the same thing. These locutions are a drag on energy and momentum. Even before John Dean gave us "at this point in time," people had stopped saying "now." They were saying "at the present time," or "currently," or "presently" (which means "soon"). Yet the idea can always be expressed by "now" to mean the immediate moment ("Now I can see him"), or by "today" to mean the historical present ("Today prices are high"), or simply by the verb "to be" ("It is raining"). There is no need to say, "At the present time we are experiencing precipitation."

A **long quotation of poetry** should also be set off in a block, but you may, if you wish, run two or three lines of poetry into your text, enclosing them in double quotation marks and indicating the end of each line with a slash mark:

> One of Shakespeare's sonnets begins: "Let me not to the marriage of true minds/ Admit impediments. Love is not love/ Which alters when it alteration finds."

When quoting, always reproduce the original exactly. You must give not only the original words but also the punctuation, spelling, and grammar, even if you think they are wrong. You may, however, omit part of what you are quoting if it is not relevant to your point and if omitting it will not change the writer's thought. Substitute three spaced dots for the omitted words. If the omission runs to the end of a sentence, add a fourth dot to indicate the period:

> Zinsser writes that "Clutter is the ponderous euphemism that turns . . . a salesman into a marketing representative, a dumb kid into an under-achiever. . . ."

You may add an explanation or comment to a quotation. To show that it is not part of the quotation, enclose it in a pair of brackets (if you are using a typewriter that has none, add them in ink):

> Zinsser writes that "before John Dean [a special adviser to former President Nixon] gave us 'at this point in time,' people had stopped saying 'now.' "

If the original contains an error of any kind—in spelling, word use, grammar, or fact—write "sic" enclosed in brackets immediately after it. This Latin word means "thus" or "in this manner" and indicates to your reader that you are aware of the error but that it appears in the original and the author wrote thus, in this manner:

> A Connecticut newspaper recently gave this household hint: "Sprinkle on the shelves a mixture of half borax and half sugar. This will poison every aunt [sic] that finds it."

Note: "Sic" is used so often that, even though it is a word in a foreign language, underlining it is no longer required.

Do use quotations to add authority and color to your writing. *Do not,* however, overload your pages with them, and *do not* use them to avoid finding ideas and words of your own.

PARAPHRASES

There are no formal conventions to follow when paraphrasing. You must rely on whatever knowledge you have of your readers to guide you in deciding how much to simplify the original writer's word choice and sentence structure. Remember that your purpose is only simplification, with the complete meaning, emphasis, and point of view of the original kept intact. If the original is fairly short, quote it in full and then paraphrase it so that your readers can see it for themselves. If it is long, incorporate a few quotations of key phrases and sentences in your paraphrase; they will add authenticity.

Follow the original sentence by sentence. If it contains long, complicated sentences that your readers will find difficult to follow, break the sentences into shorter ones. Be sure to remind your readers where the paraphrase begins and ends. If it is long, remind them in the middle as well. Remember that they will have no quotation marks to show them that these are not your thoughts. If you omit any words or phrases that are not relevant to your point, indicate the omission with dots, as in quoting, or give a short explanation such as, "Later in this paragraph, the author says. . . ."

For example, a sentence for which many readers would need a paraphrase appeared in a recent announcement by the state of South Carolina that it was issuing bonds for sale to the public in order to raise $65,000,000 for state capital improvements. As with most bond issues, these bonds will mature at various dates, some each year, starting in 1985 and ending with the last $5,000,000 in 2000. The sentence mentioned gives special information on some of the bonds:

> Bonds maturing 1994–2000 will be callable in whole or in part but if in part in inverse chronological order of maturity and if less than all the bonds of a single maturity are to be redeemed, the bonds to be redeemed shall be determined by lot within such maturity by the Registrar on March 1, 1993 and all subsequent Bond payment dates at par and accrued interest plus a premium of 2%.

To make this clear to the general reader, the paraphrase uses four sentences:

> The state may call in—insist on buying back early—some or all of the bonds due to mature between 1994 and 2000. If it does not call in the whole $5,000,000 for one of those years, it will choose the bonds to call in by having a lottery on the date when the interest is due, starting in 1993. It will buy the bonds at par—the value printed on them—which may be less than the price of the bonds on the open market. It will pay whatever interest is due up to that date along with an additional 2% interest as a premium.

SUMMARIES

The purpose of a summary—also known as an abstract, digest, or précis—is to condense the essential thoughts of a piece of writing into a short readable statement, roughly less than one fourth the length of the original and often much less than that. These steps will help you to compose an accurate summary, one that is faithful to the intention of the original.

1. Read through the entire work to see it as a whole, jotting down notes on the main points to help you later.

2. Determine the length of your summary by your needs. You may reduce a 500-page book to a tenth of its length, to a few paragraphs, or to a single sentence, depending on how much detail you require.

3. Apportion your space according to the material. The summary should be the essay in miniature, a condensation of the whole, not a selection of bits and pieces. A more or less literal reproduction of one or more important paragraphs in an essay is not a summary (unless, of course, the author has included summarizing paragraphs that you can use).

4. Select the main points. Pick your way through rhetorical devices such as figures of speech, deliberate repetitions, and narrative examples, and concentrate on the essentials.

5. Omit all extraneous comments. Do not include your own opinion of the material. The summary should be a condensation of the facts and opinions presented by the author—nothing more.

6. Paragraph according to your material, not the author's. The number of paragraphs in the summary should be determined only by the rules of good paragraph development (see Unit 1 for a discussion of paragraphing).

7. Write your summary from the author's point of view. Try to keep the flavor, the tone, of the original. Avoid such expressions as "the author says," and concentrate instead on *what* he or she says. Compare the informativeness of these two sentences summarizing Example D in Unit 14:

> **a.** Mark Twain discusses the meaning of the word lagniappe.
> **[This adds little to what the title and the author's name tell us.]**
> **b.** Lagniappe, a Spanish word we picked up in New Orleans, means something extra thrown in for good measure.
> **[This tells us not merely that Twain said something but what he said, from the first-person point of view used in the essay.]**

8. Be faithful to the author's emphasis and interpretation. A good summary is not your own interpretation of the author's material.

9. Avoid, in general, the author's phrasing and sentence structure. A summary involves no question of plagiarism, but if you depend heavily on the author's phrasing and sentence structure you will produce a copy, not a summary. Putting an idea into your own words is the best way to prove that you understand it.

10. Do not, however, write a paraphrase. A paraphrase, like any careful translation, includes every thought, and the process of simplifying will almost certainly make the paraphrase longer than the original.

Note: *Composing a summary of something you have read is an excellent way to impress it on your memory. Putting it into your own words* *forces you to come to a much closer understanding than if you merely read it. While you are a student, summarize important lectures and reading assignments; at the end of the term your summaries will make reviewing for examinations easy. Summary writing also gives excellent practice in composing clear, compact sentences and in choosing words accurately.*

* * *   * * *   * * *

The following three summaries are all of "The Fifth Freedom," which appears in the preceding unit (pages 105–107), where it is also outlined. Compare these summaries with each other and with the sentence and topic outlines to determine the advantages and disadvantages of each as a way to reduce material to its essential elements.

1. This summary reduces the essay to one-fourth its original length.

More than three centuries ago a few pioneers came to America in search of the freedoms we still cherish: freedom from want, freedom from fear, freedom of speech, and freedom of religion. Today their descendants and others are fighting to protect those freedoms everywhere. But there is a fifth freedom, basic to these four, that we are in danger of losing—the freedom to be one's best through the opportunity of developing to one's highest power. (¶¶ 1–2)

This freedom is in danger because of three misunderstandings. The first is about the meaning of democracy. This misunderstanding has defeated attempts to give special opportunities to superior students. The second is about what makes for happiness. Our culture's stress on material well-being has been reflected in the schools by too little discipline and too easy subjects. The third is about the importance of values. The recent denial of such ultimates as eternal truth, absolute moral law, and the existence of God is already reflected in increasing mass selfishness. (¶¶ 3–6)

To preserve the fifth freedom, we must do three things. First, we must give our children the most challenging curriculum of which they are capable, for only a disciplined training produces great people. Second, we must give them the right to fail, for only through standards that make for success or failure can they learn what real life is like. Third, we must give them the best values that history has given us; these will assure them of freedom. (¶¶ 7–9)

1. What supporting details are omitted in the summary?
2. Why is the first paragraph of the summary as long as the last although the original material that it condenses is only half the length of that condensed in the last paragraph?

2. This summary reduces the essay to a single paragraph and is slightly more than one-tenth the original length.

We are still fighting today to protect what the pioneers sought in America three centuries ago: freedom from want and fear, and of speech and religion. Basic to these, a fifth freedom—to be one's best by developing to one's highest power—is now endangered by three misunderstandings: of the meaning of democracy, the nature of happiness, and the importance of moral values. As a result, all our standards have deteriorated alarmingly. To preserve this freedom, we must give our children the most challenging curriculum possible, the right to fail, and exposure to the highest moral values.

3. This summary reduces the essay to a single sentence and is less than one-tenth the original length.

To preserve the traditional four freedoms for our children, we must also preserve a fifth, freedom to be one's best through full development, which we must safeguard by intellectual challenges, realistic testing, and high moral standards.

Examples

7-A   "Trees"

Guy Davenport

This essay, here complete, appears in *The Geography of the Imagination* (1981), a collection of the author's essays. Notice how he uses direct and indirect quotations, paraphrase, and summary to make his main point, that: "Trees," like many poems, draws on a variety of sources and combines them in surprising ways.

In June, 1918, the Cincinnati poet Eloise Robinson was in the wasteland of Picardy handing out chocolate and reciting poetry to the American Expeditionary Forces. Reciting poetry! It is all but unimaginable that in that hell of terror, gangrene, mustard gas, sleeplessness, lice, and 5 fatigue, there were moments when bone-weary soldiers, for the most part mere boys, would sit in a circle around a lady poet in an ankle-length khaki skirt and Boy Scout hat, to hear poems. In the middle of one poem the poet's memory flagged. She apologized profusely, for the poem, 10 as she explained, was immensely popular back home. Whereupon a sergeant held up his hand, as if in school, and volunteered to recite it. And did.

So that in the hideously ravaged orchards and strafed woods of the valley of the Ourcq, where the fields were 15 cratered and strewn with coils of barbed wire, fields that reeked of cordite and carrion, a voice recited "Trees."

Indirect quotation
Direct quotation

How wonderful, said Eloise Robinson, that he should know it. "Well, ma'am," said the sergeant, "I guess I wrote it. I'm Joyce Kilmer."   20

He wrote it five years before, and sent it off to the newly founded magazine *Poetry,* and Harriet Monroe, the editor, paid him six dollars for it. Almost immediately it became one of the most famous poems in English, the staple of school teachers and the one poem known by 25 practically everybody.

Sergeant Alfred Joyce Kilmer was killed by German gunfire on the heights above Seringes, the 30th of July, 1918. The French gave him the *Crois de Guerre* for his gallantry. He was thirty-two.   30

"Trees" is a poem that has various reputations. It is all right for tots and Middle Western clubwomen, but you are

Summary

supposed to outgrow it. It symbolizes the sentimentality and weak-mindedness that characterizes middle-class muddle. It is Rotarian. Once, at a gathering of poets at the 35 Library of Congress, Babette Deutsch was using it as an example of the taradiddle Congressmen recite at prayer breakfasts and other orgies, until Professor Gordon Wayne

Indirect quotation

coughed and reminded her that the poet's son, Kenton, was among those present. No one, however, rose to defend 40 Kipling and Whittier, at whom La Deutsch was also having.

It is, Lord knows, a vulnerable poem. For one thing, it is a poem about poetry, and is thus turned in on itself, and smacks of propaganda for the art (but is therefore 45 useful to teachers who find justifying poetry to barbarian students uphill work). For another, the opening statement is all too close to Gelett Burgess's "I never saw a Purple Cow," lines that had been flipping from the tongues of wits since 1895.   50

Partial quotation

And if the tree is pressing its hungry mouth against the earth's sweet flowing breast, how can it then lift its leafy arms to pray? This is a position worthy of Picasso but not of the *Cosmopolitan* Cover Art Nouveau aesthetic from which the poem derives. Ask any hard-nosed classi- 55

Indirect quotation

cist, and she will tell you that the poem is a monster of mixed metaphors.

And yet there is a silvery, spare beauty about it that has not dated. Its six couplets have an inexplicable integrity, and a pleasant, old-fashioned music. It soothes, and it 60 seems to speak of verities.

The handbooks will tell you that Yeats and Housman are behind the poem, though one cannot suspect from it

that Kilmer was one of the earliest admirers of Gerard
Manley Hopkins. Poems of great energy are usually distil-   65
lations of words and sentiments outside themselves.
Poems are by nature a compression. Another chestnut,
Longfellow's "A Psalm of Life," was generated by the
Scotch geologist Hugh Miller's *Footprints of the Creator*
and *The Old Red Sandstone,* books made popular in   70
America by Longfellow's colleague at Harvard, Louis
Agassiz. It is an example of the miraculous (and of the
transcendentally vague) how Longfellow, reading about
fossils in Miller, latched onto the sandstone and the ves-
tiges thereupon, to intone "Lives of great men all remind   75
us / We can make our lives sublime / And in passing leave
behind us / Footprints on the sands of time."

Poets work that way, condensing, rendering down to
essence. Another poem, as popular in its day as "Trees,"
Edwin Markham's "The Man with the Hoe" lived in Ezra   80
Pound's mind until it became the opening line of *The
Pisan Cantos*—"The enormous tragedy of the dream in
the peasant's bent shoulders."

"Trees" is, if you look, very much of its time. Trees
were favorite symbols for Yeats, Frost, and even the young   85
Pound. The nature of chlorophyll had just been discovered, and *Tarzan of the Apes*—set in a tree world—had
just been published. Trees were everywhere in art of the
period, and it was understood that they belonged to the
region of ideas, to Santayana's Realm of Beauty.   90

But Kilmer had been reading about trees in another
context that we have forgotten, one that accounts for the
self-effacing closing lines ("Poems are made by fools like
me, / But only God can make a tree"), lines that have
elevated the poem into double duty as a religious homily.   95
Kilmer's young manhood was in step with the idealism of
the century. One of the inventions in idealism that attracted much attention was the movement to stop child
labor and to set up nursery schools in slums. One of the
most diligent pioneers in this movement was the English-   100
woman Margaret McMillan, who had the happy idea that
a breath of fresh air and an intimate acquaintance with
grass and trees were worth all the pencils and desks in the
whole school system. There was something about trees
that she wanted her slum children to feel. She had them   105
take naps under trees, roll on grass, dance around trees.
The English word for gymnasium equipment is "apparatus." And in her book *Labour and Childhood* (1907) you
will find this sentence: "Apparatus can be made by fools,
but only God can make a tree."   110

Marginal labels (left column):
- Quotation of poetry incorporated in sentence
- Quotation
- Quotation
- Quotation
- Summary
- Quotation

1. In the second paragraph, Davenport quotes Kilmer directly but Robinson indirectly. What may have been his reason for this distinction?
2. Davenport devotes 20 lines to the flaws in "Trees" and to others' criticism of it but only three lines to praising it. What may have been his reasons for placing the negative criticism first and for making the praise so brief?
3. After the four-paragraph narrative that begins the essay, almost every paragraph begins with its topic sentence. Which sentence gives the topic of the ninth paragraph?
4. How has Davenport constructed the final paragraph to make it build up to a sort of climax?
5. Check the etymology, denotation and connotation of *taradiddle, "having at" someone, verities, transcendentally, rendering down.*

7-B   Sex and the Split Brain

Carol Johmann

This essay, here complete, first appeared in *Omni* in 1983. Throughout, the author uses summary, paraphrase, and quotation to present recent scientific research on the differences between men's and women's brains. For a different view of the effects of the two sides of the brain, see Stephen Jay Gould's "Left Holding the Bat" (12-F).

When she was a Ph.D. student at Columbia University, physical anthropologist Christine De Lacoste-Utamsing was dissecting human brains as part of her research. In the course of her work her attention was drawn to a flat bundle of nerve fibers, called the corpus callosum, that connects the right and left hemispheres of the brain. After examin- 5 ing specimens from nine men and five women, she noticed an odd thing: On average, the corpus callosum was larger and more bulbous in women's brains than in men's. Intrigued by this, she has since gone on to study more specimens, including the brains of both adults and fetuses. Her data have led her to one conclusion: The brains of men and 10 women are physically different.

De Lacoste is still fascinated by her work and loves to talk about it, but she is concerned that people might jump to the wrong conclusions. She worries that her discovery might be used to support a controversial hypothesis that women's brains are less specialized than men's, 15 a theory often cited by some researchers to explain why men tend to outperform women in such visual-spatial disciplines as geometry or engineering.

"Studying areas of the brain is very exciting," says De Lacoste, now at the University of Texas's Health Science Center, "but [my findings] 20 can be twisted in a very sexist way. All I've shown is that there is a difference in the number of connections between hemispheres."

"What gets me is the leap some people make," adds City University of New York psychologist Florence Denmark, who has been following this research. "They assume that brain differences between the sexes 25 always indicate differences in intelligence and ability. And somehow men always come out on top."

Such concern is hardly unwarranted. The notion that "biology is destiny" has been used repeatedly over the years to support a variety of racist, sexist, and other prejudicial attitudes. In his book *The Mis-* measure of Man, Harvard paleontologist Stephen Jay Gould points out how vulnerable a topic the brain is for misguided use of research. Bigots have long manipulated I.Q.-test results and comparative studies of brain size to support their views. What De Lacoste and others are trying to do is to put the new brain discoveries into the proper perspective before something similar happens with those findings.

Since the early Seventies there has been an increasing body of evidence that the brains of males and females differ. Studies of rat brains, for example, disclosed structural brain differences between the sexes in the hypothalamus—the section of the brain that regulates sex drive, body temperature, and blood pressure—and in the cerebral cortex, the control center for thinking, the senses, and movement. De Lacoste's research showed that there were sex-related differences in the human brain as well.

Brain researchers now assume that a larger corpus callosum means there is more communication between the right and left halves of the brain. This assumption and data from De Lacoste's research are significant when we realize how divided the brain is in its abilities, especially when we consider how that split may differ between the sexes.

The human brain is split in two ways. First, each hemisphere controls the movement of, and receives sensory input from, the opposite side of the body. Second, each half is specialized, or lateralized, as scientists like to say. The left brain handles information in an analytical, sequential manner. It is concerned with problem solving, and it excels in language skills. We use it to understand spoken instructions, for example. By contrast, the right brain appears to process information holistically; that is, more intuitively and perceptively. This is the brain half used to recognize visual patterns and three-dimensional objects.

By connecting the two halves and letting them act as a whole, the corpus callosum keeps us from feeling like some kind of two-headed, or at least two-minded, beast. So if the female's larger corpus callosum allows for more of this cross-communication, her brain may be more balanced than a man's. In short, women's brains may be less lateralized, or specialized in what they can do.

Some researchers even argue that this could help explain why boys do better in math and spatial-reasoning tasks involved in geometry but have more trouble learning how to read. With less communication going on between their hemispheres, men may have the edge on women when it comes to who uses the right side of the brain more exclusively.

In fact, several observations other than De Lacoste's suggest that the sexes are *not* created equal when it comes to lateralization. After a stroke has damaged the brain's speech center, a woman is more apt to recover the ability to speak than a man. In theory, this is because the other side of her brain can take over more easily. Another piece of 75 evidence comes from what we know of human development. The process of becoming lateralized begins in the fetus. At what point lateralization begins is not clear, although in her study of fetal brains, De Lacoste has found structural differences in fetuses as young as 26 weeks. And this process isn't finished until the onset of puberty. Since girls 80 reach puberty before boys do, their brains may have less time to lateralize.

Brains as well as bodies are shaped by sex hormones; so a difference in specialization should not be at all surprising. If a male rat is castrated at birth, for example, his hypothalamus will develop into one that 85 resembles a female's. If a female rat is given the male hormone testosterone at birth, her hypothalamus will take on male characteristics. Remove her ovaries, the source of the female hormones estrogen and progesterone, and the female's cerebral cortex will become malelike.

As De Lacoste points out, when the human brain was evolving, 90 males and females occupied different ecological niches. Female hominids gathered food and nurtured babies; males hunted. These activities, each requiring different skills, could have put different adaptive pressures on brain development. Females, for example, may have needed a more integrated understanding of the world, while males might have 95 required more specialized skills like the ability to hold three-dimensional images in their minds (perhaps for mapmaking). Pressures like these, De Lacoste speculates, may have been the environmental forces that shaped women's brains so that they became less lateralized.

"But don't misunderstand," she adds. "We don't have two brains 100 evolving separately, just one brain that reflects the differences in sex hormones and reproductive functions." More important, she adds, one shouldn't misconstrue what sex-linked brain differences mean. In itself lateralization says nothing about an individual's innate intelligence and mental capability.   105

"We're talking about differences in the way men and women screen information," De Lacoste explains. "Women seem to have a bias toward picking up information presented in a verbal fashion; men, in a visual-spatial way. Once information is selected, though, their brains function in the same way with the same potential."   110

Neither approach is better than the other, says Denmark. "It's assumed that if males have more lateralization, then it's the thing to have. But you can interpret it another way. Perhaps women have larger areas of the brain from which to draw skills."

Ultimately, both interpretations are equally irrelevant, she con- 115 cludes. Why? Because when it comes to human behavior and intelligence, biology is *not* destiny. "Regardless of structural differences, the cultural factors are enormous," explains De Lacoste. Research shows that our genes may determine which sex hormones course through our bodies, and those hormones may help sculpt our brains. But as De 120 Lacoste points out, it is the constant interplay between this genetic potential and our environment that defines our talents and abilities, and determines what we learn.

1. There are six direct quotations and many more indirect ones and summaries in this essay. What reasons may Johmann have had for quoting those six statements directly instead of quoting them indirectly or summarizing them?
2. Where does Johmann summarize opinions? What may have been her reasons for summarizing instead of quoting them?
3. Check the etymology, denotation, and connotation of *unwarranted, paleontologist, bigot, holistically, lateralized, fetus.*

Assignments

1. Compose a paraphrase of the three-paragraph passage of Johmann's essay that begins "As De Lacoste points out." Assume that your readers are other students who have not read the essay.
2. Study the three summaries carefully, comparing each with the original essay and with each other. Notice in each what is saved in space and what is lost in detail.
3. Compose a summary of the essay by Johmann in about 200 words. Consider your paragraphing carefully; remember that the number of paragraphs you use should indicate the number of main points in the original but may not be related to the number of paragraphs Johmann uses.
4. Reduce the summary you composed for assignment 3 to one paragraph of not more than 100 words; then reduce that paragraph to a single sentence of not more than 50 words.
5. Combining quotation, paraphrase, and summary, as necessary, compose a detailed account of an editorial in a recent newspaper. Include your opinion of the writer's views, and assume that your readers are classmates who have not read the editorial.

UNIT 8

Process

What's the shortest route to your house? How is lead-free gasoline produced? How can I become a better chess player? How do you start to housebreak a puppy? How do beginning writers get a book published? How do American political parties choose candidates? How are stocks sold in the over-the-counter market? How do you apply for a bank loan?

Some of these questions arise from a practical need for directions; others from a desire for more information or from simple curiosity. The answer to each requires the analysis of a process—of a series of related actions serving a particular purpose or leading to a particular goal. You have already had many occasions to answer such questions orally, and you will have many occasions to give written answers on examinations, in reports, and in your career.

In writing a process analysis, you should draw particularly on your training in *description* and *narration* because you will be describing a series of actions in chronological order. You will also need your training in *organizing* to help you decide where to give background information and, when you must describe two or more simultaneous actions, which one to take first. Most of all, you will need your training in *accurate observation.* An error on your part could make your readers take the wrong road, lose a chess game, spoil a formula, or misunderstand the operation of a machine.

Ordinarily, you will write a process analysis in answer to a question that someone else asks you, and the nature of the question will determine your specific topic. For a practice paper, however, you should choose your own topic because it must be one about which you have special knowledge. For a paper giving directions on how to do something that your readers may want to do themselves, such as housebreak a puppy, choose a process that you have performed yourself several times so that you are thoroughly familiar with it from a performer's

130

point of view. For a paper giving your readers information on how something is done, such as launching a spacecraft, choose a process that particularly interests you and that you have observed closely or read a great deal about so that you will be able to give all the necessary details.

When you have chosen a subject and decided on your purpose—to give your readers directions to follow or information to satisfy their curiosity—follow these steps in planning and writing your paper:

1. Think through the procedure from start to finish so that you see it as a whole. An overall view will help you with all the other steps in planning the paper.

2. Ask yourself what background information, if any, your readers need as an introduction to the process, such as its past history, in what locations and under what conditions it is usually performed, and so on. If time and space permit, include background information that is interesting for its own sake even though not necessary for an understanding of the process.

3. Divide the process into steps. Your practice in making subdivisions and sub-subdivisions in outlines will help you here.

4. Describe each step in the process in complete detail. You are something of a specialist in the subject you have chosen, but your readers are not. Remember that specialists are often unclear in explaining their specialties because they forget to see them from the viewpoint of the untrained person. For example, in giving the recipe for a sauce, an experienced chef may omit a detail that other chefs would take for granted, but without it an amateur will produce something that tastes like glue. Be careful not to talk down to your readers, but always assume that they are ignorant of your subject and leave no blanks.

5. Include in your description the reasons for each step you describe. Clear directions, even though followed blindly, can result in success, but your readers will appreciate an explanation of *why* a certain step is necessary as well as *how* it is to be taken. "Always work with the knife blade turned away from you so that you will not cut yourself if it slips." "Let the milk cool before adding the beaten egg, which otherwise will cook into lumps before you can stir it in."

6. Define any special terms you use. Words that have become familiar to you may be stumbling blocks to readers unfamiliar with your subject. Every field has its own vocabulary—special words or special meanings attached to common words. Words and phrases such as "empennage," "shim," and "clarify the butter" will be immediately understood by the aeronautical engineer, the carpenter, and the cook, respectively, and may be used freely by one craftsman writing for another. But for general readers, you must carefully define such terms or substitute more familiar ones.

7. Use illustrative aids whenever appropriate. Make your descriptions as definite and concrete as you can. Even a hastily drawn map is

more useful than a page of written instructions on how to go somewhere. A simple sketch or diagram will clarify a complicated procedure, as will verbal images such as "The standard gearshift moves in an
H pattern."

8. Check and doublecheck what you write for accuracy and clarity.
One or two small factual errors or ambiguities may not do serious harm
in some kinds of writing, but when you tell readers how to do something, they depend on you for their success.

* * *   * * *   * * *

The **organization for both types of process paper,** giving directions
or giving information, is the same—the chronological pattern. Time is
always involved in doing things. The sequence of parts, then, takes care
of itself. But you must choose how to group many small, separate steps
in a few clear, manageable units. Four suboperations of five steps each,
for instance, are far easier to follow and remember than twenty single
steps. The basic methods for outlining, which we applied to the imaginary topic in Unit 1 and examined in more detail in Unit 6 are the ones
to use here.

However familiar you may be with the process of starting a new
lawn, for example, you must first think through the decisions and motions involved in that procedure before you can write a process paper
on it. You may decide that these steps should be mentioned:

(1) Weeding
(2) Digging to loosen soil
(3) Liming
(4) Fertilizing
(5) Raking to distribute chemicals

(6) Seeding
(7) Raking to distribute seed
(8) Rolling
(9) Watering

When you look over these steps carefully, however, you realize that
they are not equal in importance. You can group them in a few main
units, each consisting of several related steps:

I. Preparing the soil
   A. Weeding
   B. Digging to loosen soil
II. Adding chemicals
   A. Liming
   B. Fertilizing
   C. Raking to distribute chemicals

III. Planting seed
   A. Seeding
   B. Raking to distribute seed
   C. Rolling
IV. Watering

You are at last ready to start. Cover this skeleton plan with the flesh
of words and phrases; the bones should never stick out in the body of
your finished prose. Your paper is more than a sentence outline; instead,
your plan should give your readers a pleasant sense of meaningful
order. Determine the amount of space needed for each main division
and develop your paragraphs accordingly. Use transitional devices to

hold them together and especially to clarify any shift from one division of your subject to another, but vary these devices. Do not overdo the easy but monotonous "then" and "the next step."

* * *   * * *   * * *

Catching your readers' interest can be important in a process essay. To write everyday cookbook kinds of direction-giving, you need only clarity and logical order. Someone trying to operate an unfamiliar washing machine wants brief, clear, numbered directions, but readers of an essay expect more.

Consider what attitude you should take toward your material— what tone to adopt for your intended readers. In giving directions, do not limit yourself to the formal "One does this" or the more direct "Do that." You may instead present your directions in a personal narrative and, by saying something like "I did this," add human interest. Rather than plunging directly into the first step of the procedure, you may begin in a leisurely fashion—with an account of how you came to be familiar with the process, or why you consider it worth doing. Instead of ending with the final step, you may give an account of the results of the procedure and their significance—not an essential part of direction-giving as such but often adding reader interest.

In giving general information, try to make it lively as well as intelligible. *Use fully the arts of description, narration, and exemplification as aids to exposition.* Enliven your account of a spacecraft launching with vivid descriptions of the equipment and the people involved, or with your own reactions to the scene, so that your readers feel that they are there, sharing the experience with you. Also, give special thought to composing an attention-getting beginning and a memorable ending.

Examples

In each of the following selections a process of some kind is a major feature. Other selections in which a process is important are Nemy's "Business Status" (10-H), Hall's "The Pervasive Set" (10-F), Jastrow's "Brains and Computers" (11-C), Burgess's "Splitting the Word" (11-G), *The New Yorker*'s "The Bad and Worse Sides of Thanksgiving" (11-H), 5 Conza's "Christmas Eve" (11-I), Conroy's "Death of an Island" (12-B), Huxley's "The Method of Scientific Investigation" (12-H), Keremes's "The Passing of Little Gibbs Road" (13-E), and Sullivan's "Cyclones" (14-A).

The first selection in this unit is an example of completely imper- 10 sonal direction-giving. Notice how the second writer, while describing the same basic process as the first, gives her directions a highly personal tone. In the other examples, the personalities of the writers color their descriptions in varying degrees and by varying methods.

8-A   Baked Beans

This is a standard recipe from a cookbook.

Soak 2 cupfuls of dry beans overnight. In the morning, boil until soft, and drain. Put them into a covered bean pot with ¼ lb. salt pork. Mix into ½ cup of boiling water the following: ½ tsp. baking soda, ¼ tsp. mustard, ¼ cup molasses, and salt and pepper to taste. Pour over beans, adding enough more water to cover. Bake for 6 hours in a slow 5 oven, uncovering during the last half hour to brown.

8-B   Baking Beans

Louise Dickinson Rich

This selection comes from *We Took to the Woods* (1942), an autobiographical account of the author's experience after she and her husband left their city home for what they hoped would be the "simple life" in Maine.

Now consider the baking of the beans. Baked beans have to be baked. That sounds like a gratuitous restatement of the obvious, but it isn't. Some misguided souls boil beans all day and call the lily-livered result baked beans. I refrain from comment.

We use either New York State or Michigan white beans, because 5 we like them best, although yellow-eyes are very popular, too. I take two generous cups of dry beans, soak overnight and put them on to boil early in the morning. When the skins curl off when you blow on them, they've boiled long enough. Then I put in the bottom of the bean pot, or iron kettle with a tight-fitting cover, a six-by-eight-inch square of salt 10 pork with the rind slashed every quarter of an inch, a quarter of a cup of sugar, half a cup of molasses, a large onion chopped fairly fine, and a heaping teaspoonful of dry mustard. This amount of sugar and molasses may be increased or cut, depending on whether you like your beans sweeter or not so sweet. This is a matter every man has to decide for 15 himself. The beans are dumped in on top of this conglomerate, and enough hot water is added to cover, but only cover. The baking pot should be large enough so there's at least an inch of freeboard above the water. Otherwise they'll boil over and smell to high heaven. Cover tightly and put into a medium oven—about 350° is right. They should 20 be in the oven by half past nine in the morning at the latest, and they should stay there until supper time, which in our family is at six.

So far there is no trick in making good baked beans. The trick, if it can be dignified by such a term, lies in the baking, and like a great many trade tricks, it consists only of patience and conscientious care. You have 25 to tend the beans faithfully, adding water whenever the level gets down below the top of the beans, and you have to keep the oven temperature even. If you're lazy, you can put in a lot of water and not have to watch them so closely. But to get the best results, you should add only enough water each time to barely cover the beans. This means that you'll give up 30 all social engagements for the day, because you can't leave the baby for more than half an hour at a time. I think the results are worth it—but then, I haven't anywhere special to go anyhow. My beans are brown and mealy, and they swim in a thick brown juice. They're good. I always serve them with corn bread, ketchup and pickles. 35

1. Where and how does the writer give her opinions?
2. In Example A, if anything were omitted from the directions, they would be incomplete. What could be omitted here and still leave us with adequate directions for baking beans? What would such omissions do to the overall effect?
3. Check the etymology, denotation, and connotation of *gratuitous* and *conglomerate*.

8-C Taking Care of Contacts

Marjorie Sybul (student)

Except for the light touch just before the end, this is straightforward direction-giving.

ANALYSIS
I. General problem
  A. General procedure #1
  B. General procedure #2

Contact lenses are a big investment. Before you decide to buy a pair, you should realize that hard contact lenses require much more care than does an ordinary pair of glasses. A definite procedure must be followed daily for your own safety. Unlike a pair of glasses that is casually put 5 on and taken off, contact lenses must be prepared for insertion and, when not in use, must be stored in a liquid. You must use two special solutions: a wetting agent to prepare the lenses for insertion, and a soaking agent to keep the lenses pliable. 10

II. Specific procedures: nine steps before insertion

Before touching your contact lenses, wash your hands thoroughly; bacteria trapped between the lens and the eye can cause infection. Then uncap the bottle of wetting solution and set it aside. Close the sink drain to prevent the loss of a lens if you accidentally drop it. Open the left 15 chamber of the lens case. The concave surface of the lens will be facing you. Touch the lens very gently; it will stick to your wet finger. Place it between your thumb and forefinger, and carefully rinse it with water. Now, holding the lens at its edges, squeeze one drop of wetting solution on each side. Rub the lens gently and rinse again. Put another 20 drop on the concave surface. The lens is now ready for insertion.

III. Specific procedures: four steps for insertion

At first, inserting the lens will seem very difficult, but, like many other things, it becomes easier with practice. Balance the lens on the tip of your middle finger and 25 slowly raise your finger to your eye. At the same time, be sure to cup your other hand underneath to catch the lens should it drop from your finger. Look straight ahead and bring the lens to your iris. At the slightest touch, the lens will pop into place. Now follow the same procedure with 30 the other lens.

IV. Specific procedures: six steps for removal

Removing the contact lens is fun. First open the appropriate chamber of your lens case. Then bend your head down and place one cupped hand under your eye. With the other hand, pull the outer edge of your eyelid to one 35 side as though you were imitating the shape of an Oriental eye. Blink, and the lens will pop into your hand. Place the lens in the lens case with the concave side facing you. Squeeze a few drops of soaking solution over it and close the chamber. The soaking solution will be rinsed away the 40 next time you reinsert the lens.

V. Benefits

A. Benefit #1

B. Benefit #2

C. Benefits #3, 4

This entire procedure takes only a few moments, and every step must always be followed. There are several large benefits. When any of your lensless friends happen to see you popping your lenses in or out, they are sure to 45 be impressed and fascinated by your courage and will probably gasp and groan. When you meet another lens wearer, you will immediately have a great bond in common and will be able to swap stories about the time you lost a lens in the middle of the decisive game in a tennis 50 match or on a crowded dance floor. More seriously, the small sacrifice in time and effort required to learn these procedures and follow them faithfully will be more than repaid by the great improvement in your appearance and in your peripheral vision.   55

8-D   How to Make an Ice Cream Soda

Charles Dippold (student)

In contrast to the preceding example, this has two purposes: to inform readers on making an ice cream soda and to make them laugh at the exaggerated picture of the "ideal" soda.

As a former Amalgamator of Aqueous Solutions of Carbonic Acid, I can state with authority that the ice cream soda is the acme of the soda jerker's art. Sundaes, cokes, and shakes are all secondary; anyone can ladle syrup over ice cream or mix charged water and syrup to make a coke, but it takes long experience and inspired artistic endeavor to blend together the few simple ingredients of that masterpiece of the profession, the ice cream soda. As in any art, individual technique varies, but like any artist, I believe mine to be the most satisfactory.

To begin with, a glass must be chosen. The ideal glass is tall, with thick sides to prevent breakage, and with a heavy base to prevent tipping. It should be conical in shape, since a cone has only one-third the volume of a cylinder of equal height and base, while appearing almost as large.

Equipped with the proper glass, one now chooses the syrup. I personally prefer chocolate, but with any flavor the procedure is the same. The proper amount must be judged by the soda jerker. It is generally between two and three ounces, depending upon the size of the glass and one's individual taste. A dab of stiff whipped cream is flipped upon the syrup by a dexterous tap of the spoon on the edge of the glass, and then one is ready for the most important step, adding the water.

The object is to produce a light, frothy, homogeneous mixture of charged water and syrup. To do this perfectly, the fine stream must be used. At some fountains, quality must be sacrificed to speed and the coarse stream substituted, but since we are considering the ideal soda, we may disregard this practice. One places the glass under the faucet, slowly moving the handle forward to allow the soda water to fizz out with increasing velocity, and rotating the glass carefully to insure a complete mixture of water and syrup. When the glass is about two-thirds full, the water is shut off and the soda is ready for the addition of the ice cream.

Two small scoops are better than one large one, since a large one blocks the bottom of the glass so that all of the liquid cannot be removed with the straw. The scoops must be well rounded to prevent their disintegration in the liquid. The ice cream is carefully slipped in, to avoid splashing; and now the soda is ready for its crowning glory, the cap.

Slowly and carefully the charged water is again added in a fine stream, the object being to produce as high a cap as possible without causing it to run over. If the stream strikes the floating ice cream, the water will splash out violently. This is particularly embarrassing if it lands on a customer sitting in front of the faucet. However, a really great soda jerker has so coordinated his hand and eye by constant practice that he skillfully guides the stream into the glass without splashing. When the cap has reached the highest possible point, the water is turned off, the artist quickly seizes a spoon, and both soda and spoon are nonchalantly set before the customer in one graceful motion.

What a joy it is to behold! Beads of moisture form on the cool sides, and through the foamy mass one may discern the white lumps of ice 50 cream floating like beautiful water lilies. The top, streaked with brown lines of chocolate, rises like some snow-capped mountain, inviting the epicure to partake of this nectar and ambrosia, the ice cream soda.

1. Besides giving the piece unity of content by sticking to his subject, the writer has given it unity of tone by his consistently mock-serious approach. Does this make the piece more interesting or is it annoying?
2. Given the necessary equipment and materials, could you make a good soda with only his directions to guide you, or would you be better off with a strictly informative list of steps?
3. How many paragraphs are devoted to actual direction-giving? What do the others accomplish? Are they worthwhile?
4. How many paragraphs begin with a transitional device? How many end with one, preparing us for the next paragraph?
5. At what point does the author give reasons for doing as he directs? At what point does he warn of what will happen otherwise?

8-E   How Dictionaries Are Made

S. I. Hayakawa

This is a complete subdivision of a chapter in *Language in Thought and Action* (4th edition, 1978). The author is a semanticist, a specialist in the development and changes in the meanings of words.

It is an almost universal belief that every word has a "correct meaning," that we learn these meanings principally from teachers and grammarians (except that most of the time we don't bother to, so that we ordinarily speak "sloppy English"), and that dictionaries and grammars are the "supreme authority" in matters of meaning and usage. 5 Few people ask by what authority the writers of dictionaries and grammars say what they say. The docility with which most people bow down to the dictionary is amazing, and the person who says, "Well, the dictionary is wrong!" is looked upon with smiles of pity and amusement which say plainly, "Poor fellow! He's really quite sane otherwise."

Let us see how dictionaries are made and how the editors arrive at 10 definitions. What follows applies, incidentally, only to those dictionary offices where first-hand, original research goes on—not those in which editors simply copy existing dictionaries. The task of writing a dictionary begins with the reading of vast amounts of the literature of the period or subject that it is intended to cover. As the editors read, they copy on cards every interesting or rare word, every unusual or peculiar 15 occurrence of a common word, a large number of common words in their ordinary uses, and also the sentences in which each of these words appears, thus:

> pail
> The dairy *pails* bring home increase of milk
> Keats, *Endymion*
> I, 44–45

That is to say, the context of each word is collected, along with the 25
word itself. For a really big job of dictionary writing, such as the *Oxford
English Dictionary* (usually bound in about twenty-five volumes), millions of such cards are collected, and the task of editing occupies
decades. As the cards are collected, they are alphabetized and sorted.
When the sorting is completed, there will be for each word anywhere 30
from two or three to several hundred illustrative quotations, each on its
card.

To define a word, then, the dictionary editor places before him the
stack of cards illustrating that word; each of the cards represents an
actual use of the word by a writer of some literary or historical impor- 35
tance. He reads the cards carefully, discards some, re-reads the rest, and
divides up the stack according to what he thinks are the several senses
of the word. Finally, he writes his definitions, following the hard-and-
fast rule that each definition must be based on what the quotations in
front of him reveal about the meaning of the word. The editor cannot 40
be influenced by what he thinks a given word ought to mean. He must
work according to the cards, or not at all.

The writing of a dictionary, therefore, is not a task of setting up
authoritative statements about the "true meanings" of words, but a task
of recording, to the best of one's ability, what various words have meant 45
to authors in the distant or immediate past. The writer of a dictionary
is a historian, not a lawgiver. If, for example, we had been writing a
dictionary in 1890, or even as late as 1919, we could have said that the
word "broadcast" means "to scatter," seed and so on; but we could not
have decreed that from 1921 on, the commonest meaning of the word 50
should become "to disseminate audible messages, etc., by wireless tele-
phony." To regard the dictionary as an "authority," therefore, is to
credit the dictionary writer with gifts of prophecy which neither he nor
anyone else possesses. In choosing our words when we speak or write,
we can be guided by the historical record afforded us by the dictionary, 55
but we cannot be bound by it, because new situations, new experiences,
new inventions, new feelings, are always compelling us to give new uses
to old words. Looking under a "hood," we should ordinarily have found,
five hundred years ago, a monk; today, we find a motorcar engine.

1. What larger expository purpose than is indicated by the title does this selection serve? Where is it discussed? Write a sentence that expresses what you
   believe to be the main idea of the whole essay.
2. Which paragraphs actually tell how dictionaries are made? Make a numbered list of the main steps in the process.

8-F   One of Life's Simple Joys

Joan H. Smith

This short essay was first published in the *Bangor Daily News* (Bangor, Maine) in 1983. The writer describes a specific process—how she fished for minnows—for a much larger purpose, the recreation of the simple pleasures of childhood.

Although two-thirds of my life has passed since I last fished, I still remember the smell of it—the stench of the rapids above the pool, the rot of vegetation decomposing, the damp earth, the fish.

I preferred to fish alone and would get up early summer mornings, put on the clothes I'd worn the day before, wrap two slices of bread in 5 waxed paper and take my short blue pole down to the brook that ran by my suburban home.

The brook was a farmland leftover from the time when New Jersey had acres of rolling fields and woods in the Watchung Mountain Valley. The farm had been reduced to twenty-five acres crowded by Route 22 10 on one side and a sea of identical box houses, my neighborhood, on the other. The brook is now a cement trench with rocked banks. The little strip of woods that followed it down from Watchung Mountain to the cities, where it swelled and was known as Tom's River, is gone. But before its demise, I fished it religiously.   15

The path down to the fishing pool was crossed by four fallen trees and the bare roots of others. I never stepped on the trees, always over, and between the roots like cracks in a sidewalk. I practiced silence more than fishing technique.

I began fishing at age five, soon after we'd moved to the new 20 neighborhood with red earth for front lawns and just-planted tiny shrubs at the corner of each house's identical cement steps. The natural lush green of the brook pulled me like a magnet, and my mother, who didn't want me to cross the street, gave up and let me go.

My first pole was a stick, thread and safety pin, like those I'd seen 25 in cartoons. I landed zero fish with that equipment, so my father bought me a pole and spinner tackle at Effinger's Sporting Goods on Main Street. After I stripped it of weights and bobber I caught fish, sometimes the same one a dozen times.

The five-inch minnows in that pool (shiners, red-fins, and sunnies) 30 and the suckers that milled in the deep shaded side under the bank, never went home to be eaten. Wild animals, birds or even fish were not consumed in my home, or any other in my neighborhood. I learned as an adult that little boys in Maine fished streams as I had, but they didn't throw back their catch. They stuffed them in their pockets and the fish 35 sometimes were not discovered until wash day.

I usually fished alone a half hour or so; then the others showed up. I could hear the slap of their sneakers on the path long before they reached the pool and suddenly started jumping and shouting. The fish

would dart away, but would come back to the deep part we fished by 40
the time hooks were baited.

A naked hook was nibbled; these fish were not savvy. But a hook
wound in earthworm was attacked. All the trouble it took to wrap and
puncture a worm over and over until the hook was baited did not result
in a catch nearly as often as when the bait was a gluey ball of bread. One 45
bit of bread might lure a dozen fish but be consumed by none and still
be secure on the hook when each fish, which had swallowed it whole,
was removed.

The fishermen I knew as little boys are now a lawyer and a dentist,
and another runs his father's Dunkin' Donuts franchise in Newark. 50
They were too squeamish to unhook a fish skewered through the eye
or too clumsy to roll a little piece of white bread into a tight ball to bait
the hook. One became a skilled fly caster and also caught big fish in the
ocean as his Norwegian forefathers had, but that was much later. He
showed no inherent ability at age four in his seersucker shorts.   55

The talk among us was of fish, nothing else. How many had been
already caught and thrown, how they were biting, had I seen any new
ones? We practically knew each fish, catching them over and over as
we did. Why they didn't swim on to less dangerous waters or stop biting
for the white balls of bread remains a mystery.   60

Sometimes we collected the morning's catch in an aqua plastic pail.
The little fish would circle round it and the few that we'd taken too long
to unhook would fight not to float to the top. We threw the rare fish that
died back into the brush. The others were counted and freed and
caught again the next day.   65

1. How much of the essay is specifically on the process of fishing for minnows?
   What does the rest of the essay contribute to our understanding of the
   writer's early experience?
2. What other processes does the writer mention?
3. What kinds of sensory detail do you find?
4. Why does the writer end by reminding us that she and her companions freed
   each day's catch but caught them again the next day?

Assignments

1. Look through the selections in this unit for examples of the four points of
   view from which directions can be presented: the first-person "I (or we) do
   this," the second-person "You do that," the indefinite third-person "One
   should do thus and so," and the impersonal passive "Such and such should
   be done." Compare the effects produced. Will your choice of method be
   governed by your material, your attitude toward it, or your reader?
2. Most of these selections have strictly informative titles. Try supplying more
   stimulating ones for some of them (see Unit 1, page 18).

3. For a direction-giving paper do not choose an involved subject, like how to cure inflation, or a complicated procedure, like how to play bridge, but rather some simple process for which you can give directions that will actually direct. You need not limit yourself, however, to a procedure that can be done perfectly on the first attempt; you may assume the necessity for repeated practice, as in how to perform the crawl stroke.

   Suitable subjects include how to perform a card trick, use a jigsaw, prepare a favorite dish, cast for trout, treat a snakebite, learn to ride a bicycle, write a theme, paddle a canoe, sail a boat, go waterskiing or skin diving, repair a leaky faucet or an electrical connection, shoot free throws, make an archer's bow, build a model airplane, caddy, run a trap line, develop films, drive a car, administer artificial respiration, conduct a business meeting. These topics, however, like those in other units, are meant merely as *suggestions,* to be used if you wish, but preferably to remind you of other suitable ones on which you may be even better equipped to write. When you have chosen a subject,

   a. Present it as a list of numbered steps (page 132).
   b. Make a rough outline in which you arrange these steps logically into larger related units (page 132).
   c. Write out the procedure as briefly as possible, limiting yourself to a simple straightforward account of how to do it and working from this outline.
   d. Write a second essay in which you add as much reader interest as you can —this will involve decisions as to the purpose of your paper, the kind of reader to whom it is addressed, and the attitude you wish to assume toward your subject.

4. For your informative process paper choose a subject that is so familiar to you that you can explain it accurately and interestingly to those less well informed. Remember that you can choose a larger field than for assignment 3, since you will not need to go into the exact details necessary to direction-giving. Suggested topics: How a drug store is run (compare "How to Make an Ice Cream Soda" in scope), how a fish (bird, insect, animal) lives, how an election is conducted, how calves (chickens, pigs) are raised, how something is mined or grown or harvested, how some business is run, how an airplane flies, how a ball team is managed, how a factory process (such as the manufacture of lead pencils) is carried on, how a newspaper is published, how a paper route is managed, how an amateur play is produced, how puppets are handled.

   Your subject chosen, proceed as before: Think through your material and jot down the important phases of the procedure in their proper sequence; determine the larger units into which they fall and make a rough outline; decide on your attitude toward your material—your purpose in presenting it. As an account of something with which you have had some experience, your paper will probably be cast into the form of a first-person narrative like several in this unit. But do not be distracted into writing pure narration; an account of how a summer camp is run should not be sidetracked, for example, into the more exciting story of a near-drowning that once occurred there.

UNIT 9

Comparison

Is Mark as good a skier as Bill? Which small car gets the best mileage? Is Dorado Beach as beautiful as Paradise Island? Who is best suited to be the next president of the United States? Which sweater will wear longer? Which graduate school has the best program in astrophysics?

Questions like these may range from the most important topics to the most trivial, but the answer to each involves making a comparison. Whenever we are faced with a choice, we view the various possibilities, noting the similarities and, even more important, the differences, because the differences will ultimately determine our decision.

Comparison as a pattern of thought involves holding up two similar but not identical objects, situations, people, ideas, and so on, to determine in detail their likenesses and differences (a thorough comparison must always include contrast to be complete). We follow this pattern in selecting brand-name goods, in determining contest winners, in choosing a candidate or a way of life—in any situation that involves weighing and judging.

In examinations and writing assignments of many kinds, you will often be asked to reach conclusions on a choice of objects, people, issues, or theories by comparing them. Your purpose in writing an essay of comparison may be only to determine similarities and differences or it may be to convince your readers of the superiority of one of the things you are presenting. Whatever your subject and purpose, the general mental process will be the same.

* * *   * * *   * * *

In planning and composing your paper, follow these steps:

1. Choose two things as your subject. More than two may have been involved in your original view, but we usually eliminate choices by examining them two at a time so that reaching a decision is essentially a matter of alternatives. For example, in deciding which of several cameras to buy, you will probably narrow your choice by weighing and eliminating until you arrive at the two likeliest, which you will then compare to each other in every detail.

2. Choose two things alike but different. They must be alike enough to be genuinely comparable, different enough to make the comparison fruitful through contrast. Two cars of the same make, year, and model may have some differences, despite standardized production, but such variations are usually unimportant. On the other hand, although a school bus and a space shuttle are both vehicles, they are probably too dissimilar for a comparison of them to be worthwhile.

3. Organize your information on the two things in similar ways so that your readers will easily see the basis for the comparison. The methods you learned in outlining will give you essential help in forming a pattern. If you mention a certain type of detail about one, be sure to include it or to note the lack of it in your discussion of the other. For example, if leg room is important in your choice of a car, consider that feature in both cars you are comparing.

Two patterns are appropriate for organizing information in a comparison: the *opposing pattern* and the *alternating pattern.*

a. Opposing pattern. Suppose you decide to compare education as you experienced it in high school with what you have found in college. Your chief concern will probably be to paint a vivid picture of life in each area, and your paper will consist of two main divisions: education in high school and education in college. Where you place the parts will depend on which you wish to emphasize—the more important one should be last.

To compare the two thoroughly, you must examine essentially the same phases of experience in each. Your subpoints under each main division are therefore likely to be similar—for example, activities, teachers, classes. Determine the order of these subpoints logically and then maintain it under each heading. If you decide to emphasize your experience in college, your skeleton outline for the main body of your paper may look like this:

I. Education in high school   II. Education in college
  A. Teachers   A. Teachers
  B. Classes   B. Classes
  C. Activities   C. Activities

As you write, you may merely paint two pictures, leaving your readers to draw their own conclusions; or, in your second picture, you may often point out comparisons and contrasts with the first; or you may write a conclusion tying them together and making clear your purpose in discussing them.

b. Alternating pattern. If, however, you wish to emphasize the details of the comparison instead of the larger differences, you will find an alternating arrangement more useful. In this, the levels of the points are the reverse of those used earlier, emphasizing the aspects of each way of life instead of the area. Your previous subpoints become main divisions; your main divisions, subpoints. Your skeleton outline for the main body of your paper will then look like this:

I. Teachers   II. Classes   III. Activities
  A. High school   A. High school   A. High School
  B. College   B. College   B. College

Which pattern you choose for a given paper will depend on your particular subject. For the topic of high school versus college, the first would probably be better since it emphasizes the contrast between the two pictures as a whole. But when you wish to emphasize the particular points of a comparison—one beach resort versus another, for instance, as to climate, hotels, and amusements—the second type of pattern would be better. If you completed the discussion of one resort before you started on another, the details of the first might have faded from your readers' minds before they were halfway through the second.

Notice how the patterns are used in the following examples. In the first, on two often confused objects, the *opposing pattern* emphasizes differences.

> The beginner has some trouble in distinguishing the planets from the stars, but the following difference in appearance may help. The stars are so distant that they shine only as points of light even through the largest telescopes. In consequence, their light is unsteady because of disturbances in the Earth's atmosphere, such as the rising of warm currents and the falling of cold currents. Thus the stars twinkle. The planets, on the other hand, are very much nearer—so near that with the exception of Pluto they show as discs in our large telescopes, and not as single points of light. Therefore their light is not so much affected by disturbances in our atmosphere. It is usually said that planets do not twinkle, but shine with a steady light. (Clyde Fisher, *Exploring the Heavens.*)

Introduction. Planets and stars

I. Stars   II. Planets
  A. Very distant   A. Less distant
  B. Result—twinkling   B. Result—steady light

The treatment of each part of the subject is so brief that there is no paragraph break before the second one appears in sentence 5, but "on the other hand" is a valuable transition between the two. Notice, too, the balance of "in consequence" (sentence 3) and "therefore" (sentence 6), transitions introducing in each part the comparable material on results.

The even briefer paragraph that follows is an equally clear example of the *alternating pattern.* Here, two people are compared, detail by detail.

> Irène was, like Eve, a brilliant, courageous bearer of the great Curie name, yet in every other respect the two sisters were far apart. Where Eve was a Gaullist, Irène was pro-Communist. Eve was chic and smart; Irène lived in a gray chemist's smock. Eve traveled the world and mingled with the mighty; Irène's world was the laboratory of the Curie Institute and she mingled with molecules and atoms, whose power was less visible if mightier. (David Schoenbrun, *As France Goes.*)

Introduction. Irène and Eve Curie

I. Politics	II. Dress	III. Experience
A. Eve—Gaullist	A. Eve—fashionable	A. Eve's—wide and important
B. Irène—pro-Communist	B. Irène—workaday	B. Irène's—narrow but more important

To see more precisely how the effects of these patterns differ, rewrite each paragraph according to the other pattern. The changes you find will be much greater in longer pieces.

Each pattern has limitations. The opposing pattern is not suitable for papers of more than a thousand words. Readers would forget the first part of the subject long before they finished the second part. But a writer may use the opposing pattern briefly at many points in a paper or book of any length. The alternating pattern may be as monotonous as a swinging pendulum if many of the parts are the same length. This pattern is most effective when the alternation varies from a contrast within a sentence, to one between sentences, or to one between paragraphs, depending on what is most appropriate for the particular material.

* * *   * * *   * * *

An **analogy** is like a figure of speech because its only purpose is to make something vivid and understandable. Unlike most figures of speech, however, it is always based on several points of comparison. Also, since the purpose is always practical, it appeals primarily to our sense of logic rather than to our emotions.

A familiar analogy is the description of a pump to explain the heart: the heart with its valves forcing blood through the body is compared to a pump with its valves forcing water through a system of pipes. These are two very different things—one anatomical, the other mechanical— but the relationship of their parts is comparable at point after point, and the working of the complex and unfamiliar becomes clearer through analogy with the relatively simple and familiar.

Analogies can be particularly helpful in translating measurements of some kind into familiar terms. For example, an advertisement for an airline caught the eye with "Last week we moved Chicago to Dallas." The advertisement continued: "In an average week, U.S. scheduled airlines carry three-and-a-half million passengers an average of 800 miles. That's the equivalent of picking up every man, woman, and child in Chicago and transporting them to Dallas." The advertisers made their point.

Do not expect an analogy to prove anything. The action of a pump can be used to explain that of the heart, but it does not follow that a heart is a machine whose parts can be replaced easily or that a plumber could perform open-heart surgery successfully.

* * * * * * * * *

Balanced sentence structure will give you special help in writing a comparison. It emphasizes the similarity of ideas by presenting them in similar grammatical patterns, as in "government of the people, by the people, and for the people." When the ideas are contrasting, the balance is called *antithesis* because the first part states a point, or thesis, which the second opposes or contradicts to some degree by a contrast. Two examples are "Give me liberty or give me death" and "Let us never negotiate out of fear, but let us never fear to negotiate"—sentences in American history as memorable for expression as for thought. Note the examples of antithesis in the selections that follow, especially in A, B, and F.

 # *Examples*

The writers of these selections make comparison a major feature, but you will find it used in varying degrees in many other selections in this book, notably in Granville's "A New Life" (3-C), Painter's "Conflict" (3-F), McDowell's "Ethnic Jokes" (4-C), Tysoe's "Do You Inherit Your Personality?" (4-F), Thomas's "On Societies as Organisms" (5-B), 5
Bronowski's "A Metaphor Used Twice" (5-E), Johmann's "Sex and the Split Brain" (7-B), all the essays in Unit 10, Jastrow's "Brains and Computers" (11-C), Shoglow's "Two Imperatives" (11-E), Satriale's "Dix Hills" (12-D), *The New Yorker*'s "Three Incidents" (13-A); Cohen's "The Language of Uncertainty" (13-B), Montagu's "Parentage" (14-B), 10
Neier's "Defending Free Speech" (15-A), and Carson's "David Bowie" (16-G).

The following selections all have some form of the alternating pattern. It is more flexible than the opposing pattern and therefore more useful. 15

9-A   The Seventh Continent

These paragraphs are from a travel agency's brochure on cruises to Antarctica. Notice that as the paragraphs grow longer, we move from a single sentence covering both regions to separate sentences for each, and then to more than one sentence.

Antarctica differs from the Arctic regions, which are better known to us and easier to reach. The North Pole is crossed daily by commercial airlines, whereas not a single commercial airliner operates over Antarctica.

The Arctic is an ocean covered with drifting ice and hemmed in 5 by the continents of North America, Asia and Europe. The Antarctic, on the other hand, is a continent as large as Europe and the United States put together, and surrounded entirely by oceans—the Atlantic, the Indian and the Pacific.

More than a million persons live within 2,000 miles of the North 10 Pole and the area is rich in forest and industry. There are animals and birds of many varieties. Within the same distance of the South Pole, there are no settlements apart from scientific stations which are entirely dependent on outside supplies for every need. There is not a single tree and not a single animal. It takes 70 to 80 years to grow an 15 inch of moss.

1. What do these two regions have in common that makes them comparable? In how many and what respects are they compared?
2. Rewrite this description as a comparison organized in the opposing pattern.
3. Explain the advantages and disadvantages of the two patterns in presenting this particular information.
4. What transitional devices did you use to link the parts of your comparisons? What devices are in the example?

9-B   Tolstoy's Contradictions

Henri Troyat

After two introductory sentences, this short paragraph from an article in the *Literary Guild Magazine* (1968) is the ultimate in balanced construction: all the remaining sentences match, each forming an antithesis whose parts are marked with "He preached" and "but he. . . ."

Who is Tolstoy? For me, he suffered his whole life long from an inability to match his thoughts with his actions. He preached asceticism and chastity, but he gave his wife thirteen children. He preached the joys of poverty, but he never lacked for anything. He preached the need for solitude, but he was the most surrounded and the most adulated 5 man of his times. He preached hatred of the government, but he never suffered any curtailment of his freedom, while his followers went into exile.

1. Rewrite this paragraph to make a comparison in the opposing pattern.
2. Explain the advantages and disadvantages of the two patterns in presenting this particular information.

9-C   The Downfall of Christmas

William Kirchoff (student)

Not all essays of comparison are patterned as neatly as the first two, which show the alternating pattern in its clearest and simplest form. In longer pieces, the pattern can be used more freely, as shown in this example and the ones that follow. The same questions apply, however, to their organization and sentence structure.

ANALYSIS
General
topic

I. First
   example
   A. Then

   trees

   a) color
   b) smell
   c) ornaments
   d) lights

   B. Now

II. Second
    example
    A. Then
    B. Now

    songs
    — titles

Christmas is gone. The American people have stood Christmas up against a wall and executed it, and from its grave a ghost has arisen. Strangely enough, this ghost is also named Christmas. This new Christmas is different, much different, from the one I knew not too long ago. 5 Most of the things that to me meant Christmas are gone. A little change here and a little change there have made Christmas a ghost of its former self.

A noticeable change has taken place in the tree. As I remember our trees, they were green, a green that could 10 not only be seen, but smelled. The ornaments were bright, but not gaudy. The lights were few and plain. I remember I used to have a favorite light each year, one that was in just the right place, and just the right color. All this sentiment was old-fashioned, though, and America was pro- 15 gressive. Manufacturers told us that we must always keep ahead of the Joneses and that we must always be new and unique. It is now no longer fashionable to have a green tree. One must have a silver one, a white one, a pink one, or a blue one. One must have a tree with music tinkling 20 from a hidden music box. The ornaments are no longer simple. They are now all hideous sizes and shapes, splashed with color, signifying nothing. They are all silver and sparkle, and no sentiment. The lights must bubble, flash, blink, glimmer, and do a million other things. The 25 Christmas tree is now an over-glorified monstrosity that smells suspiciously like machine oil.

Christmas songs have likewise undergone a disastrous change. It seems that no one was satisfied with "Silent Night." Now we have such pieces of trash as "I Saw 30 Mommy Kissing Santa Claus" and "Santa Rides a Strawberry Roan." Then there is the song that has done the most toward ruining Christmas, and that is "Santa Baby." It is my opinion that that is the lowest depth to which any songwriter can stoop. The modern songwriter is succeed- 35 ing in his attempts to make a farce out of Christmas songs.

III. Third example
A. Then
B. Now

santa claus
— commercialisation
— his costume
— his mentality
(character)

Poor old Santa has really been through the mill. He is no longer the kindly old gentleman who puts candy in children's stockings. He is now the man in the nylon ace- tate beard and the red satin costume (which sells for 40 twelve dollars and ninety-five cents at most downtown stores) who tells children to buy such and such from this or that store. He is now the man who comes riding into town surrounded by twenty-five Hollywood models in skimpy costumes, about a month early. Like everything 45 else, Santa has gone commercial.

IV. Fourth example
A. Then
B. Now

Season
— length

Even the Christmas season is different. Instead of a day or a week, it is now a month long and growing every year. It starts when Santa arrives in town accompanied by television and movie stars. It gets well under way when 50 Santa is starred on some program and tells gullible chil- dren what to buy and from whom. The person who spon- sors his show must feel very proud of himself.

V. Individual illustration

Merry Christmas, everybody; Peace on Earth, good will toward men, and see whose house decorations can be 55 the gaudiest. Mr. Smith is full of Christmas spirit. His house has 200 strings of light bulbs spelling out the first verse of "Jingle Bells." It looks as if no one will have a white Christmas, except Mr. Jones, who sprays his whole front lawn with 50 gallons of artificial snow.   60

Conclusion
Summary of "now"

Well, in short, that is the Christmas of today, a mere ghost of the Christmas that used to be. All the feelings are gone. Like almost everything made in this country, it smells and tastes like tin cans. It looks like a gaudy fire- works display, and sounds like Tin Pan Alley. Worst of all, 65 the feeling of Christmas is like the feeling of any other holiday when no one works. The one day of the year that was set aside for tradition is ruined by the American peo- ple who know no tradition. One day out of three hundred and sixty-five, and we had to go and ruin it. Christmas is 70 gone. It died when the true meaning of Christmas was all but forgotten, when Rudolph the red-nosed reindeer took the place of Dasher, when Mommy kissed Santa Claus, when a chorus girl in a low-cut evening gown sang "Silent Night" with a glycerin tear in her eye.   75

1. Why are the "now" sections longer?
2. Is the writer's use of colloquial words and phrases appropriate to his purpose?

9-D   The Boy Who Came to Supper

Russell Baker

This complete essay was first published in the *New York Times* (1980). The writer is a
syndicated newspaper columnist, long known for his humorous observations on life in the
United States. His most recent book is *Growing Up* (1982). Note how he combines his
references to dinner and supper in almost every paragraph.

For a long time I used to eat supper. "Supper's at 5 o'clock and
you'd better be here," my mother would say. We lived in the rural
South then, but later we moved to New Jersey and kept right on eating
supper, though sometimes it was as late as 6 o'clock.

In fact, I was still eating supper at the age of twenty-two when I 5
started working for an Eastern newspaper. Since it was a morning
paper the work hours extended from 3 P.M. to midnight with an hour
off to eat, and at 7 P.M. an editor habitually notified me that it was all
right to go to dinner.

Since all the other reporters racing for the first martini were also 10
going to dinner, I went to dinner, too. In this way I gradually became
a dinner eater, though the transition was confusing. On days off, since
I was still living at home, my mother insisted that I eat supper, though
it was often served as late as 7 P.M. now.

For a year or two, I remained in this transitional stage—a dinner 15
eater at the office, a supper eater at home. Since I was eating dinner five
nights a week and supper only twice, however, the dinner habit began
to enslave me and tensions developed at home.

"When are we going to have dinner?" I would ask my mother.
"Supper will be ready as soon as I finish frying the potato cakes," she 20
would say. We were drifting apart. Something basic we had once shared
had now eroded. I was moving into another world, the world of the
dinner eaters, while she was firmly anchored in the world of supper
eaters. I left home and have been an incorrigible dinner eater ever
since.   25

This distinction between Americans who eat supper and those who
eat dinner is one of the most striking divisions in the national life, yet
nobody has ever persuasively explained the difference between the
parties, though many sociologists have tried.

Andy Rooney, for example, holds that it defines the difference 30
between political parties. Democrats eat supper before sundown, he
states, while Republicans eat it at 8 P.M. and call it dinner.

If this is so, how does he explain why headwaiters in New York keep
me waiting at the bar past 10 P.M. while influential Democrats arriving
in limousines are promptly ushered to the dinner table I thought I had 35
reserved for 8:30?

Calvin Trillin has a theory that the distinction has something to do

with American regionalism. His three tests for identifying an Eastern
city are: "a place where nobody on the City Council ever wears white
patent-leather shoes, where there are at least two places to buy pas- 40
trami" and "where just about everybody eats supper after dark and calls
it dinner."

Trillin's theory is not supported by my experience in Newark, N.J.,
and Baltimore—indisputably Eastern cities, in which I lived for fifteen
years among people who almost universally ate supper. In fact, the 45
notion that anybody could eat dinner at the end of the day, except in
the movies, never occurred to me until the age of twenty-two.

Until then, in my experience, dinner was eaten only once a week,
always at 3 o'clock on Sunday afternoon. When somebody invited you
to dinner you assumed it would be eaten at midafternoon on Sunday 50
and the menu would be chicken. Having seen Jean Harlow and Wallace Beery in "Dinner at Eight," I realized there were unique people
who put on tuxedos and gowns to eat dinner at the hour when normal
people were taking their prebedtime cocoa, but the idea that I might
ever doll up in order to tuck into the potato cakes seemed as far- 55
fetched as the possibility of picking up Claudette Colbert on a Grey-
hound bus.

When I was in the transitional stage, learning to eat dinner with
veteran journalistic dinner eaters, I first assumed that dinner was distinguished from supper by the beverage that came with it. Supper had 60
always been accompanied by iced tea, a glass of milk or, in cold weather,
a cup of coffee, all of which were designed to wash down the potato
cakes. At dinner, the prevailing drink seemed to be gin, which was
designed to help you forget you were eating potato cakes.

This may explain why I was converted so easily, but it does not 65
explain anything more profound, since deeper investigation showed
that many supper eaters partake regularly of beer, and even bourbon
with ginger ale, while many dinner eaters are content with soda water,
a few ice cubes and a slice of lime.

Long investigation of this division among Americans forces me to 70
dismiss as myths such popular theories as: (1) that blue-collar people eat
supper while establishment people eat dinner; (2) that people with good
digestion eat supper while people prone to gastric distress eat dinner;
and (3) that people with hearty appetites are supper eaters while people
with jaded palates are dinner eaters who are really just going through 75
the motions so they will have an excuse to lap up the wine.

My studies have produced only two illuminating facts: first, that a
real supper eater wouldn't be caught dead with a Cuisinart in the
kitchen; second, that dinner eaters are five times less likely than supper
eaters to faint dead away if you serve them an artichoke.   80

1. What characteristics of "supper" and "dinner" does the writer use as the
   basis for the comparison?

2. How and where does the writer use specific details to support his points? How and where does he use narrative?

3. Most of the essay is in standard English, but occasionally the writer uses a colloquial expression, such as "wouldn't be caught dead" in the last paragraph. What others can you find and what may be the writer's purpose in using them?

4. Distinguish between these synonyms for *idea: notion, thought, opinion, concept.* What is the etymology of *jaded* and how does it differ from *tired* in meaning? What is the origin of *bourbon* as a name for whiskey?

9-E   Who Am I?

Caroline Bajsarowicz (student)

Which "me" shall I be today? This question confronts me every time I stand before my closet searching for something to wear.

Shall I dress like a JAP, a "Jewish American Princess"? (This style has become very popular around my affluent suburban neighborhood.) I could wear my black formal pantsuit and exquisitely colored scarf, a 5 gold pendant, a charm bracelet, and 14-carat gold hoop earrings. My richly colored, dark brown platform shoes and coordinating handbag would accentuate this polished outfit. My short brown hair would be blown dry so that it could lie perfectly. Then in front of my vanity mirror, I'd spend an hour polishing my nails, spraying a light mist of my 10 favorite perfume, and most important, applying my cosmetics: first foundation and blush, then eyeshadow and mascara. This outfit, with my dark green pants coat trimmed with fur, gives me the appearance of a high class snob. I become the stereotyped "rich student." (I have also been called a bitch when I dressed like this.)   15

At the other end of the closet there is a distinct odor of pine trees and outdoor freshness. My faded blue jeans with the old turtle patch in the center of twenty other brightly colored patches hang here on a peg. With them I wear a stained red T-shirt two sizes too large, old white sweat socks, and dirty hiking boots. My hair is generally tousled and 20 hidden under a blue bandanna. I pay no special attention to my appearance and use no nail polish or makeup. I throw on a shocking, bright green down jacket and pull on a pair of blue and gold checked mittens. My ghastly outfit presents me as a nonconformist.

Like the contents of my closet, the contents of my small but clut- 25 tered bedroom show my two personalities. All my brushes, cosmetics, and powders are neatly arranged on a large, mirrored vanity next to my bed. The bed is draped with a lacy orange bedspread and is covered by a dozen stuffed animals. The three scalloped shelves above my bed are filled with my collections of dolls, figurines, and souvenirs. Across the 30 room, there is a modern, bright yellow sewing chest. But above this hangs a poster of a snowcapped mountain and a cloudless blue sky.

Under my bed, hidden by the sides of the bedspread, is a down sleeping bag. My green Trailways backpack hangs next to my handbag. In my photo album, a picture of my friends at a beer party is pasted next to 35 a photograph of an altar of ice carved on a cliff.

My dual personality complicates my social life. Half of me gets along with most of the other students. I attend the many functions sponsored by the university, cheer for our sports teams, attend club meetings, and spend Friday nights dancing in the Rathskeller at the 40 weekly Beer Blasts. I ask myself, though, "Is this what everybody calls fun? Is this having a good time?" I may be smiling, laughing, joking, and acting out the gestures of amusement so that I'll seem to fit in with the group of people I'm with, but part of me doesn't want to be there. There are so many more constructive activities I'd rather be doing, such 45 as learning about musical instruments, making a needlepoint pillow, or taking a solitary walk through a park.

At summer orientation for freshmen, when we were given a list of all the clubs and sports in the university, I had many problems deciding which ones I wanted to join. The more popular clubs, such as the 50 sororities, appealed to me because I could meet so many girls in the school. I would have such privileges as exclusive rights to a table in the cafeteria and free passage into the Panhellenic Suite. But I also wanted to join the Outing Club. Although it has only four members, they appreciate those other things I like.   55

I'm a freshman with only three years left before I must answer that infamous question, "What do you want to be when you grow up?" I have spent many long hours trying to decide. How I would love to fulfill my mother's dream by marrying a wealthy doctor. My husband and I would live in an upper-middle-class, suburban neighborhood and own 60 a boat, two cars, and several pairs of skis. Probably, we would compete with the Joneses. Every time our neighbors bought something or went on a vacation, we'd buy something bigger and go to a more exclusive resort or on a more exotic cruise. It would be comfortable to settle down to familiar routine with only superficial worries.   65

But the rebellious me doesn't want this routine. That part of me would much rather go through life without ever settling down. Some people may say this free style of living is that of a bum or hippie, but I want to be independent and unrestrained so that I can see the many splendors of this world. The rebellious me doesn't want to be tied down 70 with a job or a home, nor does it want to worry about the Joneses.

How can these two very different personalities exist in one person? I have three years left to find the answer. . . .

1. Why does the author give somewhat more attention to her conventional "rich student" self than to her rebellious self?
2. Why does the author give the descriptive details of her clothes and room first rather than the larger problem she faces?

9-F   Social Control

New Society

At the beginning of this essay, two-thirds of which is given here, the anonymous writer
mentions that the riots in some British cities in 1981 made many mistakenly fear that
social order had broken down, but we should remember that, after periods of social
disorder, some kind of order usually appears—Iran, for example, after its recent revolution adopted strict Islamic law. The writer weaves together many brief comparisons and
contrasts to reach conclusions on the causes and nature of social control.

Generally, then, social order is a combination of two elements:
force (or *coercion*), and voluntary agreement (or *consensus*). Both these
elements are present in social control. We are kept in order by others,
and we also create and sustain order willingly for our mutual benefit.
The major schools of sociological thought agree that social order and 5
control are central to social life. Where they differ is over exactly what
this "order" is, how it is achieved, and in whose interests it is maintained. It is important to distinguish between two levels of order. On
a basic level, there is the order and associated control of everyday social
life—the orderliness that people need simply to communicate with 10
each other. Then there is the order of society as a whole. This involves
one of the most basic ideas in sociology, that of *social solidarity.*
      The phrase was originally coined by the French sociologist, Emile
Durkheim (1858–1917), to explain why societies stay together, even
though their individual members are constantly changing. There are 15
two kinds of solidarity, he said. One applies to pre-industrial, agrarian
societies *(mechanical solidarity)* and the other to modern industrial
societies *(organic solidarity).*
      Mechanical solidarity means that most people are essentially *alike*
—doing the same jobs, sharing the same beliefs, and probably knowing 20
each other personally. This is only possible in small, simple communities
—society has cohesion and unity because everybody is thinking the
same way.
      Organic solidarity, on the other hand, stems from the fact that in
modern society, everybody is *different.* Some are black; others are 25
white; some work in factories; others on farms; some support Liverpool,
others Everton [rival football teams]. Solidarity is attained by a lot of
people playing many different specialist roles, enmeshed with each
other *organically*—like the organs of the body—and from which all
may benefit.   30
      Or do they? This idea that "everybody benefits" has been a pro-
found source of disagreement between *functionalist* sociologists (who
follow in the tradition of Durkheim) and *marxists.*
      Is the social order of, for example, modern capitalist societies in the
interests of everybody in them ("the national interest"), or only of a 35
powerful minority? If the economic system were to be changed, would

the new order be in the interests of everybody, or simply of a different minority?

For functionalists, order is achieved through consensus, or general agreement, on certain core values, without which, they say, social life would be impossible. On the organic analogy, all parts of the organism contribute to the needs of the whole, whose continuity, stability and equilibrium are in the interests of all its elements. Socialisation is the crucial social process, and family, schools and religion are the key to the maintenance of social order and stability. Those who threaten order and the consensus must be punished and brought back into line in the interests of the whole society.

Marxists accept the same basic premise that order rests on agreement over values, but argue that this agreement is not achieved freely and voluntarily, nor is it in the interests of all concerned. The dominant class in society, which owns and controls the economic resources and thus exercises power in all other contexts, must, if it is to maintain its dominance, exercise control over all those in whose interests it would be to change the power structure.

While this could be done through force (as it has been, ironically enough, in some marxist societies like Czechoslovakia and Poland), it is far more effective through the control of ideas and of knowledge. If the people without power can be convinced of the justice, legitimacy, even the inevitability of the social system, the position of the dominant class will not be threatened. What a functionalist calls "culture" and "central value system," a marxist calls "ideology"—a set of ideas that explains and makes sense of experience by distorting it in ways that justify the status quo.

Similarly, what functionalists call the "formal agencies of social control" become, for marxists, the "repressive state apparatuses"—the police, prisons, and the armed forces. Why, it is asked, do the police spend so much time on working class crime, when really substantial crime is taking place in offices and boardrooms.

A different dimension to the argument comes from *phenomenological* sociologists, such as Peter Berger and Thomas Luckmann. They are asking the same question as the functionalists and marxists: "How is social order possible?" But, rather than stressing the way in which society influences people's behaviour, they concentrate on how order is constructed through the interaction of individuals in everyday situations.

The phenomenologists say that although most people are generally influenced by mutually accepted standards of behaviour, human conduct is highly variable, and, to a large extent, "order" only exists insofar as people actually give any meaning to it. A crime against society, for instance, has no objective meaning as such, but tends to be what a particular policeman, judge or jury thinks it is.

But what of those who do *not* behave as is expected of them? Who are they? Why do they behave in a deviant manner?

Confusing as it may seem, it is possible to regard deviance as something orderly, and even quite normal. It is not simply socially meaning- 85
less behaviour, but behaviour to which we give the meaning "deviant"
if it occurs in a context where it contravenes the rules of a particular
situation. For instance, public nakedness is normal in some contexts and
deviant in others.

To go nude on the beach at Brighton does not contravene social 90
rules because Brighton council permits nudity. But to streak at a rugby
match is reckoned to be deviant. To be nude on stage is normal in a strip
club but deviant at, say, the Royal Variety Performance. On the other
hand, it could be said that streakers are predictable these days, that
streaking is almost normal, and, whatever we may think of strippers, 95
they have an established role in our society.

In fact, if we consider all kinds of deviance, major and minor,
public and private, it is actually pretty commonplace. If sexual deviance is so unusual, how do the many mail order firms dealing in "marital aids" flourish? What proportion of the population could say, in all 100
honesty, that they had never stolen anything in their lives? We may
even begin to wonder whether the "normal" really exists, other than
as an idea.

However, there are some forms of deviance that are seen as anti-
social by everybody—violent crime, especially, comes in this category. 105
What explanations are there for the behaviour of muggers or terrorists?

Functionalist sociologists would argue that the problem is one of
defective socialisation—a failure somewhere along the line to instil the
values and norms that are necessary in a stable society. Resocialisation 110
may be possible—and this is what prisons and borstals [reform schools]
are theoretically for.

Marxists, on the other hand, would probably dispute this analysis.
Their argument might run thus: "A capitalist society concentrates on
certain acts, like terrorism, as deviant because they are a threat to those 115
who hold power. Yet other acts which may be equally destructive of life,
such as marketing a car known to be unsafe, are glossed over because
they fit in with society's ideology." The idea of what makes a terrorist
depends very much on ideological interpretation: in both Zimbabwe
and Israel, terrorists have ended up as heads of government.   120

Again, the phenomenologists tend to disagree. They are most concerned with how certain acts come to be defined as deviant, rather than
in their actual causes. But they also stress that people labelled as deviant
may see their own behavior as entirely rational and meaningful, even
normal, in the context of a situation as they interpret it.   125

Social control is, then, a matter of competing definitions of order
—and what counts as orderliness and normality is the outcome of relations of power. It is both complicated—and very basic. Together with
social order, it is at the heart of the notion of society and of social life.
To be social is to be controlled. The social is control.   130

1. What are the principal differences between mechanical solidarity and organic solidarity?
2. What beliefs separate functional sociologists, phenomenologists, and Marxists?
3. On what basis could someone argue that socially deviant behavior is orderly and normal?
4. Is violent crime always seen as a form of deviant behavior?
5. How does the writer use the examples of nudity?
6. Discuss the writer's use of specific examples, quotations, and summaries.

Assignments

1. Write an essay of comparisons, choosing as your subject two things enough alike to be comparable but with enough differences to make the comparison worthwhile. There are two chief types of topics: (1) a comparison based on periods of time—"then and now" or "now and later," and (2) a comparison based on two coexistent things—"this and that."

   Suggestions for the first type: horse and automobile, washboard and washing machine, clothing styles, early and contemporary cars, kindergarten and grade school, high school and college, your parents' childhood and yours.

   Suggestions for the second type: gasoline and diesel engines, city life and suburban life, suburban life and farm life, community colleges and universities, football and soccer, a camping vacation and a resort vacation, your home and that of a friend, your bedroom and that of a brother or sister, a book or play and the movie version, two different singers, two makes of automobile, two breeds of dogs, two TV situation comedies, two TV news analysts.

   After choosing a subject, decide which type of organization will be better for it, and make an outline showing the main points and subpoints you intend to develop.
2. Discuss the use of comparison in examples in other units, notably Unit 2-G; Unit 3-C; Unit 4-C and E; Unit 5-B; Unit 11-A and C; Unit 12-D and E; Unit 16-I.

UNIT 10

Classification

"Oh, so *that*'s where you keep the salt!" you exclaim after a long search. In your own home the salt is next to the stove because everyone likes it in most foods, but your friend keeps it in a cupboard with garlic powder, nutmeg, and other seasonings. "*Where* did you say I could find a safety pin?" In your home the safety pins are with needles and thread in your mother's sewing box, but your friend keeps them in a desk drawer with paper clips, a stapler, and thumb tacks.

You and your friends are applying logical principles of classification in choosing where to keep salt and safety pins, and your basic methods of reasoning are the same, but your criteria for establishing the classes differ. You classified the salt according to frequency of use, but your friend classified it according to purpose. You classified the safety pins according to a single purpose, fastening fabrics, and your friend classified them in the more general category of small fasteners for any purpose, but you both used classification to keep track of the salt and safety pins.

Sharing criteria for classification is like sharing a language. Without it we often have difficulty understanding each other. Scientists depend on shared criteria to communicate with other scientists. For example, biologists divide all living things into the animal, vegetable, and protist kingdoms; each kingdom is divided into phyla, each phylum into classes, each class into orders, and so on down through the family, genus, species, and variety. Anthropologists classify people according to race; businesses classify their creditors according to degrees of risk; college grading systems classify students as A's, B's, and so on.

To classify any group formally and completely involves considering every representative of that group and breaking down classes into subclasses, sub-subclasses, and so on, until the ultimate in division is reached. For most purposes, however, we need to consider only the main classes into which we can divide a given subject and to treat only the main subclasses, with perhaps a few sub-subclasses. An essay on musical instruments, for example, intended for the general reader need not have classifications covering every rare or ancient piece but may consider only those commonly used by the modern orchestra. Once the writer has divided and grouped them into kinds and described the outstanding instruments of each kind, the task of classification is, for practical purposes, complete. The purpose of such an essay is usually not total thoroughness; the writer uses classification to bring out some other point in an orderly manner.

*   *   *   *   *   *   *   *   *

To find an appropriate topic for a paper in which you use classification, follow these steps:

1. Choose a limited group. It should be small enough for you, in a brief paper, to go into some detail in describing the subgroups. "People" is too much to handle; "taxi drivers" might do nicely.

2. Choose a group with three or more subgroups. A classification with only two classes will give you the same practice in organizing as the essay of comparison in Unit 9. Classifying people into "types I like" and "types I dislike" is an example of a rather pointless division of a subject that is too large.

3. Look for a personal and original development. Many classifications already exist; for example, scientists divide meteorites into three types according to their composition: iron, iron and stone, and stone. But you may get—and give—more enjoyment with an original approach such as that of the girl who classified her dates according to the reasons for her choices into the "old school friend type," the "he drives a sports car" type, and the "he's a good disco dancer" type. (Beware of the "good-bad-average" kind of classification, which is likely to produce little originality.)

4. Choose and apply a single principle of classification. Your principle will determine the classes to be discussed. Engines may be classified according to maker, use, speed, number of cylinders—but only one at a time. An attempt to classify drivers into women drivers, truck drivers, and good drivers is no classification at all, merely a loose and purposeless discussion. The topic "women drivers" announces that the principle guiding the division is sex; "truck drivers" changes the principle to the type of vehicle driven; and "good drivers" changes it once more, this time to driving skill. Actually, there are the beginnings here of three distinct classifications:

according to sex (women, men—one of those two-part, ready-made schemes)
according to vehicle driven (truck, taxi, camper, van, passenger car)
according to proficiency (good, bad, average)

5. Do not let your classes overlap. In the scheme just presented, for example, a truck driver might also be both a woman and a good driver.

6. Make your classification reasonably complete. As mentioned earlier, your essay need not be exhaustive, but it should be adequate for your purpose. In classifying hunting dogs by breed, you might omit certain rare varieties, but you would be obliged to consider all those commonly known. To discuss horror movies you dislike and those you enjoy, you must include those you tolerate; then your classification, based on the principle of your reactions, would be adequate.

7. Introduce subclasses as needed. If there are finer divisions of any of the subgroups into which you divided your original group, you may wish to include them. In classifying students according to religious faiths—for example, as Jews, Christians, Moslems, and so on—you may want to subdivide at least the Christians into subgroups as Catholics and Protestants and the Protestants into sub-subgroups, such as Methodist, Presbyterian, Baptist, and so on. But be sure to keep such a sub-sub-grouping in its place, and do not allow your reader to confuse it with the larger classification on which your paper is based.

* * *   * * *   * * *

Your **organization**—the order in which to discuss the main classes (categories) in your classification—is the next question to consider. Sometimes this order is natural because it is inherent in your subject, leaving you no choice; sometimes you will have to decide among several possibilities, all logical. Choose the one that best suits your purpose and is likely to be clearest to your readers.

To discuss students according to their college year, you would probably use a chronological order, starting with freshmen and finishing with seniors. To classify them according to religions, you have at least three choices: (1) the chronological order in which the religions were founded; (2) the numerical size of the groups on your campus or in the nation; or (3) your own interest in them, saving until last the one you consider most interesting or important so that you can make a strong final impression on your readers and placing first the one most likely to attract your readers' attention.

Remember that the divisions and subdivisions in your outline indicate comparable groups of topics, just as they did in your essay of comparison. Each group should therefore receive similar treatment. If you write on the American Kennel Club's official classification of dogs (a somewhat arbitrary sorting into six groups: sporting, hound, working, terrier, toy, nonsporting), and if you give information on breeds, uses, and popularity for sporting dogs, your readers will expect you to cover the same areas, probably in the same order, for the other five categories. Notice that the first section suggested—breeds—will involve the kind of subclassification that a classification often includes (see paragraph 7 in the discussion of finding an appropriate topic).

Balanced sentence structure can help you to emphasize comparable topics and subtopics, as it could in writing an essay of comparison.
Study the writer's use of it in this paragraph:

> The distinctions I am making among three different kinds of culture
> —*postfigurative*, in which children learn primarily from their forebears,
> *cofigurative*, in which children and adults learn from their peers, and
> *prefigurative*, in which adults learn also from their children—are a reflec-
> tion of the period in which we live. Primitive societies and small religious
> and ideological enclaves are primarily postfigurative, deriving authority
> from the past. Great civilizations, which necessarily have developed tech-
> niques for incorporating change, characteristically make use of some form
> of cofigurative learning from peers, playmates, fellow students, and fellow
> apprentices. We are now entering a period, new in history, in which the
> young are taking on new authority in their prefigurative apprehension of
> the still unknown future. (Margaret Mead, *Culture and Commitment.*)

Notice that the three kinds of culture Mead names are listed in her first
sentence as a parallel series, each named, then followed by an "in
which" definition. The three sentences that follow take up these kinds
in the same order, explaining where each is found. Not all essays of
classification will or should show such complete balance, especially the
longer and more informal ones. But similar treatment is essential. The
preceding quotation is the opening paragraph of a small book that Mead
divides into three chapters, "The Past," "The Present," and "The Future," presenting her thoughts about these three kinds of culture one
by one in the order in which she introduced them. These long chapters
do not, of course, match in wording—but they do in purpose and accomplishment.

* * *   * * *   * * *

Your outline will give you essential help in organizing a logical
essay, but remember not to let it obtrude awkwardly. A formal classification that never goes beyond the outline stage remains a mere listing
under appropriate headings and subheadings and will not interest your
readers. Make your classification, like your essays on previous assignments, both logical and readable.

Examples

In each of these selections, classification is essential to the main
point. Other selections in which the writers use classification are Morrow's "In Praise of Serious Hats" (4-E), Kirchoff's "The Downfall of
Christmas" (9-C), *New Society*'s Social Control" (9-F), Ivins's "Why
They Mourned for Elvis Presley" (11-F), H. Gardner's "Are Television's 5
Effects Due to Television?" (12-E), Nilsson's "Why People Are Preju-
diced" (12-G); Hillary's "The Elusive Abominable Snowman" (13-J),

Ardrey's "Light from an Ape's Jaw" (13-K), all the selections in Unit 14, Mahood's "Puns and Other Wordplay" (16-C), and M. Gardner's "The Holes in Black Holes" (16-F).   10

With each selection in this unit, be sure to observe the subject being classified, the principle used, the number of classes that result, and the order in which they are presented. Also notice the transitions that connect the discussions of the various classes.

10-A   Book Owners

Mortimer J. Adler

This excerpt comes from an essay, "How to Mark a Book," first published in the *Saturday Review* in 1940.

There are three kinds of book owners. The first has all the standard sets and best-sellers—unread, untouched. (This deluded individual owns woodpulp and ink, not books.) The second has a great many books —a few of them read through, most of them dipped into, but all of them as clean and shiny as the day they were bought. (This person would 5 probably like to make books his own, but is restrained by a false respect for their physical appearance.) The third has a few books or many— every one of them dog-eared and dilapidated, shaken and loosened by continual use, marked and scribbled in from front to back. (This man owns books.)   10

1. What is the principle of classification involved here? Do these three classes constitute a "reasonably complete" discussion of the subject?
2. Notice the almost perfect parallelism of the treatment of the three classes, similar to the kind of balance we found in the development of the essay of comparison. But like the antitheses of Example B in Unit 9, this could not be sustained at length. Compare the high degree of organization here with the greater freedom in the longer selection that follows.
3. Check the etymology, denotation, and connotation of *deluded* and *dilapidated*.

10-B   The Ones Left Behind

Rebecca Lanning (student)

The Cullowhee Exodus, so much a part of the average WCU student's Friday life, begins around noon and by three o'clock is in full swing. Almost everyone who can possibly do so has wedged himself into a homeward-bound car, leaving behind only those who couldn't find a ride, those who feel they have too much studying to do, and those rare 5 and inexplicable souls who seemingly enjoy a weekend on a temporarily almost deserted campus.

The most bitter of those left behind are the No-Way-Homers. These are made up of individuals unlucky enough to have a four-o'clock class and to find no driver willing to wait until 4:50, and those who live too far away from the university to be able to travel there and back in a weekend. These two groups spend their weekend with appropriate differences: the first complaining endlessly about the stupidity of the computer that gave them such a lousy schedule, the second moaning to anyone within earshot of the folly of having any institution for higher education located so far from civilization.

The largest group of these campus weekenders, the Studiers, are less bitter than the No-Way-Homers but more disgusted. In fact, they are running over with disgust because, having wrestled with the books all week, they must now continue the match throughout the weekend. Most of the Studiers are chronic procrastinators; some are the lucky people to whom Professor Smith has given one of his little over-the-weekend take-home fifty-question "opportunity" quizzes; and the rest are the students of Sandbox 2331, who were informed in class on Friday of a term paper due the following Monday.

On Saturday afternoon the library is full of sleeping Studiers who had stayed awake far into Friday night. Some of them were scheduling their Saturday study time; others were plotting the arsenic murder of Professor Smith and his ilk. Quickly the weekend flies by, and with it the intentions of the Studiers, who when questioned later about how they spent their time, mutter something unintelligible about how much work they accomplished. In all truth, however, the only thing they really did was getting ready to get ready to study.

Neither bitter nor disgusted is the third, final, small, and entirely atypical group of those remaining behind, the Enjoyers. These rare people seem actually to relish life on an almost empty campus. They spend the entire weekend looking cool and detached as they sit drinking cokes in the Town House or strolling along the ivy-bordered walks, showing off their wonderful dispositions and making enemies right and left. The Enjoyers are considered by everyone else to be either remarkably school-spirited or downright crazy—but maybe they actually do enjoy the atmosphere of a simulated Siberia.

Time marches on (to coin a phrase), and soon it is Monday. Back troop the rest of the student population, and the No-Way-Homers, the Studiers, and the Enjoyers all blend into the renewed hustle and bustle for another busy college week. One thought, however, runs continually through most of their minds: "Just wait till next weekend; wild horses couldn't keep me here."

1. What determines the order of the three major classes of "those left behind"?
2. What subclasses and sub-subclasses are identified in the second, third, and fourth paragraphs?

10-C   Mental Depression: The Recurring Nightmare

Jane E. Brody

This excerpt, published in the *New York Times* (1977), forms the first two-thirds of an article by a writer who regularly covers health news. The rest of the article describes various treatments for depression.

ANALYSIS
Introduction

The feeling is familiar to almost everyone—nothing seems satisfying, things don't work out, you can't get yourself to do much of anything and your mental landscape is bleak. It's called depression, and few of us get through life without experiencing it at one time or another.   5

Major class
#1

Many things can get a person "down," including the weather (midwinter doldrums are an annual event for some), the letdown after the excitement and activity of the holidays, insufficient sleep, too much work and too little time in which to get it done. The ordinary everyday 10 "blues" are fortunately usually brief and self-curing and, although they take the edge off life, are not terribly incapacitating.

Major class
#2

However, for millions of Americans, depression is a far more serious, sometimes even life-threatening, situa- 15 tion. Most serious depressions are reactions to stressful life events—loss of a job or a spouse, serious financial setback, a serious illness or injury, the end of a love affair. After a reasonable number of weeks or months, most such depressions lift and the world and life begin to seem brighter. 20

Major class
#3

But for some people, depression is a recurring phenomenon that is provoked by events that others seem to weather with little difficulty or get over very quickly. And for others, depression happens "out of the blue," unrelated to any particular situation, and totally incapaci- 25 tates the victims. Many accomplished people suffered from severe depression, including Sigmund Freud, Abraham Lincoln, Nathaniel Hawthorne, Winston Churchill and the astronaut, Edwin E. Aldrin.

Importance
of major
class #3

The National Institute of Mental Health estimates 30 that each year between 4 and 8 million Americans suffer depressions severe enough to keep them from performing their regular activities or compelling them to seek medical help. Perhaps 10 to 15 million others have less severe depressions that interfere to some extent with the per- 35 formance of normal activities.

All told, depression is clearly "the mental illness of the '70's," rivaling schizophrenia as the nation's number one mental health problem and currently increasing significantly among people below the age of 35.   40

Theories on causes of major class #3
Some experts say the social tensions of the times—the erosion of trust, diminished personal impact, unrealistically high expectations for success, disintegration of the family, social isolation and loss of a sense of belonging to or believing in some stable, larger-than-self institution—   45
foster a society especially prone to depression.

Subclasses of #3
Subclass #1
Recognizing depression, should it strike you or someone you know, can sometimes be very difficult. In its classic, undisguised form, depression has three main characteristics: 50

Sub-subclass #1
¶Emotional—A dull, tired, empty, sad, numb feeling with little or no pleasure from ordinarily enjoyable activities and people;

Sub-subclass #2
¶Behavioral—Irritability, excessive complaining about small annoyances or minor problems, impaired   55
memory, inability to concentrate, difficulty making decisions, loss of sexual desire, inability to get going in the morning, slowed reaction time, crying or screaming, excessive guilt feeling;

Sub-subclass #3
¶Physical—loss of appetite, weight loss, constipation,   60
insomnia or restless sleep, impotence, headache, dizziness, indigestion and abnormal heart rate.

Subclass #2
But in many cases, the symptoms of depression are "masked," disguised in a form that makes recognition by the depressed person, his family, friends and even his phy-   65
sician difficult. "The exhausted housewife, the bored adolescent and the occupational underachiever are often suffering from depression just as truly as the acutely suicidal patient or the one who refuses to get out of bed," according to Dr. Nathan Kline, a New York psychiatrist.   70

The patient with disguised depression may complain of headache, backache or pains elsewhere in the musculoskeletal system. He may have a gastrointestinal disorder, such as chronic diarrhea, a "lump" in the throat, chest pain or a toothache.   75

Or his depression may be disguised in sexual promiscuity, overeating, excessive drinking or various phobias.

Depression in children is usually masked, presenting symptoms like restlessness, sleep problems, lack of attention and initiative.   80

Other causes of major class #3
In addition to stressful events that cause depression (called "reactive" or "exogenous" depression), and unknown internal, probably biochemical, causes (called "endogenous" depression), depression can result from organic

diseases, including viral and bacterial infections, such as 85
hepatitis, influenza, mononucleosis and tuberculosis; hor-
monal disorders, such as diabetes and thyroid disease, and
such conditions as arthritis, nutritional deficiencies, ane-
mia and cancer.

1. Why is "Masked" not listed as a fourth classification of the symptoms of
   depression, after "Emotional," "Behavioral," and "Physical"?
2. What distinction is the author drawing between "emotional" and "behavioral" symptoms?

10-D   The South Africans

E. J. Kahn, Jr.

The following paragraphs are from *The Separated People* (1968), a study of South Africa,
and were first published in *The New Yorker.*

The peculiar composition of South Africa's population . . . has given
the country its character and its controversiality. There are four principal kinds of South Africans. Largest in number and least in influence are
its twelve and a half million black-skinned people. There are almost two
million others, of mixed blood, who are known as "Colored." Their skins 5
range in hue from white to black, but whatever a Colored man's color,
his rights are meager. There are slightly more than half a million Asiat-
ics, most of them of Indian ancestry and all of them second-class citizens. First class is reserved for three and a half million Whites, who, as
they never forget, constitute the largest concentration of white people 10
in Africa. Johannesburg, the Republic's main metropolis, with a total
population of 1,250,000, has the biggest white population of any city on
the continent. Johannesburg also has the biggest black population. It is
in large part because of such unique distinctions that contemporary
South Africa is so uniquely vexed.   15
    The mere identification of the various categories of South Africans
can confuse outsiders. The Whites—who rarely have anyone else in
mind when they use the term "South African"—are often known as
"Europeans," although in fact most of them have firm African roots;
some of their family trees were planted in African soil a dozen genera- 20
tions ago. (The few Japanese in South Africa also rate as Europeans,
because most of them are businessmen and it suits the South African
government to treat them—although Chinese do not get the same
break—as honorary Whites.) In the Transvaal province—wherein are
located both Johannesburg and Pretoria, the country's administrative 25
capital—"non-European" means "non-White." In the province of the
Cape of Good Hope, however, wherein lies Cape Town, the country's
legislative capital (the highest judicial body sits in still another province,

at Bloemfontein in the Orange Free State), the only non-Whites considered non-European are the Coloreds, most of whom live in the Cape. 30
Throughout South Africa the darkest and most downtrodden of its
residents are called either Africans, as they themselves prefer to be
designated, or Bantu, as the government prefers to designate them (in
many African languages, "Bantu" means "people"), or natives, or
kaffirs, a word of Arabic origin that means infidels and is akin to the 35
American "niggers." Only bigots and Africans use "kaffir."

South Africa is extremely conscious of the variety and disparity of
its inhabitants. Where else on earth would the head of a government
refer, as Prime Minister Balthazar John Vorster did in the winter of
1967, to "my country and my *peoples*"?   40

1. This selection suggests some of the need for and difficulties of classifying.
   What is the principle of classification here?
2. How do you account for the order in which the classes are presented? Could
   it have been reversed?
3. Check the etymology, denotation, and connotation of *unique*. How does it
   differ from *unusual* and *rare*?

10-E   Outer Limits

Jane Panzeca (student)

A good student need not be on the honor role or a whiz at taking
tests. He or she must, however, view learning as a way to expand and
grow as a human being and as a way to contribute to society.

There are four basic types of students: Regurgitators, Magicians,
Sluggards, and Generators. The Regurgitators are the ones who cough 5
up information as it was dictated to them. They do well on tests but
never offer an opinion or idea of their own. The Magicians are the
deceivers; they view schooling as a means of getting a high-paying job.
They are the master cheaters who pull top grades from midair but who
perform a disappearing act when the going gets tough. The Sluggards 10
are habitually lazy. They lack motivation and regard school as useless.
They must be pushed to learn, even though they have the ability to do
well. The Generators are the dedicated students who take part in all
class discussions. They see learning in a different light. Although they
are not all honor students, they are curious and in touch with the world 15
around them. They will view even the most common things differently
from their peers.

If one representative of each group were taken by an instructor to
a stream and asked to throw a pebble into the water and then to express
a thought, each would react differently. The Regurgitator might say, 20
"Well, what is *your* opinion?" The Magician might reply, "Are we going
to be asked this on a test?" The Sluggard might say, *"I'm* not going to

throw the stone; you throw it for me!" The Generator might reply, "I get the idea! It reminds me of an earthquake. The rock hitting the water generates ripples. Earthquake waves are like the vibrations in the 25 water."

A student who is curious and interested will see even very ordinary devices in a provocative way. For such a student, learning is like the pebble causing circular waves, a never-ending process; for, after all, learning has no limits.   30

10-F   The Pervasive Set

Edward T. Hall

This essay, here complete, forms a chapter in *The Silent Language* (1959), a study of the many ways that people communicate with and without words. The author is an anthropologist.

As a general rule, a set is a group of two or more constituent components that is perceived as being set apart from other things. Material objects such as chairs, tables, desks, and myriad other assemblages of things can be considered sets. So can words, periods of time, special measurements like the mile, and governing bodies, to mention 5 only a few of the less tangible appurtenances of life which fit our definition. Because there are different types of sets, however—formal sets, informal sets, and technical sets—some sets are perceived more easily than others. Formal sets, for example, are those things which people take for granted and which seem natural: words, buildings, govern- 10 ments, families, the day, the months, and the year. Yet all these dissolve as satisfactory sets once one begins to look at them technically. We cannot think of words without languages, buildings without a civilization, time without periods.

At whatever level, sets are seldom perceived in isolation. Normally 15 they appear in context and as one of many in a series of similar or related events. In the cross-cultural situation the first thing that a person will learn about another society is the existence of certain formal sets. These are either pointed out right away or they are so obvious that they cannot be missed. Yet in many cases the newcomer never gets 20 beyond this first step. For example, he may learn a great many words (or sets) of a foreign language but still use the linguistic isolates of his mother tongue—which gives him an accent. Moreover, he may, without knowing it, fit the foreign words into the constructions, or patterns, of his native tongue—which can render his thoughts unintelligible. To 25 take another example, we in America perceive all makes of cars as automobiles, whereas in certain parts of the Arab world only one make, the Cadillac, is considered an automobile. In such cases the foreigner (i.e., an Arab) feels he has mastered a set quite different from the ones

he is familiar with and has the illusion of having understood another 30
culture. In reality only the first hesitant step has been taken. To master
a foreign culture it is necessary to master its patterns and isolates as well
as its sets.

Sets are limited only by the number of possible combinations of
their isolates and patterns. To try to deal with a foreign culture by 35
learning more and more sets is a hopeless task. To collect sets in your
mind is easy, but to decipher a pattern is difficult. Talking about sets
without bringing in patterns is like talking about bricks without saying
anything about houses. Thus, though this chapter is primarily devoted
to sets, it is necessary to introduce the concept of pattern frequently. 40

If people can recognize a pattern, it doesn't much matter what
specific events they perceive. These can, in fact, be quite different and
still be part of the same pattern, just as houses are still houses even
though made of different materials. Throughout the Middle East, for
example, bargaining is an underlying pattern which is significantly dif- 45
ferent from the activity which goes under that name in our culture. Yet
what is perceived on the surface (i.e., Arab methods of bargaining) looks
familiar and is assumed to be the same. Nothing could be farther from
the truth. Our first mistake is in the assessment of the value of bargaining in the Middle East and the role it plays in everyday life. Americans 50
tend to look down on people who haggle. They restrict their serious
trading to houses and automobiles. To the Arab, on the other hand,
bargaining is not only a means of passing a day but actually a technique
of interpersonal relations. However, it is not just the value placed on
bargaining that is different in the Middle East but the pattern as well. 55

What we perceive on a first visit to an Arab country is a series of
interactions that we recognize as something akin to bargaining. That is,
we perceive the sets: the actions, the motions, the rises in the tone of
voice, increases in loudness, the withdrawal, the handling of the merchandise. With all this going on before our eyes we do not ordinarily 60
reflect on how our own pattern differs from this ostensibly familiar one.
The American asks, "What percentage of the asking price shall I give
as my first offer?" What he doesn't know is that there are several asking
prices. Like the Eskimo who has many different words for snow, the
Arab has many different asking prices, each with a different meaning. 65
The American pattern is that the two parties have hidden prices above
and below which they will not go, and an asking price which is perceived and thought of as having some sort of fixed relationship to the
hidden prices.

To return to sets, the principal point to remember is that they are 70
the first thing to be observed, their number is unlimited, and the interpretation of their significance depends upon a knowledge of the patterns in which they are used.

There are additional generalizations which one can make about
sets, however. These can be of use to the field worker, for they point 75
the way to deeper patterns.

A large part of the vocabulary of a culture is devoted to sets. By looking at the vocabulary you can get a rough idea of the content of a culture and the things that are valued. The fact that we have only one word for snow while the Eskimos have several is a case in point. A highly 80 developed technical vocabulary reflects a technical culture. Americans think nothing of having their advertising filled with words once known only to scientists and engineers, such as chlorophyll, thermonuclear, chloromycetin, cardiovascular, and the like.

The same set may be *valued* differently. The Latin American is 85 likely to ask, if he comes from a place like Venezuela, why we emphasize something so dirty and unpleasant as plumbing. He may even want to know why we put the toilet in the bathroom. In Japan, to take another example, emotion or feeling is ranked very high. They call it *kimochi* or *dojo*. Logic, as we think of it, is ranked low. Our ranking of 90 these two sets is, of course, almost the reverse of the Japanese.

Comparable sets are also composed of different components in different cultures. We think of a set of china as being primarily the dishes, cups, and saucers made from the same material and bearing the same pattern or in the same style. In Japan this does not hold. One of 95 the many sets which I saw in the modern department stores in the Ginza was a "coffee set" in a box. It included five cups, five saucers, five spoons (all china), one aluminum percolator (kitchen variety), one cut-glass cream pitcher, and one plain sugar bowl with a plastic top. In the United States, no stretch of the imagination could put these diverse 100 items in the same set.

Another important point is that the same sets are *classified differently* as one moves about the globe. This provides us with some additional stumbling blocks and gives us the illusion that we are really learning something different. In English, nouns are not classified as to 105 sex. In Arabic, they are. You have to know the sex of the noun if you are to use it properly. We, on the other hand, classify everything into animate and inanimate, which would mean that a Trobriand Islander who does not make these distinctions would have to remember every time he referred to something whether we thought it was alive or not. 110 He would also experience some difficulty with our animal and vegetable classifications, because he conceives of vegetables as being like animals and able to migrate from one garden to the next. (A good gardener to him is like a shepherd who is able to keep his own vegetables home and possibly even to entice a few, but not too many, of his neighbor's vegeta- 115 bles to enter his garden.)

English also has mass and non-mass nouns. Mass nouns comprise such things as sand, snow, flour, and grass. They are indicated by the phrase, "Give me some—." Non-mass nouns include such objects as man, dog, thimble, and leaf. The phrase, "Give me a—" is the linguistic 120 clue to their existence. The foreigner always has to learn, pretty much by rote, which nouns are mass and which are not. Grass is, leaf isn't; there is no known consistent logic as to why a noun exists in one category and not another. In fact, it is true of sets generally that there is a good deal of plain old repetitious learning involved in their use. Vocab- 125 ulary, wherever and however you find it, always has to be memorized.

We also distinguish between the various states of things—that is, whether they are active or passive. How the person speaking relates to natural events also varies. We say, "I'll see you *in* an hour." The Arab says, "What do you mean, 'in an hour'? Is the hour like a room, that you 130 can go in and out of it?" To him his own system makes sense: "I'll see you before one hour," or "I'll see you after one week." We go out *in* the rain. The Arab goes *under* the rain.

Not only are sets classified, but they are broken down into further categories. An analysis of the number of sets in a given category can sometimes tell you the relative importance of an item in the over-all 135 culture. The first person to speak scientifically about this trait was Franz Boas in his discussion of such things as the Eskimo's use of several different "nouns" for the many states of snow. In our culture one can get some idea of the importance of women by examining the tremendous proliferation of synonyms for females, particularly the young ones 140 —cupcake, doll, flame, skirt, tomato, queen, broad, bag, dish, twist, to mention only a few. Each indicates a different variety or a subtle distinction in the ranking scale.

An additional attribute of sets, indicated by the above, is that they are almost always ranked within their category. The ranking, of course, 145 varies as one moves about. White men are ranked above Negroes in the United States. In Liberia it's the other way around. In fine watchmaking, gold is ranked above steel when elegance or social display is the goal. If one is a sportsman, steel may take precedence. To the American public as a whole, Cadillac ranks Buick, which ranks Chevrolet. 150

As a matter of fact, the ranking of sets is so subtle that one has to be more specific. It is not enough to say that sets are ranked. The categories of rankings, which reveal a pattern themselves, are of equal importance. In essence there are three different ways in which the set is ranked: (a) formally as a traditional item in a system of valued sets 155 (lead, copper, gold, platinum); (b) informally, according to the taste of the observer or the demands of a situation (rare, medium, well-done steaks; red, green, blue, yellow); (c) technically, as points in a pattern: "Potatoes are selling for $5.00 a lot; yesterday they went for $4.95." The pattern in this case is the so-called law of supply and demand. On the 160 Trobriand Islands a comparably comestible item like the yam was valued according to a completely different pattern. It was ranked according to its size, shape, when it was harvested, and who was to receive it. Supply and demand had nothing to do with the case.

Americans treat colors informally as a whole—that is, situationally. 165 We may use a spot of yellow or of red, or yellow and red to accent a gray wall. We would be unlikely to put the yellow and the red next to each other. The colors in themselves have little or no value. If they do, the criterion is taste. To the Navajo the situation is quite different; colors are

ranked just as we rank gold and silver—only more intensely. Not realiz- 170
ing this caused considerable embarrassment to a number of Indian
Service employees years ago. In their attempt to bring "democracy" to
the Indians these well-meaning souls tried to introduce a system of
voting among the Navajo. Unfortunately a great many Navajo were
illiterate, so someone conceived of the idea of assigning the various 175
candidates for the tribal council different colors so that the Navajo could
go into the booth and check the color he wanted. Since blue is a good
color and red bad, the result was to load the dice for some candidates and
against the others. Nowadays photographs are used on the ballots.

Though Westerners tend to be impressed by big numbers and have 180
an aversion to thirteen, one number is as good as the next now that
superstition has dwindled away. Numbers become meaningful only in
a technical context. The Japanese, however, have numbers that mean
good luck, wealth, bankruptcy, and death. This fact complicates the
Japanese telephone system. Good numbers bring a high price, unlucky 185
ones are palmed off on foreigners.

It is quite clear then that one of the readily perceivable differences
between cultures is the category to which a set is assigned and, once it
is assigned, how it is treated: formally, informally, or technically.

In summary, we might point out that the only meaning which can 190
be assigned to sets as sets is what we can call *demonstrational* meaning:
This is a "dog"; that is a "man"; there goes an "airplane." By themselves,
sets are neutral. In patterns, on the other hand, sets take on all sorts of
more complex types of meaning.

1. Where does Hall use examples?
2. What may have been his reasons for giving examples for some points but not
   for others?
3. What kinds of information can we gather about the culture of another people
   by observing how they use the sets in their vocabulary?
4. Which paragraphs begin with a topic sentence?
5. Check the etymology, denotation, and connotation of *appurtenances* and
   haggle.

10-G   American Magazines and American Culture

Peter McGrath

This excerpt forms three-quarters of an article that appeared in *New Society* (July 1980).
It begins with the recent rescue from bankruptcy of *Harper's,* a highly respected, 130-
year-old magazine. The writer uses his classification of successful magazines to support
his opinions on the dangers of current American attitudes.

Last year *Harper's* lost more than $1.5 million according to pro-
spective buyers who claim to have seen its books. It had a long-term
subscription liability reported at $4 million, and an unfavourable con-
tract with an advertising sales agency. Its circulation of 300,000 made

it one of the five best-read magazines of its kind. But its kind was the 5
wrong kind, from an advertiser's point of view.

The fact is that general-interest magazines have about as much of
a future in the American market as Socrates would have as a talk-show
host on commercial television. No matter how good the material, the
audience will never be suitable for advertisers. *Harper's* once indulged 10
in demographic testing and found it had an elite readership: good
education, high income, nice homes in Scarsdale and Chevy Chase. But
no one could figure out what these people were interested in consum-
ing, other than ideas. They had money, but were they whisky drinkers
or wine buffs? Sports car drivers or eminently sensible owners of Volvo 15
estate wagons? The *Harper's* readership didn't define itself with anything like enough precision.

Thirty years ago, when magazines were fewer in number, and the
field was dominated by a few fat general-interest publications—the
Saturday Evening Post, Life, Look, and *Collier's,* now all gone, though 20
two have been revived in different form—defining your readers wasn't
so important. Your competition was other general-interest magazines.
But in the past ten years, partly because prime-time television has
priced itself beyond the reach of all but the richest advertisers, the
magazine business has been thriving. Therefore crowded. Therefore 25
competitive.

And the business has changed. If you want to start a magazine today,
you target a particular readership. You appeal to a particular interest,
defining it as narrowly as possible. For instance: it is not narrow enough
to concentrate on women simply, as *Redbook* does; there must be 30
magazines for liberated women *(Ms.),* career women with children
(Working Mother), even fat women—*Big Beautiful Woman,* introduced earlier this year. It's not enough that there are general sports
magazines like Time Incorporated's excellent *Sports Illustrated;* there
must be separate magazines for each separate sport—*Golf Digest* has a 35
million readers, and its chief competitor *Golf* has over 700,000. . . .

Among the magazines with revenues of at least $2.7 million last
year, more than a dozen are devoted to automobiles. There are six more
for motorcyclists alone, and these are subdivided according to the split
between road and trail bikers. A magazine called *Pickup, Van and 4WD* 40
(for four-wheel drive), took in as much money as *Harper's* did—about
$5,150,000—but did so with a circulation 75,000 lower.

How? Because its readership is so easily defined. They want the tiny
refrigerators that fit inside vans, and the compact stereo systems you
can conceal in the wall panels of your truck. They want the plexiglas 45
tops that convert a pickup truck into a camper. With *Pickup, Van and
4WD,* as with *Big Beautiful Woman,* an advertiser knows exactly what
he's getting. . . .

Even literate readers segment themselves in this way. There is now
a boom in science magazines; one of these, *Science 80,* was started by 50

the hyper-scholarly American Association for the Advancement of Science and features ads for high-tech items like a Sony radio with a "memory scan" device that lets you hear exactly 3.5 seconds of each of eight preselected stations before you have to make your choice.

. . . There is no reading public any more; there are only markets. 55 Once upon a time a man would start a magazine because he thought he had some idea worth hearing, or knew of some writers worth reading. Publishing was almost a missionary activity, and the intimate relationship that readers had with magazines testified to this. People knew the exact day of the week or month their magazines came out on— 60 hence names like *Saturday Review*—and would look forward to those dates as one would look forward to the visit of a friend. And as they turned the pages, they would find voices that were personal, even eccentric, but always distinctive and familiar—think of H. L. Mencken at *American Mercury,* or Walter Lippmann at the early *New Republic.* 65

Today's entrepreneur, though, starts a magazine out of no inner compulsion. He simply spots a market that isn't being served. Do affluent, suburbanite professionals in their mid-forties with 2.2 children lack a publication to call their own? For them there will be *Prime.* Are flat dwellers neglected in a country that makes a fetish of home ownership? 70 They will need *Apartment Life,* which has a current circulation of over 830,000. The modern publisher picks his subject according to its advertising possibilities, and gradually the line between advertising and editorial content begins to disappear.

But whose fault is this? Certainly not the advertisers; they're only 75 seizing an opportunity. Not the publishers—you can't demand that a man lose money, though you might applaud him when, like Martin Peretz at the *New Republic,* he does so for the sake of keeping a point of view in circulation.

The market favors single-interest magazines because Americans 80 have become a single-interest people. It's no coincidence that this age of publications like *Pickup, Van and 4WD* is also an age of so-called "single-issue" politics.

Single-issue politics is the politics of the anti-abortion groups, of the gun owners who oppose limits on access to the weapons. For such 85 people there is one standard and one only by which to judge a politician: his stand on the issue they care most about. One slip and he's dead, no matter how much they may like his record in other areas. In 1978, Senator Dick Clark, a liberal Democrat from Iowa, was astonished to find liberal Democrats voting against him simply because he supported 90 federal aid for abortions for the poor; he lost to a lack-lustre candidate he was expected to beat easily. This year the pro-abortion politician is an endangered species.

The problem with single-issue politics is that it distorts the democratic process. In the tug-of-war for politicians' hearts and minds, it 95 gives an advantage to people whose views are narrow. It favors conflict over consensus, rigidity over flexibility. It mocks the man who tries to make of his opinions a coherent whole. At bottom, it is authoritarian.

Single-issue politics is a product of single-interest culture. And this culture, of which today's magazines are so accurate a reflection, is in- 100 dividualism's ultimate achievement, pluralism gone berserk. The American ideology encourages people to pursue their own happiness in their own way, but there's a point beyond which a narrow pursuit of happiness, of one's own personal interests, undermines the system that makes it all possible. As Robert Frost once remarked in an interview, 105 the reason "we've got a good arrangement here" is that "we're minding our own business a certain amount, and we're minding each other's business a certain amount." If Americans don't start minding each other's business a little more, they're going to find no business left to mind.   110

1. What principles of classification does the writer use?
2. What may be his reasons for choosing them?
3. What transitional devices do you find?
4. How well does he support his conclusion? Do you agree with it?
5. Check the etymology, denotation and connotation of each of these words: *elite, buffs, entrepreneur, consensus, berserk.*

10-H   Business Status—How Do You Rate?

Enid Nemy

This article, given here almost complete, appeared in the *New York Times* (August 1980). The writer's tone is half-joking; how accurate do you think her observations are?

You arrive for a business appointment. First you spend twenty minutes in the waiting room, leafing through January's *Reader's Digest* and the April *New Yorkers.* Then the receptionist tells you to go in— the first corridor on the right, the fifth door on the left.

Right then, you should know that you don't rate. According to 5 unofficial office protocol, you're a one or two on a scale of 10. Not quite the bottom of the totem pole—a zero wouldn't have been granted an appointment at all—but next thing to it.

Still, if it's any comfort, you may find that the person with whom you have the appointment isn't a 10 either, or even a six or seven. His 10 rating, or hers, may be just as pathetic as your own.

There are two distinct aspects to business status. The first encompasses the actual office space you occupy, and the second is how you are treated and greeted when you arrive in someone else's office for an appointment.   15

In the matter of office space, it is as well to know that anyone without an office, that is, a physical space with walls, is probably not worth wasting time on. This includes all or most newspaper reporters.

Cubicles also aren't worth much. At most, they're half a step up, but that's only if they have doors. Cubicles without doors are considered about as impressive as Princess telephones.

It is, however, in the genuine private offices that the status game is played seriously. For example, it's a good thing to be on friendly terms with men and women who have suites of rooms on high floors. Executives of this ilk can be very useful. As can the occupants of large corner offices with two walls of windows or, at the very least, with lots of window, or even one big window.

Windows, in fact, apparently are as essential to office prestige as Christmas is to retailing. Even at the United Nations, where legend has it that the building was designed so that there could be no corner offices, the expanse of glass in individual offices is said to be a dead giveaway as to rank. Five windows are excellent, one window not so great.

In addition to a lofty floor number and windows, a carpet is another feature to look for. At a certain corporate level, offices almost always have carpets. If they don't, the assumption is that the occupants don't wish to have them. But they practically all do, so there is rarely need to assume.

As though all this weren't enough, some cities have additional hierarchical clues. There are Washington officeholders who would hang their heads in shame if they didn't have a big flag and a personally inscribed picture of the President. And areas, best unnamed, where an office without a bar and refrigerator is, well, naked.

As for visiting other offices, the signals are equally clear. An important visitor is not kept waiting after his presence is made known. He is met and escorted to the inner office by a private secretary. That is about as well as most people can do, other than the few who rate the big gun himself or herself coming out to the reception area to do the escorting personally. This treatment usually entails a similar kind of farewell—the caller is escorted right out to the elevator by his host.

Assuming that one doesn't rate the biggie greeting, but the scene of the appointment is finally reached, what happens then? It's a bad sign if the person is talking on the telephone and indicates with a casual wave of a hand that you be seated. Better, much better, if the telephone conversation is terminated immediately, and the greeting is done by a figure at least on its feet.

The nuances are endless. For example, once a business meeting has begun, it's a sign of the visitor's importance if there are no interruptions. This generally means that the outside office has been told to hold telephone calls. If calls are accepted, the situation still isn't hopeless so long as the conversation is confined to saying that the call will be returned later.

If you're kept waiting in the reception area, told how to find the right office yourself, are faced with a hand holding a telephone and another hand waving you to a chair and are constantly interrupted by long telephone conversations, be advised: There is nowhere to go but up.

1. The writer has two main classes; how does she arrange the subclasses of each?
2. Check the etymology, denotation, and connotation of *protocol* and *entails.*
3. What is the effect of the writer's occasional use of such colloquialisms as *dead giveaway, big gun,* and *biggie?* What other colloquial words and phrases do you find?

Assignments

1. For an essay of classification you have a wide choice of subject matter. For example, you may write of classes already existing in guns, boats, airplanes, engines, welding processes, ways of preparing food, swimming strokes, trees, crops, cattle, pets, advertising, music, musical instruments, mathematics, curricula. Some of these subjects also lend themselves to more original handling, depending on the principle of classification you adopt and on the attitude you take toward the material. But more likely to demand originality of treatment are subjects such as love, patriotism, weather, television commercials, books, movies, fraternities.
2. You may especially enjoy a personal and original classification of some limited group of people: students, teachers, "dates," pledges, grandparents, salespeople, customers, employers, dog lovers, service-station attendants, taxi drivers, bridge players, pilots, amateur fishermen, news commentators, ballplayers, sports fans, dancers, hitchhikers.
3. Having chosen your subject, decide on a single principle of classification and keep it firmly in mind as you jot down the classes that you will include, making sure that they represent a reasonably complete treatment of the subject. Next, determine the most effective order in which to present these several classes, and then make a brief outline, indicating not only the classes and their order, but, with subpoints, the kind of information that you will include under each. (Remember that the information should be approximately the same and presented in approximately the same order for each class.)

PHOTOGRAPHS FOR UNIT 10

How good an observer are you? Test yourself by answering the questions on the next page. Be honest with yourself and do not turn back to look at the photographs until you have finished the test. If you can answer six questions correctly you are a good observer.

Photograph A   Teresa Sabala/NYT Pictures (Census Bureau-computer disk file)

Photograph B   Edward Hausner/NYT Pictures

QUESTIONS ON THE PHOTOGRAPHS FOR UNIT 10

Photograph A
1. What is the man wearing?
2. Can we see both of his hands or only one?
3. How many rows of disks are on each side of the aisle?
4. How many empty places show where discs have been removed?

Photograph B
1. What bird is near the ceiling in the corner of the room?
2. How many pictures of Mickey and/or Minnie Mouse can be seen?
3. How many Coca Cola signs can be seen?
4. In what position are the left arm and leg of the man seated near the center of the picture?
5. What time does the clock say?
6. Where is the telephone?

Writing assignments based on the photographs for Unit 10
1. Assume that these photographs are to be published in your college newspaper and compose a title and a statement of about 50 words for each to attract the readers' attention.
2. Assume that these photographs are to be published together as a contrast in ways to organize things. Compose an essay of about 250 words in which you discuss the methods of classification suggested by the two pictures.

UNIT 11

Analysis

What did you put in this soup? How is the city government organized? What are the structural patterns of Rembrandt's painting, *The Night Watch?* What are the departments in this engineering company? What chemicals are in aspirin? What are the parts of a sonata? What materials are in this sweater?

The soup eater, the city resident, the art student, the business employee, the medical student, the music lover, the clothing shopper, have different questions, but they are all asking for an analysis. They share the need to know in detail the parts, whether tangible or intangible, that make up a whole so that they can understand and use both the whole and its parts intelligently. There are several methods to apply, singly or in combination, to analyze anything.

1. Division. The simplest kind of analysis is a form of division—we split a subject in the way we section an apple, to make it yield comparable parts. The results are not like those of classification (Unit 10), however, because they come from breaking down a single thing rather than a group. Apples in the mass may be classified—into sizes, colors, varieties; but one apple will be divided into halves or quarters. We use division when we think of a year as twelve months or of a day as morning, afternoon, and evening. We use it when we think of the world as composed of continents, or of a nation as composed of states.

2. Dissection. The process that we shall for convenience call dissection operates on a deeper level of analysis than division. Dissection yields not similar sections of the apple but its different components: skin, flesh, core, stem. Some subjects lend themselves to either kind of breakdown. We divided the day into comparable time periods, but we can dissect it into logical rather than chronological components: classes, outside activities, recreation (see pages 7–8). Many subjects that can be analyzed by dissection would not lend themselves to division. A pencil could be

181

dissected into graphite, wood, and paint, or divided into inch-long pieces; but although you can easily dissect a radio, you cannot divide it.

The analytical process, however, goes far beyond apples and radios. You may use it, of course, in the relatively simple matter of explaining the parts composing a given mechanism (it will then be similar to the simple informative type of description discussed in Unit 2), but you may also use it in the far more difficult task of discovering the issues in a complex problem. You may be interested in listing the components of a diesel engine or in setting forth what you believe to be the elements of Homer's greatness as an epic poet. In either task, the process of analysis by dissection is essentially the same.

3. Enumeration. How often in serious discussions do we find expressions like these: "Three questions remain to be considered"; "Five courses of action are possible"; "Two reasons for his success emerge"; "Several misconceptions must be corrected."

When we analyze by division or dissection we determine the number of parts or phases of our subject and examine them one by one. How many there are will be determined largely by the subject and our purpose, but there are limits. We can never divide it in less than two, since by definition analysis implies a breaking down, and we are not likely to need more than five or six, since a larger number becomes unwieldy. Reasonable completeness, in analysis as in classification, (page 161, item 6), will suffice.

Here, too, it is of prime importance to choose a principle to guide you through the breakdown of your subject so that your result will be neatly ordered pieces making up a logical whole. Whether they are parts of a simple mechanism or abstract qualities making up a reputation, they must be comparable. The tone is not an item in enumerating the parts of a radio, although it is the result of the parts; nor is the title "General" one of the qualities of Washington's character that you may list as contributing to his greatness. Recognize elements that are logically similar and omit the unrelated.

The order of the parts you finally choose as suitable will be determined, of course, by the usual patterns of arrangement for emphasis (see pages 8–9). Because the parts are comparable, you may often find that numbers make the best transitions: "1," "2," "3," or "first," "second," "third," and so on (the forms "firstly," "secondly," "thirdly" are no longer popular). Other transitions like "next" and "another" may also serve to emphasize your arrangement.

4. Focusing on a problem. Your analysis need not stop with an enumeration of parts. You can apply it as a logical process in problem solving. To find a solution, you must discover the exact nature of the problem; to discover its nature, you must break it down into its component parts. Whether you are hunting for an error in your bank balance, choosing a career, or settling one of the world's major ills, the general procedure will be the same.

You may make a preliminary analysis in order to eliminate any aspects of the subject that are irrelevant to your view of the problem, just as when, asked to determine the chemical composition of an unknown substance, you rule out rapidly the more unlikely possibilities. Martin Luther King described doing this in *Stride Toward Freedom.* Having found three ways in which oppressed people might react to oppression—by acquiescence, violence, and nonviolent resistance—he ruled out the first two as unsuitable and concentrated on the third. You may analyze the psychological pressure on the average student, for instance, into the academic, economic, and social aspects, and decide to eliminate the first two from your discussion in order to devote yourself to the third, the one over which the student has most control. You will then proceed to break down the chosen part of the problem into its subordinate parts (dormitory life, dating, extracurricular activities, etc.), and on the basis of these parts, clearly stated, you will work through to a logical solution of the problem.

Although such an analysis is often applied to problem solving, it does not necessarily include a solution. It may imply an answer, or it may merely lay bare the issues for the reader's consideration; clarification is the central purpose of the analytical process.

5. Stating the essentials. To help your readers understand the parts of an analysis and see how they fit together, you may begin by summing up instead of breaking down—by setting forth the essence, the root principle, the key to the whole subject. This procedure may not seem to be "analysis" at all, in the sense in which we have been using the word; but in a wider sense it is one of the most valuable parts of this logical process. Analysis may mean not only dissection, a breakdown into parts, but also a reduction to a simpler form—to the bare essentials. Such a reduction is likely to precede the normal taking-apart process (especially in the handling of abstract and complex subjects) to give the dissection clarity and purpose.

A writer might, for example, begin an analysis of the depression of the thirties by reducing that complex economic phenomenon to a basic description, such as starvation in the midst of plenty, before breaking it down into its causes, results, manifestations, or whatever other aspects interest the writer. The essentials will serve as a unifying guide among the aspects. One writer reduces the greatness of Lincoln to the fact that he was able to make such a reduction out of the confusion of his time:

> The greatness of Lincoln consisted precisely in the fact that he reduced the violence and confusion of his time to the essential moral issue and held it there against the cynical and worldly wisdom of the merchants of New England and the brokers of New York and all the rest who argued for expedient self-interest and a realistic view. (Archibald MacLeish, *A Time to Act*)

Examples

Analysis has a major role in the selections in this unit. It is also a contributing factor in almost all the other selections in the book, most notably in Mencken's *"Le Contrat Social"* (4-B), Thomas's "On Societies as Organisms" (5-B), Jackson's "Challenge" (5-D), Bronowski's "A Metaphor Used Twice" (5-E), *New Society's* "Social Control" (9-F), Hall's "The Pervasive Set" (10-F), H. Gardner's "Are Television's Effects Due to Television?" (12-E), Gould's "Left Holding the Bat" (12-F), and all the selections in Units 12, 13, 14, 15, and 16.

11-A   The Structure of a Comet

C. C. Wylie

This example of objective description, analyzing a comet, is taken from *Astronomy, Maps and Weather* (1942), a book intended for the general reader.

The head of a comet is a hazy, faintly shining ball. This head, or *coma,* is the essential part of the comet and gives it its name. Inside the coma there is usually, but not always, a *nucleus.* The nucleus is formed as the comet approaches the Sun and is seen as a starlike point near the center of the coma. Naked-eye comets always, and telescopic comets often, form a *tail* as they approach the Sun. The tail is formed by matter streaming off in a direction opposite to the Sun. Usually the tail attains its maximum length and brightness a little after the comet passes perihelion.

In volume, comets are the bulkiest members of the solar system. The head, or coma, is rarely smaller than the Earth in diameter, and for one or two comets the diameter of the head has surpassed that of the Sun. The length of the tail of a spectacular comet may be as much as one hundred million miles, or about the same as the distance of the Earth from the Sun.

The mass of any comet is exceedingly small—so little that it cannot be measured directly. Calculations from the amount of light reflected indicate that the mass of Halley's Comet, one of the most spectacular, was a little less than that of the rock and dirt removed in excavating the Panama Canal. From its mass and volume the density of the head of Halley's Comet was estimated as being equivalent to twelve small marbles per cubic mile. It is believed that the head of a comet is composed of dust and small particles surrounded by gas. The density of the tail of a comet is almost inconceivably small. For Halley's Comet the density has been calculated as equivalent to one cubic centimeter of air at sea level pressure expanded to two thousand cubic miles.

1. What principle of organization has the writer used?
2. Can you think of a different method of organization that would make the material as clear?
3. What similarities and differences do you find in purpose, organization, and general style between this example and Unit 2-D, Unit 4-F, and Unit 9-A?
4. Check the etymology and denotation of *perihelion*.
5. Where and how does Wylie use figures of speech to make his description clear?

11-B   Male Humor

Isaac Asimov

Why do conversations among men so often become exchanges of dirty jokes? Why don't women's conversations do the same? This essay, here complete, and two letters commenting on it, appeared in the *New York Times* in 1983.

ANALYSIS
General
introduction
Main topic

Most of us, if we are male, have gathered in groups that happened to be exclusively masculine. On those occasions, at least according to my experience, it is extremely common to have conversation turn to an exchange of off-color jokes. Such is the glee with which such jokes are told, 5 and such the delight with which they are received, that one of the most serious objections to admitting women to the gatherings is that the presence of the female of the species would inhibit these exchanges and destroy much of the joy of the occasion.   10

Analytic
questions

But think about it. Why should jokes of this sort be told at all? Why should they be considered funny and why *are* they (when told well) unfailingly funny at that? Why do even the most respectable and well-mannered men tell them and listen to others tell them? We might almost 15 paraphrase Shakespeare and say, "One touch of smut makes the whole male world kin."

Two specific
areas

But is it really a mystery? Sex and elimination—the two basic staples of such jokes—are unmentionable in polite society (in theory) and yet are always with us. They are 20 simply unavoidable, though the rules of the etiquette books tell us they don't exist.

What a horror is introduced into life by refusing to mention what we cannot escape. What a torture of roundabouts we are plunged into as a result.   25

Example #1
of area #1

Have you ever watched television commercials push laxatives and talk about the dread disease of "irregularity"? Irregularity of what? In fact, even irregularity has become suspect, and no abnormal condition at all is mentioned by name. It has all sunk into a tight-lipped look 30 of gentle concern. The tight lips give it away, I think.

Example #2
of area #1
Example #3
of area #1

When you dash for the washroom, is it a wild desire to wash your hands that fills you? Is it for a nice rest that you go to the rest room, for a chance to lounge about that you retreat to the lounge, a last-minute adjustment to the 35 top hat that makes it necessary to retire to the little room austerely marked "Gentlemen"? No civilized man from Mars could possibly guess the function of such rooms from the names we give them.

Example #1
of area #2

And is there a married couple (or an unmarried one, 40 for that matter) that doesn't invent some coy and innocuous phrase to serve as a signal that indicates a desire for sex? What's yours? A meaningful clearing of the throat?

Dissection of
examples

What relief it is, then—what sheer release of tension —to tell some story that involves the open admission that 45 such things exist. Add that release of tension to the natural humor such a joke might contain and the laugh can be explosive. It might even be argued that, given the distortions introduced by our social hypocrisy, the dirty joke is an important contributor to the mental health of males. 50

Dissection of
women's
reactions

But don't women suffer from the same social hypocrisy as men do? Aren't women repressed even more than men, since women are supposed to be "ladylike" and "pure"? Of course! And it is my experience that women laugh as hard at dirty jokes as men do, and show even 55 greater tolerance for those that are not really very funny, but *are* very dirty.

Dissection of
men's
reactions

Why, then, do men persist in believing that the presence of women will spoil their fun? Partly, I suppose, it is because they are victims of the myth of feminine purity, 60 but partly it is because one of the important components of the dirty joke is unabashed male chauvinism. Women are almost always the butts and victims of such jokes, and, indeed, a male chauvinist joke can be extremely successful even when there is no hint of any element of either sex or 65 scatology.

Dissection of
men's
reactions
Example #1

Again, it's no mystery. Men are tyrannized by women from birth (or feel themselves to be—which comes to the same thing, of course). The young boy is hounded unmercifully and continually by his mother, who is perpetually 70 at him to do what he does not want to do, and to *not* do what he *does* want to do. (The father is inevitably a more distant creature and, unless he is a monster, is more easily handled.)

Example #2　　The young man in love is constantly tantalized by the　75
young woman he desires, and the young groom is harried
to fulfill his campaign promises to his young bride. And,
eventually, as married life settles down, the husband is
hounded unmercifully and continually by his wife, who is
perpetually at him to do what he does not want to do; and　80
to *not* do what he *does* want to do. (At least, this is how
it seems to him to be.)

Results:
problem
given at
start

　　Naturally, then, the male gathering is the one place (it
seems to the man) where he can escape from this unend-
ing, lifelong feminine domination, and where he can retal-　85
iate, in safety, by telling jokes in which women get what
they deserve.

　　You might argue that there's no harm in it. When all
the jokes are done, he goes back home, having undergone
a useful catharsis, and says his "Yes, dear" with far greater　90
efficiency than he would have otherwise. Here again, such
jokes may be essential to male mental health.

　　Do I approve?

Suggestions
for
solution

　　No. I don't like male chauvinism—but let's not repress
the jokes that serve a useful psychological purpose. I　95
would, instead, prefer to invite women into the charmed
circle and have them tell their jokes, too, which perhaps
will help remove some of *their* hang-ups.

Opposition
to
solution

　　The trouble is that they leave the jokes to the men.
Women by the hundreds have said to me, after having　100
laughed fiendishly at some joke I have told: "Oh, I wish I
could repeat it, but I never seem to be able to remember
jokes, and when I do, I can't tell them."

　　Haven't we all heard that line?

　　Well, *why* can't women remember jokes? Have they　105
poor memories?

　　Nonsense! They remember the price of every garment they have ever bought, and the exact place they
have bought it. They know where everything in the
kitchen is, including the mustard jar that any husband will　110
swear, after a thorough search, is nowhere in the house.

Dissection
Further
conclusion

　　They're just defaulting on their responsibilities, and,
as long as they do, they encourage us men to put our heads
together and tell our chauvinist jokes after a nervous
glance hither and thither assures us that no woman can　115
hear us.

1. Asimov claims that men enjoy off-color jokes that make fun of women because they are reacting against a "lifelong female domination." Do you agree
or disagree with this controversial opinion?

2. Do you agree or disagree with Asimov's claim that women are "defaulting on their responsibilities" by not joining men in telling off-color jokes?
3. Where does Asimov use rhetorical devices such as questions and repetition to emphasize his ideas?
4. Read the two letters replying to Asimov that follow and then reread his essay. Does he leave himself open to their criticisms?
5. Check the etymology, denotation, and connotation of *scatology, tantalize,* and *catharsis.* Who was Tantalus?

This letter by Richard A. Gardner, a professor of child psychiatry at the College of Physicians and Surgeons of Columbia University, was published as a reply to Asimov. Notice the writer's use of dissection to reach his conclusions.

Isaac Asimov's article certainly provides some plausible explanations regarding why men engage in joke-telling more than women and remember jokes more frequently. However, he makes no mention of two additional factors that I consider central to the phenomenon.

The first factor relates to our "courting" patterns. Recent changes 5 notwithstanding, the male is still very much the pursuer and the female the passive one in the "mating game." In their attempts to "win" women, men use a wide variety of techniques. One of these is entertaining the woman, and such entertainment involves making her laugh. The social pattern, then, is one in which the man's role is to tell the jokes 10 and the woman's role is to laugh at them.

The other factor not mentioned by Isaac Asimov is competition. When men get together to swap jokes, they generally compete to be considered the best joke-teller or the one with the largest repertory.

The man with a large repertory of good jokes, then, is at an advan- 15 tage in his pursuit of women and in his competition with other men. I believe that these social factors, rather than some biologically based difference, cause men to collect more jokes than women and to remember them more efficiently.

This letter by Clare D. McGorrian was also published as a reply to Asimov:

Isaac Asimov concludes by accusing women of "defaulting" on their responsibility to remember jokes and thereby encouraging the male-chauvinist joke session. He has trivialized the issue to be that of men needing a "useful psychological" outlet. In so doing, Mr. Asimov overlooks the other functions that such gatherings serve, that of build- 5 ing and maintaining an "old-boy" network which denies women access to the power structure in this country and worldwide. Mr. Asimov states that he would prefer to admit women into the "charmed circle" to tell their jokes and thereby rid themselves of "hang-ups." Has Mr. Asimov considered that women do not derive pleasure from telling such jokes 10 because to us male domination is a reality and not merely a perceived wrong or a neurotic Oedipal obsession?

1. If the people quoted in "When Is a Joke Not a Joke" (4-C) were to read Asimov's essay, what would their reactions probably be?
2. What would their reactions probably be to the two letters replying to Asimov?

11-C   Brains and Computers

Robert Jastrow

This essay forms a complete chapter in *The Enchanted Loom* (1981), the third volume in a trilogy with *Red Giants and White Dwarfs* and *Until the Sun Dies.* This volume, Dr. Jastrow says, "focuses on intelligence and the brain: how the brain evolved, the way it works, how it balances instinct and reason, what it is evolving into."

Circuits, wires and computing are strange terms to use for a biological organ like the brain, made largely of water, and without electronic parts. Nonetheless, they are accurate terms because brains work in very much the same way as computers. Brains think; computers add and subtract; but both devices seem to work on the basis of the same funda- 5 mental steps in logical reasoning.

All arithmetic and mathematics can be broken down into these fundamental steps. Most kinds of thinking can also be broken down into such steps. Only the highest realms of creative activity seem to defy this analysis, but it is possible that even creative thinking could be broken 10 down in this way, if the subconscious mind could be penetrated to examine the processes that appear at the conscious level as the flash of insight, or the stroke of genius.

The basic logical steps that underlie all mathematics and all reasoning are surprisingly simple. The most important ones are called AND 15 and OR. AND is a code name for the reasoning that says, "If 'a' is true *and* 'b' is true, then 'c' is true." OR is a code name for the reasoning that says, "If 'a' is true or 'b' is true, then 'c' is true." These lines of reasoning are converted into electrical circuits by means of devices called "gates." In a computer the gates are made out of electronic parts 20 —diodes or transistors. In the brain of an animal or a human, the gates are neurons or nerve cells. A gate—in a computer or in a brain—is an electrical pathway that opens up and allows electricity to pass through when certain conditions are satisfied. Normally, two wires go into one side of the gate, and another wire emerges from the other side of the 25 gate. The two wires coming into the gate on one side represent the two ideas "a" *and* "b". The wire going out the other side of the gate represents the conclusion "c" based on these ideas. When a gate is wired up to be an AND gate, it works in such a way that if electrical signals flow into it from both the "a" *and* the "b" wires, an electrical signal then 30 flows out the other side through the "c" wire. From an electrical point of view, this is the same as saying, "If 'a' *and* 'b' are true, then 'c' is true."

When the gate is wired as an OR gate, on the other hand, it permits electricity to pass through the outgoing, or "c", wire if an electrical signal comes into the other side through either the "a" wire *or* the "b" 35 wire. Electrically, this is the same as saying, "If 'a' *or* 'b' is true, then 'c' is true."

How do these two kinds of gates do arithmetic? How do they carry on a line of reasoning? Suppose a computer is about to add "1" and "1" to make "2"; this means that inside the computer a gate has two wires 40 coming into it on one side, representing "1" and "1", and a wire coming out on the other side, representing "2". If the gate is wired as an AND gate, then, when electrical signals come into it through both of the "1" wires, it sends a signal out the other side through the "2" wire. This gate has added "1" and "1" electrically to make "2".   45

Slightly different kinds of gates, but based on the same idea, can subtract, multiply and divide. Thousands of such gates, wired together in different combinations, can do income tax returns, algebra problems and higher mathematics. They can also be connected together to do the kinds of thinking and reasoning that enter into everyday life. Suppose, 50 for example, that a company distributes several different lines of goods, and its management assigns a computer the task of keeping a continuous check on the inventories in these various product lines. Inside that computer, certain gates will be wired as AND gates to work in the following way: two wires coming into one side of the gate carry signals 55 that indicate "stock depleted" and "sales volume heavy." If the stock is depleted *and* the sales are brisk, the gate opens, and a decision comes through: Order more goods!

OR gates are just as important in reasoning. Suppose that the same company also relies on its computer for guidance in setting prices. That 60 means that a certain gate inside the computer is wired as an OR gate; coming into one side of this gate is a wire that indicates cash flow, another wire that indicates prices charged by a competitor for similar products, and a third wire that indicates the inventory in this particular product. If the company needs cash, *or* it is being undersold by its 65 competitors, *or* it has an excess inventory, then the decision gate opens and a command comes through: Cut prices!

In a simple computer, the gates are wired together permanently, so that the computer can only do the same tasks over and over again. This kind of computer comes into the world wired to do one set of 70 things, and can never depart from its fixed repertoire. A computer that solves the same problems in the same way, over and over again, is like a frog that can only snap at dark, moving spots; if either kind of brain is presented with a novel situation, it will react stupidly, or not react at all, because it lacks the wiring necessary for a new response to a new 75 challenge. Such brains are unintelligent.

Larger, more complex computers have greater flexibility. In these computers, the connections between the gates can be changed, and they can be wired up to do different kinds of things at different times; their repertoire is variable. The instructions for connecting the gates to 80 do each particular kind of problem are stored in the computer's memory banks. These instructions are called the computer's "program." When a computer expert wants his machine to stop one kind of task and start another, he inserts a new program into the computer's memory. The new program automatically erases the old one, takes command of 85 the machine, and sets about doing its appointed task.

However, this computer is still not intelligent; it has no innate flexibility. The flexibility and intelligence reside in its programmer. But if the memory banks of the computer are extremely large a great advance in computer design becomes possible; that marks a highlight 90 in the evolution of computers comparable to the first appearance of the mammals on the earth. A computer with a very large memory can store a set of instructions lengthy enough to permit it to learn by experience, just like an intelligent animal. Learning by experience requires a large memory and a very long set of instructions, i.e., a complicated program, 95 because it is a much more elaborate way of solving problems than a stereotyped response would be. When a brain—electronic or animal— learns by experience, it goes through the following steps: first, it tries an approach; then it compares its result with the desired result, i.e., the goal; then, if it succeeds in achieving its goal, it sends an instruction to 100 its memory to use the same approach next time; in the case of failure, it searches through its reasoning or computations to pinpoint the main source of error; finally, the brain adjusts the faulty part of its program to bring the result into line with its desires. Every time the same problem arises, the brain repeats the sequence and makes new adjustments 105 to its program. A large computer has programs that work in just that fashion. Like a brain, it modifies its reasoning as its experience develops. In this way, the computer gradually improves its performance. It is learning.

A brain that can learn possesses the beginnings of intelligence. The 110 requirements for this invaluable trait are, first, a good-sized memory, and, second, a wiring inside the brain that permits the circuits connecting the gates to be changed by the experience of life. In fact, in the best brains—judging brain quality entirely by intelligence—many circuits are unwired initially; that is, the animal is born with a large number of 115 the gates in its brain more or less unconnected with one another. The gates become connected gradually, as the animal learns the best strategies for its survival. In man, the part of the brain filled with blank circuits at birth is greater than in any other animal; that is what is meant by the plasticity of human behavior.   120

Large computers have some essential attributes of an intelligent brain: they have large memories, and they have gates whose connections can be modified by experience. However, the thinking of these computers tends to be narrow. The richness of human thought depends

to a considerable degree on the enormous number of wires, or nerve 125
fibers coming into each gate in the human brain. A gate in a computer
has two, or three, or at most four wires entering on one side, and one
wire coming out the other side. In the brain of an animal, the gates may
have thousands of wires entering one side, instead of two or three. In
the human brain, a gate may have as many as 100,000 wires entering 130
it. Each wire comes from another gate or nerve cell. This means that
every gate in the human brain is connected to as many as 100,000 other
gates in other parts of the brain. During the process of thinking innumerable gates open and close throughout the brain. When one of these
gates "decides" to open, the decision is the result of a complicated 135
assessment involving inputs from thousands of other gates. This circumstance explains much of the difference between human thinking and
computer thinking.

Furthermore, the gates in the brains of an animal or a human do
not work on an "all-or-nothing" basis. The AND gate in a computer, for 140
example, will open only if *all* the wires coming into it carry electrical
signals. If one wire entering a computer gate fails to carry a signal, the
gate remains shut. If every one of the 100,000 pathways into a gate in
a human brain had to transmit an electrical signal before that gate could
open, the brain would be paralyzed. Instead, most gates in the brain 145
work on the principle of ALMOST, rather than AND or OR. The AL-
MOST gate makes human thought so imprecise, but so powerful. Suppose that 50,000 wires enter one side of a gate in a human brain; if this
were an AND gate in a computer, all 50,000 things would have to be
true simultaneously before that gate opened and let a signal through. 150
In real life, 50,000 things are rarely true at the same time, and any brain
that waited for such a high degree of assurance before it acted would
be an exceedingly slow brain. It would hardly ever reach a decision, and
the possessor of a brain like that would not be likely to pass its genes
on to the next generation.   155

Real brains work very differently. Wired largely out of ALMOST
gates, they only require that, say, 10,000 or 15,000 things out of 50,000
shall be true about a situation before they act, or perhaps an even
smaller number than that. As a consequence, they are inaccurate; they
make mistakes sometimes; but they are very fast. In the struggle for 160
survival, the value to the individual of the speed of such a brain more
than offsets the disadvantages in its imprecision.

1. According to Jastrow, what basic steps underlie all reasoning?
2. How does Jastrow fit together the many comparisons and contrasts that he
   uses?
3. What specific examples does Jastrow give to explain his main point?
4. What does he mean by the "plasticity of human behavior"?
5. Check the etymology, denotation, and connotation of *depleted, repertoire,*
   and *plasticity.*

11-D   And If We Hanged the Wrong Man?

Maryon Tysoe

This essay, here almost complete, first appeared in *New Society* in 1983. The cases on which it is based are all British, but the problem is universal.

James Hanratty, "hanged by the neck until dead" for the A6 [Highway] murder in 1963. George Ince, tried for the Barn restaurant murder in 1973. Laszlo Virag, convicted as a gun-toting parking-meter thief in 1969. George Davis, convicted for armed robbery in 1975. Peter Hain, tried for bank robbery in 1976. The link? In each case, the main 5 evidence against them was the testimony of eyewitnesses; each of them was later found (or, in the case of Hanratty, strongly suspected) to be innocent.

People, including murder trial juries, tend to find it hard to believe that eyewitnesses can be so wrong. We're inclined to think that our 10 perceptions and memory work like a movie camera—you record what you see and file it away. But perception and memory are both flexible and selective, and we can only register a small part of what we see.

Elizabeth Loftus, a psychologist from the University of Washington and a leading expert on eyewitness testimony, wrote recently (with 15 colleague Katherine Ketcham): "People in general, and jurors in particular, are so ready to believe eyewitness testimony because for the most part our memories serve us reasonably well. But precise memory is rarely demanded of us. When a friend describes a vacation, we don't ask, 'Are you sure your hotel room had two chairs, not three?' Or, after 20 a movie, 'Are you sure Warren Beatty's hair was wavy, or was it curly?' But precise memory suddenly becomes crucial in the event of a crime. . . . To be mistaken about details is not the result of a bad memory, but of the normal functioning of human memory." We don't play back a "memory tape." Rather, we reconstruct what we did take in in a way 25 that makes sense.

Unfortunately, witnessing a crime is precisely the sort of situation where distortions of perception and memory can easily occur. The incident will probably be over quickly; it may be dark; the witness may not realise a crime is being committed and therefore won't be paying 30 full attention. The witness may be shortsighted, or drunk.

It also makes a great deal of difference if the incident is violent— as in the case of murder. Clive Hollin, a psychologist at Leicester University, says, "It is a stable finding that memory of a violent event is not as good as that of a non-violent event." In one experiment that he did 35 with Brian Clifford of North East London Polytechnic, they showed students a film either of a man assaulting a woman and robbing her of her handbag, or asking her for directions. The man was sometimes alone, and sometimes with companions. Then they showed the partici-

pants various mugshots. They found that recognition of the principal 40
man was very poor regardless of the violence of the film: overall, only
27 percent of witnesses picked the right man. All the same, the people
who had watched the non-violent films described him significantly
more accurately than did those who had seen the violent ones.

Why is this? Hollin says, "I think it's because emotional arousal 45
interferes with memory." Watching violence churns us up a bit. Indeed,
if there's a weapon involved, Loftus has suggested that we can become
transfixed by that and fail to notice much about the person who's carrying it.

Even assuming you have adequately perceived what was happening 50
at the time, there *is* the problem of remembering it. Loftus has shown, in
many experiments, that if we hear any misleading information between
witnessing the crime and having to recall it, this can become added on to
—or even alter—our memory. In one study, three of her students acted
out a mock crime in train stations, bus depots and shopping centres. Two 55
women would leave a large bag on a bench and go off to study a
timetable. Then a male student "lurked over," pretended to pull something out of the bag, stuffed "it" under his coat and walked off. The
women returned and began to lament that a tape recorder was missing.
They then asked the genuine eyewitnesses for their telephone numbers, 60
in case they were needed "for insurance purposes." A week later, an
"insurance agent" rang up, asked what details they could remember,
and inquired, "Did you see the tape recorder?" Lotus says, "Although
there was in fact no tape recorder, over half of the eyewitnesses 'remembered' seeing it, and nearly all of these could describe it in reasonably 65
good detail." Sometimes it was grey, sometimes black; sometimes it had
an antenna, sometimes it didn't.

What is happening here, according to Loftus, is that the original
memory is becoming blended with the later information to form a new
"memory." And this can happen with memory for faces as well as 70
events. For example, Loftus has shown that if witnesses heard another
witness refer to a misleading feature (like a moustache), over one third
of the first witnesses included that detail in their own description—and
they used the exact wording that the other witness had used.

Remembering faces is, of course, often a crucial part of eyewitness 75
testimony. In murder trials, if the accused were on trial for their life,
it could hardly be more vital that it was correct. In one experiment,
witnesses were asked to identify from a line-up a "criminal" they had
seen about six days before. But they were also asked to look at some
mugshots four days before attending the line-up. And 29 per cent of 80
them then identified an "innocent" person they had seen among the
mugshots. Other experiments have shown that *bystanders* to a crime
are quite likely to be picked out.

What is happening is that the participants can remember having seen the person before—but not where or when, and they mistakenly link the person with the crime. A real-life example of this "unconscious transference" was the case where a railway ticket agent selected a sailor at an identification parade, claiming that he was the armed robber who had held him up. Fortunately for the sailor, he had an unbreakable alibi. It turned out that the ticket agent had seen the sailor three times before —buying tickets from him.

Apart from this kind of mix-up, identification parades are fraught with other perils. One psychologist, Helen Dent, while researching identification parades at Nottingham University, found that people were more likely to pick the "criminal" they had seen in a filmed incident if they viewed colour slides—or looked at a parade through a one-way screen—than if they were present at a live parade (although they were just as likely to pick the wrong person). She says, "I found that witnesses find it difficult to look at people in the live parade. They are embarrassed, fearful, they have problems with social things like staring, and there's the stress of going up and down the line." Screens and slides seem less anxiety-making.

Sometimes, events conspire to make the suspect—even if innocent —likely to be picked out by more than one person. Hadyn Ellis has pointed out that the stand-ins may unwittingly stand further from the suspect than from each other. They may inadvertently cast sidelong glances at him or her. The suspect may look the most nervous; may appear the most disreputable because of the time spent in custody; and may (poor creature) look like a stereotypical murderer or rapist. And according to a review of studies of parade bias by an American psychologist, Robert Buckhout, the stand-ins are not always chosen very successfully. The result is that the suspect sticks out like a sore thumb. (This seems to have played a part in the Hanratty case twenty years ago.) Witnesses may also feel under pressure to make a choice and then they will simply choose the "best resemblance."

Eyewitness testimony clearly plays an important part in the legal process, all the way from the time of the crime itself to the courtroom (if the case gets that far). Fears about the unreliability of such testimony led to the Devlin report on identification evidence in 1976. But most of its suggestions for ways of minimising the problem have been ignored or watered down. Even though judges are now supposed to draw juries' attention to the quality and nature of the identification evidence, juries still seem to place greater weight on it than may be warranted (as in the case of Christopher Scales, reported in *New Society*, 24 February 1983). Experiments on mock jurors show that they are likely to be misled by a witness's confidence, whereas in fact confidence is *not* always related to accuracy.

Saying that eyewitness testimony may quite often (though *not* in-variably) be unreliable does not, of course, seem terribly helpful. The judicial process could hardly operate without it. But the system for 130 helping witnesses's recall *could* be more sensitive. The research in this area does have some positive implications, for example, the need, to avoid the dangers of leading questions (which can occur when inter-rogators let their own theories about events colour the questions they ask). Better understanding of how we remember faces may lead to a 135 better (though not perfect) composite system than photofit. Identity parades could be viewed through one-way screens (though this would entail a change in current regulations) and composed more carefully. More precise guidelines for juries could be developed.

Finally, psychologists may have some new techniques to offer that 140 might help witnesses to remember more accurately. Graham Davies and his colleague, Alan Milne, have arranged for people to witness an unexpected intruder in a room where they were completing a test. They found that taking the witnesses "back" mentally, helping them to recall the original incident step-by-step (the details of their arrival, how 145 they were feeling, and so on) improved the quality of the facial compos-ites they constructed of the intruder. Having them recall the incident in the actual room where it took place also helped, but not as much as the "memory guidance."

Debra Bekerian and John Bowers of the MRC Applied Psychology 150 Unit, Cambridge, have also found that reconstructing the original inci-dent can help "restore" the original memory, even when the person has been exposed to misleading information that should, according to Lof-tus, actually *alter* the memory. It looks as though Freud may be partly right—perhaps some memories do resemble, as he said, great fishes 155 resting on the bottom of a very deep pond—and there may be tech-niques we can use to winch them out. This may not, Loftus says, be true for many memories—which *may* really be changed.

Memory can be a fragile entity. But perhaps, as Graham Davies says, "I'm sure we can get much closer to exploiting the limits of human 160 memory than we are doing at the moment."

Should the accused in a criminal trial become the subject of a life-or-death experiment in the limits of human memory? This is one thing we'd risk by a return to capital punishment.

1. Tysoe describes six common causes of inaccurate eyewitness testimony—what are they?
2. Where does Tysoe use examples? direct quotations? indirect quotations?
3. Tysoe concludes with a question. On the basis of her essay, what do you think her answer probably is? What is your own answer?
4. Check the etymology, denotation, and connotation of *stable* (as used here in "stable finding"), *transfixed, crucial, fraught.*

11-E   Two Imperatives in Conflict

Richard Shoglow (student)

There is some evidence in the world that the phenomenon called the "territorial imperative," or something very like it, exists, and this can lead to pessimistic conclusions about the future of the human race. Ardrey, in his essay called "Of Men and Mockingbirds," points out some evidence to support the idea of "territoriality." For instance, he reports 5 on twenty-four different primitive tribes in various separate areas around the world. Although they were unable to learn from each other, they all formed similar social bands occupying specific permanent territories. This showed the unlearned, perhaps genetic, need of human beings for their own territory.   10

A second example of these territorial instincts is, I think, in the Middle East today. The situation there is a struggle for possession of an area. Both the Israelis and the Palestinians are in battle over this territory—one to keep it and the other to obtain it. Both regard this land as necessary for their existence and as belonging to them.   15

Among my neighbors and even in my own family, I have seen further evidence of a territorial imperative. My father, for instance, was very worried when a neighbor decided to build a boathouse near the property boundary of our house. Although we had plenty of land to spare, my father was worried about losing a little part of it. I have seen 20 arguments between neighbors about trees that cross property boundaries and even disputes over whether a boundary marker had been moved a foot or so. If this phenomenon is instinctive, innate, it is therefore inevitable that people must clash for living space. The increasing pressure of a growing population and a severely limited world space 25 may lead to a catastrophic battle, such as a nuclear war, that could mean the end of the world.

But while the potential for disaster may exist in our territorial imperative, there is some evidence that a "social imperative" may also exist. This "social imperative" is our ability to share and to cooperate 30 with our fellow human beings. If this exists, then there is hope for our future. Maybe many of our problems will be solved eventually. Ardrey's article mentions that there are some animals, such as the elephant, the antelope, and the gorilla, who have no territorial bond. These animals wander constantly, moving where food can be found. They have no 35 wars. There is no competition over a particular territory. They move together, sharing the space and the food. The Middle East dispute is in an uneasy equilibrium as both sides, with the help of negotiators, search for a compromise solution that can bring peace. If their "territorial imperative" gets the better of either of them, a terrible conflict may erupt, but 40 as long as both sides are willing to cooperate, they can avoid war. If

traditional enemies can really join and share for the betterment of
mankind, perhaps there can be a more optimistic view of man's future.

We are born with a genetic structure that helps to determine the
adjustment we make in this world. But we are also subject to the influ- 45
ences of our social environment. We can learn new behavior and we
can modify our predispositions. If this were not true, all constructive
influences such as education would be worthless. I believe—or at least
hope—that we will learn to modify our genetic need for territory by
accepting the modern reality. We all inhabit the same rapidly shrinking 50
earth populated by a rapidly rising number of people. We must share
and cooperate, because there is no other way.

1. This essay was written in response to one of the readings assigned in the
   course. What use does the writer make of analogy, narration, and comparison
   in his analysis of the "territorial imperative"?
2. By what methods does he analyze the "social imperative"?
3. The writer refers to his own individual experience and also to a major international problem. What is the effect of this use of both small-scale and large-
   scale examples?

11-F   Why They Mourned for Elvis Presley

Molly Ivins

This example, a complete news article, first appeared in the *New York Times* (1977).

Why did 25,000 people stand for hours in an almost unbearable
heat, in a truly unbearable crush, trying to get a glimpse of a rock-and-
roll singer? Why did so many drive all night, take plane trips they
couldn't afford, set out from half a continent away without money or
comforts or plans, solely to attend the funeral of Elvis Presley?   5

The people who came to mourn offered only one reason: "Because," they said over and over, "we love him."

Those who make it their business to explain such phenomena offered a multitude of reasons. Mass hysteria, they said. Ghoulishness.
Suppressed sexual yearnings. An acting out of class antagonisms. Nostal- 10
gia for lost innocence and youth. They attributed it to generational
identification, to Freudian repression, to a mad media overkill.

But if some observers seemed condescending or embarrassed by
the open displays of sentimentality, mawkishness and love, Mr. Presley's fans saw nothing to be ashamed of in glorying in their sorrow. They 15
were not offended by an instant commercialization of their grief, by the
T-shirts reading "Elvis Presley, In Memory, 1935–1977" that were on
sale for $5 in front of Mr. Presley's mansion.

The Memphis police, whose courtesy was remarkable, carefully
carried water out to the waiting fans, gently carried away the fainters, 20
and played with the children. When fans emerged distraught after

viewing Mr. Presley's body, the police walked up to them, put an arm around their shoulders and walked away with them, talking soothingly until the fans were calmer.

The police became unpopular at one point, when they shut out at 25 least 10,000 waiting fans on Wednesday evening. "Why are you treating us like this?" shouted a man as he was pushed away from the gate. "Why do you have all those helicopters and cops here?"

"We're afraid of a riot," replied a sheriff's deputy.

The fan was outraged, "You don't understand," he said. "We're not 30 troublemakers, we didn't come here to . . . we're, we're *family*. We came because we love him."

One seldom expects the country's President to adequately note the passing of a rocker, but Jimmy Carter's assessment of Elvis Presley's appeal—"energy, rebelliousness and good humor"—is remarkably 35 close to the mark. When he started out in the 1950's he looked like a hood, he sang sensually. Part of his appeal in the 1970's was our remembering what we thought was "sexy" back then. Underneath that greaser hairdo, he had the profile of a Greek god. Besides, our parents didn't like him, so what could be better? And the music? Well, the music can 40 be left to the music critics, who by and large seem to think it's pretty good. A teenage foot that never tapped to "Heartbreak Hotel" in the 50's probably belonged to a hopeless grind.

A large proportion of the mourners in Memphis were the girls who once screamed and cried and fainted at Elvis Presley concerts in the 45 1950's. They grew up, but they never got over Elvis.

The idols of one's adolescence tend to endure—you never forget how you worshipped them. There is never anyone quite so wonderful as the people who were seniors when you were a freshman. And the intense crushes of adolescent girls helped create the phenomenon of 50 Elvis Presley.

The fans who came to Memphis, especially the women, tended to have been Elvis fans "from the beginning." Many of them said they had married right out of high school and that their last memories of girlhood are of passionate feelings about Elvis Presley—"My first love." 55

"I told my husband he'd always be second to Elvis." "I loved him then and I love him now." They never stopped being Elvis fans. They kept up their Elvis Presley scrapbooks. They went to his concerts and grabbed the scarves he used to give away, and had them framed. Some of them seemed to realize that it was, perhaps, a little silly, but he 60 seemed to represent the only rebellion they ever knew, the dreams of their youth.

Oh, there were some who came to Memphis because "it's what's happening, man." Just to be there, to be seen, to see, without caring. But for the most part, Memphis was awash with genuine emotion for 65 three days. It is too easy to dismiss it as tasteless. It is not required that love be in impeccable taste.

1. According to the author, what reasons did some observers give for the arrival of 25,000 people from all over the country in Memphis to pay their last respects to Elvis Presley?
2. What additional reasons does the author find for the large number of mourners?
3. What descriptive and narrative touches does the author use to bring out her main point and to make the scene vivid?

11-G   Splitting the Word

Anthony Burgess

These paragraphs begin the chapter on words in *Language Made Plain* (1964), a book explaining the basic principles and terminology of linguistics to the general reader. A phoneme is any one of the smallest units of sound of which words are composed and which distinguish one word from another. In English these are often not indicated by spelling. For instance, the only phonemic difference between *though* and *those* is the *z* sound in *those.*

For the moment—but only for the moment—it will be safe to assume that we all know what is meant by the word "word." I may even consider that my typing fingers know it, defining a word (in a whimsical conceit) as what comes between two spaces. The Greeks saw the word as the minimal unit of speech; to them, too, the atom was the minimal 5 unit of matter. Our own age has learnt to split the atom and also the word. If atoms are divisible into protons, electrons, and neutrons, what are words divisible into?

Words as things uttered split up, as we have already seen, into phonemes, but phonemes do not take *meaning* into account. We do not 10 play on the phonemes of a word as we play on the keys of a piano, content with mere sound; when we utter a word we are concerned with the transmission of meaning. We need an appropriate kind of fission, then—one that is *semantic,* not *phonemic.* Will division into syllables do? Obviously not, for syllables are mechanical and metrical, mere 15 equal ticks of a clock or beats in a bar. If I divide (as for a children's reading primer) the word "metrical" into "met-ri-cal", I have learned nothing new about the word: these three syllables are not functional as neutrons, protons, electrons are functional. But if I divide the word as "metr-; -ic; -al" I have done something rather different. I have indicated 20 that it is made of the root "metr-," which refers to measurement and is found in "metronome" and, in a different phonemic disguise, in "metre," "kilometre," and the rest; "-ic," which is an adjectival ending found also in "toxic," "psychic," etc., but can sometimes indicate a noun, so that "metric" itself can be used in a phrase like "Milton's 25 metric" with full noun status; "-al," which is an unambiguous adjectival ending, as in "festal," "vernal," "partial." I have split "metrical" into three contributory forms which (remembering that Greek *morph-* means "form") I can call *morphemes.*

1. How does the author use analogy? metaphor?
2. Why does he use "fission" in the third sentence of the second paragraph instead of "division" or "splitting"?
3. Why does the author mention dividing words into syllables since he immediately says that doing so gives him no new information about the words?

11-H   The Bad and Worse Sides of Thanksgiving

The New Yorker

This example is taken from an unsigned satire published in the "Notes and Comments" section of *The New Yorker* (November 1978).

At last, it is time to speak the truth about Thanksgiving. The truth is this: it is not a really great holiday. Consider the imagery. Dried cornhusks hanging on the door! Terrible wine! Cranberry jelly in little bowls of extremely doubtful provenance which everyone is required to handle with the greatest of care! Consider the participants, the mer- 5
rymakers. Men and women (also children) who have survived passably well through the years, mainly as a result of living at considerable distances from their dear parents and beloved siblings, who on this feast of feasts must apparently forgather (as if beckoned by an aberrant Fairy Godmother), usually by circuitous routes, through heavy traffic, at a 10
common meeting place, where the very moods, distempers, and obtrusive personal habits that have kept them happily apart since adulthood are then and there encouraged to slowly ferment beneath the cornhusks, and gradually rise with the aid of the terrible wine, and finally burst forth out of control under the stimulus of the cranberry jelly! No, 15
it is a mockery of a holiday. For instance: *Thank you, O Lord, for what we are about to receive.* This is surely not a gala concept. There are no presents, unless one counts Aunt Bertha's sweet rolls a present, which no one does. There is precious little in the way of costumery: miniature plastic turkeys and those witless Pilgrim hats. There is no sex. Indeed, 20
Thanksgiving is the one day of the year (a fact known to everybody) when all thoughts of sex completely vanish, evaporating from apartments, houses, condominiums, and mobile homes like steam from a bathroom mirror.

Consider also the nowhereness of the time of the year. The last 25
week or so in November. It is obviously not yet winter: winter, with its death-dealing blizzards and its girls in tiny skirts pirouetting on the ice. On the other hand, it is certainly not much use to anyone as fall: no golden leaves or Oktoberfests, and so forth. Instead, it is a no man's land between the seasons. . . . 30

Consider for a moment the Thanksgiving meal itself. It has become a sort of refuge for endangered species of starch: sweet potatoes, cauliflower, pumpkin, mince (whatever "mince" is), those blessed yams. Bowls of luridly colored yams, with no taste at all, lying torpid under

a lava flow of marshmallow! And then the sacred turkey. One might as 35
well try to construct a holiday repast around a fish—say, a nice piece of
boiled haddock. After all, turkey tastes very similar to haddock: same
consistency, same quite remarkable absence of flavor. But then, if the
Thanksgiving pièce de résistance were a nice piece of boiled haddock
instead of turkey, there wouldn't be all that fun for Dad when Mom 40
hands him the sterling-silver, bone-handled carving set (a wedding
present from her parents and not sharpened since) and then everyone
stands around pretending not to watch while he saws and tears away
at the bird as if he were trying to burrow his way into or out of some
grotesque, fowllike prison.   45

What of the good side to Thanksgiving, you ask. There is always a
good side to everything. Not to Thanksgiving. There is only a bad side
and then a worse side. For instance, Grandmother's best linen tablecloth is a bad side: the fact that it is produced each year, in the manner
of a red flag being produced before a bull, and then is always spilled 50
upon by whichever child is doing poorest at school that term and so is
in need of greatest reassurance. Thus: "Oh, my God, *Veronica,* you just
spilled grape juice [or "plum wine" or "tar"] on Grandmother's best
linen tablecloth!" But now comes worse. For at this point Cousin Bill,
the one who lost all Cousin Edwina's money on the car dealership three 55
years ago and has apparently been drinking steadily since Halloween,
bizarrely chooses to say, "Seems to me those old glasses are *always*
falling over." To which Auntie Meg is heard to add, "Somehow I don't
remember *receivin'* any of those old glasses." To which Uncle Fred
replies, "That's because you and George decided to go on vacation to 60
Hawaii the summer Grandpa Sam was dying." Now Grandmother is
sobbing, though not so uncontrollably that she cannot refrain from
murmuring, "I think that volcano painting I threw away by mistake got
sent me from Hawaii, heaven knows why." But the gods are merciful,
even the Pilgrim-hatted god of cornhusks and soggy stuffing, and there 65
is an end to everything, even to Thanksgiving. Indeed, there is a gran-
deur to the feelings of finality and doom which usually settle on a house
after the Thanksgiving celebration is over, for with the completion of
Thanksgiving Day the year itself has been properly terminated—shot
through the cranium with a high-velocity candied yam. At this calendri- 70
cal nadir, all energy on the planet has gone, all fun has fled, all the
terrible wine has been drunk.

But then, overnight, life once again begins to stir, emerging, even
by the next morning, in the form of Japanese window displays and
Taiwanese Christmas lighting, from the primeval ooze of the nation's 75
department stores. Thus, a new year dawns, bringing with it immediate
and cheering possibilities of extended consumer debt, office-party flirta-
tions, good—or, at least, mediocre—wine, and visions of cheapskate
excursion fares to Montego Bay. It is worth noting, perhaps, that this
true new year always starts with the same mute, powerful mythic cere- 80

mony: the surreptitious tossing out, in the early morning, of all those horrid aluminum-foil packages of yams and cauliflower and stuffing and red, gummy cranberry substance which have been squeezed into the refrigerator as if a reënactment of the siege of Paris were expected. Soon afterward, the phoenix of Christmas can be observed as it slowly 85 rises, beating its drumsticks, once again goggle-eyed with hope and unrealistic expectations.

1. What subdivisions does the writer make in analyzing the subject? Can you think of others that would also be appropriate?
2. Would a different sequence for presenting the material be equally clear and effective?
3. Check the etymology, denotation, and connotation of *forgather, aberrant, distempers, pirouetting, no man's land, yams, torpid, repast, pièce de résistance, grotesque, bizarrely, nadir, surreptitious, phoenix.*
4. How and where does the writer use figures of speech, narration, and characterization to complete the satire?

11-I   Christmas Eve

Christine Conza (student)

This essay was written after a class discussion of the preceding essay (11-H). Notice how Conza uses the organization of a process description to make a critical analysis of a traditional family gathering.

Christmas Eve arrives at my house each year accompanied by the same heraldry. The center of the celebration is dinner. My mother spends the five preceding days preparing an exotic assortment of sea creatures, including eels, squid, and dried codfish. The guest list is fairly consistent. It is composed of my Aunt Marcy and her husband, my 5 oldest brother, Sal, his wife, and their four children, my sister, Joann, her husband, and their two children, and my second brother, Richard, his wife, and their two children.

My aunt and uncle always come laden with enough pastries and wine for George Washington's troops at Valley Forge. My brother Sal 10 and gang invariably show up an hour early and empty handed. Joann's group is usually late and apologetic. Richie and clan generally arrive on time, bearing gifts for everyone. I have the responsibility of getting the Christmas tree. Remaining in my usual character of the great procrastinator, I emerge through the door, struggling with my half-priced, 15 over-sized evergreen just as the spaghetti is being served.

In keeping with the tradition of over-indulgence, there are two varieties of pasta from which to choose. For the daring, there is the garlic and oil sauce, with anchovies thrown in for good measure. For the more conservative, like me, there is crab sauce. After the spaghetti, the 20 seafood is brought out. All the hours of preparation are wolfed down in a matter of minutes. It is an Italian tradition to have fish on Christmas Eve. Along with the yearly repetition of menu comes the yearly repetition of conversation.

My father always dwells on how difficult his childhood was for him. 25 Everyone comments on how good the food tastes and on how "Mom" is the only one who can cook a meal such as this one. My mother then gives a thorough rundown on all the supermarkets from which the fish was purchased. This begins our period of comparison shopping. For at least thirty minutes, we try to outdo each other mentioning the bar- 30 gains we have found. For example, Joann will mention that Waldbaum's had a sale on coffee, only $2.50 a pound. Then Sal will mention that his wife bought coffee for $1.99 at King Kullen, and Richie will top that by saying that his wife paid only $1.70 at Pathmark using a forty cent coupon during double-coupon week. 35

Meanwhile, the kids are starting to grow restless. It is all downhill for them after the spaghetti. Since the dinner conversation does not interest me anyway, I usually end up playing the role of Miss Louise of Romper Room fame. Mom then brings out a mound of fruit and nuts, and trays of Aunt Marcy's pastries. These are met with a chorus of oohs 40 and aahs from the group, who have already eaten more than their share. The evening dies slowly.

This annual gathering occurs out of habit. If my mother did not sponsor this event, we would not know what to do with ourselves. Personally, I do not feel the need to be with a crowd on Christmas Eve. 45 Christmas Eve, to me, is a quiet time, a time for reflection. It is the anniversary of a night on which Mary and Joseph were cold and without a place to stay. It seems ludicrous to remember a night of such poverty and simplicity with such over-indulgence and revelry. The excessive noise and confusion of this gathering contradicts my feelings about 50 Christmas. The "celebration" stains the dignity of the holiday—or, better named, the holy day.

Assignments

1. The simplest subjects for analysis by dissection are definite objects such as a ball point pen or mechanical pencil, a sailboat, a tennis court, a football team —in all of which the parts are easily discoverable. More challenging is the analysis of an institution (school, church, government) or a work of art (a poem, a painting, a symphony), in which the existing parts are less readily discernible.
2. Use the analytical process to solve some problem, such as a strongly felt but perhaps hitherto unexamined like or dislike of your own (for a person, a course, a custom), the popularity of something (a sport, a fad, a curriculum), the success of something or someone (a program, a campaign, an individual).

3. Approach through a statement of root principle the analysis of a leader, a form of government, war, peace, success, the American way of life.

4. Whatever subject you choose or whatever approach you decide on, keep your purpose clearly in mind. A textbook, for example, can be analyzed as an object by dissecting the physical parts of which it is composed, or it can be analyzed by dissecting the content. But do not confuse two purposes: A red cover is not to be mentioned in the same breath with a clear-cut literary style.

5. Analysis is such a common method by which the mind works that you can find it illustrated to some extent in every unit in this book. It operates most conspicuously in Unit 15, where you will find it essential to support an argument, in Unit 16 for critical writing, and in Unit 17 for the research paper. Study its use in the next unit in all the examples, particularly in E, F, G, and H.

UNIT 12

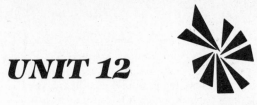

Cause and Effect

Two cars collide in the morning rush hour. The immediate cause is obvious to everyone who sees the accident. Although the traffic light had been yellow for some time, one driver tried to beat it as it turned red and speeded into the narrow intersection when the driver on his right was already moving briskly forward. But what caused the first driver to try to beat the light? Was he late for an appointment with an important client? What caused him to be late? Did an emergency at home delay him? What caused the emergency? Was his little boy scratched by the family cat? What caused the ordinarily gentle cat to turn suddenly fierce? Was the child teasing it? and if so, why? and so on.

The immediate effect of the accident is also obvious to everyone— a badly dented fender on each car, two drivers exchanging identification in the road, and backed-up traffic in both directions. But what are the later effects the bystanders cannot see?—the first driver's important client growing impatient over the delay, being rude to the secretary, and canceling the appointment; the second driver's embarrassment when he explains to his sister that her car is damaged; the bruised elbow of his passenger who will now not be able to play in a tennis tournament that week; the conversation between two passengers in another car who had just met that morning, which results in their making a dinner date (with subsequent dates eventually resulting in their marriage); the decisions by three drivers to increase their collision insurance and the resolve by four drivers to start for work earlier; and so on.

One of our most common logical problems is to discover the true causes behind the effects or to trace from the causes the effects that have already resulted or that probably will result. They may be single, as when cough medicine brings relief, or numerous, as when an antibiotic produces several side effects. They may be closely related, as a knife is to a cut, or separated by time, as is contact with poison ivy from blisters the next day. We may see the connection of cause and effect clearly, or we may discover it only after careful analysis. In this unit we shall concentrate on this relationship. But first we should look at some of the *fallacies*—the wrong beliefs—involved.

1. Do not mistake a time relationship for a cause. This confusion results in the popular *post hoc* fallacy (named from the Latin *post hoc, ergo propter hoc,* meaning "after this, therefore because of this"). This fallacy is responsible for the origin of many of our superstitions. A black cat crosses our path, and bad luck follows; therefore a black cat is believed to have caused the bad luck. Breaking a mirror, walking under a ladder, and so on—these belong to the mythology of our culture and are attempts to explain something whose true cause is unknown or too unpleasant to be faced. Certainly, we might see these as causing bad effects if we were scratched by the cat or cut by the mirror or spattered with paint; but, as intelligent people, we would look for other, plausible causes of any *unrelated* misfortune that follows. Before we can attribute a series of storms to atomic tests, we need much more research. The tests *may* prove to be a contributing cause, but they may not—after all, we had bad storms long before the atom was split. Note the continuing debate among scientists over the links between some foods and cancer.

2. Do not mistake for a cause something actually unrelated. Akin to the *post hoc* fallacy is the assumption that two things that usually happen at the same time must have a causal relationship—for instance, popular opinion holds that leaves turn color in the fall because of the first frost of fall, although scientists insist that the change usually precedes the frost. A causal relationship is often attributed to many pure coincidences: someone who seems to be following you down a lonely street may merely be going in the same direction at the same speed.

3. Do not settle for one cause if there are more. One effect may have been produced by multiple causation. Comic books may contribute to juvenile delinquency, but so do many other social forces. If a normally cheerful man appears surly, he may have had an argument with his neighbor about the neighbor's dog, received an unexpectedly large telephone bill, been criticized by his boss, had a flat tire on the way to work, or be coming down with a cold. More probably, a combination of these causes has affected him—the proverbial last straw did not break the camel's back all by itself.

4. Do not mistake cause for effect or effect for cause. Some medieval philosophers believed that the great European rivers sprang up where the great cities were built; the modern historian sees the process in reverse. The old farmer who said, "If I'd known I was going to have such nice children, I'd have picked a better mother for 'em," might also stand correction.

5. Distinguish between immediate and remote causes. Asked why you are here in college, you could truthfully answer, "Because my father and mother married," but the inquirer is probably concerned with more recent causes directly connected with the effect in question.

6. Be sure the cause could produce the result. If a large dog is left unwatched in the kitchen and three pounds of hamburger disappear, the dog is a likely suspect—particularly if, as with the disappearance of the teapot and spoons in Huxley's essay (Example I in this unit), there is other circumstantial evidence as well, such as distended ribs and a greasy muzzle and paws. On the other hand, a small puppy may be exonerated, not from lack of motive but of capacity.

7. Allow for causes that may nullify predicted effects. Corn needs rain, but a heavy rainfall does not assure farmers of a good crop; it may instead prevent them from planting in time or, if heavy enough, may drown the corn they have already planted. Wage increases do not necessarily result in more buying power; they may instead contribute to an increase in the cost of living.

8. Avoid predicting contradictory effects. The campaign promises of politicians to lower taxes and also expand the public works program are not taken seriously by experienced voters.

9. Avoid the pitfall of rationalization. In the search for causes and effects, especially the causes of your own opinions or the effects of your own actions, you may be tempted to use false or superficial explanations that let you avoid facing the truth. For instance, drivers involved in car accidents often blame road conditions or mechanical failure, denying their own carelessness; and students may excuse their failure to study adequately by pleading that the assignment was too long or that they needed sleep, rather than admit their laziness.

 ## *Examples*

The relationship between cause and effect is particularly evident in the selections in this unit, but it can be found, in varying degrees, in every other selection in this book, perhaps most notably in Smith's "One-Man Show" (1-B), Wright's "A Loaf of Bread and the Stars" (3-B), Mencken's *"Le Contrat Social"* (4-B), Bolinger's "We Reduced the Size" (4-H), Jackson's "Challenge" (5-D), Johmann's "Sex and the Split Brain" (7-B), *New Society*'s "Social Control" (9-F), McGrath's "American Magazines" (10-G), and Jastrow's "Brains and Computers."

12-A   Living on the Altiplano

Georgie Anne Geyer

These paragraphs are taken from a travel article in the *Atlantic Monthly* (1967).

The Altiplano, that high plain which balances at 14,000 feet like a
slate between the two spectacular black ridges of the Andes, has formed
and influenced the life of the Incas more than anything else. Its thin
stern air has even affected the bodies of the Indians, giving them larger
lungs to bear the strain and more red corpuscles to stand the cold.   5

It is a stunning part of the world, with broad barren valleys and
purple mountains dotted by floating clouds that can suddenly erupt in
convulsive showers. Historians say that the very barrenness of the land
and its prohibitiveness are what prodded the Incas into their astonish-
ing accomplishments. They had to use every piece of land, to terrace   10
and burrow and organize and work together, to be able to live there.

1. The author mentions several possible effects of living on the Altiplano. Which
   ones can be tested scientifically to determine whether or not there is a
   genuine cause-and-effect relationship and which can only be a matter of
   opinion? Why?
2. What difference in wording is there in presenting the provable effects and
   the ones that are opinion?

12-B   Death of an Island

Pat Conroy

These paragraphs are from *The Water Is Wide*, an autobiographical account of the author's year on a small island off the coast of South Carolina. Unit 2-F is also about the
island.

ANALYSIS Effect	[Yamacraw] is not a large island, nor an important one, but it represents an era and a segment of history that is rapidly dying in America. The people of the island have changed very little since the Emancipation Proclamation. Indeed, many of them have never heard of this proclama- 5 tion. They love their island with genuine affection but
Cause	have watched the young people move to the city, to the lands far away and far removed from Yamacraw. The is- land is dying, and the people know it.
Background	In the parable of Yamacraw there was a time when 10 the black people supported themselves well, worked hard, and lived up to the sacred tenets laid down in the Protes- tant ethic. Each morning the strong young men would

take to their bateaux and search the shores and inlets for
the large clusters of oysters, which the women and old 15
men in the factory shucked into large jars. Yamacraw oysters were world famous. An island legend claims that a
czar of Russia once ordered Yamacraw oysters for an imperial banquet. The white people propagate this rumor.
The blacks, for the most part, would not know a czar from 20
a fiddler crab, but the oysters were good, and the oyster
factories operating on the island provided a substantial
living for all the people. Everyone worked and everyone
made money.

Cause

Effect

Effect

Effect

Effect

Cause

Effect

Effect

Effect

Then a villain appeared. It was an industrial factory 25
situated on a knoll above the Savannah River many miles
away from Yamacraw. The villain spewed its excrement
into the river, infected the creeks, and as silently as the
pull of the tides, the filth crept to the shores of Yamacraw.
As every good health inspector knows, the unfortunate 30
consumer who lets an infected oyster slide down his throat
is flirting with hepatitis. Someone took samples of the
water around Yamacraw, analyzed them under a microscope, and reported the results to the proper officials. Soon
after this, little white signs were placed by the oyster 35
banks forbidding anyone to gather the oysters. Ten thousand oysters were now as worthless as grains of sand. No
czar would order Yamacraw oysters again. The muddy
creatures that had provided the people of the island with
a way to keep their families alive were placed under per- 40
manent quarantine.

Since a factory is soulless and faceless, it could not be
moved to understand the destruction its coming had
wrought. When the oysters became contaminated, the island's only industry folded almost immediately. The great 45
migration began. A steady flow of people faced with starvation moved toward the cities. They left in search of jobs.
Few cities had any intemperate demand for professional
oyster-shuckers, but the people were somehow assimilated. The population of the island diminished consid- 50
erably. Houses surrendered their tenants to the city and
signs of sudden departure were rife in the interiors of
deserted homes. Over 300 people left the island. They left
reluctantly, but left permanently and returned only on
sporadic visits to pay homage to the relatives too old or too
stubborn to leave. As the oysters died, so did the people. 55

1. Here the relationship of cause and effect is plainly visible. Where does it
   start?
2. List the sequence of effects that follow the initial cause of trouble.

3. What words suggest that the writer feels certain that his analysis of the cause-and-effect relationship is correct?
4. Check the etymology, denotation, and connotation of *tenets, intemperate, assimilated, sporadic* (*bateaux,* the French for *boats,* is borrowed from the French settlers of Louisiana).

12-C   The Decisive Arrest

Martin Luther King, Jr.

In these paragraphs from his book, *Stride Toward Freedom* (1958), Dr. King shows a real cause that has been obscured by more obvious but false ones. Note that here he tries to explain only why Mrs. Parks broke the law; she was not the *cause* of the great bus strike but rather, as King wrote later, a "precipitating factor." The immediate effect was her arrest, but this in turn touched off a series of larger effects that are still operating. Another example of Dr. King's writing is in Unit 20.

On December 1, 1955, an attractive Negro seamstress, Mrs. Rosa Parks, boarded the Cleveland Avenue Bus in downtown Montgomery. She was returning home after her regular day's work in the Montgomery Fair—a leading department store. Tired from long hours on her feet, Mrs. Parks sat down in the first seat behind the section reserved 5 for whites. Not long after she took her seat, the bus operator ordered her, along with three other Negro passengers, to move back in order to accommodate boarding white passengers. By this time every seat in the bus was taken. This meant that if Mrs. Parks followed the driver's command she would have to stand while a white male passenger, who 10 had just boarded the bus, would sit. The other three Negro passengers immediately complied with the driver's request. But Mrs. Parks quietly refused. The result was her arrest.

There was to be much speculation about why Mrs. Parks did not obey the driver. Many people in the white community argued that she 15 had been "planted" by the NAACP in order to lay the groundwork for a test case, and at first glance that explanation seemed plausible, since she was a former secretary of the local branch of the NAACP. So persistent and persuasive was this argument that it convinced many reporters from all over the country. Later on, when I was having press confer- 20 ences three times a week—in order to accommodate the reporters and journalists who came to Montgomery from all over the world—the invariable first question was: "Did the NAACP start the bus boycott?"

But the accusation was totally unwarranted, as the testimony of both Mrs. Parks and the officials of the NAACP revealed. Actually, no 25 one can understand the action of Mrs. Parks unless he realizes that eventually the cup of endurance runs over, and the human personality cries out, "I can take it no longer." Mrs. Parks's refusal to move back was her intrepid affirmation that she had had enough. It was an individual expression of a timeless longing for human dignity and freedom. She 30 was not "planted" there by the NAACP, or any other organization; she

was planted there by her personal sense of dignity and self-respect. She
was anchored to that seat by the accumulated indignities of days gone
by and the boundless aspirations of generations yet unborn. She was a
victim of both the forces of history and the forces of destiny. She had   35
been tracked down by the *Zeitgeist*—the spirit of the time.

1. What words show that Dr. King feels certain that his analysis of the cause-
   and-effect relationship is correct?
2. Check the origin of the word *boycott.*
3. How does the connotation of *plausible* differ from that of its synonym *credible?* How do the etymologies of *intrepid* and *aspiration* help us to understand their meanings?

12-D   Dix Hills: The Grown-Ups' Toy

Donna Satriale (student)

Note the writer's attention to both immediate and long-term effects.

My first glimpse of Dix Hills was from the back seat of my mother's
'62 Falcon as we drove from one model home to another. Dead, brown
leaves dangled from the twisted branches of scrawny trees. The ground
was a smear of coagulated mud, rippled in places and strewn with
rivulets. It sucked my sneakers from my feet as I walked past the naked   5
skeletons of houses until we came to the one which Dad said was ours.
We went there often, as if we were visiting a sick relative in the hospital.

We were one of the first families to move in. My sister and I thrived
among the pounding hammers and roaring bulldozers. The unfinished
houses invited us to romp in them. Every empty lot was our play-   10
ground. We were French explorers discovering exotic lands, archaeolo-
gists digging up the ruins of an ancient Palestinian city, medieval
knights conquering a fortress, and messengers struggling through the
Egyptian desert. Dix Hills was a land of make-believe where a child's
creative imagination could expand.   15

A shabby cornfield marked the end of our pebbly street. Carefree,
we sprinted between the bristly stalks, playing tag and hide-and-seek
as if the field were ours and it was the only place on earth. We lost shoes,
toys, and hair ribbons there. Sometimes we lost ourselves, dozing between the mounds with the silver sunlight filtering through the corn.   20

As time went on we found that we had to go farther and farther
away to play in the empty housing lots. More families were constantly
moving in. Shiny, civilized moving vans replaced the ferocious bulldozers, velvety sod carpeted our digging sites, and cars interrupted our
kickball and hop-scotch games. The cornfield was plowed under, and   25
more houses were built.

Across the street was a dense patch of woods, and we began to play there. Mighty forts were built, traps set, and holes dug. We climbed trees and swung on vines, scratching our arms and legs. Afterwards, we were afraid to go home because we were coated with dirt and were 30 often the victims of "creeping crud" or poison ivy. But they knocked down our forts, our trees, and our woods to expand the parking lot for the public library.

Because the library was so close, we did a lot of reading. We read about faraway places where children played in untouched cornfields 35 and open woods—children who were not trapped in suburbia.

It wasn't long until everything was frosted with an upper-middle-class snobbery. Dix Hills was suddenly ripped from the hands of the children and given to the grown-ups. There was nothing left for the children to do except to play the adults' games. Cliques and clubs 40 formed even among the children. It was no longer "My Pop can lick your Pop," but "My father makes $45,000 a year, what does your father make?"

Today, there are no children playing kickball in the street. They are in air-conditioned houses watching "Sesame Street" or swimming 45 in private, fenced-in pools. The neighbors rarely communicate, and when they do the falseness of their artificial smiles shines from their gleaming capped teeth. It is a quiet community, and the people like it that way. For me, it is too quiet. It is sterile.

1. Compare this presentation of changes in a place with the presentation of changes in Example B in this unit.
2. Could this writer have made more extensive use of the alternating pattern of comparison to emphasize the cause-and-effect theme underlying her material?

12-E   Are Television's Effects Due to Television?

Howard Gardner

This essay, here complete, first appeared in *Psychology Today* (1980) and is reprinted in a collection of the author's essays, *Art, Mind, and Brain* (1982). Dr. Gardner, a psychologist currently conducting research at Harvard Project Zero and the Boston Veterans Administration Medical Center, raises questions about common current assumptions that television harms children. Notice his frequent use of summary, quotation, paraphrase, and example.

Nearly all of the ills of our sorely afflicted society have at one time or another been blamed on television. The drop in College Entrance Examination Board scores, the decline in literacy, the lack of political involvement on the part of many citizens, the upsurge in violent crimes, the mediocre artistic tastes of large segments of our culture— 5 these and countless other lamentable trends have all been attributed to this pervasive medium. A deluge of articles, books, and even television programs have chronicled the evil effects of television. Marie Winn had deplored *The Plug-In Drug,* and Gerry Mander has issued *Four Arguments for the Elimination of Television.*   10

To be sure, one occasionally hears whispers about possible dividends from television: an earlier mastery of certain basic skills (courtesy of "Sesame Street"), greater access to information by neglected pockets within the society, an increase in the rate or efficacy of visual thinking, and, possibly, the speedier erection of Marshall McLuhan's "global vil-   15 lage." Yet for the most part, when television is spoken of, the medium that has been viewed by more individuals for longer periods of time than any other in human history receives a dismal press.

When such a consensus is voiced, it requires some boldness (or foolhardiness) to call it into question. Yet in my view we know astonish-   20 ingly little about the actual effects of television. For the most part, we do not know what things are caused by television. And even when we can establish probable cause, it is difficult to confirm that the medium of television *per se* is at fault. Put another way, it might be that any pursuit, or at least any medium with which one were engaged for   25 twenty to thirty hours a week, would yield similar results—in which case the various trends cited above are hardly due to television itself. Our "vast wasteland" of ignorance about television's effects stems from the fact that researchers claiming to study television have failed to tease out those effects due directly to television from those that might have   30 resulted from any mode of presentation. And so, to anticipate my conclusions, only if we systematically compare television to other media of communication will we be able to determine which sins—and which virtues—can legitimately be laid at the base of the ubiquitous console.

Television and Human Behavior, a recently published exhaustive   35 compendium of more than 2,500 studies, provides an important case in point. This thoughtful book compiled by George Comstock and his colleagues inundates us with information about television in this country—the number of sets, the number of hours they are watched by members of every age and demographic group, and the preferences   40 and dislikes of the gigantic viewing audience. Appropriately, the largest section of the book is devoted to the aspect of television that has generated the most controversy—the effects of the medium on children. In fact, it takes more than a hundred pages simply to survey the several hundred studies in this area.   45

I read through these pages with mounting disappointment. The millions of research dollars spent on this issue seem to have yielded only two major findings, each of which might easily have been anticipated by the experimenter's proverbial grandmother. As the authors constantly remind us, "it has now been established" that children will   50 imitate behaviors they see on television, whether these actions be aggressive, violent, or benignly "prosocial." Moreover, "it has also been established" that the younger the child, the more likely it is that he will believe in the contents of commercials, urging parents to purchase what has been advertised and confusing commercial fare with other television content.

Some recent research efforts have adopted a more cognitive approach to children and television: they have implicitly viewed the child as a fledgling explorer trying to make sense of the mysterious lands visible on the handful of channels beamed to every household. And these studies have furnished the reassuring headline that, much as children pass through stages in the other realms of existence probed by psychologists, so children pass through "stages of television comprehension." But again, these pioneering studies have not revealed much that would surprise an observant parent or a shrewd grandparent.

Why do we know so little? Why have the thousands of studies failed to tell us more about television *per se* and about the minds of children who view it? A number of answers spring to mind. First of all, just as a new medium usually begins by presenting the contents previously transmitted through older media (for example, movies initially conveyed celluloid theater, and television at first amounted to visual radio), so, too, initial lines of research on television have largely adopted methods and questions that had once been applied to other media or to "unmediated" behavior. Only when a generation reared on television undertook research in this area did studies become attuned to the special or "defining" properties of television. Another limiting dimension has been the "mission" orientation of most television research. Because society has been (justifiably) vexed about violence and about commercials, it has twisted researchers' arms to grapple with these issues.

But probably the chief stumbling block to imaginative and generative television research has been the fact that everyone (and his grandmother) has a television set. Thus the crucial experimental control—comparing individuals with televisions to those without—cannot be done. The few eccentrics who do not have television are too different from their viewing counterparts to serve as a meaningful control group. Those scattered societies not yet blessed (or traumatized) with television are also sufficiently different to render comparisons of little value. When the gifted social psychologist, Stanley Milgram, was asked to study the effects of television on violence, he had a very logical idea which was, alas, soon dashed. Milgram's first impulse was to divide the country in half, remove all violence on television west of the Mississippi, enact laws so that no one could move from one part of the country to the other, and then observe what happened over a period of years. "It turned out not to be practical," he wryly admitted to an interviewer, "so I had to work with what I had."

I have recently encountered a few strands of research that address more directly the distinct features of television. In trying to determine which aspects of television compel children's attention, researchers

Aletha Huston-Stein and John Wright of the University of Kansas have 100
focused on the medium's "formal features"—the quick cutaways, sound
effects, and frenetic activity, in which commercial television revels.
They have documented that the younger the child, the more likely he
is to attend to these features of television, independent of the kind of
content being presented. In contrast, older children will watch a pro- 105
gram for extended periods of time even when such formal features are
not heavily exploited. Huston-Stein and Wright make the interesting
suggestion that violence or aggression are unnecessary for capturing
the attention of preschool children. So long as a show is fast-paced,
contains action, and is laced with interesting visual and sound effects (as 110
is, for example, much of "Sesame Street"), the youngsters will remain
hooked.

Another innovative researcher, Gavriel Salomon of the Hebrew
University in Jerusalem, has also focused on those features that prove
unique to television. He has paid special attention to such features as 115
the zoom—the shot that begins with a panoramic overview and then
rapidly "zooms" in upon a tell-tale detail. According to Salomon, children with difficulty attending to relevant detail can be greatly aided by
a television segment replete with zooms: the medium can "supplant"
a skill that the child needs but that, for one or another reason, he has 120
not yet developed on his own. Salomon has not only documented an
effect linked specifically to television but has also pointed the path to
a positive pedagogical payoff.

Yet because they employ only television, even these isolated oases
in the wasteland of research do not permit a determination of the 125
effects of television *per se.* One line of research that *does,* however, was
initiated by Laurene Meringoff, my colleague at Harvard Project Zero,
and is now being continued in conjunction with several other colleagues. Exploiting the fact that television transmits certain contents,
such as narratives, that have traditionally been conveyed by other 130
media, these researchers have compared with as much precision as
possible the differential effects wrought by such story content when it
is presented on television, as opposed to when it is presented in book
form. And they have uncovered some very intriguing findings.

Let me describe their procedures. To begin with, members of the 135
research team select stories of high quality and interest. Using materials
developed at Weston Woods, a studio which produces stories in various
media for children, they prepare book and television versions that are
virtually identical save in the medium of transmission.

As an example, the research team has worked extensively with *The* 140
Three Robbers by Tomi Ungerer. In this tale three hitherto ferocious
bandits abandon their violent ways after stopping a stagecoach that was
carrying the charming orphan Tiffany. Turning their backs on a life of
crime, the trio of robbers goes on to help abandoned girls and boys
throughout the land. In a typical study, one group of subjects hears the 145
story read by an experimenter and sees the accompanying pictures—

the "book version." Another group of subjects views a film of equivalent
length, based on the book, on a television monitor; in this "television
version," the specially recorded sound track uses the voice of the book
narrator and the animated film presents the same illustrations that 150
appear in the printed text. Thus, while respecting the essential properties of each medium (movement within the image in the case of television, discrete static imagery in the case of a picture book), the two
versions are about as similar as can be imagined. (Of course, reading a
book oneself is different from having it read aloud to one at a preor- 155
dained rate, but the researchers were interested in attempting to simulate the latter experience.)

A quartet of studies carried out thus far by the Project Zero team
revealed a consistent and instructive picture. To begin with, adults who
watched the television program remembered about as much of the 160
story on their own and were able to select as many items from multiple
choice as did the matched adults who had the picture book read to
them. But when subjects were asked to make inferences that went
beyond the text, modest effects of medium were found. For example,
subjects were asked to evaluate how a character felt or how difficult it 165
was for the robbers to carry out an action. In these cases, adults who saw
the story on television were more likely to make inferences based on
the visual portions of the story (such as the expression on a character's
face), while those exposed to the book were more likely to rely on the
plot they heard (although both groups were exposed to identical sound 170
tracks and saw a similar set of visual images, one static and one dynamic).

With children the differences across media proved far more dramatic. Compared to the video youngsters, the book children remembered much more of the story on their own and were also better able 175
to recall information when they had been cued. When it came to recall-
ing precise wordings and figures of speech, differences proved especially dramatic: the book children were surprisingly skilled at repeating
just what they heard (phrases such as "visit her wicked aunt"), while the
television children, when they remembered linguistically presented 180
information at all, were prone to paraphrase.

To my mind, the most intriguing differences with children
emerged when inferences were called for. Both groups of children
tended to reach the same conclusions—for instance, an equal number
of television and book children concluded that the robbers' axe was easy 185
to wield, or that Tiffany felt happy. But the lines of reasoning used to
buttress the inferences were different. Television children relied overwhelmingly on what they had seen—how difficult an action looked, how
someone appeared to feel. They rarely went beyond the video information, either to attend to what was said or to draw on their own experi- 190
ence. In contrast, book children were far more likely to draw on their
own personal experiences or to apply their own real-world knowledge
("It's hard for me to hold an axe—it's way too heavy"). Estimates of time

and space were also more constrained for the television children. That is, when asked how long an action took or how far from one another two 195 sites were located, television children made more modest estimates, suggesting a reliance on the superficial flow of information rather than a consideration of what was plausible.

In all, television emerged as much more of a self-contained experience for children, and within this bounded realm the visual component 200 emerged as paramount. The book experience, in contrast, allowed for greater access to the story's language and suggested greater expanses of time and space; it also encouraged connections to other realms of life —thus buttressing some of the very claims bibliophiles have made in the past. 205

One possible outcome of such research is to comfort critics of television—those troubled souls whose Cassandran cries I initially branded as premature. And it seems to be true that the younger the child, the greater the gap between comprehension of television and comprehension of books. Yet, in my own view, the significance of this research does 210 not rest primarily in its favoring one medium over another. For one thing, the largely verbal measures used thus far could well be charged with being "pro-book." It could be that other more visual measures might have favored television, as has in fact proved to be the case in subsequent studies. Or it could be that the kinds of skills actually engen- 215 dered by television (for example, being able to create or recreate in one's mind a vivid visual sequence) cannot yet be tapped by our experimental methodology. Rather, the importance of the research may lie in its demonstration of qualitative differences in the effects of these media: exposure to television apparently highlights a set of contents and en- 220 genders a line of inference quite different from that stimulated by experience with books. Thus the individual who views television intensively and extensively may well develop different kinds of imaginative powers or, as Marshall McLuhan might have claimed, a different "ratio among imaginations" from that of an individual weaned on another 225 medium, such as books.

We are left with an even more tantalizing thought. Ever since the time of Immanuel Kant, it has been assumed by most philosophers that individuals perceive experience in terms of certain basic categories— time, space, and causality. Indeed, one has no choice but to conceive 230 of life in such terms—they are "givens." While psychologists do not necessarily accept these categories as part of the human birthright, they assume that eventually all normal individuals will come to possess similar versions of these basic categories of knowing.

If, however, one adopts an alternative perspective, if one affirms 235 that some of our knowledge of time, space, and causality comes from the media of communication that happen to proliferate in one's culture, then this research has an additional implication. Put simply, it makes little sense to talk of the child's sense of time or space as a single undifferentiated entity. Rather, the ways in which we conceptualize 240 our experience may reflect the kinds of media with which we have been engaged. And so the temporal and spatial outlook—and, *a fortiori,* the imagination of the television freak may have a different flavor from that of the bookworm. While such a finding from television research is perhaps not as immediately sensational as those involving violence or commercials, it can have potentially far-reaching educational implications. For instance, the ways in which one teaches history (with its time frames) or geometry (with its spatial components) might differ depending on the media with which children happen to have been raised *and* the media in which lessons are conveyed. And the findings can also help to reveal something about our own era. Based on comparisons between two pervasive cultural media—books and television—research results can pinpoint differences between individuals of our era and those of earlier times, and also suggest which of those differences might be due to television alone.

1. What stumbling blocks to research on the effects of TV does Gardner mention?
2. What characteristics of TV may help children to learn?
3. Gardner uses many transitional words and phrases to lead the reader from paragraph to paragraph and, within paragraphs, from sentence to sentence. Starting after the first paragraph, choose any sequence of three paragraphs and make a list of all the transitional devices you find.
4. What was Cassandra famous for? Who was Immanuel Kant?
5. Check the etymology, denotation, and connotation of *lamentable, efficacy, consensus, ubiquitous, compendium, compiled, inundate, demographic, benignly, cognitive, implicitly,* per se, *attuned, generative, crucial, traumatized, wryly, frenetic, unique, panoramic, replete, supplant, differential, wrought, discrete* (not to be confused with *discreet*), *preordained, simulate, inferences* (not to be confused with *implications*), *buttress, plausible, bounded* (as used here in "bounded realm"), *component, paramount, bibliophiles, engendered, methodology, causality, proliferate, implication, undifferentiated, entity, conceptualize,* a fortiori, *pervasive.*

12-F   Left Holding the Bat

Stephen Jay Gould

This essay, here complete, first appeared in *Vanity Fair* in 1983. The author, a professor of palaeontology at Harvard, has written many books on science for the general reader, most recently *The Mismeasure of Man* (1981) and *Hen's Teeth and Horse's Toes* (1983). Notice his use of statistics, direct and indirect quotations, and summaries to present the opinions of others and to support his own.

It is the job of advertising to create a desire for objects not really needed. Fads and fashions, advertising's analogue in the realm of ideas, can be recognized in the same way: they substitute strained and farfetched explanations for simple common sense or honest and appropriate ignorance. Since the separation of insight from fashion ranks high on any list of worthy intellectual pursuits, this criterion for identifying fads may be worth exploring.

Of all current psychological fads, none has transgressed the border between fact and overextended fantasy so far as the supposed distinction between right and left brains. This fashion, like so many, has a root in firm and fascinating fact. The two halves of our brain are not mirror images, and the asymmetry of form underlies important distinctions of function. Language and most sequential, logical operations are generally localized in the left brain. Spatial and other styles of perception often labeled as gestalt or analog are monitored by the right brain. In one study, for example, people were asked to think about a piece of music. Those who tried to remember the melody activated their right brains, while those who visualized the notes on a staff of music activated their left brains. Cerebral asymmetry also runs beyond our own species; songs of most male birds are more profoundly altered by experimentally induced lesions of the left brain than of the right.

Overextended, even silly, speculation has issued from this interesting foundation—speculation fostered, I suspect, by the apparent resonance of left and right brains with several facile dichotomies of our popular press. The left brain is rational, the right intuitive; the left reflects linear and logical Western culture, the right, contemplative and integrative Eastern thought. The left, Harvard pretension; the right, California psychobabble. This invalid extension often overwhelms common sense, thus meeting our criterion for identifying fads.

For example, neurologists have long known that a curious crossover occurs between brain and body, so that the left brain regulates the right side of the body, while the right brain controls the left side. Our culture also displays a lamentable prejudice toward right-handedness, a bias deeply embedded in nearly all Western languages, where right is dextrous (from the Latin *dexter,* or right), *Recht* (or justice in German), *droit* (or law in French) and, well, just plain right—while left is sinister (from Latin for left) or gauche. If we overextend the theme of cerebral asymmetry, we might be tempted to trace this prejudice to our Western bias for rational over intuitive thought, since the favored left brain controls the valued right side.

Fritjof Capra makes such a claim in *The Turning Point,* his polemic against reductionist thinking in Western science. Our preferences for right-handedness, he claims, reflect "our culture's Cartesian bias in favor of rational thought." Yet this proposal, superficially attractive, makes no sense on further reflection. The originators of our language had no notion of neurological crossover and, if they thought about it at all, would probably have figured that each brain controlled its own side (a right-minded view)—if they even knew about divided brains. The obvious reason for our prejudice lies in the simple frequencies of handedness and our unfortunate tendency to despise, and even to fear, the uncommon. For some unknown reason, right-handedness prevails overwhelmingly in all human cultures—and most of these cultures have tried to convert their deviants to the path of righteousness. My grandmother, a natural lefty—I am a righty by the way—wrote haltingly with her right hand because her left had been tied behind her back in 55 turn-of-the-century Hungarian schools. Common sense dictates that the source of our pro-right prejudice lies in simple frequency nurtured by xenophobia—not in neurological knowledge that our ancestors could not have possessed. Jesus sits at the right hand of the Father because most of us skewer our enemies and write our Bibles with the same hand. 60

Right-handedness is so much more common that we might ask whether lefties follow the usual distinction of right and left brains—or whether their cerebral hemispheres might not be reversed as well. In fact, we find both patterns. Most lefties show the standard distinction, with language in the left brain and most spatial patterning in the right, 65 but some display the reversed difference, with language in their right brains. Lefties often exhibit another interesting distinction from righties—and mark this well, for it is the source of the bogus claim we shall soon discuss: their brains are often less lateralized than those of righties; that is, the two hemispheres of lefties are often more similar in their performance, with much overlap of function and less distinction be- 70 tween linear and integrative skills. Thus lefties are often more imperfectly handed, and closer to ambidextrous in their performance, than righties. (Handedness, by the way, also extends beyond the human species. Cats and dogs show paw preferences, and rats tend to turn one way or the other.) 75

We love fads, none more these days than overextensions of legitimate differences between right and left brains. We hear that women are right-brained, that Chinese are right-brained, that we'd all be better off if we heeded our neglected right brains. I suppose it had to spill over into baseball some day, where the oldest of ancient observations pro- 80 claims that left-handed hitters have a small but certain edge over righties. Aha, it must be those right brains that critics of Western culture are trying so hard to cultivate. But wait, before we get too intrigued with another extension of a hot fad, let's consider the equally ancient and obvious commonsense explanation for the edge that lefties enjoy. It is also well known that batters do better against pitchers of the opposite 85 hand—for the obvious reason that balls served from the opposite side are more clearly seen. Righties do better against left-handed pitching, lefties against righty pitchers; switch-hitters invariably face their opponents from the opposite side. (I would also not discount the equally old argument that lefties gain a slight advantage from standing closer to 90 first base—that must be good for beating out a few infield hits per season.)

The standard explanation for higher batting averages among lefties invokes the same argument about frequency that invalidated Capra's claim. Since most people are righties, most pitching comes from the 95

right side and lefties gain their traditional edge. I counted the first 1,000
pitchers listed in *The Baseball Encyclopedia,* and 77 percent of them
are or were righties. This explanation is so commonsensical and, well, 100
right-minded that I can't imagine any other serious contender. But
challenged it was, and, of all places, in the staid *New England Journal
of Medicine* for November 11, 1982, in a note by John M. McLean,
M.D., and Francis M. Ciurczak, Ed.D., titled "Bimanual Dexterity in
Major League Baseball Players: A Statistical Study." 105

McLean and Ciurczak first found that lefties are overrepresented
among baseball players; the well-known edge is clearly exploited.
Among current major league players, they count 324 righties and 177
lefties, or 35 percent lefties (in contrast with the 23 percent I calculated
for pitchers). When we consider the top hitters of all time, lefties are 110
in the majority, 76 to 63.

McLean and Ciurczak then considered batting averages, but first
they divided left-handed batters into "pure" lefties, who both bat and
throw with their left hands and "mixed" lefties, who bat left but throw
right. The pure lefties had higher batting averages, while mixed lefties 115
neatly match the righties in both categories. For all players active in
1980, righties average .264, lefties who throw right .260, and pure
lefties .281. For the top hitters of all time, righties average .314, lefties
who throw right also .314, and pure lefties .322.

McLean and Ciurczak reason that since lefties who throw right 120
apparently enjoy no advantage in hitting, the traditional explanation
must be abandoned—for these mixed lefties also face as much right-
handed pitching and stand as close to first base as their pure colleagues.
As an alternative, they probe the current fad and come up with a
hypothesis based on right and left brains. Only the pure lefties, they 125
argue, display the relative weakness of lateralization discussed above—
that is, pure lefties do not have as strong a dominant hand as either pure
righties or lefties who throw right. Thus lack of a strongly dominant
hand must confer some advantage, since bats are held with both hands.
They conclude, in typically dense, but decipherable, scientific prose: 130
"This relative but pervasive lack of lateralization in left-handers may in
some manner contribute to the motor function of the nondominant
hand, thereby enhancing a dexterity that clearly requires the concert
of both hands."

I reject this explanation and believe I can show, from McLean and 135
Ciurczak's data, and from some of my own compilation, that the commonsense explanation based on greater frequency of right-handed
pitching still holds. If I am correct, I must provide an explanation for
why lefties who throw right do not bat as well as pure lefties.

Forgive the appeal to philistinism, but I well remember that on my 140
stickball court all us righties were incessantly experimenting and trying
to hit left-handed, while the few natural lefties among our friends were
smugly content with their lot. We all knew the advantages that accrue

to lefties, and we tried to avail ourselves of them, usually without much luck. 145

Yet some experimenters are undoubtedly successful and manage to convert themselves into left-handed hitters. Most of these people will continue to throw right. Thus many left-handed hitters who throw right are not true lefties, but natural righties who have trained themselves to bat left. This must exact some toll upon batting averages. I also 150 assume that most people who both bat left and throw left are natural lefties. Therefore, lefties who throw right tend to bat more poorly than pure lefties because many of them are not natural lefties and they balance the edge that they enjoy swinging left with the disadvantage of playing against a natural bent. Thus pure lefties do better not because 155 their brains are less lateralized, but for the traditional reason: they see more right-handed than left-handed pitching and, as natural lefties, suffer no compensating disadvantage of playing against an inborn disposition.

My traditional explanation would gain some support if I could show 160 that large numbers of players really do force themselves to hit lefty against a natural inclination. McLean and Ciurczak's own data supply such a hint. I was surprised by the high frequency of lefties who throw right in their study—they actually outnumber the pure lefties in all categories. Among all recorded players, 1,069 bat left but throw right, 165 while only 694 are pure lefties. Among active players, 91 are mixed, 86 pure, while for top hitters, 45 are mixed and 31 pure. By comparison, righties who throw left are rare birds. Among top hitters, we find only 2, in contrast with 45 lefties who throw right.

But McLean and Ciurczak also counted some controls—high school 170 and grammar school students not headed toward the major leagues. In these data, two items support my claim. First, pure lefties now outnumber those who hit left but throw right (25 to 10 for high school students and 11 to 3 for grammar school students). Second, lefties who throw right are no longer more common than righties who throw left (10 vs. 175 12 for high schools and 3 vs. 5 for grammar schools). It seems that nonbaseball players are not struggling to bat left, and that the exaggerated number of mixed lefties among major league players must therefore represent, largely, a group of natural righties who have forced a change upon themselves and must pay for it with lower batting 180 averages than pure lefties.

I was able to corroborate this conclusion by my own compilation of pitchers. I reasoned that since pitchers do not pay much attention to their own hitting (where absence of a designated hitter rule still permits them to bat), we would not find the same concentration of lefties who 185 throw right among pitchers. On counting the first 1,000 pitchers listed in *The Baseball Encyclopedia*, I found 686 pure righties, 171 pure lefties, 84 who bat left and throw right, and 59 who throw left and bat right. The differences between batters and pitchers are much greater

than I would have imagined and must, I believe, be explained as I 190
propose—by the argument that many batters who are natural righties
have trained themselves to bat left, and pay a price for it.

To reiterate, among all players, 694 are pure lefties, while 1,069 bat
left but throw right; but among pitchers, 171 are pure lefties, while only
84 bat left and throw right. Moreover, among pitchers, lefties who 195
throw right are about as common as righties who throw left, while
among hitters, lefties who throw right seem to be about ten times as
common as righties who throw left.

I won't close with the yahoo's blare of gimme that old-time religion,
the traditional way has triumphed over newfangled science. Rather, 200
simple common sense about handedness seems to edge out a faddist
proposal based on overextended reasoning, just as pure lefties continue
to edge out us poor, dextrous, ordinary, right-minded, northpaws.

1. Gould begins with his thesis—that much of the current interest in the two
   sides of the brain is only a fad and that it includes some farfetched explanations of behavior. In the rest of the essay, where does he state explicitly that
   he thinks some theories are foolish or at least mistaken?
2. Where does Gould show the relationship between cause and effect to support
   his attack on some theories?
3. Check the etymology, denotation, and connotation of *analogue, criterion,
   transgressed, gestalt, analog, lesions, facile, dichotomies, rational, intuitive,
   lamentable, polemic, Cartesian, deviants, xenophobia, bogus, lateralized,
   philistinism, corroborate, reiterate, yahoo, faddist.*

12-G   Why People Are Prejudiced

William Nilsson (student)

Many words have been written about the various racial and religious aversions still extant among large segments of the population.
Thinking people everywhere have stressed the evils of prejudices, have
shown them to be illogical and unfounded, have demonstrated the
harm they do and the benefits to be derived from abandoning them. It 5
occurs much less often that someone endeavors to point out objectively
the reasons why people have prejudices and seeks out the primary roots
from which prejudices stem. Perhaps it is only through an examination
of these fountainheads of prejudice that any ultimate solution can be
arrived at.   10

A good starting point might be a definition of the word. A prejudice
may be defined as a preconceived aversion to a person, place, or thing
without adequate acquaintance with said person, place, or thing. A good
example of a common prejudice is the dislike for certain foods. In many
cases this can be proved to be based completely on preconceived ideas. I 15
know a woman who says that she dislikes cheese, but on several occasions
she has eaten it in sauces and liked it when she didn't know it was there. A

certain man who professes an intense dislike for a particular kind of meat has eaten it many times without complaint when his wife told him it was something else. Such dislikes can often be traced to childhood impres- 20 sions. The child who hears his father scorn salad as "rabbit food" will often adopt this dislike purely through suggestion and not because of any taste aversion. The small child whose mother bribes him with rewards for eating certain foods will come to think of them as something unpleas- ant. Parental attitudes and example, therefore, are among the most 25 significant factors in the development of prejudices. Certainly they also play a major role in the fostering of racial and religious bias. The child who hears his parents speak disparagingly of certain racial and religious groups, associating them with dishonesty, boorishness, and other unde- sirable character traits, will accept these ideas without much question. 30 After all, don't Mother and Father know what is right?

Another source of prejudice is feelings of inferiority. The person who claims to dislike symphonic music, painting, or serious literature invariably knows little about them and has never made any effort to become acquainted with them. He will usually tell you that such things 35 are for snobs and "highbrows," or are boring. What he is really express- ing is his feelings that he is somehow intellectually incapable of ap- preciating them. Since such a feeling of inferiority is naturally unpleas- ant, he counteracts it by decrying and belittling that which he believes he cannot learn to understand.   40

Still another reason for prejudice may be found in man's basic fear of the unknown, the unfamiliar. Immigrant groups, newly arrived in the United States, usually settle in neighborhoods where there are many other people who speak their language. Because of linguistic limitations, they develop a clannishness which an American might eas- 45 ily interpret as hostility. They keep strange customs that may make him ill at ease in their company and give him that uncomfortable feeling of "not belonging." He may wonder if they are talking about him when they speak a language he doesn't understand.

Economic factors, too, may have a strong influence on prejudices. 50 A certain group may be feared as a threat to the economic security of another. The Chinese and Japanese, up to recent times, have been bitterly resented on the West Coast because their willingness to work for low wages caused unemployment and a lower standard of living among native Americans in the area. On the other hand, it may be very 55 profitable for one group to keep another one in an inferior status. One of the main reasons for the well-to-do Southerner's long desire to keep the Negro from full equality was his unwillingness to lose a source of cheap labor, a loss which has followed the Negro's increasing awareness of his rights, both economic and social. An idea of the importance of 60 economic factors in fostering prejudice can be derived from an exami- nation of workmen's compensation insurance statistics, which show the unbelievably low wages paid to Negroes by, for example, Southern lumber camp owners.

The question that may follow from this is why the occasional lynch- 65
ings and other acts of violence against Negroes in the South were usually
done not by the well-to-do but by the extremely poor "white trash" who
derive no profit from Negroes' labor. These people must do backbreaking toil themselves in order to eke out the barest living. This uncovers
still another cause of prejudice, the need of a scapegoat, the need of an 70
outlet for hostilities and frustrations built up by a life of fruitless toil for
meager returns. It was this same emotional need that the Nazis used to
stir up popular sentiment against the Jews in a Germany impoverished
by World War I and the injustices of the Versailles Treaty. It was this
need that was taken advantage of by wealthy Polish and Russian land- 75
lords in Czarist times whenever peasants showed signs of discontent
with their economic lot. The peasant's hostilities were diverted by
blaming his poverty on the Jews, thus providing a tangible something to
vent his grievances on, and touching off the notorious pogroms.

Bad example acquired in childhood from parents and other adults, 80
innate feelings of inferiority, distrust of the unknown and unfamiliar,
fear of economic competition, desire for profit through exploitation, the
need for a scapegoat—these are the main sources from which prejudices spring. While this essay does not attempt a solution of the problem, it does suggest that such a solution cannot be a simple one, with 85
the causes of prejudice so numerous, so diverse, and so deep-seated.

1. How does the writer lead up to a statement of his general topic at the end
   of the first paragraph?
2. In his second paragraph how does he make the examples of his definition lead
   to a cause of prejudice? In the rest of the essay how much space does he
   devote to examples to support his analysis of causes?
3. What transitional words and phrases does the writer use? How is the final
   paragraph related to the rest of the essay?

12-H   The Method of Scientific Investigation

Thomas H. Huxley

This example is a famous lecture on the scientific method by the nineteenth-century
writer who helped to publicize Darwin's theory of evolution and was noted for his ability
to clarify difficult abstract concepts, largely through the use of simple narrative examples.
This example is placed at the end of this unit because it not only shows cause and effect
but also makes the logical processes of induction and deduction remarkably clear. These
processes, the subject of the next two units, are closely related to the logic of cause and
effect.

The method of scientific investigation is nothing but the expression
of the necessary mode of working of the human mind. It is simply the
mode at which all phenomena are reasoned about, rendered precise
and exact. There is no more difference, but there is just the same kind
of difference, between the mental operations of a man of science and 5

those of an ordinary person, as there is between the operations and methods of a baker or of a butcher weighing out his goods in common sales, and the operations of a chemist in performing a difficult and complex analysis by means of his balance and finely graduated weights. It is not that the action of the scales in the one case, and the balance 10 in the other, differ in the principles of their construction or manner of working; but the beam of one is set on an infinitely finer axis than the other, and of course turns by the addition of a much smaller weight.

You will understand this better, perhaps, if I give you some familiar example. You have all heard it repeated, I dare say, that men of science 15 work by means of induction and deduction, and that by the help of these operations, they, in a sort of sense, wring from Nature certain other things, which are called natural laws, and causes, and that out of these, by some cunning skill of their own, they build up hypotheses and theories. And it is imagined by many, that the operations of the com- 20 mon mind can be by no means compared with these processes, and that they have to be acquired by a sort of special apprenticeship to the craft. To hear all these large words, you would think that the mind of a man of science must be constituted differently from that of his fellow men; but if you will not be frightened by terms, you will discover that you 25 are quite wrong, and that all these terrible apparatus are being used by yourselves every day and every hour of your lives.

There is a well-known incident in one of Molière's plays, where the author makes the hero express unbounded delight on being told that he had been talking prose during the whole of his life. In the same way, 30 I trust that you will take comfort and be delighted with yourselves, on the discovery that you have been acting on the principles of inductive and deductive philosophy during the same period. Probably there is not one here who has not in the course of the day had occasion to set in motion a complex train of reasoning, of the very same kind though 35 differing of course in degree, as that which a scientific man goes through in tracing the causes of natural phenomena.

A very trivial circumstance will serve to exemplify this. Suppose you go into a fruiterer's shop, wanting an apple—you take up one, and, on biting it, you find it is sour; you look at it, and see that it is hard and 40 green. You take up another one, and that too is hard, green, and sour. The shopman offers you a third; but, before biting it, you examine it, and find that it is hard and green, and you immediately say that you will not have it, as it must be sour, like those that you have already tried.

Nothing can be more simple than that, you think; but, if you will 45 take the trouble to analyze and trace out into its logical elements what has been done by the mind, you will be greatly surprised. In the first place, you have performed the operation of induction. You found that, in two experiences, hardness and greenness in apples went together with sourness. It was so in the first case, and it was confirmed by the 50 second. True, it is a very small basis, but still it is enough to make an induction from; you generalise the facts, and you expect to find sourness in apples where you get hardness and greenness. You found upon that a general law, that all hard and green apples are sour; and that, so far as it goes, is a perfect induction. Well, having got your natural law in this way, when you are offered another apple which you find is hard and green, you say, "All hard and green apples are sour; this apple is hard and green, therefore this apple is sour." That train of reasoning is what logicians call a syllogism, and has all its various parts and terms—its major premise, its minor premise, and its conclusion. And, by the help of further reasoning, which, if drawn out, would have to be exhibited in two of three other syllogisms, you arrive at your final determination, "I will not have that apple." So that, you see, you have, in the first place, established a law of induction, and upon that you have founded a deduction, and reasoned out the special conclusion of the particular case. Well now, suppose, having got your law, that at some time afterwards, you are discussing the qualities of apples with a friend: you will say to him, "It is a very curious thing—but I find that all hard and green apples are sour!" Your friend says to you, "But how do you know that?" You at once reply, "Oh, because I have tried them over and over again, and have always found them to be so." Well, if we were talking science instead of common sense, we should call that an experimental verification. And, if still opposed, you go further, and say, "I have heard from the people in Somersetshire and Devonshire, where a large number of apples are grown, that they have observed the same thing. It is also found to be the case in Normandy, and in North America. In short, I find it to be the universal experience of mankind wherever attention has been directed to the subject." Whereupon, your friend, unless he is a very unreasonable man, agrees with you, and is convinced that you are quite right in the conclusion you have drawn. He believes, although perhaps he does not know he believes it, that the more extensive verifications are—that the more frequently experiments have been made, and the results of the same kind arrived at—that the more varied the conditions under which the same results are attained, the more certain is the ultimate conclusion, and he disputes the question no further. He sees that the experiment has been tried under all sorts of conditions, as to time, place, and people, with the same result; and he says with you, therefore, that the law you have laid down must be a good one, and he must believe it.

In science we do the same thing; the philosopher exercises precisely the same faculties, though in a much more delicate manner. In scientific inquiry it becomes a matter of duty to expose a supposed law to every possible kind of verification, and to take care, moreover, that this is done intentionally, and not left to a mere accident, as in the case of the apples. And in science, as in common life, our confidence in a law is in exact proportion to the absence of variation in the result of our experimental verifications. For instance, if you let go your grasp of an article you may have in your hand, it will immediately fall to the

ground. That is a very common verification of one of the best established laws of nature—that of gravitation. The method by which men   100
of science established the existence of that law is exactly the same as
that by which we have established the trivial proposition about the
sourness of hard and green apples. But we believe it in such an extensive, thorough, and unhesitating manner because the universal experience of mankind verifies it, and we can verify it ourselves at any time;   105
and that is the strongest possible foundation on which any natural law
can rest.

So much, then, by way of proof that the method of establishing laws
in science is exactly the same as that pursued in common life. Let us
now turn to another matter (though really it is but another phase of the   110
same question), and that is, the method by which, from the relations of
certain phenomena, we prove that some stand in the position of causes
towards the others.

I want to put the case clearly before you, and I will therefore show
you what I mean by another familiar example. I will suppose that one   115
of you, on coming down in the morning to the parlor of your house, finds
that a teapot and some spoons which had been left in the room on the
previous evening are gone—the window is open, and you observe the
mark of a dirty hand on the windowframe, and perhaps, in addition to
that, you notice the impress of a hobnailed shoe on the gravel outside.   120
All these phenomena have struck your attention instantly, and before
two seconds have passed you say, "Oh, somebody has broken open the
window, entered the room, and run off with the spoons and the teapot!"
That speech is out of your mouth in a moment. And you will probably
add, "I know there has; I am quite sure of it!" You mean to say exactly   125
what you know; but in reality you are giving expression to what is, in
all essential particulars, an hypothesis. You do not *know* it at all; it is
nothing but a hypothesis rapidly framed in your own mind. And it is an
hypothesis founded on a long train of inductions and deductions.

What are those inductions and deductions, and how have you got   130
at this hypothesis? You have observed, in the first place, that the window is open; but by a train of reasoning involving many inductions and
deductions, you have probably arrived long before at the general law
—and a very good one it is—that windows do not open of themselves;
and you therefore conclude that something has opened the window. A   135
second general law that you have arrived at in the same way is that
teapots and spoons do not go out a window spontaneously, and you are
satisfied that, as they are not now where you left them, they have been
removed. In the third place, you look at the marks on the windowsill,
and the shoemarks outside, and you say that in all previous experience   140
the former kind of mark has never been produced by anything else but
the hand of a human being; and the same experience shows that no
other animal but man at present wears shoes with hobnails in them such
as would produce the marks in the gravel. I do not know, even if we

could discover any of those "missing links" that are talked about, that 145
they would help us to any other conclusion! At any rate the law which
states our present experience is strong enough for my present purpose.
You next reach the conclusion, that as these kinds of marks have not
been left by any other animals than men, or are liable to be formed in
any other way than by a man's hand and shoe, the marks in question 150
have been formed by a man in that way. You have, further, a general
law, founded on observation and experience, and that, too, is, I am sorry
to say, a very universal and unimpeachable one—that some men are
thieves; and you assume at once from all these premises—and that is
what constitutes your hypothesis—that the man who made the marks 155
outside and on the windowsill, opened the window, got into the room,
and stole your teapot and spoons. You have now arrived at a *vera causa*
—you have assumed a cause which, it is plain, is competent to produce
all the phenomena you have observed. You can explain all these
phenomena only by the hypothesis of a thief. But that is a hypothetical 160
conclusion, of the justice of which you have no absolute proof at all; it
is only rendered highly probable by a series of inductive and deductive
reasonings.

I suppose your first action, assuming that you are a man of ordinary
common sense, and that you have established this hypothesis to your 165
own satisfaction, will very likely be to go off for the police, and set them
on the track of the burglar, with the view to the recovery of your
property. But just as you are starting with this object, some person
comes in, and on learning what you are about, says, "My good friend,
you are going on a great deal too fast. How do you know that the man 170
who really made the marks took the spoons? It might have been a
monkey that took them, and the man may have merely looked in afterwards." You would probably reply, "Well, that is all very well, but you
see it is contrary to all experience of the way teapots and spoons are
abstracted; so that, at any rate, your hypothesis is less probable than 175
mine." While you are talking the thing over in this way, another friend
arrives, one of that good kind of people that I was talking of a little while
ago. And he might say, "Oh, my dear sir, you are certainly going on a
great deal too fast. You are most presumptuous. You admit that all these
occurrences took place when you were fast asleep, at a time when you 180
could not possibly have known anything about what was taking place.
How do you know that the laws of Nature are not suspended during the
night? It may be that there has been some kind of supernatural interference in this case." In point of fact, he declares that your hypothesis is
one of which you cannot at all demonstrate the truth, and that you are 185
by no means sure that the laws of Nature are the same when you are
asleep as when you are awake.

Well, now, you cannot at the moment answer that kind of reasoning. You feel that your worthy friend has you somewhat at a disadvantage. You will feel perfectly convinced in your own mind, however, that 190

you are quite right, and you say to him, "'My good friend, I can only be guided by the natural probabilities of the case, and if you will be kind enough to stand aside and permit me to pass, I will go fetch the police." Well, we will suppose that your journey is successful, and that by good luck you meet with a policeman; that eventually the burglar is found 195 with your property on his person, and the marks correspond to his hand and to his boots. Probably any jury would consider those facts a very good experimental verification of your hypothesis, touching the cause of the abnormal phenomena observed in your parlor, and would act accordingly. 200

Now, in this supposititious case, I have taken phenomena of a very common kind, in order that you might see what are the different steps in an ordinary process of reasoning, if you will only take the trouble to analyze it carefully. All the operations I have described, you will see, are involved in the mind of any man of sense in leading him to a 205 conclusion as to the course he should take in order to make good a robbery and punish the offender. I say that you are led, in this case, to your conclusion by exactly the same train of reasoning as that which a man of science pursues when he is endeavoring to discover the origin and laws of the most occult phenomena. The process is, and always must 210 be, the same; and precisely the same mode of reasoning was employed by Newton and Laplace in their endeavors to discover and define the causes of the movements of the heavenly bodies, as you, with your own common sense, would employ to detect a burglar. The only difference is, that the nature of the inquiry being more abstruse, every step has 215 to be more carefully watched, so that there may not be a single crack or flaw in your hypothesis. A flaw or crack in many of the hypotheses of daily life may be of little or no moment as affecting the general correctness of the conclusions at which we may arrive; but, in a scientific inquiry, a fallacy, great or small, is always of importance, and is sure 220 to be in the long run constantly productive of mischievous, if not fatal, results.

Do not allow yourselves to be misled by the common notion that an hypothesis is untrustworthy simply because it is an hypothesis. It is often urged, in respect to some scientific conclusion, that, after all, it is 225 only an hypothesis. But what more have we to guide us in nine-tenths of the most important affairs of daily life than hypotheses, and often very ill-based ones? So that in science, where the evidence of an hypothesis is subjected to the most rigid examination, we may rightly pursue the same course. You may have hypotheses and hypotheses. A man may 230 say, if he likes, that the moon is made of green cheese: that is an hypothesis. But another man, who has devoted a great deal of time and attention to the subject, and availed himself of the most powerful telescopes and the results of the observations of others, declares that in his opinion it is probably composed of materials very similar to those of 235 which our own earth is made up; and that is also only an hypothesis. But

I need not tell you that there is an enormous difference in the value of the two hypotheses. That one which is based on sound scientific knowledge is sure to have a corresponding value; and that which is a mere hasty random guess is likely to have but little value. Every great step 240 in our progress in discovering causes has been made in exactly the same way as that which I have detailed to you. A person observing the occurrence of certain facts and phenomena asks, naturally enough, what process, what kind of operation known to occur in Nature applied to the particular case, will unravel and explain the mystery? Hence you have 245 the scientific hypothesis; and its value will be proportionate to the care and completeness with which its basis has been tested and verified. It is in these matters as in the commonest affairs of practical life: The guess of the fool will be folly, while the guess of the wise man will contain wisdom. In all cases, you see that value of the result depends on the 250 patience and faithfulness with which the investigator applies to his hypothesis every possible kind of verification.

1. In the example of the apple, what steps are the basis for the conclusion?
2. In the example of the teapot, what steps are the basis for the conclusion?
3. What is the basis for rejecting the suggestion by the first friend? by the second friend?
4. What use does Huxley make of narrative, of analogy, and of comparison to make his points clear?
5. Check the etymology, denotation, and connotation of *mode, phenomena, graduated, beam, axis, induction, deduction, hypothesis, theories, syllogism, premise, verification, hobnailed, unimpeachable, presumptuous, suspended, supposititious, abstruse, fallacy;* what is the singular form of *phenomena?* of *hypotheses?* (Note that *apparatus* may be either singular or plural.)

Assignments

With all these assignments, be sure to look beyond the first causes that come to mind. Find the causes behind them and then the causes behind those, and so on.

1. What made you decide to become a college student and why did you choose the college you now attend? Be sure to go beyond easy explanations, such as that an education will prepare you for a career and that the college has a good reputation.
2. Everyone has prejudices—strong feelings on some subject, for or against, which exist without much thought or reason (see Example G in this unit). If you have noticed a prejudice held by one of your friends, ask what your friend believes to be its cause; then examine the answer and decide whether it is reasonable or whether your friend has been guilty of rationalization. Try the same experiment with a prejudice of your own (areas of taste, religion, politics, and race are good hunting grounds).

3. Choose some incident in your own life that at first seems to have been pure "accident," and search for causes. Consider all possibilities, rejecting those that do not bear up under scrutiny and explaining why you believe others to be the true ones. Determine what you believe to be the cause or causes of one of your present strong interests or hobbies. Then test the validity of your conclusions by checking them against the list of warnings on pages 207–208.
4. Examine some local phenomenon—a campus tradition, a dating custom, a strong interest in some kind of activity (from sports to studies), the presence or absence of the honor system—and try to determine the cause or causes behind it.
5. Write an essay with a title such as "I Changed My Mind" or "I Used to Think So" in which you organize your material into three sections: your original attitude toward something (a sport, activity, profession, person); the cause of your change of mind; your present attitude. Devote most of your attention to the cause of the change and its effects.
6. Choosing as your subject some situation, policy, or plan on your campus, write an essay predicting what the outcome will be. For example, what effects can logically be expected to follow an increase in tuition or enrollment? a change in entrance or degree requirements? the relaxation or tightening of rules regarding class attendance, drinking, visiting hours in dormitories?

UNIT 13

Inductive and Deductive Reasoning

If a new restaurant opens in your neighborhood, how do you decide whether to try it? Probably, you first check its general appearance from the street. If that seems attractive, you look for a menu posted on the door or a window. If you find one, you glance over it rapidly to determine the general type of food served and the range of choices. If these are satisfactory, you read the menu more closely and check the prices. If you are still attracted to the restaurant, you try to peek through the window to see the interior. If several tables are occupied by people who look pleasant and who seem to be enjoying their food, if the tables are comfortably large with plenty of space between them, if each table looks clean and has sparkling glasses and shining silverware, if the lighting is at a level you like, and if the general decoration is pleasing, you now feel safe in drawing the conclusion that the restaurant is worth trying.

You have used inductive reasoning to reach this conclusion, and you based each step in the process on earlier experiences in reaching conclusions about restaurants—for instance, you had learned from many experiences which types of cooking and which special dishes you like most and what prices are reasonable, what seating arrangements you prefer, how people behave when they are enjoying a good restaurant meal, and so on.

With inductive reasoning we add one piece of information to another until we have enough evidence to draw a conclusion. Usually, we know in advance what question we are trying to answer ("Is that new restaurant worth trying?") and search for relevant information, like the members of a jury who listen to evidence in a criminal case to prepare themselves to answer the question "Guilty or not guilty?" (Sometimes, of course, we may unexpectedly happen on the answer to a question we have not asked, like Sir Alexander Fleming, who was conducting research on the influenza virus when he chanced to notice the antibacterial effect of penicillin on staphylococcus germs.)

With deductive reasoning we use earlier conclusions, reached inductively by ourselves or others, to answer new questions about material. For example, suppose that, after eating several good meals at the restaurant, you learn that the owner has two other restaurants not far away. Curious to see if they are as good as the one you visited, you try both, examine them closely, and conclude that they equal the first in every way. When several of your friends, who also like the first restaurant, try the others and agree with you, your conclusion has further support. If you then hear that the owner plans to open a fourth restaurant and you are so convinced that it will meet the standard set by the others that you recommend it warmly, you have used deductive reasoning to reach a conclusion: you have relied entirely on a previous conclusion to form your opinion about a new case instead of testing it as you did the others.

This kind of thinking can be expressed as a **syllogism,** the classic pattern of deductive reasoning. A syllogism is composed of two statements, called premises, and a conclusion that derives from them. The classic example is this:

> *Major premise*—All men are mortal.
> *Minor premise*—Socrates is a man.
> *Conclusion*—Therefore Socrates is mortal.

In making your recommendation about the fourth restaurant, you derived your conclusion by the same process:

> *Major premise*—All of X's restaurants are good.
> *Minor premise*—Y is one of X's restaurants.
> *Conclusion*—Y is a good restaurant.

The conclusion reached through syllogistic reasoning is logically valid only if the terms are accurate and correctly related to each other. Three kinds of errors are common in trying to draw logical conclusions. Consider this faulty syllogism: "All fish can swim; John can swim; therefore John is a fish." Here, "swimming" includes "fish" and "John," but fish are not the only creatures who swim, and so John's ability to swim does not make him a fish. Also consider this: "All men drown in deep water; John is a man; therefore John will drown in deep water." Here the major premise is an inaccurate generalization; "drowning" does not include "all men," only those who cannot swim, and if John can swim, he will not automatically drown in deep water. Finally, consider this: "All mammals nurse their young; turtles are mammals; therefore turtles nurse their young." Here, the minor premise is inaccurate. Although all mammals nurse their young, turtles are not mammals, and therefore the major premise does not apply to them. Remember that the truth of a valid conclusion depends entirely on the reliability of the premises and of their relationship to each other.

Syllogistic reasoning may seem only a kind of game, but its importance becomes clear when we examine the logic behind some of our own hasty conclusions. "Bob shouldn't apply to law school; he's one of the stupid Joneses." What is the reasoning here? Part of it looks like the following when we supply the unexpressed but implied major premise:

> Stupid people should not apply to law school.
> Bob is a stupid person.
> Therefore he should not apply to law school.

The generalization in the major premise seems reasonable, but what of the minor premise—what evidence have we that Bob is stupid? For this we must go back to an earlier *implied* deduction:

> All the Joneses are stupid.
> Bob is a Jones.
> Therefore Bob is stupid.

Here the major premise is harder to accept. It may prove on closer examination to be based only on gossip, or at least to be an overstatement; perhaps some of the Joneses are stupid but Bob is one of the exceptions. Or if we are able to accept the generalization, the minor premise may not hold; perhaps Bob is adopted. In any event, by examining of our reasoning we may become less satisfied with our first casual conclusion and concede that we should let Bob's fitness for law school be determined by his performance on entrance examinations.

A football player once wrote in a theme that the trouble with his college was that "Writing is taught to too great an extent, thus causing players to be ineligible, games to be lost, and the college to lose its standing among institutions of higher learning." One suspects that even a devoted football fan, faced with the "general truth" lurking behind this remark, would not attempt to defend it, for arranged syllogistically, the major deduction runs something like this:

Major premise: All reputable colleges should have as their primary purpose the winning of football games.
Minor premise: This is a reputable college.
Conclusion: Therefore this college should have as its primary purpose the winning of football games.

Many of our conclusions rest, as do these examples, on general assumptions—often unstated, sometimes not clear even to ourselves, and sometimes found on analysis to be false. An excellent way to learn to analyze the thinking of others and to think more accurately ourselves is to uncover underlying assumptions and check their validity. To do this, we should examine the sources of every generalization; they will probably be one or more of these:

a. an unquestionable assumption like "All men are mortal"—we need not test it because it has been reaffirmed by experience from the beginning of time;
b. an inductive conclusion not yet firmly established—we may need to examine the evidence on which it rests;

c. a conclusion reached through a previous syllogistic deduction, as in the example of Bob's stupidity—we may need to examine the validity of the deductive reasoning that produced it;

d. a statement by a person whose expertise is not known—we need to establish his or her authority adequately;

e. an assumption that we fix arbitrarily by definition—we could, for example, deduce whether or not to classify a certain type of music as good if we accept the assumption that "good music is music that we dance to easily."

     * * *   * * *   * * *

For a paper in which you practice using inductive and deductive reasoning to reach a conclusion of some kind, choose a topic about which you are really curious because investigating it may take some time. But choose a fairly limited topic so that you will be able to explore it thoroughly in the time allowed. There are several specific suggestions in "Assignments" at the end of this unit.

To convince yourself and others that you have drawn a logical conclusion, follow these guidelines:

1. Keep an open mind as you work toward a conclusion. Do not decide in advance what it will be; a preconceived opinion will prejudice you. Your object is to arrive at whatever truth emerges from the evidence, not to select evidence to support your previous idea of the truth. Certainly, an inkling of what you hope to determine can help you to start your investigation, just as scientists begin experiments with a hypothesis—a tentative formulation of the truth they are working to establish. However, like scientists, you must be willing to abandon your hypothesis if the facts fail to uphold it. For example, you might start to investigate the effect of extracurricular activities on student grades because you suspect that the activities interfere with study. But you may find that students study more effectively after relaxing with those activities. Your final generalization must be whatever the evidence supports—not what you would like it to support.

2. Do not lose sight of the problem you are investigating. To determine the effect of extracurricular activities on grades, for instance, you must not be distracted by the question of whether such activities help in developing a well-rounded personality, which is quite another matter.

3. Consider a reasonable number of instances. Drawing conclusions does not mean jumping to them. A *hasty generalization,* the most common fallacy in inductive reasoning, is one made on insufficient evidence. Your conclusion about the effect of extracurricular activities will have little validity if you based it on observations of only three or four students. What constitutes a "reasonable" number of instances will depend partly on the subject. For example, an investigation of which background, city or rural, has produced more presidents of the United States could easily include all the presidents, but a similar study of

American doctors could be reasonably done through a sampling. The number of instances necessary will also depend on your intention. For practical purposes, you will not need nearly so many as scientists do; their studies may require hundreds, even thousands, of instances, but you may need only a few well-chosen ones. Moreover, you do not have to give the details of all the instances but only the evidence you draw from them.

4. Use fair instances. Get a representative sampling. Do not let your preconceptions or haste to finish influence you. Public opinion research-ers use elaborate techniques to get fair samples. If you are studying the effects of activities on the grades of students in general, do not limit your examples to those with high or low grades; make a cross section.

5. Consider carefully any contrary evidence you may find. Charles Darwin, the nineteenth-century naturalist, kept special records of any evidence that tended to disprove his hypothesis concerning evolution, on the grounds that he could easily remember the data that supported his theory but needed reminders of contrary evidence.

6. Be cautious in drawing conclusions and generalizing. Do not conclude, because you know two drama club members, who are on probation, that drama club members in general have low academic averages.

The more carefully you guard against any suggestion of prejudice, any loading of the dice, in your choice and analysis of instances, the more reliable and convincing your conclusions will be.

* * *   * * *   * * *

In organizing your paper, you may choose between the inductive and deductive rhetorical patterns or use them in combination. These are named after the two patterns of thinking just examined, but each can be used to describe an investigation by either method.

1. To use the inductive pattern, start with little or no indication of the conclusions you finally reached in your investigation. Make your readers imagine that they are accompanying you in your examination of material and your search for meaning in it. The conclusions you draw will therefore form a climax at the end of the paper. For example, to write a paper organized inductively on whether to try a particular restaurant, you would begin with whatever first brought the restaurant to your attention and give all the information in precisely the order in which it came to you, including any false leads you followed. You would also give your interpretations and conclusions on the material in exactly the sequence in which you made them, and your final decision, that the restaurant was worth visiting, would form the end of the paper, much as the solution to the crime forms the end of a detective story.

Advantages in using the inductive pattern: Readers have a sense of sharing the investigation with you, and their curiosity will be aroused as to the outcome.

Disadvantages in using the inductive pattern: If the material is at all complex or unfamiliar to your readers, they may have difficulty in following the steps and may not accept your interpretation of the evidence.

2. To use the deductive pattern, begin by briefly stating your conclusion. Then describe the steps by which you reached it.

Advantages in using the deductive pattern: Your readers will know from the start precisely where you are leading them and will therefore know what to look for in the evidence you present. You can describe false leads very briefly and thus emphasize your conclusions more firmly.

Disadvantage in using the deductive pattern: The ending will be an anticlimax unless you can present it in particularly forceful words that catch your readers' imaginations.

3. To combine the two patterns, start with a hint about the conclusions you reached and then present your investigation chronologically, ending with a full explanation of your conclusions. In writing on the restaurants mentioned earlier, you could, for example, start by presenting your conclusion as a question: "Is X's fourth restaurant good?" You would then give the evidence on the other restaurants, starting with your first view of the first one and ending with your answer to the question—your conclusion that you are sure that it is good. Sir Edmund Hillary uses a question effectively to begin his essay, which is in this unit. You might, instead, start by presenting your conclusion in the form of a general opinion that can be seen as open to discussion or, at the very least, in need of explanation and support—for example, "The quality never varies in any of the restaurants of a careful owner." The third sentence of Example A in this unit and the first sentences of Examples B, C, and D present such opinions.

* * *   * * *   * * *

In planning, writing, and revising your paper, keep the following points in mind:

1. Assemble an adequate quantity of evidence—if you fear you have too much, use phrases such as "A minor example of this point is . . ." or "Some additional support is . . ." to let readers know that they can read those parts rapidly.

2. Examine all your assumptions to be sure that they are based on good sources (the checklist given earlier about Bob Jones will help you), and explain them fully to your readers.

3. Define your terms.

4. Test the validity of your evidence at every step and show your readers that you have done so.

5. Remember that analogies are never evidence, merely rhetorical devices that clarify what they describe (see pages 146–147). Make sure that any analogies you use are well chosen. The fact that swimming, being a skill, requires not only an understanding of technique but also much practice may well illustrate the point that writing, although a very different sort of skill, also requires a study of technique and much practice. But a country doctor's need for a car is too far removed from the international scene to make a good analogy with a nation's need for a merchant marine, even though both situations involve transportation.

6. Emphasize the logic of your deductions by presenting the steps clearly.

7. Be cautious in wording generalizations. Never overstate your claims. You may not be able to arrive at an absolutely certain conclusion, but there is value in suggesting significant trends. In writing your paper, limit the scope of your conclusions by giving percentages or by carefully chosen words such as *nearly all, probably, usually, likely, possibly, sometimes, few, seldom, rarely.* (See Example B in this unit.)

8. Sharpen your thinking throughout by imagining a very skeptical, "show me!" kind of reader who doubts and questions you at every step.

Examples

In the selections in this unit, reasoning by inductive and deductive methods is essential, but it plays such an important part in all thinking that you will find it present, at least to some extent, in every other selection in this book. For a particularly notable example, go back to Huxley's "The Method of Scientific Investigation" (Unit 12-H) and re- 5 read the first six paragraphs.

13-A   Three Incidents

The New Yorker

This unsigned essay, here complete, appeared in *The New Yorker* in 1980. The writer is surprised by a conclusion reached inductively.

I am fully aware that anecdotal evidence is no longer, if it ever was, in good scientific repute. Nevertheless, in the course of the past few months I have been witness to three aberrations of nature that seem to me to be worth noting. They suggest, if nothing else, that, contrary to much received understanding, man is not the only form of life that is 5 capable of making a fool of itself.

The first of these incidents occurred in the spring, just under the eaves on our front veranda. There is a fixture up there, a galvanized-iron box about the size and shape of a thick paperback book (it has something to do with the outdoor lights), that forms a kind of shelf. I came out on the veranda one morning in time to see a bird—a little 10 red-breasted house finch—make a landing there on the top of the box and deposit a beakful of grass. I stood on tiptoe and craned my neck, and saw the beginnings of a nest. It was in many ways an excellent nesting site—dry, airy, nicely sheltered. But it was also as slippery as glass. And, as I watched, a gust of breeze came along and the nest slid off and blew away in pieces. Well, that, I thought, is that. The bird, however, thought differently. It went to work again, retrieving the scattered grasses, and started another nest. Another doomed nest, I should say. Because another little breeze came along and scattered that nest, too. But the finch was undismayed. I watched it start still another nest, and I watched that nest blow away. That was enough for me. I went on with my own affairs. But every now and then through the rest of the day I went over to the door or the window and looked out. The finch was always there—sitting on the box, fluttering away, swooping back with a wisp of grass. And there was still nothing more than the pathetic beginnings of a nest.

The second incident occurred in the house, in the attic. I went up there a couple of weeks ago to look for something or other. I was feeling my way toward an old chest of drawers when something odd caught my eye. It was a strand of ivy espaliered on the wall above the little end window. It was two or three feet long, its leaves were a sickly yellowy green, and it had forced itself, at God knows what exertion, through a tiny crack in the window frame from the life-giving sunlight into the deadly dusk of the attic.

And then, just the other day, I was out weeding the garden and sat down on the bench to rest and noticed an anthill at my feet. There was much coming and going around the hole—a stream of foraging workers. I leaned down and watched a worker emerge from the hole, race away through the grass, pounce on a tiny something—a seed, maybe, or an egg or a minuscule creature—and head quickly back toward the hole. Only, it headed in the wrong direction. It raced this way and that, back and forth, farther and farther away from home. I had to get up from the bench to follow it. I finally lost it, in a weedy jungle, a good eight feet (the equivalent, perhaps, of a couple of miles) from where it wanted to be. I went back to the bench and sat down again and wondered. It might be possible, I thought, to somehow see the strivings of the finch as an example of determination, an iron procreative perseverance. And the ivy: its suicidal floundering, too, might be explained—as an evolutionary thrust, an urge (like that of some aquatic organism feeling its way up a beach) to try a new environment. But the ant! There was no way of rationalizing that: the phenomenon of a worker ant—an ant bred exclusively to forage for its queen—unable to find its way home. It shook and shattered the concept of a knowing and nurturing instinct, of a computerized infallibility, in nature. I felt a tug of something like sympathy for that errant ant. And also for the finch and the ivy. They gave me a new vision of nature: a nature unmechanized, a nature vulnerable, a nature appealingly natural.

1. The writer gives the three incidents chronologically—in the order in which they occurred. Do you find any additional reason for this sequence?
2. Where does the writer use specific, concrete details? specific, concrete words?
3. Check the etymology, denotation, and connotation of *aberrations, received understanding, espaliered, foraging, minuscule.*

13-B   The Language of Uncertainty

John Cohen

In these paragraphs from an essay in *Scientific American* (1957) Cohen reports the results reached **inductively** through experiments and suggests applying them **deductively** in intelligence testing.

ANALYSIS
General
conclusion
Examples

    Uncertainty pervades our lives so thoroughly that it dominates our language. Our everyday speech is made up in large part of words like *probably, many, soon, great, little.* What do these words mean? "Atomic war," declared a recent editorial in the London *Times*, "is likely to ruin 5 forever the nation that even victoriously wages it. How

Analysis of
example

exactly are we to understand the word *likely?* Lacking any standard for estimating the odds, we are left with the private probability of the editorial writer.

Analysis of
conclusion

    Such verbal imprecision is not necessarily to be con- 10 demned. Indeed, it has a value just because it allows us to express judgments when a precise quantitative statement is out of the question. All the same, we should not and need not hide behind a screen of complete indefiniteness.

General
purpose of
experiments

Often it is possible to indicate the bounds or limits of the 15 quantitative value we have in mind.

Classification
of data

    The language of uncertainty has three main categories: (1) words such as *probably, possibly, surely,* which denote a single subjective probability and are potentially quantifiable; (2) words like *many, often, soon,* which are 20 also quantifiable but denote not so much a condition of uncertainty as a quantity imprecisely known; (3) words like *fat, rich, drunk,* which are not reducible to any accepted number because they are given values by different people.   25

Specific
purpose of
experiments
Method for
analyzing
data

    We have been trying to pin down, by experimental studies, what people mean by these expressions in specific contexts, and how the meanings change with age. For instance, a subject is told "There are many trees in the park" and is asked to say what number the word *many* 30 means to him. Or a child is invited to take "some" sweets from a bowl and we then count how many he has taken. We compare the number he takes when alone with the number when one or more other children are present and are to take some sweets after him, or with the number he 35 takes when instructed to give "some" sweets to another child.

Category #1: Results of analysis Examples

First, we find that the number depends, of course, on the items involved. To most people *some friends* means about five, while *some trees* means about twenty. How- 40 ever, unrelated areas sometimes show parallel values. For instance, the language of probability seems to mean about the same thing in predictions about the weather and about politics: the expression *is certain to (rain,* or *be elected)* signifies to the average person about a 70 per cent chance; 45 *is likely to,* about a 60 per cent chance; *probably will,* about 55 per cent.

Category #2: Results of analysis Examples

Secondly, the size of the population of items influ- ences the value assigned to an expression. Thus, if we tell a subject to take "a few" or "a lot of" beads from a tray, 50 he will take more if the tray contains a large number of beads than if it has a small number. But not proportion- ately more: if we increase the number of beads eightfold, the subject takes only half as large a percentage of the total. 55

Category #3: Results of analysis Deductive application of results Examples

Thirdly, there is a marked change with age. Among children between six and fourteen years old, the older the child, the fewer beads he will take. But the difference between *a lot* and *a few* widens with age. This age effect is so consistent that it might be used as a test of intelli- 60 gence. In place of a long test we could merely ask the subject to give numerical values to expressions such as *nearly always* and *very rarely* in a given context, and then measure his intelligence by the ratio of the number of *nearly always* to the one for *very rarely.* We have found 65 that this ratio increases systematically from about 2 to 1 for a child of seven to about 20 to 1 for a person twenty-five years old.

1. The writer gives the results of the experiment, not all the data on which they were based (presumably these are available on request). Are the results convincing without the data?
2. What is the principle of classification of the general subject in ¶3? What is the principle of the classification of the results of the analysis in ¶5–7?
3. Check the etymology, denotation, and connotation of *quantitative, subjec- tive, quantifiable, denote, contexts.*

13-C   Letter from Home

William Zinsser

Zinsser was a member of the Yale faculty when this essay, here complete, appeared in the *New York Times* (1977). His most recent books are *On Writing Well* and *Writing with a Word Processor*. Here, in his analysis of the problems he found students facing, Zinsser applies deductions he had made much earlier on the importance of freedom. What opinions does he share with Hiatt (13-H) and St. John (6-A)? Do the students you know have similar problems? For a student's reply to Zinsser, read Cooper's essay (13-E).

Now is the edgy time for Yale seniors. In three weeks they will graduate and join the rest of us out here in the real world. It is a place that they are inordinately afraid of.

Not all of them, of course, will take the icy plunge. Quite a few will stay on the academic assembly-line—in law school or medical school or 5 graduate school—to study for three or four years more. This doesn't mean that they necessarily want to be lawyers or doctors or scholars. Some are continuing their education because their parents want them to. Some are doing it just to postpone the day of decision. Some are doing it because lawyers and doctors make a good living. Some are 10 doing it to acquire still another degree to impress a society in which they think credentials are the only currency. Some—the lucky ones— really do want to be lawyers, doctors, scholars or specialists in a field that requires further skill.

But they all are driven—those who are leaving Academia and those 15 who are staying—by one message: Do Not Fail. It is a message that has been echoing in their heads since they were admitted to the pre-kinder-garten of their choice, beating less competitive toddlers. Score high, test well, play it safe. Next month's graduates have been so obsessively bent for four years on measurable achievement (grades) and a secure 20 future (jobs) that they have hardly had time to savor the present and to grow as well-rounded people. They know that the outside world is wary of experimenters, of late starters and temporary losers.

I'm talking about Yale students because I live in their midst and know them well. (I am Master of Branford College, one of Yale's twelve 25 residential colleges. In our house I can lie awake and listen to some of the loudest stereo sets in the East. That, in fact, is why I lie awake.) And I'm talking about seniors because they are the ones who are most on my mind right now: panicky that they won't have enough A's to persuade an employer to hire them, though they are men and women I'd like to 30 have working for me, if I were an employer, for qualities of intelligence and humor and humanity that don't show up on any chart.

But I could just as well be talking about Yale's juniors, sophomores and freshmen—or, I suspect, about the students at most colleges today. They are studying more and enjoying it less. At Yale, they play in fewer 35 plays and musical groups, join fewer campus organizations, take part in fewer sports, carve out fewer moments just to linger and talk and put a margin around their lives. They are under pressure to do too much work in too little time.

If all their friends are studying in the library until it closes at 40 midnight (and they are), they feel guilty if they want to go to a Woody Allen movie, though there is as much to be learned from a Woody Allen movie as from a book—much, in fact, that they will never learn from a book. Not surprisingly, their emotional health is often far from healthy. I see a lot of psychic disarray. 45

It is not that I don't wish them fame and fortune, especially the seniors as they lurch toward graduation, more stuffed with learning and shorn of money than they probably ever will be again. Obviously I do. But I also wish them a release from fear of the future. They should know that fame and fortune are not end products that they will automatically 50 win if they follow a straight and safe route, but by-products that will accrue to them if they dare to poke down the unmarked side roads that lead to life's richest surprises.

Risk and change, art and music, joy and affection, the unexpected friendship of strangers—these are some of the essential tonics. "To 55 affect the quality of the day, that is the highest of the arts," said Thoreau. I wish it could be chiseled over the door of every school, college, corporation and home.

Home is where the words "Do not fail" are first instilled and constantly repeated. One of next month's Yale graduates came to me on 60 her first day as a freshman in 1973 and said: "I want to be a great journalist—what courses should I take for the next four years?" She wanted a blueprint at seventeen. Many students come to me in the middle of their sophomore year, afraid of changing the curriculum that they mapped but no longer think is the one that they want to pursue. 65 "If I don't make all the right choices now," one of them said, "It will be too late."

Too late at eighteen? Sad words. They are growing up old and set in their ways. They have been told to prepare for one career—preferably one that will reflect well on their parents—and to stick to it and 70 succeed. They are not told that they have a right to try many paths, to stumble and try something else, and to learn by stumbling. The right to fail is one of the few freedoms not granted in our Bill of Rights. Today it is more acceptable to change marriage partners than to change careers. 75

"Victory has very narrow meanings and can become a destructive force," writes Bill Bradley in his book, *Life on the Run*. Bradley was an Ivy Leaguer himself and a Rhodes Scholar—an earlier member of the same elite that is now so preoccupied with success—before starting his ten-year career of professional basketball, which has just come to an 80 end. "The taste of defeat," he writes, "has a richness of experience all its own. To me, every day is a struggle to stay in touch with life's subtleties. No one grows without failing."

The fault is not with our children, but with the narrowness of the flowerbed in which we expect them to germinate. We are stunting their growth if we tell them that there is only one "right" way to get through their education or to get through life. America has always been nourished by mavericks and individuals—men and women not afraid to go against the grain. 85

1. What, if anything, does Zinsser gain by delaying the statement of his major premise almost to the end?
2. The only analogy in the essay is at the very end, but many examples of figurative language are scattered throughout, beginning with "icy plunge" and "assembly line" in the second paragraph. What others can you find and what do they contribute to the effectiveness of the essay?
3. Check the etymology, denotation, and connotation of *inordinately, credentials, currency, wary, lurch, accrue, tonics, elite, mavericks;* check the origin of *against the grain.*

13-D   After Graduation, What Next?

Fred Hiatt

Hiatt was a Harvard senior when he wrote this essay, here almost complete. It appeared in the *Boston Globe* in May 1977. He began by quoting a classmate who claimed that many seniors were as concerned with correcting social injustices as the students in the '60s had been.

One of my goals this year has been to teach the mechanics of typing to a cat I know, a cat who has always been fascinated by manual typewriters, pawing at the letter rods as they jumped out and watching with frustration when they lie quietly beyond his reach. I have spent hours pushing his paws on the keys and encouraging him to see the causal 5 connection, to see that the letters have no life of their own. But the cat, as fascinated as ever, still vainly hopes to catch one alive.

Similarly, many seniors are concerned, even fascinated, by their society and by its injustices, but baffled by the causal links, uncertain where the injustice comes from or what they could do about it. And so, 10 though they are concerned—"quiescent, but not acquiescent," as Harvard sociology professor David Riesman said—within a few years even many who are not yet pre-business will have lost interest in "working towards change."

Most of us, then, will pursue lucrative careers in business, law, or 15 medicine. A survey of 1971 Harvard graduates showed more than 50 per cent choosing one of the three within five years, and while the number of 1977 graduates going to law school may drop a bit, more will probably end up in business school.

Many will go not because they've wanted to be executives or attor- 20 neys, nor just to make money, but because they don't know what else to do. Part of the appeal of the professional career is the desire, or need, for individual recognition. In school we learned to judge the quality of our work by the grade somebody else assigned it. At college we scrabbled for the prominent byline or the leading role on stage.   25

Now the reputation of the law school seems to matter more than what we will do as lawyers, the prestige of the newspaper more than what we'd like to say in print. Only power and fame can bring "success" and happiness.

To opt for the cooperative, to work in legal aid without heading the   30
office, to write without a byline, would be to reject everything we've been trained to be. And that rejection would be doubly hard for women, who, instead of receiving praise for spurning ego-gratification, would be blamed by many for regressing to old passive roles.

Then, many seniors just don't see other options. Up to now, we've   35
always been most rewarded for performing the expected. To depart from the expected now—to choose a career that doesn't guarantee power and $35,000 a year five years from now—takes courage. Many Harvard graduates, though certainly not all, can afford more easily than other college graduates to pass up the best-paying job; their family   40
background and their degree render future starvation unlikely.

Yet, most of us won't dare pass up that job. In a few years, we will persuade ourselves that we "need" a car, a sunnier apartment, a winter vacation—and that we "need" more money than we can imagine needing now. And as we grow discouraged by the potential for real social   45
change, working "within the system" will seem more and more sensible —until one day we suddenly find ourselves not infiltrators, but bulwarks, of that system.

Going to professional school is not the same as selling out, of course, and for many women and minority graduates the struggle is just begin-   50
ning. But many of us seem to be headed past quiescence into acquiescence itself. Maybe the only thing that can bring about a profound change is sex, the search for new structures of romance. . . . At least some feminist values have seeped into the undergraduate consciousness and, together with the seriousness with which most women face   55
their careers, have prompted new problems, new ground rules, new questionings of old assumptions. Whose job should take priority—until now a problem for only a few, middle-class career couples—is an issue, real or potential, for almost every graduate. If he follows her, will the relationship suddenly seem more permanent than they want it to be?   60
If she follows him, is she giving in to sexist pressures?

Where political principles and the quest for adventure once stood in the way of pure ambition, now only love interferes. He may work in a dead-end job to help her through law school; she may settle for a second-rate medical school to stay by his side.   65

It will be interesting to see, when we gather for our five-year reunion, whether we have settled into our law firms with housewives and househusbands at our sides, whether we have forsaken coupledom entirely—or whether the compromises forced on us by relationships have derailed us from the straight, ambitious track in a way that, for 70 most of us, the search for adventure and the commitment of political activism no longer can.

1. On what premises does Hiatt base his conclusions?
2. What specific, concrete details does he use?
3. What relationships can you see between Hiatt's opinions and those of Zinsser in the preceding example? of Bell in 4-D?
4. How appropriate is the analogy of the inability of the cat to understand cause and effect?
5. Check the etymology, denotation, and connotation of *camaraderie, quiescent, acquiescent, bulwarks.*

13-E   A Reply to Zinsser and Hiatt

Chris Cooper (student)

Today's college students face a multitude of decisions. With rising tuition costs, most students graduate not only with a diploma but with a pile of debts. Can we attend college for personal fulfillment alone and place no monetary value on the degree? I think not, but I do feel that learning to appreciate art, acquiring social skills, and interacting with 5 others are vital parts of a college education. Students must not relinquish their right to question, to disagree, and to be wrong.

According to Zinsser in "Letter from Home," most students are so intent on success, on "making it" in the "real world," that they want to follow a formula instead of experimenting. As a result, he says, they are 10 missing a lot. Some of the true treasures of life are on the "unmarked side roads"—the rewards of human interaction, of art, of individualism, and even of occasional failure, which Zinsser claims can be one of life's best educators.

Fred Hiatt makes some of the same points in "After Graduation, 15 What Next?" He believes that most students are not in college or professional school for an education but to get a high-paying job afterwards, and he wishes that they cared more about correcting social wrongs and were more willing to risk being unconventional. Zinsser, on the other hand, does not put down the students' desire for success but instead 20 argues that a lasting success can be better achieved by suffering from a few pitfalls along the route.

Both authors have valid arguments, but only within the limits of the kinds of colleges they know. I have been a student on three different campuses—a state college, a city college, and a private college. I agree 25 with Zinsser that students are afraid of failure, but I think their fears are valid. Students today are seeing their middle-aged parents suddenly out of work. The American dream of following the right routes and being sure of success does not always come true. I cannot sympathize readily with Hiatt's argument. Since he was a Harvard senior when he wrote the essay, it was fairly easy for him to advocate working for social change instead of personal success. He admits himself that Harvard graduates can usually afford to pass up a job opportunity without risking starvation, unlike graduates of other colleges. Both authors are writing about Ivy League students but are trying to apply their deductions to *all* college students. I do not think that these deductions are general truths. For many students at city and state universities, it is a struggle just to attend class—their parents would rather that they work to help support the family. I do believe, however, that students should not be afraid to take risks or change their minds—a little experimentation is good, even when we have to pay for our mistakes. But many of the students that I know are expressing their individuality by attending college in the first place.

1. In your opinion, does the writer present Zinsser's and Hiatt's arguments accurately?
2. The writer relies on his own personal experience to make his reply. Is this an adequate basis? Do you agree or disagree with this writer?

13-F   An Open Letter to Black Parents: Send Your Children to the Libraries

Arthur Ashe

This essay, here complete, is from the *New York Times* (1977). Ashe, an international tennis champion, retired from professional sports in 1980 because of heart trouble but continues as captain of the U.S. Davis cup team and is a sports commentator. He has compiled a reference book, *The History of the Black Athlete in America* (1984).

Since my sophomore year at University of California, Los Angeles, I have become convinced that we blacks spend too much time on the playing fields and too little time in the libraries.

Please don't think of this attitude as being pretentious just because I am a black, single, professional athlete. I don't have children, but I can make observations. I strongly believe the black culture expends too much time, energy and effort raising, praising and teasing our black children as to the dubious glories of professional sport.

All children need models to emulate—parents, relatives or friends. But when the child starts school, the influence of the parent is shared by teachers and classmates, by the lure of books, movies, ministers and newspapers, but most of all by television. Which televised events have the greatest number of viewers?—Sports—the Olympics, Super Bowl, Masters, World Series, pro basketball playoffs, Forest Hills. ABC-TV

even has sports on Monday night prime time from April to December. 15
So your child gets a massive dose of O. J. Simpson, Kareem Abdul-
Jabbar, Muhammad Ali, Reggie Jackson, Dr. J and Lee Elder and other
pro athletes. And it is only natural that your child will dream of being
a pro athlete himself.

But consider these facts: For the major professional sports of 20
hockey, football, basketball, baseball, golf, tennis and boxing, there are
roughly only 3,170 major league positions available (attributing 200
positions to golf, 200 to tennis and 100 to boxing). And the annual
turnover is small. We blacks are a subculture of about 28 million. Of the
13½ million men, 5 to 6 million are under twenty years of age, so your 25
son has less than one chance in 1,000 of becoming a pro. Less than one
in a thousand. Would you bet your son's future on something with odds
of 999 to 1 against you? I wouldn't.

Unless a child is exceptionally gifted, you should know by the time
he enters high school whether he has a future as an athlete. But what 30
is more important is what happens if he doesn't graduate or doesn't land
a college scholarship and doesn't have a viable alternative job career.
Our high school dropout rate is several times the national average,
which contributes to our unemployment rate of roughly twice the national average.   35

And how do you fight the figures in the newspapers every day? Ali
has earned more than $30 million boxing, O. J. just signed for $2½
million, Dr. J. for almost $3 million, Reggie Jackson for $2.8 million,
Nate Archibald for $400,000 a year. All that money, recognition, atten-
tion, free cars, girls, jobs in the offseason—no wonder there is Pop 40
Warner football, Little League baseball, National Junior Tennis League
tennis, hockey practice at 5 A.M. and pickup basketball games in any
center city at any hour.

There must be some way to assure that the 999 who try but don't
make it to pro sports don't wind up on the street corners or in the 45
unemployment lines. Unfortunately, our most widely recognized role
models are athletes and entertainers—"runnin' " and "jumpin' " and
"singin' " and "dancin.' " While we are 60 percent of the National
Basketball Association, we are less than 4 percent of the doctors and
lawyers. While we are about 35 percent of major league baseball, we 50
are less than 2 percent of the engineers. While we are about 40 percent
of the National Football League, we are less than 11 percent of construction workers such as carpenters and bricklayers.

Our greatest heroes of the century have been athletes—Jack Johnson, Joe Louis and Muhammad Ali. Racial and economic discrimination 55
forced us to channel our energies into athletics and entertainment.
These were the ways out of the ghetto, the ways to get that Cadillac,
those alligator shoes, that cashmere sport coat.

Somehow, parents must instill a desire for learning alongside the
desire to be Walt Frazier. Why not start by sending black professional 60

athletes into high schools to explain the facts of life? I have often addressed high school audiences, and my message is always the same. For every hour you spend on the athletic field, spend two in the library. Even if you make it as a pro athlete, your career will be over by the time you are thirty-five. So you will need that diploma. 65

Have these pro athletes explain what happens if you break a leg, get a sore arm, have one bad year or don't make the cut for five or six tournaments. Explain to them the star system, wherein for every O. J. earning millions there are six or seven others making $15,000 or $20,-000 or $30,000 a year. 70

But don't just have Walt Frazier or O. J. or Abdul-Jabbar address your class. Invite a benchwarmer or a guy who didn't make it. Ask him if he sleeps every night. Ask him whether he was graduated. Ask him what he would do if he became disabled tomorrow. Ask him where his old high school athletic buddies are. 75

We have been on the same roads—sports and entertainment—too long. We need to pull over, fill up at the library and speed away to Congress and the Supreme Court, the unions and the business world. We need more Barbara Jordans, Andrew Youngs, union cardholders, Nikki Giovannis and Earl Graveses. Don't worry: we will still be able 80 to sing and dance and run and jump better than anybody else.

I'll never forget how proud my grandmother was when I graduated from U.C.L.A. in 1966. Never mind the Davis Cup in 1968, 1969, and 1970. Never mind the Wimbledon title, Forest Hills, etc. To this day, she still doesn't know what those names mean. What matters to her was 85 that of her more than thirty children and grandchildren, I was the first to be graduated from college, and a famous college at that. Somehow, that made up for all those floors she scrubbed all those years.

1. As the title indicates, Ashe has written a letter, not a formal argument, but his advice is based on the deduction that there are very few chances for success in professional athletics. What follows from this deduction?
2. What support does he give the deduction?
3. What use does he make of narrative, analogy, and analysis to support his argument?

13-G   The Child in January

Gordon D. DeLetto (student)

All forms of activity lead to boredom when performed on a routine basis. We can see this principle at work in people of all ages. On Christmas morning, children play with their new toys and games. But the novelty soon wears off, and by January those same toys can be found tucked away in the attic. The world is well stocked with half-filled stamp 5 albums and unfinished models, each standing as a monument to someone's waning interest. When parents bring home a pet, their child gladly grooms it. Within a short time, however, the burden of caring for the animal is shifted to the parents. Adolescents enter high school with enthusiasm but are soon looking forward to graduation. A similar fate 10 befalls the young adults going on to college. How many adults, who now complain about the long drives to work, eagerly drove for hours at a time when they first obtained their licenses? Before people retire, they usually talk about doing all of the interesting things that they never had time to do while working. But soon after retirement, the golfing, the 15 fishing, the reading and all of the other pastimes become as boring as the jobs they left. And, like the child in January, they go searching for new toys.

1. Why has the author arranged his data in a chronological pattern?
2. What criticism of people is implied by the author's use of the analogy of the behavior of children with toys?

13-H   A Red Light for Scofflaws

Frank Trippett

This essay, here complete, first appeared in *Time* in 1983. On the basis of many observations, the author concludes that we may be turning into a "terminally foolish society," unable to govern our own behavior for the good of others.

Law-and-order is the longest-running and probably the best-loved political issue in U.S. history. Yet it is painfully apparent that millions of Americans who would never think of themselves as lawbreakers, let alone criminals, are taking increasing liberties with the legal codes that are designed to protect and nourish their society. Indeed, there are 5 moments today—amid outlaw litter, tax cheating, illicit noise and motorized anarchy—when it seems as though the scofflaw represents the wave of the future. Harvard Sociologist David Riesman suspects that a majority of Americans have blithely taken to committing supposedly minor derelictions as a matter of course. Already, Riesman says, the 10 ethic of U.S. society is in danger of becoming this: "You're a fool if you obey the rules."

Nothing could be more obvious than the evidence supporting Riesman. Scofflaws abound in amazing variety. The graffiti-prone turn public surfaces into visual rubbish. Bicyclists often ride as though two- 15 wheeled vehicles are exempt from all traffic laws. Litterbugs convert their communities into trash dumps. Widespread flurries of ordinances have failed to clear public places of high-decibel portable radios, just as earlier laws failed to wipe out the beer-soaked hooliganism that plagues many parks. Tobacco addicts remain hopelessly blind to signs that say 20 NO SMOKING. Respectably dressed pot smokers no longer bother to duck out of public sight to pass around a joint. The flagrant use of cocaine is a festering scandal in middle- and upper-class life. And then there are (hello, Everybody!) the jaywalkers.

The dangers of scofflawry vary wildly. The person who illegally 25 spits on the sidewalk remains disgusting, but clearly poses less risk to others than the company that illegally buries hazardous chemical waste in an unauthorized location. The fare beater on the subway presents less threat to life than the landlord who ignores fire safety statutes. The most immediately and measurably dangerous scofflawry, however, also 30 happens to be the most visible. The culprit is the American driver, whose lawless activities today add up to a colossal public nuisance. The hazards range from routine double parking that jams city streets to the drunk driving that kills some 25,000 people and injures at least 650,000 others yearly. Illegal speeding on open highways? New surveys show 35 that on some interstate highways 83% of all drivers are currently ignoring the federal 55 m.p.h. speed limit.

The most flagrant scofflaw of them all is the red-light runner. The flouting of stop signals has got so bad in Boston that residents tell an anecdote about a cabby who insists that red lights are "just for decora- 40 tion." The power of the stoplight to control traffic seems to be waning everywhere. In Los Angeles, red-light running has become perhaps the city's most common traffic violation. In New York City, going through an intersection is like Russian roulette. Admits Police Commissioner Robert J. McGuire: "Today it's a 50–50 toss-up as to whether people will 45 stop for a red light." Meanwhile, his own police largely ignore the lawbreaking.

Red-light running has always been ranked as a minor wrong, and so it may be in individual instances. When the violation becomes habitual, widespread and incessant, however, a great deal more than a traffic 50 management problem is involved. The flouting of basic rules of the road leaves deep dents in the social mood. Innocent drivers and pedestrians pay a repetitive price in frustration, inconvenience and outrage, not to mention a justified sense of mortal peril. The significance of red-light running is magnified by its high visibility. If hypocrisy is the tribute that 55 vice pays to virtue, then furtiveness is the true outlaw's salute to the force of law-and-order. The red-light runner, however, shows no respect whatever for the social rules, and society cannot help being harmed by any repetitive and brazen display of contempt for the fundamentals of order.   60

The scofflaw spirit is pervasive. It is not really surprising when schools find, as some do, that children frequently enter not knowing some of the basic rules of living together. For all their differences, today's scofflaws are of a piece as a symptom of elementary social demoralization—the loss by individuals of the capacity to govern their 65 own behavior in the interest of others.

The prospect of the collapse of public manners is not merely a matter of etiquette. Society's first concern will remain major crime, but a foretaste of the seriousness of incivility is suggested by what has been happening in Houston. Drivers on Houston freeways have been show- 70 ing an increasing tendency to replace the rules of the road with violent outbreaks. Items from the Houston police department's new statistical category—freeway traffic violence: 1) Driver flashes high-beam lights at car that cut in front of him, whose occupants then hurl a beer can at his windshield, kick out his tail lights, slug him eight stitches' worth. 2) 75 Dump-truck driver annoyed by delay batters trunk of stalled car ahead and its driver with steel bolt. 3) Hurrying driver of 18-wheel truck deliberately rear-ends car whose driver was trying to stay within 55 m.p.h. limit. The Houston Freeway Syndrome has fortunately not spread everywhere. But the question is: Will it?   80

Americans are used to thinking that law-and-order is threatened mainly by stereotypical violent crime. When the foundations of U.S. law have actually been shaken, however, it has always been because ordinary law-abiding citizens took to skirting the law. Major instance: Prohibition. Recalls Donald Barr Chidsey in *On and Off the Wagon:* "Law- 85 breaking proved to be not painful, not even uncomfortable, but, in a mild and perfectly safe way, exhilarating." People wiped out Prohibition at last not only because of the alcohol issue but because scofflawry was seriously undermining the authority and legitimacy of government. Ironically, today's scofflaw spirit, whatever its undetermined origins, is 90 being encouraged unwittingly by government at many levels. The failure of police to enforce certain laws is only the surface of the problem; they take their mandate from the officials and constituents they serve. Worse, most state legislatures have helped subvert popular compliance with the federal 55 m.p.h. law, some of them by enacting puny fines that 95 trivialize transgressions. On a higher level, the Administration in Washington has dramatized its wish to nullify civil rights laws simply by opposing instead of supporting certain court-ordered desegregation rulings. With considerable justification, environmental groups, in the words of *Wilderness* magazine, accuse the Administration of "destroy- 100 ing environmental laws by failing to enforce them, or by enforcing them in ways that deliberately encourage noncompliance." Translation: scofflawry at the top.

The most disquieting thing about the scofflaw spirit is its extreme infectiousness. Only a terminally foolish society would sit still and allow 105 it to spread indefinitely.

1. Where and how does the author combine analysis and examples of lawbreaking?
2. How does he organize the large number of examples he gives?
3. To what extent does this essay complement "Social Control" (Unit 9-F)? Would Trippett agree that social control is at the heart of social life?

13-I   The Passing of Little Gibbs Road

Connie Keremes (student)

My neighborhood is dying. The houses know it. They creak and groan at the slightest breeze. The trees know it. Their bare limbs rasp dryly together in the wind. The people know it. They gaze out of dusty windows and sigh at the falling leaves.

The houses in my neighborhood are ancient and dilapidated. Many 5 years ago, they were fine, well-cared for buildings with fresh paint and neat lawns. Now, however, the houses, more than fifty years old, have become quite tumbledown. They are simply too old and weathered to endure another fierce winter. The houses are sagging structures. They never seem to stand straight but, rather, they lean heavily to one side 10 as if they might topple over at any moment. The rotting beams and frames groan under the weight of roofs which look like patchwork quilts of mending slate. The shingled fronts are discolored from many winters of snow and ice. Several shingles have come loose from many of the houses and, left unrepaired, creak back and forth in the wind. Every 15 stoop and walk is crumbling and cracked. A few homeowners have placed potted plants on the stoops in an attempt to hide the many cracks—but the plants make the deep fissures all the more apparent. The houses appear more pathetic than ugly in their dilapidation, for their squeaking paint-chipped doors and groaning frames seem to say 20 these once fine homes will soon crumble to dust.

The houses are not alone in their deterioration, for the trees are also decaying. At one time, the trees along my street were tall and leafy, but now they are bent and twisted with age. The tops of many trees have been sawed off because their branches had been tangling the 25 telephone wires. Such trees have now become rotting stumps overrun with burrowing insects. Those trees which are standing are gnarled and diseased. Vandals have carved obscenities in the trunks of several trees, boldly leaving their names and dates beside the deed. A few leaves cling to the twisted branches, but for the most part the trees are barren. They 30 bend low as the wind whines through their bare limbs. These wasted old trees will easily be uprooted by the first strong blast that blows this year. They undoubtedly will not survive the winter.

The people themselves seem to be wasting away. Only very old people live in the neighborhood, for the children who once lived there 35 have all grown up and moved away. No one ever moves into the neighborhood—only out. The old people who live here are very frail. They walk slowly along the cracking sidewalks, their kerchiefed heads bent against the gusty winds. In passing each other along the street, the old people no longer smile or stop to talk, but merely nod grimly and 40 continue along their way. They lack the strength to climb up on their roofs to patch a hole or fasten a loose shingle, and as a result their houses become progressively more dilapidated. Aware of their failing strength and inability to make repairs on the decaying neighborhood, the old people resign themselves to staying indoors and staring dully out at the 45 leaves that swirl across the cracking sidewalks and past the gnarled trees. There is nothing left for them to do but to watch the neighborhood die.

1. The subject and main point here are similar to those of Examples B and D in the preceding unit. What differences and similarities do you find in the three authors' methods of presentation?
2. Why does the author save her discussion of the people until the last?

13-J   Epitaph to the Elusive Abominable Snowman

Sir Edmund Hillary

This essay, here complete, first appeared in *Life* (1961). The writer, a mountaineer from New Zealand, was a member of the first expedition to climb Mt. Everest.

Does the yeti, or "abominable snowman," really exist? Or is it just a myth without practical foundation? For the last four months our Himalayan scientific and mountaineering expedition has been trying to find out—and now we think we know the answer.

There has been a growing pile of evidence in favor of the creature's 5 existence: the tracks seen by many explorers on Himalayan glaciers, the complete conviction of the local people that yetis roam the mountains, the yeti scalps and hands kept as relics in the high monasteries, the many stories about people who claim to have seen them.

But despite the firm belief of many Himalayan explorers and of 10 some anthropologists, I began the search for the yeti with some skepticism. My own experience had been limited to two incidents. In 1951 a tough and experienced Sherpa (Sherpas are a mountain people of Tibetan stock) had told me with absolute conviction that he had seen a yeti and watched it for some time. In 1952 Explorer George Lowe and 15 I had found a tuft of black hair at an altitude of 19,000 feet, a tuft that our Sherpas swore was yeti hair—and immediately threw away in obvious fear.

Last September we set off from Katmandu in Nepal and walked for a hundred miles through rain and leeches to the 12,000-foot-high 20 Sherpa village of Beding. For eight days we were immobilized by weather, but we made profitable use of our time by interrogating the villagers and the lamas in the local monastery. One of our expedition members, Desmond Doig, speaks the language of Nepal with great fluency and has the ability, quite unprecedented in my experience, to 25 gain the confidence and liking of the local peoples.

We confirmed much that we already knew and learned more besides. The Sherpas believe there are three types of yetis:

1. The chuteh: a vast, hairy, ginger-and-black creature, sometimes eight feet tall, generally vegetarian and not harmful to man unless disturbed or annoyed.
2. The miteh: usually four to five feet tall with a high, pointed skull. His feet are said to be placed back to front. He has a decidedly unpleasant temperament and delights in eating any humans who come his way.
3. The thelma: a small creature from 18 inches to two feet high who lives down in the jungle, has human features and takes great pleasure in piling sticks and stones into little mounds.

We couldn't find any Sherpa who had actually seen a yeti, but several had heard them—usually when the winter snowfalls lay deep on the ground and the villagers were confined to their houses. Then, one gathered, the sound of the yeti was frequently heard at night, and next morning tracks were seen by the frightened Sherpas.

One of our own Sherpas, Ang Temba, now proved to be a veritable Sherlock Holmes. He scoured the villages for information and brought us the exciting news that there was a yeti skin here, the prized possession of a lama and his wife. The lama was away, and at first the wife refused to show us the skin. But Ang Temba and Desmond Doig were a formidable combination, and after much persuasion and chinking of rupees the skin became ours. In our opinion it was a fine specimen of the very rare Tibetan blue bear, but all our Sherpas disagreed emphatically. It wasn't a bear at all, they said, but undoubtedly the chuteh, or biggest type of yeti. Nothing we said could sway this belief.

When the weather cleared, we moved up the Rolwaling valley and began our search for signs of the yeti. Several weeks later our efforts were rewarded by the discovery of many tracks on the Ripimu glacier between 18,000 and 19,000 feet. These tracks were positively identified by our Sherpas as those of yetis, and they certainly fulfilled the required specifications: large broad feet with clear toe marks.

We devoted much care to the examination of these tracks and made some interesting discoveries. When we followed a line of tracks to a place where the footprints were in the shade of rocks or on the cold north side of a snow slope, the yeti tracks suddenly ceased to exist. In their place we found the small footprints of a fox or wild dog, bunched closely together as the animal bounded over the snow. Again and again we saw precise evidence of the effect of the sun on those bunches of small tracks. The warmth melted them out, ran them together, completely altered their contours and made as fine a yeti track as one could wish.

Probably the best known photographs of yeti tracks are those taken by Explorer Eric Shipton and Dr. Michael Ward on the Menlung glacier in 1951. The tracks that we discovered were less than two miles from the Shipton tracks and at a similar height and time of the year. Dr. Ward, who came back to the Himalayas as a member of my physiological team, said that among the yeti tracks on the Menlung glacier he and Shipton had noticed a number of small animal tracks, but at the time they had not thought them significant. 75

In November we continued our investigations in the Khumbu region at the foot of Mr. Everest. In the villages of Namche Bazar and Khumjung we obtained two more blue bear skins. Whenever we showed these skins to a Sherpa, we got the confident reply, "Chuteh." 80

Doig and Marlin Perkins, our zoologist, carried out a thorough enquiry among the Khumbu villages and monasteries. All the Sherpas believed in the yeti, but it was practically impossible to find anyone who, under careful questioning, claimed to have seen one. Even in the Thyangboche monastery, traditionally the source of much yeti lore and many yeti sightings, we were unable to find anyone who had seen a yeti. In fact, the two oldest lamas, who had lived in the monastery since its founding over 40 years ago, said they had neither seen a yeti nor knew of anyone who had. 85

90

Relics of the yeti in the monasteries of Khumjung, Pangboche and Namche Bazar came in for special attention. The bones of a hand in the Pangboche monastery were thought by our medical men to be those of a man—possibly the delicate hand of a lama. The yeti scalps we were shown in these monasteries were more of a puzzle. They were in the shape of high, pointed caps covered with coarse reddish and black hair and seemed to be very old. If they were authentic scalps, their very form indicated that they belonged to no known animal. Although they had no seams or needle marks, there was the chance that they had been cleverly fabricated many years before out of the molded skin of some other creature. 95

100

Doig and Perkins worked hard on this second possibility. Ang Temba produced two skins which had hair similar in texture to the scalps. We made high, pointed molds out of blocks of wood. The skins were softened, then stretched over the molds and left to dry. The resultant scalps were similar enough to the yeti scalps we saw in the monastery to indicate that we might be on the right track. 105

We realized that unless we could get an authoritative answer on the scalps, they would remain a constant challenge to any theories about the yeti. But the village elders of Khumjung firmly believed that their community would suffer a plague, earthquake, flood or avalanche if their relic scalp ever was removed. They insisted that it was the remains of a famous yeti slaughter that took place 240 years ago, when there were so many man-eating yetis about that the Sherpas resorted to ruse to eliminate them. The Sherpas pretended to get drunk and to kill each other with wooden swords. At night the Sherpas substituted real swords, which they left lying about. The yetis, 110

115

who had been watching them and were great imitators, proceeded to drink heavily also, slashed at each other with the real swords and killed each other off.   120

After much negotiation with the Khumjung elders, we persuaded them to lend us the scalp for exactly six weeks. In exchange I promised I would try to raise money for a school which they will share with nearby Sherpa villages. To guarantee that we would bring the scalp back, the elders said they would hold as hostages our expedition's three   125 head Sherpas, as well as their property and possessions.

Our faithful Sherpas unhesitatingly agreed. Then the villagers chose Kunjo Chumbi, the keeper of the village documents, to accompany us and bring the scalp back. For his first trip to the West, he wondered if he should take Sherpas traveling rations with him—a dried   130 sheep carcass, wheat flour and some of the local brew. After talking it over with Doig, he settled instead on some cakes of Tibetan brick tea and his silver teacup.

He, Doig, Perkins and I covered the 170 miles of steep country to Katmandu in 9½ days. From there we flew to Chicago, Paris and Lon-   135 don and showed the scalp and the chuteh skins to zoologists, anthropologists and other scientists. Their decision was unanimous: the yeti scalp was not a scalp at all. It had been molded out of some other skin, and the scientists agreed that it was the skin and hair of the serow, a rather uncommon Himalayan member of the large goat-antelope   140 family. Also our chuteh skins were confirmed to be Tibetan blue bear.

We now know that a yeti track can be made by the sun melting the footprints of a small creature such as a fox or wild dog. The same effect could occur with the prints of snow leopards, bears and even humans. We know that the large furs so confidently described by our Sherpas as   145 chutehs are in fact the Tibetan blue bear. There is the strong possibility that some of these big, unfamiliar creatures strayed down from their only known habitations in eastern Tibet and crossed the Himalayan range. The small thelma in its habits and description sounds very much like the rhesus monkey. And the pointed scalps of the miteh have   150 proved to be made from the skin of the much less frightening serow.

There is still much to be explained. Our theory on the tracks does not cover every case. We have not yet found a satisfactory explanation for the noise of the yeti which many Sherpas claim to have heard. But all in all we feel we have solved some of the major problems surround-   155 ing this elusive creature. Of course, the yeti still remains a very real part of the mythology and tradition of the Himalayan people—and it is undoubtedly in the field of mythology that the yeti rightly belongs.

1. Does the title spoil Hillary's effort to create suspense?
2. What hypothesis did Hillary have when he began the search?
3. How much attention does he give to each piece of evidence? Which pieces seem most important to him? to you?

4. Proof that something exists is naturally easier to find than proof that something does not exist, and Hillary is understandably cautious in his final paragraph. Do you think that he is nevertheless convinced of the nonexistence of the yeti? Are you convinced?
5. What is a lama? a rupee?
6. Check the etymology, denotation, and connotation of *formidable, chinking, lore, ruse.*

13-K　　　　　Light from an Ape's Jaw

Robert Ardrey

This essay is part of a chapter in *African Genesis* (1961), Ardrey's account of his efforts to find traces of the earliest human beings. In Johannesburg he studied under Raymond Dart, a palaeontologist and anatomist noted for his discoveries of the fossils of prehistoric manlike apes.

Johannesburg brooded on its golden reef in the golden, southern autumn. A last rare storm of the rainy season darkened Dart's upper-floor office at the Medical School. My mood of discouragement returned. Fossil bones of extinct animals piled up before me. Unfamiliar Latin names assailed my eardrums. Despite all the best efforts of this 5
sandy, smiling, persuasive, india rubber man, I could gain no brainhold on concepts so fearfully specialized. Then I found in my hands what seemed a human jaw.

I mentioned in passing, in the introductory chapter of this account, the jaw of a twelve-year-old southern ape which Raymond Dart showed 10
me on our first meeting. This was that jaw. And as I held it for the first time—staring into its headless, disconnected history as into the darkness surrounding Cardinal Newman's aboriginal calamity—my discouragement fell away. My sense of incompetence vanished. One needed nothing but the lay common sense of a juryman to return a verdict that 15
at some terrible moment in most ancient times, murder had been done.

The jaw was heavy. Three-quarters of a million years of residence on the floor of a dolomite cave had turned its bone and dentine to stone. The jaw seemed human. The cusped pattern of the teeth would have been familiar to any dentist. And the jaw seemed young. Several of the 20
permanent molars were only partially erupted. One canine tooth had not yet come in at all, though I could see its point hovering in the tooth canal. But the jaw while both young and heavy with antiquity was not human; for had the skull been attached, it would have revealed a brain-case little larger than that of a chimpanzee. 25

What I held in my hand was the last remains of an adolescent australopithecine whose life had been brought short by a heavy blow. The four front teeth were missing. Just below was a cracked, abraded area where the blow had fallen partially splitting the jawbone on the left side and breaking it quite through on the right. The injury could 30 scarcely have occurred as some post-mortem indignity of nature afflicted on an old jaw lying about the cave, for in that case the fragments would have been scattered about. Flesh must have held the fragments together to be fossilized as a single whole. Nor could the blow —or other simultaneous blows—have resulted in anything but death. 35 There was no least sign of knitting along the lines of the fracture.

My mind struggled to recapture the situation. Could the injury have been acquired accidentally? By a fall, for instance? It seemed unlikely. When falling, one inclines to land on almost any sector of one's anatomy other than the point of the jaw. I thought of the cave in which 40 the mandible had been found. Could a rock jarred loose from the cave roof have been the instrument of accidental injury? But to provide such a target for a falling fragment, one would have to visualize the youthful man-ape as sleeping on the cave floor with his jaw directed neatly to heaven, and even this unlikely situation brought difficulties. The scar on 45 the jawbone, rough and abraded, had an area of less than a square inch. No falling rock so small as to leave a scar of this dimension could conceivably be heavy enough to produce the damage.

I dismissed accident as the mother of injury. The youthful creature had died of purposeful assault.   50

I considered the means by which death might have been administered. Could a fist have done it? Yes, a human fist to a human child. But the jawbone of the southern ape, lacking a chin eminence, is more heavily constructed than ours. This child's jaw had the thickness of bone that one would find in a man. The aggressor, on the other hand, could 55 have swung no such power as an adult human male. *A. robustus* is not found at Makapan. And *A. africanus,** we recall, stood four feet tall and weighed, at the outside, ninety pounds. To visualize a fist causing such injury one would have to see a ninety-pound human boy with a single swing knock out his father's front teeth and break the jaw in two places. 60

A fist seemed unlikely. I inspected the point of impact where the blow had landed. It was a rough place, very slightly flattened. Would a piece of stone, grasped up impetuously from the cave floor and driven or thrown against the jaw leave a scar of this order? It was possible, but it was not probable. A jagged, sharp-cornered, uneroded rock fragment 65 such as one finds in caves, to have achieved fractures of the jaw on both sides, would almost surely at its point of impact have left a more decisive mark. As compared with the likelihood of a purposeful bludgeon of some sort—a bone or wooden club which would have left a flattened, roughened mark precisely like that beneath my thumb—the use of an 70 expedient stone shrank into moderate improbability.

The afternoon darkened with a fleeting thunderstorm. A window rattled with the earth movement of a collapsing tunnel in the gold reef

---

*Australopithecus robustus and *Australopithecus Africanus* are the scientific names of two types of prehistoric apemen.

a mile below us. I had put the jaw on Dart's desk, just before me, and
it jiggled. Dart stood at the window looking out at the storm while I 75
contemplated the remnant of antique assassination. Evidence for murder lay clearly before me, but the mere question of murder shrank
rapidly in significance. A specter far and away more grisly entered the
dark periphery of my consciousness. Long before the time of man, had
this creature surrendered his life to a weapon?   80

1. Would Ardrey agree with Huxley that much scientific reasoning is simply
   "lay common sense" (Unit 12-H, opening paragraphs)?
2. What steps of reasoning does he take to reach each of these conclusions: (a)
   the ape died young; (b) it died from a blow; (c) it was killed by another
   creature; (d) it was struck by a weapon?
3. Which steps or parts of steps require only "lay common sense" and which
   require some special knowledge?
4. Check the etymology, denotation, and connotation of *brooded, assailed,
   india rubber, aboriginal, calamity, dolomite, dentine, cusped, molars,
   erupted, canine tooth, canal, australopithecine, abraded, mandible, assault,
   bludgeon, expedient, assassination, periphery.*

Assignments

1. Discuss the differing kinds of particulars that would be necessary in order
   to justify the following general statements:
   a. We have a football team.
   b. We have a good football team.
   c. We have the best football team we have had in ten years.
   d. We have the best football team in the state.
   e. We have the best football team in the United States.
2. From one of the biological or physical sciences that you have studied,
   choose an example of inductive reasoning, preferably one in which you
   yourself have performed experiments, and write it up, showing the particulars involved and the generalization that can be drawn from them.
3. The first paragraph of Mark Twain's essay (Unit 15-C) recounts particular
   experiences through which he finally arrived at an understanding of the
   general meaning of the word *lagniappe.* Write an account either of your
   own gradual acquaintance with some previously unfamiliar technical word
   or phrase encountered since you came to college, or of how you arrived,
   through inquiries and listening, at the meaning of some new slang phrase
   not yet in the dictionaries.
4. Write an essay in which you discuss what you have found to be the prevailing opinion on your campus or among your classmates on an issue, such as
   working one's way through college, engaging in extracurricular activities,
   cheating on examinations, supporting student protesters, joining fraternities or sororities, living in coeducational dormitories. Or if you prefer, write
   on student opinion on some state, national, or international issue. Be sure
   that your generalization fits the evidence that you are able to produce and
   that you make allowances for the size of your sample.

5. After reading "The Language of Uncertainty" (Unit 13-B), decide what percentages you yourself might reasonably imply by, or infer from, each of the following statements. Compare your figures with those of other members of the class.
   a. Everybody voted in the election.
   b. Nearly everybody voted in the election.
   c. Most people voted in the election.
   d. Many people voted in the election.
   e. Some people voted in the election.
   f. A few people voted in the election.
   g. Nobody voted in the election.
6. To test the validity of the following statements, supply the general assumptions that underlie them and arrange them in syllogistic form. Then point out any flaws revealed in the facts or the logic.
   a. I'm glad to find that both my new chemistry professors are fat, because they're sure to be good-natured and easygoing.
   b. Jack must be at least twenty-one because he just got married.
   c. American automobiles are getting better every year: They have more equipment and more different styles and are more expensive.
   d. Maggie must be Irish because she comes from Boston, which has a large Irish population, and her name sounds Irish.
   e. Tom and Jane will never be honor students; they're both Phys Ed majors.
7. Note the interdependence of the forms of reasoning discussed in Units 11–13.
   a. Go back to Unit 12, "Cause and Effect," and reread Huxley's "The Method of Scientific Investigation" (Example H), examining his illustrations of the deductive reasoning that accompanies the inductive method.
   b. Go to Unit 15, and read Krutch's "Killing for Sport" (Example H). Notice the implied generalization in paragraph 2 that "all activity that lessens the amount of vitality in the world is evil." Complete the syllogism and discuss it, as fact and as logic. Do the same with the assumption in paragraphs 5 and 6 that "all pleasure resulting from cruelty is wrong." What evidence does he offer in support of this generalization?
8. Look through a copy of a popular magazine, examining the advertisements in search of examples of deductive reasoning. Do not be discouraged by the absence of an expressed major premise in such appeals as "Use——, the choice of thousands." Supply the underlying generalization, decide on its source (see page 236), and determine its soundness and the truth and validity of the deductions made from it. (You may have to draw up more than one syllogism in order to express all the implications of the implied reasoning.)
9. In a short story, "The Other Side of the Hedge," E. M. Forster pictures the confusion of a man from the contemporary world who enters a world where athletes run and swim for the joy of the sport, with no one to race against, and singers sing for the joy of singing, even with no one to listen. Being as objective as possible, examine the assumptions underlying some ordinary activities, such as choosing a new pair of slacks, watching a popular TV show, cheering for the home team, participating in student government, joining a fraternity or sorority, playing a musical instrument in private, playing one in public, or refusing (for reasons of time? health? morality?

religion?) to enter into some activity that others indulge in and urge on you. Do not be satisfied with the first explanation that comes to mind. Push your thinking as far back into your basic assumptions as you can. When you have found a subject among these possibilities (or among others suggested by them), write an essay that makes clear the deductive logic, or lack of logic, involved.

10. Examine carefully one of your own strongly held and perhaps frequently voiced opinions, or an opinion held by a friend, a relative, a teacher, or a political leader, to determine on what assumption or assumptions it is based. Then write an essay on the subject, using deductive reasoning.

UNIT 14

Definition

"By *my* definition, he's too drunk to drive." "Why isn't child psychology considered one of the humanities?" "You may call their behavior rude, but I think they're just silly." "What's a metaphor?" "How dare you call me 'crazy'!"

To explain anything or to get credit for knowing something, we usually must define the thing. It can be surprisingly difficult, however, to make accurate, generally acceptable definitions in our own words, especially if what we are trying to define is thoroughly familiar to us.

A **formal definition** is based on a concise, logical pattern that lets the writer give a maximum of information in a minimum of space. It has three parts: the **term** (word or phrase) to be defined; the **class** of object or concept to which the term belongs; and the **differentiating characteristics** that distinguish what the term defines from all others of that class.

term		*class*	*differentiating characteristics*
Water	is	a liquid	made up of molecules of hydrogen and oxygen in the ratio of 2 to 1.
An owl	is	a bird	with large head, strong talons, and nocturnal habits.

Practice in writing such formal definitions is a good mental discipline and an excellent training in conciseness and care in the use of words. Follow these guidelines:

1. Keep your class small but adequate. It should be large enough to include everything covered by the term you are defining but no larger. To define the term *lieutenant,* the class *soldier* is too small, because there are lieutenants in the Navy and police as well as in the

Army and Marines. On the other hand, the class *officer* is too large because it includes the noncommissioned and commissioned. *Commissioned officer* is a happy compromise.

2. Do not define a word by mere repetition. "A baked potato is a potato that has been baked" adds nothing to what the term "baked potato" has already told us.

3. State the differentiating characteristics precisely. "A flute is a musical instrument played by blowing" is too general because it covers many musical instruments that are not flutes.

4. Define a word in simpler and more familiar terms. The purpose of definition is to clarify, not to confuse. In his eighteenth-century dictionary, Samuel Johnson humorously defined "network" as "anything reticulated or decussated at equal distances with interstices between the intersections"—a well-known example of how *not* to define. Compare it with the definition of the same word in your own college dictionary.

5. Do not define a word with *is* or *are when* or *is* or *are where*. In "Vacations are when people don't work" and "A grocery is where food is sold," the "when" and "where" clauses modify the verbs "are" and "is" because they follow them, instead of modifying "vacations" and "grocery." In a definition, *is, are, was,* and *were* function like equal marks; the word or group of words forming the definition should match the grammatical structure of the word or words it defines. "Vacations are times when people don't work" ("Vacations = times"); "A grocery is a store where food is sold"; "To run is to move quickly"; *"Lambent* means *softly bright."*

> Exercise: In your own words, without help from a dictionary, write formal one-sentence definitions of the following familiar terms: (1) apple; (2) cow; (3) dictionary; (4) eye; (5) typewriter; (6) vinegar; (7) microscope; (8) foul ball; (9) professor; (10) democracy. Then check the five "warnings" and make any necessary revisions and corrections before handing in your definitions.

*   *   *   *   *   *   *   *   *

In the **essay of definition,** unlike the preceding brief definitions, you may write as much as necessary to make your definitions accurate, clear, and useful for your readers. Try to catch and hold your readers' interest. A formal one-sentence definition usually has as little interest for readers as a mathematical equation. The essay of definition, however, can be personal, amusing, vigorous, stimulating, memorable. In it you may use, singly or in combination, any of the expository methods we have examined.

Always remember, however, that your first duty is to define. It is not essential to include a formal definition, but your paper must be an expansion of the basic material that you would use to make such a definition, never an evasion of it. Without this fact in mind, you may find that you have written a charming informal essay on a given subject, but not defined it.

Choose a generic subject, not a specific one. We define a dog, for instance, rather than our Rover; a cathedral, rather than Notre Dame of Paris; supersonic aircraft, rather than the Concorde. (Note the kinds of topics suggested at the end of this unit.) But use specifics of all kinds to illustrate your subject and make it vivid for your readers. To develop your definition, you will find some or all of the following helpful:

1. Descriptive details are often valuable. For example, the bare definition of a dog as a "carnivorous domesticated mammal of the family Canidae" will be clearer with descriptive details as to size, build, color, use, and so on.

> The *masonquo* is a six-stringed lyre having a hollow leather-covered sound-chamber much like that of a banjo. It has a bridge and, since it lacks a neck or fingerboard, the strings are stretched to a framework of sticks. The keys are primitive but ingenious and effective. All six strings are struck simultaneously with a small piece of leather or a feather. (Harold Courlander, *Musical Quarterly.*)

2. Examples and incidents (narration) can make the definition of a general subject more specific. Protestantism might be clarified by reference to the Lutheran or other denomination. Or incidents may be used to make abstract terms concrete: the old story of Abe Lincoln's walking miles to return a few cents was popular because, by illustrating honesty in action, it made the idea of that virtue much more vivid than could any discussion of honesty in the abstract.

> Drop a cricket ball from your hand and it falls to the ground. We say that the cause of its fall is the gravitational pull of the earth. In the same way, a cricket ball thrown into the air does not move on forever in the direction in which it is thrown; if it did, it would leave the earth for good and voyage off into space. It is saved from this fate by the earth's gravitational pull, which drags it gradually down, so that it falls back to earth. The faster we throw it, the farther it travels before this occurs; a similar ball projected from a gun would travel for many miles before being pulled back to earth. (Sir James Jeans, *The Universe Around Us.*)

3. Comparisons may define the unfamiliar by showing how it resembles the familiar or differs from it.

> Like gliding, ballooning depends for movement on luck with thermals, which are air currents rising off sun-warmed fields and hills; unlike gliding, ballooning gives a pilot no control of direction—except up and down. *(The New Yorker.)*

A strange object may be described through likeness as having "the shape of a hen's egg" or "the color of a tomato."

To the wanderer from temperate zones, the papaya might be a dwarfed Tom Watson or an unripe cantaloupe. This interesting native of the torrid zone assumes a variety of shapes and sizes. It may be elongated like a watermelon, or almost spherical, or even slightly compressed on one end, like our crook-neck squash. Within, it is much like a muskmelon, with a multitude of seeds which cling tenaciously to a firm, thick, salmon-colored lining which is its edible part. (G. W. James, student, the *Green Caldron.*)

On the other hand, a thing may be described through difference as "larger than a tennis ball" or "not so sour as a lemon." The following example is from a definition of the word *tact.*

A great many would-be socialites entertain the illusion that politeness and tact are the same thing. That is why they are only would-be's. Politeness is a negative, and tact a positive, virtue. Politeness is merely avoiding trampling on another person's toes, while tact is placing a Persian carpet under his feet. (Margaret Van Horne, student, the *Green Caldron.*)

4. Negative comparisons may be helpful. Explaining what a thing is *not* can clear the ground for explaining what it *is.* This method is particularly useful in eliminating things that might otherwise be confused with the thing to be defined: "Botanically speaking, a tomato is not a vegetable." "A leprechaun is not to be confused with a ghost."

Research is a word that is often used narrowly, but I am using it not in any mean and cramped sense. It is not, for instance, restricted to the uncovering of specific new facts, or the development of new scientific processes, although it is partly this. It is not encompassed by learned papers in scholarly journals, although it is certainly this among other things. By research I mean, as well as all this, the publication of a biography, or a volume of poetry, or the delivery of a lecture that sets off a mental chain reaction among students. (Claude T. Bissell, *What the Colleges Are Doing.*)

5. Classification can extend the definition of a term that denotes a group by indicating the classes of which it is composed; a definition of service organizations might include the major kinds of clubs—Rotary, Kiwanis, and so on.

I found the Negro community the victim of a threefold malady—factionalism among the leaders, indifference in the educated group, and passivity in the uneducated. All of these conditions had almost persuaded me that no lasting social reform could ever be achieved in Montgomery. (Martin Luther King, Jr., *Stride Toward Freedom.*)

6. Analysis is another logical means of expanding a basic definition. You may break down the object to be defined into the parts composing it: "A good composition has a beginning, a middle, and an end."

A power mower, so popular with householders today, consists of a source of power, usually a small gasoline engine; a cutting blade, usually rotary; a transmission system by which the power is applied to the blade; and a frame to support the mechanism, a set of wheels to make it movable and a handle by which the operator can guide it.

7. The **origins and causes** are essential for definitions of some subjects. The meaning of a word like *radar* is implicit in its origin (it is composed of "ra" for *radio,* "d" for *detection,* "a" for *and,* and "r" for *ranging*); and a phenomenon like a geyser or a volcano can best be explained through its cause.

The meter was originally intended to be one ten-millionth of the distance from the equator to the pole of the earth, measured on the surface. The measurements by means of which the first meter was prepared were inaccurate, however, and the real meter is the distance, measured at the freezing point of water, between two marks on a bar of platinum-iridium kept at the International Bureau of Weights and Measures at Sèvres, France. (W. A. Noyes, *Textbook of Chemistry.*)

8. The **results, effects, and uses** are also essential for some subjects. *Christianity* and *communism,* for example, should be explained in terms of their results as well as of their origins, and *war* and *depression* in terms of their effects. Definitions of mechanisms and processes (radar is again an example) are equally likely to involve a discussion of the uses to which they are put.

In adjusting to his new way of life the hunting ape developed a powerful *pair-bond,* tying the male and female parents together during the breeding season. In this way, the females were sure of their males' support and were able to devote themselves to their maternal duties. The males were sure of their females' loyalty, were prepared to leave them for hunting, and avoided fighting over them. And the offspring were provided with the maximum of care and attention. (Desmond Morris, *The Naked Ape.*)

*   *   *   *   *   *   *   *   *

For the **organization** of your essay of definition you have a wide choice of patterns. No one simple pattern or plan can be laid out for it. You may successfully combine any or all of the patterns mentioned in the list. Your plan will depend entirely on the demands of your subject, the needs of your readers, and your own preference as a writer. A definition of Americanism, for instance, might involve a detailed breakdown of the term into the qualities that you believe it covers; it might include examples of true Americanism in action, a comparison of real Americanism with false varieties or with other "isms," and a discussion of its origins and effects on a people and the world. How best to arrange and combine this ample and varied material would depend on your intended readers and your particular purpose.

Examples

In the following selections, the main purpose of each writer is to arrive at a definition, but you will find definitions are important in many other selections, most notably in the *Encyclopedia Americana*'s "The Hellbender" (2-D), Mencken's *"Le Contrat Social"* (4-B), McDowell's "When Is a Joke Not a Joke?" (4-C), Jackson's "Challenge" (5-D), Baker's 5 "The Boy Who Came to Supper" (9-D), Wylie's "The Structure of a Comet" (11-A), Neier's "Defending Free Speech" (15-A), Lerner's "The ACLU's Grievous Mistake" (15-B), Morrow's "Holding the Speaker Hostage" (15-C), and in all the examples of critical writing in Unit 16.

These selections vary in subject matter from the tangible to the 10 abstract, in style from expanded formal definitions to informal essays, and in length from a single paragraph to a couple of pages. Determine for each, as has been done for Example A, what methods have been used in development.

14-A   Cyclones

Walter Sullivan

This report from *The New York Times* (November 1977), here complete, is by a writer whose special field is science. It was published shortly after a cyclone caused severe damage in Bangladesh and parts of India.

ANALYSIS
Introduction

November is the month dreaded by coastal residents in India and Bangladesh, for it is then that the most devastating cyclones occur.

Comparison

These storms are essentially the same in the way they form and behave as the hurricanes of the western Atlantic 5 and western Mexico and the typhoons of the western Pacific.

In the Indian Ocean they are known as cyclones, although they have no relationship to the "cyclone" that transported Dorothy to the Land of Oz. That was a Mid- 10 dle-Western usage referring to a tornado—a localized, funnel-shaped cloud.

Historical
example

Indian Ocean cyclones have caused some of the greatest disasters in history. In November 1970, such a storm swept across the Ganges delta in what was then East Pakis- 15 tan, and is now Bangladesh. It drove the sea far inland over the flat landscape, flooding countless villages. The death toll may have reached a half million.

Historical
example

At the start of November 1971, a similar storm struck the east coast of India and many more thousands died. 20

When a cyclone hit Darwin, on the north coast of Australia, in 1974 two-thirds of the city's homes were destroyed, but only 49 people were killed.

Causes and effect in example

The explanation for the disparity in the death tolls appears to be that because of flimsy construction, dense 25 population and flat landscape in the deltas of India and Bangladesh, those living there are highly vulnerable. Air

in general

pressure drops so radically during such storms that high tides rise far above normal. The 1970 disaster occurred at

in example

a time in the lunar cycle when tides would have been very high in any case. 30

Details

Torrential rains add further to the flooding and high waves are driven inland by the violent winds.

Cause and effect in general

Such storms are typically born in the intertropical convergence zone. This is the region where converging 35 trade winds of the Northern and Southern Hemispheres meet and form an updraft. When that zone is far enough north or south of the Equator for the earth's rotation to impart circular motion to the converging winds a storm may be born. The motion is counterclockwise when the 40 process occurs north of the equator and clockwise when it occurs in the Southern Hemisphere.

Cause and effect in general

Small at first, the storm feeds on the hot, moist air that it sucks in from surrounding areas. As the air rises inside the storm, the moisture condenses into heavy rains. The 45 latent heat that evaporated that moisture in the first place is released to drive the rotating winds even faster, and more air is drawn in.

Effect

Thus the storm swells to cover an area several hundred miles in diameter. Like an upside-down whirlpool, it 50 rotates about an open funnel in the center—the "eye"— in which skies are clear and winds minimal. Once over land the storm loses energy for lack of moist oceanic air and fades away.

Details

The ideal time for Indian Ocean cyclones is Novem- 55 ber. In the Atlantic, the Caribbean Sea and Gulf of Mexico the hurricane season extends from June to October.

Cause and effect

Modest efforts have been made to tame such storms by seeding clouds in front of them, thus dumping their rain before the clouds are drawn into the storm and feed 60 it energy. Until the effects of such action can be more accurately predicted than at present, it is feared that, following such treatment, a storm might change its path and head for a populated center instead of remaining harmlessly at sea. 65

1. To define cyclones in the region of Bangladesh and India for American readers, what information must Sullivan give besides that directly describing the cyclones themselves?
2. What use does he make of comparison, both literal and figurative?
3. Check the etymology, denotation, and connotation of *typhoons, tornado, disparity, latent, seeding.*

14-B   Parentage and Parenthood

Ashley Montagu

This paragraph is from *The American Way* (1967), an anthropological and sociological study. Note how Montagu defines the two terms by drawing distinctions between them.

It is apparently very necessary to distinguish between parenthood and parentage. Parenthood is an art; parentage is the consequence of a mere biological act. The biological ability to produce conception and to give birth to a child has nothing whatever to do with the ability to care for that child as it requires to be cared for. That ability, like every 5 other, must be learned. It is highly desirable that parentage be not undertaken until the art of parenthood has been learned. Is this a counsel of perfection? As things stand now, perhaps it is, but it need not always be so. Parentage is often irresponsible. Parenthood is responsible. Parentage at best is irresponsibly responsible for the *birth* of a 10 child. Parenthood is responsible for the development of a human being —not simply a child, but a human being. I do not think it is an overstatement to say that parenthood is the most important occupation in the world.

1. How are parentage and parenthood defined in an unabridged dictionary?
2. To what extent do the dictionary definitions show—or fail to show—the distinctions Montagu draws?

14-C   Lagniappe

Mark Twain

These paragraphs are from Twain's *Life on the Mississippi* (1875). Note how the student writer of Example E makes use of Twain's definition.

We picked up one excellent word—a word worth traveling to New Orleans to get; a nice, limber, expressive, handy word—"Lagniappe." They pronounce it *lanny-yap.* It is Spanish—so they said. We discovered it at the head of a column of odds and ends in the *Picayune* the first day; heard twenty people use it the second; inquired what it meant 5 the third; adopted it and got facility in swinging it the fourth. It has a restricted meaning, but I think the people spread it out a little when they choose. It is the equivalent of the thirteenth roll in a "baker's dozen." It is something thrown in, gratis, for good measure. The custom originated in the Spanish quarter of the city. When a child or a servant buys something in a shop—or even the mayor or the governor, for aught I know—he finishes the operation by saying:

"Give me something for lagniappe."

The shopman always responds; gives the child a bit of licorice root, gives the servant a cheap cigar or a spool of thread, gives the governor —I don't know what he gives the governor; support, likely.

When you are invited to drink—and this does occur now and then in New Orleans—and you say, "What, again?—no, I've had enough," the other party says, "But just this one time more—this is for lagniappe." When the beau perceives that he is stacking his compliments a trifle too high, and sees by the young lady's countenance that the edifice would have been better with the top compliment left off, he puts his "I beg pardon, no harm intended," into the briefer form of "Oh, that's for lagniappe." If the waiter in the restaurant stumbles and spills a gill of coffee down the back of your neck, he says, "F'r lagniappe, sah," and gets you another cup without extra charge.

1. What words and phrases indicate Twain's humorous intention?
2. Classify the different kinds of situations in which Twain says *lagniappe* could be useful.
3. Which of the kinds of writing listed on pages 267–269 does Twain use here to enliven his definition?

14-D   "No Sweat"

John D. Myers (student)

"No sweat" is one of the most descriptive slang terms that I have ever encountered. I first heard the term used in Korea, where it appeared in almost every conversation among the American soldiers stationed there. It is admittedly a somewhat vulgar expression for formal use, but for saying much in a few words, it is hard to beat.

Strangely enough, "no sweat" does not refer to the amount of work involved in doing something, nor yet to the temperature. It refers to the absence of worry and apprehension involved in a certain action. Used properly, it carries a note of reassurance; it is a short way of saying, "Don't work yourself up over this matter, as it is all taken care of."

For example, let us suppose that a lovely young lady, in backing her car out of a parking lot, accidentally scrapes a young man's fender. The young man gallantly releases her from all responsibility by saying cheerfully, "No sweat," and the situation probably terminates in a date instead of a lawsuit.

But the expression means more than a release from obligation, as can be seen from the following example: a production engineer calls in his foreman and explains that he will need four thousand brake units by the end of the week. The foreman replies, "No sweat," and the production engineer knows he is safe in telling the company's sales 20 representative to confirm delivery.

If "no sweat" had been current in New Orleans at the time Mark Twain wrote "Lagniappe," the restaurant scene in which the waiter spilled coffee down the customer's neck would have had a different outcome. Before the careless fellow had had time to make any kind of 25 apology, the injured patron would have looked up with a smile and said, "No sweat," and the incident would have been closed.

Which of the kinds of writing listed on pages 267–269 does the writer use here to enliven his definition?

14-E   On Maturity

Carlos Moras (student)

This essay and the one following it were written for the same assignment—a definition of maturity. Moras draws on his readings in social psychology, his major, to give a traditional kind of definition.

Maturation involves two processes: internalizing the constraints society puts on us and shifting away from self-centeredness toward an awareness that we are not the only ones on the face of the earth.

When we're children we have to be told what to do. Our parents, teachers, and other authority figures act as mediators between us and 5 that complicated world where "right" and "wrong" don't exist as easily discernible extremes. In our world there are too many shades of "right" and "wrong." Our childish minds are incapable of making a choice from among so many alternatives, and so we have rules. We spend a large part of our childhood obeying or disobeying these rules. As we grow 10 older we begin to see the reasons behind some of them, and we start doubting the validity of others. At this point the internalizing process begins. Our adolescence is a period of rebellion against constraints imposed by others. We want to rule ourselves. But soon many of us come to realize that rules are important in a society as complicated as 15 ours. We then become our own arbitrators between "right" and "wrong," our own rule-makers and enforcers.

Maturity is also a shift away from self-centeredness toward a more realistic image of ourselves. A baby's actions are all directed toward itself. The self-centered infant can't be blamed for its selfish attitude, 20 because its world doesn't extend beyond itself. As the baby grows older, its world's boundaries extend, and it then notes that others exist as well. First the baby notes that it has a mother on whom it depends for food.

The selfish baby exploits this relationship. It cries until it is fed. It also cries until it receives attention. Quite early in life, the baby learns to see the rewards it can get from this relationship. Later on, the child learns from interactions with the family what a "give and take" relationship is and then starts to shift away from self-centeredness.

As we mature we should become aware of our position in relation to others in our world, a position no greater and no less than that of any other person. Not everyone succeeds in developing a realistic concept of self, and not everyone is able to internalize the constraints society puts on each of us. Thus, mental maturity, unlike physical maturity, does not come automatically to all.

1. Are there any specific details to enliven this generalized definition?
2. How has the writer used classification as an organizing principle?

14-F   Learning Has No End

Irma Cruz (student)

This essay was written for the same assignment as the preceding essay. The writer, a middle-aged student who had just begun her college career, draws on personal experience to enliven her remarks.

Mature people have a growing understanding of themselves, of others, and of social, moral, and ethical problems. They have the ability to translate words into meanings, to grasp the ideas presented, and to sense the mood suggested. They have curiosity and enthusiasm for a wide variety of experiences, directly and also indirectly through reading, and they relate new ideas to previous experiences. Thus, they acquire new and deeper understandings, broadened interests, rational attitudes, and richer and more stable personalities.

I have few memories of my early childhood. My parents were poor and so involved in the struggle to survive that they could offer me little or no personal enrichment. No books were given or read to me, there were no trips to museums, zoos, theaters, or movies, there was no money to buy the kinds of toys that would have stimulated my imagination. My early days in kindergarten were bright days. I remember looking forward to the mornings that I would spend in school, but another memory like a rainfall, bitter in taste, is of being labeled by the system as a remedial child. I was made to feel that I was not going far in life. A year later when my younger sister joined me in school, my parents and teachers gave me the message that she was bright and I wasn't. From that moment on I imprisoned my soul with the ridiculous challenge of proving that I too had abilities.

In my early twenties I fell in love and married. I can truly say, as I look back many years later, that on the day of my marriage I was born again; I wish that I could change my entire name to suit my second

birth. I entered marriage with no identity, no sense of myself, no experi- 25
ence of life whatever. Through my husband's patience, through my
struggles with everyday life, through bearing children, caring for them
and trying to meet their needs in a more conscious way than mine were
met, through reading more and reading with a more critical view, and
through developing my love for art, I began to grow and continue to 30
grow.

I have chosen a career in education and have worked as a para-
professional teaching "target" children, children who need to catch up.
I am in college, an activity which my relatives and I had thought I would
never be capable of but which I had always wanted. I look forward with 35
great hope to continuing to experience and to grow more mature in life,
for learning has no end.

14-G   The Meaning of "Negro"

Negro History Bulletin

This essay was published as an editorial in an issue of the *Bulletin* in 1971.

The word "Negro" has a long history. The Spanish and Portuguese
with their Latin background began the African slave trade. They called
black Africans "Negroes" because *negro* meant black in their languages. During most of the 19th century, black Americans preferred
the terms African or Colored or African-American. Those who favor the 5
latter point out that many Americans are called by the name of their
ancestors' land, Italian-American, Polish-American, Jewish-American;
and others prefer the word "black" and are using it widely, so that books
and magazine articles carry it, as the opposite to "white." However,
black is a misnomer, just as white is, for neither white nor black convey 10
adequately the color or race of the people described; and certainly,
there is genetically neither a white race nor a black race.

The word "Negro" is mainly a sociological word and has little relation to biology. Persons who by appearance are "white" have been
designated as Negroes because there were some ancestors who were 15
Africans. Accordingly, the study of "the Negro" in the United States has
to face first of all the difficulty of definition. It is difficult to give a fixed
and definite meaning to this word. It has been used in its narrow sense,
to include the primitive group of darker African peoples, characterized
by darker skins, curly hair, broad facial features and dolichocephalic 20
[long] heads; their colors varied from nearly black to light brown and
yellow. Their original habitation was Africa, south of the Sahara and
north of the line running southeast from the Gulf of Biafra to the Tana
River, and they have never numbered more than a million persons. In
its widest sense, it has been used in the United States, especially, to 25
embrace all of the peoples—not only those of dark skin, but also any

person whose ancestors have been Negroes. In few cases of racial designations is the term more loosely used and in no case is it more difficult to fix an established meaning. The term "white" and "black" are equally indefinite and are used as loosely without scientific exactness. 30

In the United States, one may be called a Negro and be white in appearance. In Africa one may be called a Negro only if he is one of the definite Negroid types, who perhaps have never been in relatively large numbers as the continent goes. The brown, the yellow and some of the black peoples of Africa are excluded in the African use of the term. If 35 we use the term "Negro" in its American use—for if one is a Negro for all negative purposes, certainly the positive purposes do not make one any less a Negro—we then find that the Negroes of Africa and the United States have been the creators of a valuable civilization, and have no need to hide themselves under the umbrella of a new name. 40

There has not been and there is not one unvarying Negro type. Persons of various colors and features have been found in Africa. Many of the Bantus, for instance, have been known to have "Caucasian-like features." The pygmies have been described by some observers as coffee-brown, and at times, by others as red and light yellow. The 45 Fellatahs and Nigritians vary in color from light brown to dark brown. The Fellatah girls were described by one traveller as having beautiful forms which with their complexions "of freshest bronze" gave him the impression that they could not be "excelled in symmetry by the women of any other country." Another seventeenth century contemporary 50 wrote, "The women of Nekans (in north) are handsome body'd and fair, with black and shining hair, which makes them take pride to frequent the Bathes." The Bahima people were a "tall and finely formed race of nutty brown color with almost European features." This variation of color has been so typical over the African continent that one student 55 of the problem has been led to conclude that the mulatto is as typically African as the black man.

The Negroes in America are essentially Americans and not Africans. There is little except color which shows their relationships to Africa and there are Negroes whose color does not show it, but who are 60 proud of their African background. They have learned the language and social techniques of the United States, the country in which they lived. But they came to this country from a culture which had been developing in Africa through many centuries. There are few traces of African culture in Negro life in America, and the Negro-American 65 seems not to be essentially different in this respect from the Irish-American, the German-American, the Jewish-American, the Scotch-American, or any other American types so far as the cultures of the lands of their ancestors are concerned. Millions of Europeans have come to America and millions of Africans have been brought from 70 Africa to America. They have all become a part of the American population.

These Africans, designated as Negroes, have been marching forward in all lines of endeavors and achievement. They are proving that civilization and contributions to it are not based on race or color but upon the individual men or women of ability who seek to advance themselves, be they white or black. In these respects God is no respecter of persons, whatever their names and colors. 75

1. Where does the writer use classification in developing the definition?
2. What specific examples does the writer use to illustrate or explain generalizations?
3. How is the essay organized?

Assignments

1. There are many types of terms from which you may draw subjects for essays of definition:
   a. Words like *ruana, sukiyaki, goober, pedicab,* which may be in common use in some areas but which are so limited in locale that they are unfamiliar to many readers.
   b. Technical terms like *azimuth, ombudsman, recidivism, onomatopoeia,* which are so specialized as to be either unknown to most readers or not well understood by them.
   c. Slang terms like *gam, smokey, pad, spiv, skedaddle,* which are either too dated or too limited in use to be generally understood in all their implications.
   d. Abstract terms like *culture, sportsmanship, education, freedom,* which continually require specific definition because of the variety of interpretations possible.
   e. Familiar terms like *freshman, spring fever, conscience, homesickness,* which are known to all but which may have a special personal meaning for you that you would like to express.
2. Many words may be usefully defined in pairs to overcome frequent confusion of the two: courtesy and etiquette, job and profession, art and science, knowledge and intelligence, house and home, infer and imply, naturalist and biologist, religion and theology, possibility and probability.
3. When you have chosen a subject,
   a. Write a formal one-sentence definition.
   b. Expand that definition into a paragraph by increasing the differentiating details, but keep it formally informative.
   c. Expand it into a longer essay of definition by using devices and adding information that will make it enjoyable as well.
4. The importance of definition can be seen by the number of times that it is used in the examples of other units. See Unit 2-D; Unit 6-A; Unit 9-D; Unit 10-A and C; 11-G. In which is it needed more? In Unit 3-A the failure to accept each other's choice of words brings a waitress and customer into conflict.

UNIT 15

Argument and Persuasion

"What she did was terrible. How can you defend her?" "The critics panned the show, but there's a great scene in it." "You're carrying your right to free speech too far—that's libel." "Despite your objections, I recommend that the committee approve this resolution."

The more a subject is open to different opinions, the more strongly you must try to persuade others to accept your views. The writers of all the examples in this book try to catch our attention and convince us that their interpretations, analyses, and deductions are correct or at least deserve consideration. Notice, for instance, how the general tone of the examples in "Process" (Unit 8) differs from that of the examples in "Inductive and Deductive Reasoning" (Unit 13). The writers in Unit 8 can safely assume that their readers want to learn how to do something or will quickly see the advantages of using the methods described. In Unit 13, however, the writers assume that their readers may have opposing views or that the deductions they present may not be self-explanatory. As a result, most of these writers use the techniques of argument and persuasion.

In composing a persuasive argument, you will find that all the advice and suggestions given in the earlier units are helpful and that the methods of definition, analysis, and inductive and deductive reasoning are essential. These guidelines will also help you:

1. Define the problem that forms your subject or underlies it. You may define it by means of description, narration, classification, analogy, analysis, or cause and effect. Most probably, you will need a combination of some of these, perhaps of all.

2. Analyze the nature of the problem fully. Be sure to include specific examples. Choose only the best, of course. A few good ones thoroughly explained will be more effective than a superficial description of a large number. For the analysis you will probably need to summarize, compare, contrast, and classify parts of your material. To make your presentation vivid you may need description, narration, and characterization. To make it logical you will need induction and deduction.

3. Include a full recognition of the opposing points of view and analyze them to show their strengths and weaknesses. A one-sided argument convinces no one for long. Moreover, recognizing your opposition will show your fair-mindedness and the thoroughness of your research.

4. Resist the temptation to oversimplify the problem or the opinions of the opposition. An oversimplification may make your position seem stronger for the moment, but as soon as your readers have had time to think about it, they will realize that you are slanting the evidence. Do not, for instance, blame voter apathy alone as the cause of a low turnout in a particular election if you know that the candidates ignored local problems or that the weather was stormy on election day.

5. Give your solution to the problem, if you have a solution, but admit it frankly if you have none. If your solution is relatively simple and straightforward, you may be able to present it in a single section of your essay. If, however, it is complex or requires making several steps, your reader will probably follow it more easily in a presentation that takes it up point by point and relates each to the appropriate points of the problem. The advice in Unit 9 for organizing comparisons and contrasts will help you here.

6. End with your most convincing material, such as a brief restatement of your solution that your readers can remember easily, or a clinching example or analogy, or a quotation from an eminent authority.

7. Support your argument throughout the main body of your essay. Remember that your readers may know little or nothing about your subject or that they may hold views very different from yours. A mere assertion of your opinion, with no support, will tell them only that you hold that opinion and will not change their minds. Give as much factual evidence as you can, such as statistics, historical background, newspaper reports, your own experience, your direct observation of the experience of others, and references to books and articles that present such observations. When you can, support your opinions by briefly quoting or summarizing the views of the experts.

8. Strengthen your argument by giving your qualifications. The less your readers are likely to know about you or the more specialized your subject is, the more fully you should describe your qualifications to write on the problem. For example, in writing to your college newspaper to support a candidate in a student election, you would need to say only how long you have been at the college and in what situations you had observed the candidate; but in writing to the editor of a newspaper with a large circulation to give your views on energy conservation, you would need to show that you have special knowledge from your academic training or practical experience. In presenting yourself, be honest about your limitations. If your readers suspect that you are exaggerating your experience or abilities, they will distrust everything you say.

9. **Appeal to your readers' interests and sympathies.** An argument based entirely on logic may convince your readers that your opinion is correct, but it may not move them to action. The most effective argument is also a persuasion. It makes readers want to do or believe what you say by appealing to their emotions. This does not mean that you should rely on a sprinkling of emotionally "loaded" words such as "foul" and "heroic." These may add drama to your essay and show the strength of your convictions, but you must go further. Whenever possible, appeal to your readers' own needs and beliefs. Elderly people in a retirement community may not see why their tax dollars should be spent on improving the playground in a local park, but if you can demonstrate that the rest of the park will be quieter and neater as a result of the playground and that outdoor activity improves children's health and social development, and if you remind them of their own childhood pleasures, you will appeal to their concern for their own comforts, to their sense of duty toward the development of good citizens, and to their sentiments. If you know that other retirement communities elsewhere have supported similar projects, you can also use the "bandwagon" effect—suggesting that your readers join the general trend.

 Examples

The writers of many other selections, besides those in this unit, use the techniques of argument, persuasion, or both, in their efforts to convince their readers, most notably Ward in "Yumbo" (3-A), Wright in "A Loaf of Bread and the Stars" (3-B), Manganiello in "The Greatest Welterweight in the World" (4-A), Jackson in "Challenge" (5-D), St. 5 John in "The Fifth Freedom" (6-A), Kirchoff in "The Downfall of Christmas" (9-C), McGrath in "American Magazines" (10-G), Asimov in "Male Humor" (11-B), Tysoe in "And If We Hanged the Wrong Man?" (11-D), *The New Yorker* in "The Bad and Worse Sides of Thanksgiving" (11-H), Conza in "Christmas Eve" (11-I), Nilsson in "Why People Are Preju- 10 diced" (12-G), Zinsser in "Letter from Home" (13-C), Cooper in "A Reply to Zinsser and Hiatt" (13-E), Ashe in "An Open Letter to Black Parents" (13-F), Trippett in "A Red Light for Scofflaws" (13-H), and all the selections in Unit 16.

The following selections differ considerably in emotional intensity 15 because they differ in purpose and subject matter and therefore in word choice and the degree to which they emphasize logic. Be sure to take all these features into account in judging their effectiveness.

15-A   Defending Free Speech for Those We Despise Most

Aryeh Neier

This editorial, published in *Civil Liberties* (November 1977), states the position of the ACLU (the American Civil Liberties Union) in agreeing to defend an American Nazi group that had been refused permission to march through a Jewish neighborhood in Skokie, Illinois. The ACLU is ordinarily considered politically liberal. Following this editorial, a letter to the *New York Times* (16-B) presents an opposing view.

ANALYSIS
Definition of
problem by
description

A letter I received from a woman in Ohio gave a different twist to a criticism of the ACLU's defense of free speech for Nazis. Many critics say that, while they recognize that interference with the Nazis' right to march in Skokie violates the First Amendment, the ACLU should 5 use its limited resources elsewhere. My usual response is that we could have ducked the issue by talking about limited resources—but it would have been false.

Analysis of
problem

The ACLU takes all free speech cases. We have always viewed free speech as our prime responsibility. Other 10 cases—prison, mental commitment, juvenile rights, political surveillance, abortion, race and sex discrimination, privacy—require major commitments of resources. Not so with free speech cases. They usually don't require the construction of complete evidentiary records. They are 15 generally simple and straightforward and it would be untrue to say we don't have the resources to handle them.

Cause and
effect

The woman in Ohio made a point, however, which could not be so readily answered. ACLU is losing a lot of members and a lot of money because we defend free 20 speech for Nazis. This means, she rightly pointed out, that we will have less resources to handle other cases. Is it really so important to defend the rights of Nazis that we are willing to make ourselves less able to defend the rights of others? 25

Redefinition
of problem

Further
analysis

The same thought crossed the minds of many of us who make day to day decisions for the ACLU. Do a few contemptible Nazis deserve to wreck some important ACLU programs? Some of my colleagues have even wondered out loud whether the real purpose of the Nazis and 30 the KKK is to harm the ACLU by presenting themselves as clients in free speech cases.

Specific,
immediate
problem
defined

Regardless of such dark speculations, however, we have to recognize what is at stake in Skokie. Skokie tests whether we really believe that free speech must be de- 35 fended for all—even for those we despise most.

<table>
<tr><td>

Author's
qualifica-
tions
Definition
by examples

</td><td>

As a Jew, and as a refugee from Nazi Germany, I have
strong personal reasons for finding the Nazis repugnant.
Freedom of speech protects my right to denounce Nazis
with all the vehemence I think proper. Free speech also 40
protected the right of Al Wirin, the ACLU of Southern
California's long-time general counsel, to picket a high
school where a rightwing rally was being held—after
Wirin had won in court a decision allowing the rally to be
held.   45

</td></tr>
</table>

Deduction

If the ACLU does not maintain fidelity to the principle that free speech must be defended for all, we do not
deserve to exist or to call ourselves a civil liberties organization. Caving in to a hostile reaction—some of it from
ACLU members—would only advance the notion that 50
speakers may be silenced if listeners are offended. That is
the issue in Skokie, as it has been in a very large number
of the free speech cases ACLU has taken on over the years.

Comparisons
with
similar
examples

Did the wobblies have a right to speak in company
towns? Did Jehovah's Witnesses or birth control advocates 55
have a right to pass out leaflets in Catholic neighborhoods?
Did Norman Thomas have a right to speak in Frank
Hague's Jersey City? Did Paul Robeson have a right to sing
at a concert in Peekskill, New York? Did Martin Luther
King, Jr., have a right to march in Selma, Alabama or in 60
Cicero, Illinois?

Further
comparisons

Did the Jewish Defense League have a right to picket
the Soviet embassy or the home of someone they say was
a Nazi war criminal? Did anti-war demonstrators have a
right to demonstrate at a military base? Did opponents of 65
Richard Nixon have a right to picket the White House? Do
Nazis have a right to hold a demonstration in Skokie?

Cause and
effect

A lot of examples I have cited resulted in violence.
Wobblies were murdered in many Western cities. Jehovah's Witnesses were stoned. Norman Thomas narrowly 70
escaped a lynch mob in Jersey City. There was a riot in
Peekskill and scores of people were injured. Civil rights
marchers were attacked all over the South, in Chicago and
its suburbs, and in many other places.

Analogy

Are any of these instances analogous to shouting fire 75
falsely in a crowded theater? Of course not, although with
the hindsight we know that violence took place. Free

Analysis of
problem

speech—as Justice Holmes said and as the great majority
of the thousands of letters about Skokie I have received
point out—does not protect the shouter of fire. On the 80
contrary, shouting fire falsely in a crowded theater is the

antithesis of speech. No other point of view can be heard.
A panic takes place too quickly.

Comparison
and
contrast
Deduction

By contrast free speech could operate in Skokie. Opponents of the Nazis are free to speak and to condemn the 85
Nazis. There is no need for opponents of the Nazis to
respond violently, but if they do, their violent response is
no reason to silence the Nazis. Speakers must not be silenced because their listeners do not like what they say.

Cause and
effect

It is disheartening to get letters from members quit- 90
ting the ACLU over defense of free speech for the Nazis
and the KKK. These letters ask the ACLU to betray its
very reason for existence. I take pride in saying that I
detect no weakening of resolve in the ACLU's leadership.

Solution
Deduction

We will continue to defend free speech for everyone. 95
It is costing us a great deal and it is forcing us to cut back
on some of the things we should be doing. But if we cannot
ourselves hold to the principle that the right to express
views must be defended even when the views offend listeners, including ACLU members, we can hardly call on 100
governments to follow that principle.

1. Who were the "wobblies" (line 54)? Who are the other persons and organizations mentioned in this paragraph?
2. What is the origin of the word *lynch?*

15-B   The ACLU's Grievous Mistake

Abba P. Lerner

This letter to the editor of *The New York Times* (March 1978) is representative of the
reasoned arguments against the ACLU's position given in the preceding example (Unit
16-B). The writer is a professor of economics at Florida State University.

The American Civil Liberties Union has been sticking to its principles in defending the right of the American Nazi Party to march in a
demonstration through a Jewish-populated area where it will outrage
victims and relatives of victims of the German Nazi bestialities. The
officers of the ACLU feel it is their duty, although a very unpleasant one, 5
to defend the Nazis' right to such demonstrations in the course of
defending the general right of freedom of speech for everyone. They
fear that if freedom of speech is denied to some this opens the way to
denial of freedom of speech to others.

Their intention is noble, but their understanding of their duty is 10
faulty. The overriding purpose of the ACLU is to promote and defend
a democratic social order in which freedom of speech is secure. If this
purpose comes into conflict with freedom of speech directed at destroy-

ing such a democratic social order, their obligation is surely to protect the social order of free speech rather than the free speech of its destroy- 15 ers.

It is true that unpopular as well as popular speech must be kept free —popular speech does not need to be defended—but it is not the *unpopularity* of Nazism that deprives Nazis of free speech rights. It is their opposition to that right for all, and their intention to destroy it, 20 that make it monstrously impertinent for them to claim it. It is a grievous mistake for the ACLU to accept Nazism as merely another unpopular point of view to be defended against prejudice and intolerance.

There is a similar confusion in the nature of the complaints about the use of a Berkeley city park by a Nazi group. The police are perfectly 25 right in claiming that they cannot refuse the park to the Nazis just because they limit participation in their meetings. Other groups also limit participation. But surely this is not the true objection to the Nazis. All would not be remedied if they invited everybody to attend their hate indoctrination sessions. The true objection is that they would not 30 permit Jews or free-speakers to survive, beginning with barring Jews from public parks; and nobody has a valid claim to a right he would deny to others.

Protecting democratic rights of Nazis is often defended by the plea that to deprive them of these rights would make us as intolerant as the 35 Nazis themselves. But, as in mathematics, negatives cancel each other. Intolerance of intolerance is not intolerance, just as the negative of a negative is not negative. It is the *toleration* of intolerance that allows it to grow and to threaten our freedoms.

1. Which of the "aids" to writing an argument listed earlier does the writer use here? (His qualifications were indicated by his title as a university professor, given beneath his signature.)
2. Where has the writer used balanced sentences for emphasis?

15-C Holding the Speaker Hostage

Lance Morrow

Is heckling a speaker a form of free speech? This essay, here complete, first appeared in *Time* in 1983.

Heckling is both a primitive art form and a kind of low-grade amateur guerrilla warfare, a nonviolent intellectual terrorism. Done properly, it produces roughly the effect achieved by releasing a bagful of garter snakes and rats in a cathedral: a spiritual shambles, the sermon in ruins, the bishop standing speechless at the altar.   5

Some sentimentalists, of course, think of heckling as a democratic dialogue, a roughhewn give-and-take of language. But it can turn strident and ultimately sinister. The shriek from the floor can become a different medium altogether. It turns into street theater. Anarchy crashes the hall, like a motorcycle leaping through the window and 10 blasting down the aisle toward the podium. The sound is an anti-language, a gust of obliterating noise from below that is designed precisely to subvert the process whereby words arrive as ideas at their destination in people's brains.

When practiced at certain universities, heckling to silence and 15 expel the intruder achieves a tribal quality; it becomes a gesture of group solidarity, a way that certain zealots in the academic capsule reaffirm the received wisdom of their tribe and symbolically slay the stranger. As such, it is after all a comparatively harmless practice. If academe were more profoundly primitive, undergraduates might have 20 to initiate themselves into the group by, say, ritually mutilating a Republican.

Some politicians, notably the British, cultivate an amiable relationship with hecklers. A man would shout "Rubbish!" during one of former Prime Minister Harold Wilson's stump speeches, and Wilson would 25 imperturbably answer, "Sir, we will get to your area of special interest in just a moment." Other politicians have got down to the darker possibilities. Once in 1921, Adolf Hitler led a gang of Brownshirts into a meeting that was to be addressed by a Bavarian federalist named Ballerstedt. "We got what we wanted," Hitler said. "Ballerstedt did not 30 speak." Hitler explained, "The National Socialist Movement will in the future ruthlessly prevent, if necessary by force, all meetings or lectures that are likely to distract the minds of our fellow countrymen."

The distractions in U.S. halls have increased lately. Disruptive little creatures have been loose—not at political meetings, where hecklers 35 may have more legitimate business, but in university auditoriums. Two months ago in Berkeley, the cradle of the Free Speech Movement in 1964, a group of them managed to jeer U.N. Ambassador Jeane Kirkpatrick from the stage, temporarily. She canceled her lecture scheduled for the next day. The student senate, in a masterpiece of smug non 40 sequitur, sent a letter of regret that observed, "We cannot help but find it somewhat inconsistent that you feel such great concern for your own freedom of speech while blithely accepting . . . so much misery and lack of freedom throughout the world."

Kirkpatrick ran into similar trouble at the University of Minnesota 45 last month. Even before she began her speech, student protesters shouted epithets and chanted, "Murderer! Nazi! Fascist, go home!" (The "Nazi" vocabulary is promiscuously adaptable.) Smith College invited Kirkpatrick to be its commencement speaker this spring, and prepared to award her an honorary degree. The school then decided it could not 50 guarantee decorum if Kirkpatrick came to speak, and so she withdrew.

Other speakers have had trouble lately being heard in academe. Former Black Panther Eldridge Cleaver, now, improbably, a conserva-

tive born-again Christian, was drowned out by several hundred scream- 55
ing protesters when he tried to speak at the University of Wisconsin.
Saudi Arabian Oil Minister Sheik Ahmed Zaki Yamani began a talk at
Kansas State University. A roar of protest erupted from the back of the
auditorium. The room had to be cleared for eighty minutes.

Finally last week, the American Council on Education, joined by
the American Association of University Professors and three national 60
student organizations, decided that the spectacle had grown both embarrassing and morally dangerous. The groups issued a statement that
condemned heckling that silences speakers on college campuses. "Unless there is freedom to speak and to teach," the statement said, "even
for those with whom we differ on fundamentals, and unless there is 65
freedom for all to listen and to learn, there can be no true college or
university."

Both students and teachers are casting an apprehensive eye toward
this spring's graduation ceremonies. Some administrators are afraid
that the crowd manners of the '60s are on the way back. They may be. 70
The operative logic then, as now, was what might be called the Doctrine of Overriding Outrage. This doctrine holds that the issue at hand
—U.S. policy in El Salvador, for example—is too important to be left to
the flaccid (two sides to every question) processes of free speech and
calm discussion. Why tolerate ideas that are so obscenely wrong? His- 75
tory is not high tea. As the Marxist philosopher Herbert Marcuse wrote
in his essay *Repressive Tolerance,* under the free-speech practices of a
liberal regime, "the stupid opinion is treated with the same respect as
the intelligent one, the misinformed may talk as long as the informed."
History is not the *MacNeil-Lehrer Report* either. Should one grit one's 80
teeth and recite the First Amendment when, say, American Nazis decide to march in a Chicago suburb (Skokie) inhabited by many Jews who
survived the Holocaust? Suppose that a man (William Shockley) wishes
to tour American lecture halls suggesting that blacks are inherently
inferior to whites? 85

The Doctrine of Overriding Outrage also rests on the submerged
premise that since the established power owns the microphone and
podium, the process of so-called free speech is part of the problem, not
the solution. The heckling zealot wishes to reroute the entire discussion:
hijack the issue and force it to a wilder jurisdiction. Hecklers take ideas 90
hostage.

Those who disrupt, of course, are almost always a tiny minority of
the audience. They achieve theatrical results far out of proportion to
their size. They traffic in a publicity of anger, not in ideas. For too long,
universities have, rather sweetly, rather weakly, feared to come down 95
hard on those whose screaming silences speakers. Administrators did
not wish to be thought intolerant of dissent; they do not want to interfere too much with youth supposedly acting out its ideals. They need
the character to enforce the prerequisites of intellectual inquiry. They

need to think more clearly about an essential distinction: if a disrupter 100
is removed from the hall and arrested, it is not the disrupter's opinions
that are being censured, but the disruption. A society that will not
defend its basic principles of order is off on a brainless drift. If free
speech has meaning, it must be defended against both cretins and
idealists.

105

1. Compare and contrast the position taken by the American Council on Education (lines 61–67) with the positions taken by Neier and Lerner (Examples
   A and B). What is your opinion?
2. Read the essay by Frederick Douglass (20-B) for an opinion expressed more
   than a century ago. To what extent would Douglass agree with the writers
   of Examples A, B, and C in this unit?
2. Check the etymology, denotation, and connotation of *zealots, received wisdom, non sequitur, flaccid, high tea, cretins.*

15-D   A Crime of Compassion

Barbara Huttmann

This essay, here complete, first appeared in *Newsweek* in 1983. The author is a nurse and
teacher.

   "Murderer," a man shouted. "God help patients who get *you* for
a nurse."
   "What gives you the right to play God?" another one asked.
   It was the Phil Donahue show where the guest is a fatted calf and
the audience a 200-strong flock of vultures hungering to pick at the 5
bones. I had told them about Mac, one of my favorite cancer patients.
"We resuscitated him fifty-two times in just one month. I refused to
resuscitate him again. I simply sat there and held his hand while he
died."
   There wasn't time to explain that Mac was a young, witty, macho 10
cop who walked into the hospital with thirty-two pounds of attack
equipment, looking as if he could single-handedly protect the whole
city, if not the entire state. "Can't get rid of this cough," he said. Otherwise, he felt great.
   Before the day was over, tests confirmed that he had lung cancer. 15
And before the year was over, I loved him, his wife, Maura, and their
three kids as if they were my own. All the nurses loved him. And we
all battled his disease for six months without ever giving death a
thought. Six months isn't such a long time in the whole scheme of
things, but it was long enough to see him lose his youth, his wit, his 20
macho, his hair, his bowel and bladder control, his sense of taste and
smell and his ability to do the slightest thing for himself. It was also long
enough to watch Maura's transformation from a young woman into a
haggard, beaten old lady.

When Mac had wasted away to a sixty-pound skeleton kept alive by liquid food we poured down a tube, i.v. solutions we dripped into his veins and oxygen we piped to a mask on his face, he begged us: "Mercy . . . for God's sake, please just let me go."

The first time he stopped breathing, the nurse pushed the button that calls a "code blue" throughout the hospital and sends a team rushing to resuscitate the patient. Each time he stopped breathing, sometimes two or three times in one day, the code team came again. The doctors and technicians worked their miracles and walked away. The nurses stayed to wipe the saliva that drooled from his mouth, irrigate the big craters of bedsores that covered his hips, suction the lung fluids that threatened to drown him, clean the feces that burned his skin like lye, pour the liquid food down the tube attached to his stomach, put pillows between his knees to ease the bone-on-bone pain, turn him every hour to keep the bedsores from getting worse and change his gown and linen every two hours to keep him from being soaked in perspiration.

At night I went home and tried to scrub away the smell of decaying flesh that seemed woven into the fabric of my uniform. It was in my hair, the upholstery of my car—there was no washing it away. And every night I prayed that Mac would die, that his agonized eyes would never again plead with me to let him die.

Every morning I asked his doctor for a "no code" order. Without that order, we had to resuscitate every patient who stopped breathing. His doctor was one of several who believe we must extend life as long as we have the means and knowledge to do it. To not do it is to be liable for negligence, at least in the eyes of many people, including some nurses. I thought about what it would be like to stand before a judge, accused of murder, if Mac stopped breathing and I didn't call a code.

And after the fifty-second code, when Mac was still lucid enough to beg for death again, and Maura was crumpled in my arms again, and when no amount of pain medication stilled his moaning and agony, I wondered about a spiritual judge. Was all this misery and suffering supposed to be building character or infusing us all with the sense of humility that comes from impotence?

Had we, the whole medical community, become so arrogant that we believed in the illusion of salvation through science? Had we become so self-righteous that we thought meddling in God's work was our duty, our moral imperative and our legal obligation? Did we really believe that we had the right to force "life" on a suffering man who had begged for the right to die?

Such questions haunted me more than ever early one morning when Maura went home to change her clothes and I was bathing Mac. He had been still for so long, I thought he at last had the blessed relief of coma. Then he opened his eyes and moaned, "Pain . . . no more . . . Barbara . . . do something . . . God, let me go."

The desperation in his eyes and voice riddled me with guilt. "I'll stop," I told him as I injected the pain medication.

I sat on the bed and held Mac's hands in mine. He pressed his bony fingers against my hand and muttered, "Thanks." Then there was one soft sigh and I felt his hands go cold in mine. "Mac?" I whispered, as I waited for his chest to rise and fall again. 75

A clutch of panic banded my chest, drew my finger to the code button, urged me to do something, anything . . . but sit there alone with death. I kept one finger on the button, without pressing it, as a waxen pallor slowly transformed his face from person to empty shell. Nothing 80 I've ever done in my forty-seven years has taken so much effort as it took *not* to press that code button.

Eventually, when I was as sure as I could be that the code team would fail to bring him back, I entered the legal twilight zone and pushed the button. The team tried. And while they were trying, Maura 85 walked into the room and shrieked, "No . . . don't let them do this to him . . . for God's sake . . . please, no more."

Cradling her in my arms was like cradling myself, Mac and all those patients and nurses who had been in this place before who do the best they can in a death-denying society. 90

So a TV audience accused me of murder. Perhaps I am guilty. If a doctor had written a no-code order, which is the only *legal* alternative, would he have felt any less guilty? Until there is legislation making it a criminal act to code a patient who has requested the right to die, we will all of us risk the same fate as Mac. For whatever reason, we devel- 95 oped the means to prolong life, and now we are forced to use it. We do not have the right to die.

1. In your opinion, are the metaphors in lines 4, 25, and 35 appropriate?
2. What may be Huttmann's reasons for using questions and direct quotations?
3. Huttmann raises a highly controversial issue. As medical knowledge on ways to prolong life increases, we shall probably see many more cases like the one she describes. What is your opinion?

15-E   The Farmer—An Endangered Species?

Richard M. Ketchum

This essay, here complete, appears in *Second Cutting* (1981), a collection of the author's essays on the problems faced by the owners of small farms. Notice his use of statistics and other facts to support his claims.

A statistician in the U.S. Department of Agriculture has concluded that the forty-year decline in the number of American farms has "bottomed out." Checking the records, he noticed that fewer farms vanished in 1974 than in the previous year, and this convinced him that things are looking up. 5

It may be uncharitable of us to be skeptical about this hopeful news, but we are. For one thing, when you have only half as many farms today as you had four decades ago, it seems reasonable to expect that fewer of them will go on the auction block. But for another—and it pains us to say this—we no longer take much stock in official pronouncements. We don't know whether to rejoice or to mourn when we hear one, on the theory that it may be denied or declared inoperative the next morning.

Ours is the reverse of the fable about the boy who cried wolf. Having been gulled by so many big statements during the past decade, we no longer believe the little ones. Probably it is inevitable in this disposable society that government officials—like the rest of us—should come to think that nothing is durable or worth hanging on to. Like plastic drinking cups and the packaging for Big Mac hamburgers, their pronouncements are thought of as throwaways, to be trashed in case of a change of heart.

An example of how things work occurred one May, when the government began spreading the word that an upturn in the economy was imminent. After so many dreary months of bad news and gloomy predictions, someone in Washington decided it was time for a change. So they announced that there were "serious flaws in the old composite index," and conjured up a new index that would prove how rosy the picture is—unemployment, inflation, business failures, and the like notwithstanding.

We don't mean to pick on the USDA, which is having enough problems without us, God knows, but we have observed little to suggest that the farm decline is really "bottoming out," as they put it. On the contrary, the signs point to the fact that there is little in store for most small farmers but continued hard work and prices that don't begin to provide a decent return for their efforts. We see tired men and women unable to continue on the homestead in which they have invested a lifetime of backbreaking drudgery, unable to find new hands willing to take on the kind of work farming means, unable to comprehend a society that gives its farmers the short end of the stick.

Look at it this way: fifteen years ago the dairy farmer received $4.60 per hundredweight for milk (a figure that translates to 10 cents a quart). Ten years later nearly everything the farmer has to pay for—grain, fertilizer, machinery, labor—has doubled in price, and some items have tripled; yet he receives only 17 cents a quart for his milk. Which means that he gets 30 percent less for what he has to sell than for what he has to buy.

Go to the butcher shop and buy a porterhouse steak. Then ask the beef producer what he got for that steer he sent to auction.

Somehow, somewhere, a lot of cream is being skimmed off the middle—the difference between what the farmer gets for his produce and what the customer has to pay. We know the farmer isn't getting it, and neither is the retailer: that fellow in the white apron at the butcher shop is making a net profit of about 4 cents a pound on the steak he sells you, and surely you won't begrudge him that.

It's customary to blame all this on the mysterious "middleman." 55 Now, we have never met a middleperson, but we suspect that all this middlemoney we are fussing about is going not to any one person but to an army of them—buyers, wholesalers, processors, packagers, truckers, commission men, and what have you.

So, rather than try to pin the onus on anyone in particular, maybe 60 we should view this problem as an argument for more locally produced food. Why should the Vermont dairy farmer send milk to Boston at 17 cents a quart, only to have to buy it back for 42 cents a quart? And when the Maine potato farmer may receive as little as $2.40 a hundredweight for his crop, why should his neighbors have to pay five times that for 65 potatoes in the supermarket?

In Vermont a number of people are taking matters into their own hands. In 1850, 75 percent of the land in the state was cultivated or pastured; and it has been estimated that only 18 percent was being farmed by 1979. But some interesting changes are afoot. Almost over- 70 night, it seems, thirty thousand Vermonters have become members of food cooperatives; there are now twelve thousand community gardens in the state (not counting the backyard variety); and suddenly seventeen farmers' markets are flourishing, providing the local farmer with an outlet and the community with fresh produce at lower prices.   75

In Massachusetts, Frederic Winthrop, Jr., the commissioner of agriculture, made increased food production the number one priority for his state. Alarmed by the relentless erosion of agricultural acreage, Winthrop told anyone who would listen that "the time is coming when we will need every bit of farming land we have." A similar message 80 comes from Connecticut, where the Governor's Task Force for the Preservation of Agricultural Land recommended that the state take steps to preserve enough farmland to produce one-third of the food its citizens require.

Connecticut, incidentally, is also the state whose senate voted to 85 designate *Homo sapiens* as the state animal. We don't know how Connecticut struggled along without a state animal all these years, but the notion advanced by David H. Neidetz, a West Hartford Democrat, appeals to us. As he put it, a species that is so threatened by taxes, unpaid bills, and a deteriorating environment deserves recognition for 90 its plight, and a majority of his fellow senators agreed. But it was a short-lived moment of glory for old *Homo sapiens;* outraged animal lovers complained so vociferously that the bill was sent back to committee to die.

The idea got us to thinking, though. Perhaps, if Connecticut's vot- 95 ers aren't willing to give this plum to man in general, they would consider bestowing it on a subspecies—the farmer—who appears to be low man on everyone's totem.

1. What does Ketchum emphasize by his use of similes in the third paragraph and by balanced sentence structure?
2. Would Ketchum's argument have been easier to follow if he had used such expressions as "nearly twice the price" or "much more expensive" instead of statistics?
3. All Ketchum's references are limited to New England and the only farm products he mentions specifically are milk, beef, and potatoes. In your opinion, would his argument have been stronger if he had mentioned other parts of the country and included a greater variety of farm products?
4. Check the etymology, denotation, and connotation of *gulled, onus, vociferously, totem.*

15-F   Where Is My Child?

Dorothy Collier

This essay, here complete, appeared in the *London Sunday Times* (1977). For reasons that the essay makes clear, the writer has used an assumed name. In forty of the United States, laws, like those in England, keep adoption records sealed so that parents who gave up their children cannot get information later on their whereabouts or welfare and the children cannot trace their parents.

Franklin D. Roosevelt once announced, in a voice choked with emotion, that December 7, 1941 was "a date that would go down in the annals of infamy." I feel much the same about November 26, 1976.

On that date the Children Act came into operation. This permits adopted people to gain access to their own birth records and thus to find 5 out who they are. Many of them, though by no means all, want to go further than that and find out if their natural parents, and in particular their mothers, are "all right." The implicit question here is: Did my mother recover from the shock of parting with me, did she pick up the pieces of her life? 10

I have no quarrel with that Act. It was wise, it was humane, and, in light of recent evidence from America, it puts Britain in the forefront of the caring Nations. My point is that the Act is infamously incomplete.

Two principles underlie the Act. The first is that everybody, whether adopted or not, has a need to know about his lineage, his 15 background, his family. Cut out that knowledge, and, whether the child be adopted, fostered or placed in a Home, he will feel a basic sense of insecurity, a feeling of incompleteness. There is plenty of clinical evidence to support that view, and I myself have been in such close contact with so many adopted people that I know it to be true. I also know how 20 "finding out" brings peace of mind.

The second principle is that, in the majority of orthodox adoptions, the child was too young to understand what was happening. Something was done to him without his knowledge or consent, and justice demands that when he reaches a more mature age he should reach his own 25 conclusions. When you come to think of it, there is an analogy here with Christian practice, whereby a child is baptised soon after birth and later confirms—or doesn't confirm—his attitude to life.

What is now emerging, ever more clearly, is that just as the baby does not know what is happening when the Adoption Order is made, neither does the mother.

In 1943 I was a young married woman. I had fallen out of love with my husband and into love with another man. The situation was such that when I became pregnant—or rather when I could no longer conceal my pregnancy—the expected baby could not possibly have been my husband's.

He turned me out. I had nowhere to go, and he took me back again. I was permitted the full term of pregnancy. I was permitted to go into hospital and have my baby delivered. I was permitted to take my little son home and to suckle him. One evening I was informed that he would be taken from me that following morning and placed for adoption. From the moment of that announcement I was frozen; I remained frozen for many years.

I would like to make it clear that the baby was not snatched from me, I didn't struggle. I handed over my son as a robot might have handed him over. A few weeks later I signed papers, presumably consents to his adoption, and I was literally unconscious at the time. The enormity of what was happening was too great for my mind to handle, either in intellectual or in emotional terms, and it shut itself off. It was many years later, after acutely disruptive emotional disorder, that my mind reopened itself to the shock. By that time my husband was dead. Whatever arrangements he made for my child, whatever knowledge he had of my son, died with him. I am prohibited now from finding out if my boy is "all right."

My purpose in writing is not to seek sympathy for myself. Over and over and over again I have spoken with mothers whose stories are similar to my own. My conviction is that the female psyche cannot cope with carrying a child full term—feeling him quicken, feeling him kick —with the delivery of him, with hearing his first cry, with learning that he is safe and well, even, as in my case, with feeding him at the breast and *then* with severance. Emotional paralysis is, I am sure, inevitable; when she signs her consent to adoption, the mother cannot "know" what she is doing.

But of course the lawmakers are mostly male, aren't they?

The child cannot know what is happening, the mother cannot know. If the child needs to know about lineage retrospectively, the mother needs to know prospectively—that her line continues. If the child needs to know about grandparents, the mother needs to know about grandchildren. If the child needs to know that Mum's "all right," the mother needs to know—oh, how desperately!—that her son flourishes and is well.

Yet the law applies only to the child. He has all the rights and all the initiatives. If my son, the child that I bore, is dead, I am denied even the right to know where his body lies. I cannot believe that that right should be abrogated by the stroke of the pen at a time when the mind 75 has ceased to function. I believe firmly that, with the same safeguards as now apply to the children, the right to know, the right to acquire basic information, should be granted to the natural parents of adopted persons.

1. In the fourth and fifth paragraphs the writer clearly labels two principles that form the basis of her argument. What principles are implied in other parts of her essay?
2. Why does the writer wait until the sixth paragraph to state the problem explicitly?
3. Check the etymology, denotation, and connotation of *infamy, implicit, lineage, orthodox, enormity, psyche, severance, abrogated.*

15-G   Campus Vandalism

James Brown (student)

This essay was an in-class exercise. The writer had a choice of three topics and took "How serious is vandalism on our campus and what can be done to reduce it?"

"Hey, grab that cat!" screamed one student, and a friend jumped to block the cat's escape.
"I got him!" shouted a third as he lunged for the animal.
The three students proceeded to spray-paint the entire cat green. They dissolved into hysterical laughter as the terrified creature fled into 5 *the bushes.*

This is a fictional episode, but, who knows, spraying cats green may be next year's favorite campus stunt.

Major contributors to vandalism are students who don't know what to do with their spare time. Many children go through stages of petty 10 larceny and destructiveness and get a thrill from stealing a stick of gum from the local candy stores or smashing pop bottles in vacant lots. The students who destroy their own campus have never outgrown that stage. They have never found a way to be noticed except to brag to their friends that they have performed such great deeds as pouring glue over 15 the box of spoons in the campus cafeteria. One of my roommates goes around stealing anything he can get his hands on. To date, in our room we have a "University Dining Room" sign, two extra chairs, a McDonald's flag, several road signs from nearby streets, and a blinking light used to warn cars of a road block. If this is what just one person can 20 collect in a semester, imagine what the entire student body may have stowed away.

Many of these stunts are amusing and may seem harmless. But even the most seemingly harmless practical jokes can be destructive in the end, and most cause expenses for repairs. This contributes to our ever- 25 increasing tuition charges. Why must mature, innocent students pay for the silly behavior of the childish, guilty ones?

The main reason vandals are not apprehended is that they are protected by their peers. No student wants to come forth and "rat" or "snitch" on another. For the university to eliminate some of the vandal- 30 ism, there must be a system for students to identify a vandal without having to do so face to face. In the outside world many people are intimidated by criminals when they are asked to testify, and that is exactly what these campus vandals are—criminals, young students who are finally free of family rule and who want to explore all the things they 35 could not do at home.

Also, fraternities and sororities have a duty to try to stop the ritual of destruction, instead of encouraging it. In hazing, they must not force pledges to destroy a car to qualify for membership. Think how good the results would be if instead they required pledges to police the campus 40 every day for a month.

Vandals must be dismissed from the university. After one or two are found guilty and expelled, vandalism will decrease dramatically. Every student must understand that he is not helping a friend by protecting him; he is only allowing the friend to continue hurting every- 45 one, including himself. If everyone works together, maybe we'll never have to see a green cat.

1. Is the narrative beginning effective? Would a less dramatic but true example have been better?
2. Which of the other "aids" to argument does the writer use?

15-H   Killing for Sport

Joseph Wood Krutch

These paragraphs form about one-quarter of an essay that first appeared in *The American Scholar* (1956). The topic has gained increasing attention, and now many groups are active in protecting the lives of wild animals from hunters.

It wouldn't be quite true to say that "some of my best friends are hunters." Still, I do number among my respected acquaintances some who not only kill for the sake of killing but count it among their keenest pleasures. And I can think of no better illustration of the fact that men may be separated at some point by a fathomless abyss yet share else- 5 where much common ground. To me, it is inconceivable that anyone can think an animal more interesting dead than alive. I can also easily prove, to my own satisfaction, that killing "for sport" is the perfect type of pure evil for which metaphysicians have sometimes sought.

Most wicked deeds are done because the doer proposes some good for himself. The liar lies to gain some end; the swindler and the thief want things which, if honestly got, might be good in themselves. Even the murderer is usually removing some impediment to normal desires. Though all of these are selfish or unscrupulous, their deeds are not gratuitously evil. But the killer for sport seems to have no such excusable motive. He seems merely to prefer death to life, darkness to light. "Something which wanted to live is dead. Because I can bring terror and agony, I assure myself that I have power. Because of me there is that much less vitality, consciousness and perhaps joy in the universe. I am the spirit that denies." When a man wantonly destroys one of the works of man, we call him "Vandal." When he wantonly destroys one of the works of God, we call him "Sportsman."

The hunter-for-food may be as wicked and as misguided as vegetarians sometimes say, but he does not kill for the sake of killing. The ranchers and the farmers who exterminate all living things not immediately profitable to them may sometimes be working against their own best interests; but whether they are or are not, they hope to achieve some supposed good by the exterminations. If to do evil, not in the hope of gain but for evil's sake, involves the deepest guilt by which man can be stained, then killing for killing's sake is a terrifying phenomenon and as strong a proof as we could have of that "reality of evil" with which present-day theologians are again concerned.

Despite all this, I know that sportsmen are not necessarily monsters. Even if the logic of my position is unassailable, the fact remains that men are not logical creatures, that most, if not all, are blind to much they might be expected to see, and that the blind spots vary from person to person. To say, as we all do, "Any man who would do *A* would do *B*" is to state a proposition mercifully proved false almost as often as it is stated. The murderer is not necessarily a liar, any more than the liar is necessarily a murderer. Many have been known to say that they considered adultery worse than homicide, but not all adulterers are potential murderers and there are even murderers to whom incontinence would be unthinkable. The sportsman may exhibit any of the virtues—including compassion and respect for life—everywhere except in connection with his "sporting" activities. It may even be too often true that, as "antisentimentalists" are fond of pointing out, those who are tenderest toward animals are not necessarily the most philanthropic. They, no less than sportsmen, are not always consistent.

Yet, if the Puritans really did forbid bearbaiting, not because it gave pain to the bears but because it gave pleasure to the spectators, they were not necessarily so absurd as Macaulay has made us believe. That particular pleasure *was* evil in itself, and to this day the Puritan logic is also that of the Roman Catholic position (based on St. Thomas): namely, that cruelty to animals is wrong, not because animals have any rights, but because cruelty corrupts men. And I am so sure this is true 55 that I was offended when President Eisenhower told reporters that on his vacation he hoped to find time "to shoot a few crows." I have no doubt that crows have to be kept down. But I have strong doubt that killing them ought to be a pleasure.

If anyone asks me why we shouldn't get a little fun out of a neces- 60 sary activity, I will reply: "For the same reason that legal hangings are no longer made a public spectacle. The fallacy is precisely that of the Mikado, whose sublime object it was to 'make each prisoner pent / Unwillingly represent / A source of innocent merriment / Of innocent merriment.' "*   65

1. Krutch states in ¶1 that he can establish to his own satisfaction the generalization that "killing 'for sport' is the perfect type of pure evil." Does he establish it to your satisfaction as well?
2. List the examples he gives of other killings whose evil he finds less "pure." What is the basis for his claim?
3. Does his admission later that sportsmen may have some virtues in other areas weaken his case?
4. Why does he uphold the Puritans' objection to bearbaiting and the Roman Catholic position on cruelty to animals? Why does he object to Eisenhower shooting crows and to the Mikado making prisoners "a source of innocent merriment"?
5. Check the etymology, denotation, and connotation of *fathomless, abyss, gratuitously, wantonly, phenomenon, theologians, incontinence, compassion, bearbaiting,* the *Mikado, pent.*

Assignments

1. Reread the examples in this unit. Is there an author with whom you disagree, wholly or in part? If so, write an argumentative essay of about 500 words replying to the author.
2. Choose a recent editorial from your college or local newspaper and write a 500-word argumentative essay, directed to the paper's readers, explaining why you agree or disagree with it. If you agree, be sure to support your argument in ways and with material not used in the original.
3. What improvement do you think is most needed in the neighborhood in which you live? Write an argumentative essay urging the residents and the appropriate officials to make the improvement. Be sure to choose something specific such as a traffic light at a dangerous intersection, better parking facilities in a particular area, a summer recreation program for children, a stricter enforcement of regulations about unleashed dogs, or a bigger selection of books and magazines in the public library.

---

*The quotation is from a song in the operetta *The Mikado,* by Gilbert and Sullivan.

4. What change do you think is most needed at the college or university you are attending? Choose something specific and write an argumentative essay urging the other students or the appropriate members of the faculty or administration to make the change.

5. What annoying or dangerous habit does one of your friends or a member of your family have that you think can be corrected? Write a tactful argument persuading him or her to break the habit.

UNIT 16

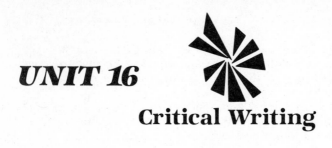

Critical Writing

When you criticize something, do you look only for faults? or do you also look for good points?

Criticism, in the larger sense, is not mere fault-finding but an analysis of strengths as well as weaknesses. It is a dissection and evaluation of all the characteristics of a particular subject. Most of your college instructors will ask you to write critically about assigned readings, such as scholarly articles, chapters of a book, whole books, and works of literature. They will expect you to go beyond what you may have written for high school "book reports," which were probably only summaries of your reading. Instead, you will be expected to compare, contrast, evaluate, and reach conclusions on what an author has to say.

In choosing a subject, you may, depending on the assignment, criticize a complete work, covering all its main points and the methods of presentation, or concentrate on a particular aspect or section. Professional book reviewers, drama and music critics, and so on, cover a whole work or performance because they are writing about new ones and therefore must give their readers an overall view. But critics writing on an established work usually concentrate on a section or an aspect of it that they think has been neglected by the critics or inaccurately evaluated or interpreted.

You are unlikely, for example, to have anything new to say about the whole of Shakespeare's *Hamlet,* at least until you have become an authority on Shakespeare, but you may have some interesting thoughts on a small element of the play, such as one of the minor characters, or two or three lines in an important speech. You may also find that a comparison and contrast between a minor character in *Hamlet* and one in another of Shakespeare's plays sheds light on one or both characters.

A specific critical approach may help you to form a new interpretation. In writing about a minor character in *Hamlet,* for example, you might consider primarily that character's psychology as revealed in words and actions, explaining to your readers the exact psychological theory you are applying and why you chose it. You might examine the same character from a historical point of view to determine Shakespeare's degree of accuracy in portraying the attitudes and customs of a historical period, his own or an earlier one. You might apply linguistic analysis to the words in several lines, determining both their etymology and use by Shakespeare's contemporaries, to arrive at a fuller understanding of his use of language.

When writing on something that others have already criticized, you should take their criticism into account and tell your readers why there is room for another view—yours. The professional criticism can itself be a subject for a critical paper. Instead of giving a new interpretation of a minor character in *Hamlet,* you could show why the interpretation by critic X is better than the interpretations by critics W, Y, and Z—assuming, of course, that X made little or no reference to W, Y, and Z, because if X attacked them effectively you will probably have nothing significant to add.

To find a subject for a critical paper, apply the same principles you used to find subjects for the other kinds of writing discussed in this book. The broader your topic is and the more familiar it is to others, the less likely you are to have something new and forceful to say. Just as you were advised in Unit 1, you should narrow your topic so that you can handle it thoroughly and have something fresh to say.

In writing any criticism, you will find helpful all the skills discussed earlier, particularly analysis, classification, comparison, and definition. Whatever methods you use, be sure to include the four points in this guideline:

1. Classify the work with which you are dealing. For example, if it is a written work, you must tell your readers whether it is a biography, a novel, a report on an economic survey, a political analysis, and so on. You must also tell them what areas it covers and to which readers it seems directed. A dictionary, as Mark Twain remarked humorously, can scarcely be blamed for having little plot. Similarly, we apply one set of critical standards to an article on a particular problem in foreign policy if the article appears in a scholarly journal and a rather different set of standards to another article on the same problem that appears in a general circulation magazine.

2. Indicate the scope and nature of your critical approach. If you are going to limit your discussion to a minor character in *Hamlet,* tell your readers exactly that and explain your interest in that character. If you are going to base your criticism on a psychological theory, define that theory and say why you are using it.

3. Summarize the content of the work. An adequate summary gives your criticism a firm foundation; however, be brief—include only the essential features of the work, and remember that your main purpose is to criticize it, not to save your readers the effort of reading it for themselves. It is customary to use the present tense to summarize the main actions of any narrative, whatever the literary form, because you then have the past and future tenses to refer to events before and after the part of the narrative under immediate consideration. With paintings, musical compositions, and other works in nonverbal media, give a brief description. If the work is very well known, *Hamlet,* for example, or Beethoven's Fifth Symphony, a summary or description is not necessary, but be sure to let your readers know which section you are discussing so that they can recognize it quickly and easily. (**Note:** for a discussion of summary writing, read the introductory section of Unit 7.)

4. Interpret and evaluate the work by using as many of the skills discussed earlier as are appropriate. Make your remarks convincing by using the argumentative methods discussed in Unit 15. Have the courage of your convictions and do not feel intimidated by the fame of the writer or artist whose work you are criticizing or of the critics with whom you disagree. As in argumentative writing, use objective analysis and logic as the basis of your criticism and rely on emotional words and phrases only to add vitality and color to it. Be sure to explain how your interpretation and evaluation resembles or differs from those of major critics. Support your remarks with specific illustrations from the work and with any relevant information, such as the historical background, and explain how the illustrations and information support them.

*   *   *   *   *   *   *   *   *

Satire is a special kind of criticism. Writers use it to attack something they think is wrong. Instead of stating their beliefs and objections directly, they take the risk of being indirect. They try to make their readers think for themselves and look through the literal meaning on the surface to the deeper meaning. By doing this, successful satire can often be more effective than straightforward critical writing. Only a few specialists are now familiar with Jonathan Swift's direct attack on the causes of poverty in eighteenth-century Ireland but his satiric attack, "A Modest Proposal," has become such a classic that any piece now using that title immediately announces to every educated reader that it is satiric.

To be made fun of is always more painful than simply to be scolded, and satire makes what it attacks ridiculous. It may grossly **exaggerate,** as Orwell does in his novel *1984* by taking totalitarian control far beyond what it had reached when the book was published in 1949. It may **reverse** the facts, as Swift does in the fourth book of *Gulliver's Travels,* with human beings (the Yahoos) as savage beasts and with horses (the Houyhnhnms) as intelligent, virtuous creatures. Or it may **transfer** the situation to a different area where its ridiculousness will be apparent, as a writer annoyed by the excesses of time-and-motion studies in a government bureau once did when he applied the efficiency experts' principles to conducting a symphony orchestra.

When you write satire, whatever your method, make sure that your readers will know that it is satire. If you choose exaggeration, you must exaggerate grossly; if you choose to reverse or transfer the facts, you must give clues to your satiric purpose early in your essay.

Examples

Criticism is the primary purpose of the writers of the following selections, but it has an important part in many other selections in this book, most notably in Manganiello's "The Greatest Welterweight" (4-A), McDowell's "When Is a Joke Not a Joke" (4-B), Bronowski's "A Metaphor Used Twice" (5-E), Kirchoff's "The Downfall of Christmas" (9-B), McGrath's "American Magazines and American Culture" (10-G), Asimov's "Male Humor" (11-B), *The New Yorker*'s "The Bad and Worse Sides of Thanksgiving" (11-H), Conza's "Christmas Eve" (11-I), Cooper's "Reply to Zinsser and Hiatt" (13-E), Ashe's "An Open Letter to Black Parents" (13-F), Trippett's "A Red Light for Scofflaws" (13-H), and almost all the selections in Unit 15.

The critical methods in the following examples can be applied to any subject. Since most of your critical writing in college will be on what you read, six of the examples are criticisms of written works. The first five show some of the many critical approaches possible even when the work—in this case, Shakespeare's *Romeo and Juliet*—has been criticized many times before. All the writers include enough information on the play to make their points clear. **To follow their criticism, you do not need to have read the play.**

Of the remaining examples, one is a review of two scientific books and another of an album of a popular singer; the last three are humorous.

16-A   Misadventures in Verona

Brendan Gill

These paragraphs begin a review of a 1977 production of *Romeo and Juliet*. The writer, the chief drama critic for *The New Yorker*, first states his general opinion of the production—it was "an honorable failure"—and then, to show the basis for his judgment, gives his interpretation of the play. In the rest of the review, omitted here, he explains how the production failed to fulfill his expectations.

The new production of *Romeo and Juliet* at the Circle in the Square is an honorable failure. The director of the play, Theodore Mann, has evidently worked hard with a large and motley cast, but he is not known for having a light touch, and, oddly enough, it is a light touch that the play requires. For *Romeo and Juliet* is a tragedy that must be played as if it were a comedy, or it won't succeed; tether it to solemnity and it becomes an earthbound recounting of a series of preposterous misadventures. Because its tone is continually at odds with its content, it is a play far more difficult to perform than one would expect from a mere reading acquaintance with it. From first to last, bodies pile up on the stage at a fearful rate, and the emotions aroused in us by a carnage almost as ample as that in *Hamlet* ought surely to be pity and terror, but no such thing: the language of the play is so lyrical, so springlike, so charged with the

energetic hopefulness of first love that we scarcely take in the grim
evidence of our senses. After an ideal performance, we leave the theatre   15
elated rather than deeply moved, remembering Romeo and Juliet not as
corpses in a tomb but as dear, harmless, amorous children. Though
Romeo takes two men's lives and is a suicide, these formidable offenses
against God and the state strike us, in their romantic context, as only
mildly reprehensible. Moreover, if *Romeo and Juliet* were an authentic   20
tragedy instead of a nominal one, the protagonists would be, of course,
Capulet and Montague, who by their senile pride and other flaws of
character bring ruin to those presumably dearest to them.

That Shakespeare himself intended the play to be taken lightly is
hinted at in its last words, spoken by Escalus, Prince of Verona: "For   25
never was a story of more woe/Than this of Juliet and her Romeo." The
couplet reduces the play to a pretty toy, which one may be grateful for
but need not take too seriously; the effect is startlingly like that evoked
by the ending of *A Midsummer Night's Dream,* which Shakespeare is
thought to have written a year or so earlier. Both plays are washed in   30
the same blue moonlight, and the celebrated "aria" describing Queen
Mab could have been given as readily to Theseus as to Mercutio. The
passage has, at the very least, the look of being a delectable leftover, too
precious to discard.

1. To support his claim that the play "is a tragedy that must be played as if it
   were a comedy," what use does the writer make of specific examples? of
   quotation? of comparison with other plays?
2. Check the etymology, denotation, and connotation of *motley, tether, preposterous, formidable, reprehensible, nominal, protagonists, senile, aria, delectable.*

16-B   Clues to Meaning

John Hankins

These paragraphs are from a 3000-word essay introducing a widely used paperback
edition of *Romeo and Juliet.* The essay is intended to give the general reader an overall
view of the play and the chief critical interpretations.

ANALYSIS   In recent years numerous attempts have been made to
Classification   state a central theme for the play. One critic views it as a
#1
analysis   tragedy of unawareness. Capulet and Montague are unaware of the fateful issues which may hang upon their
quarrel. Romeo and Juliet fall in love while unaware that   5
they are hereditary enemies. Mercutio and Tybalt are both
unaware of the true state of affairs when they fight their
duel. In the chain of events leading to the final tragedy,
even the servants play a part and are unaware of the results
of their actions. The final scene, with Friar Laurence's long   10
explanation, is dramatically justified because it brings Mon-

tague, Capulet, Lady Capulet, and the Prince to at least a partial awareness of their responsibility for what has happened. Supplementing this view of the play is one which finds it to be a study of the wholeness and complexity of things in human affairs. The issues of the feud may appear to be simple and clear, but in reality they are highly complex, giving rise to results which are completely unforeseen. The goodness or badness of human actions is relative, not absolute, an idea symbolically set forth in Friar Laurence's opening speech on herbs which are medicinal or poisonous according to the manner of their use.

Classification #2 analysis

15

20

Other clues to the meaning of the play may be found in the repetitive imagery employed by Shakespeare. The images of haste, of events rushing to a conclusion, are found throughout. When Romeo says, "I stand on sudden haste," Friar Laurence answers, "They stumble that run fast," and thus expresses one moral to be drawn from the play. Romeo and Mercutio symbolize their wit-combat by the wild-goose chase, a reckless cross-country horse race. "Swits and spurs," cries Romeo, using the imagery of speed. Numerous other instances may be found.

Classification #3

analysis

25

30

Closely allied to the imagery of haste is the violence expressed in the gunpowder image. The Friar warns that too impetuous love is like fire and powder, "which, as they kiss, consume." Romeo desires a poison that will expel life from his body like powder fired from a cannon. This may identify the Apothecary's poison as aconite, since elsewhere Shakespeare compares the action of aconite with that of "rash gunpowder" (*2 Henry IV,* IV, iv, 48). Violence is also expressed in the image of shipwreck which may end the voyage of life. Capulet compares Juliet weeping to a bark in danger from tempests. Romeo describes his death as the shipwreck of his "seasick weary bark." Earlier, after expressing a premonition that attendance at Capulet's party will cause his death, he resigns himself to Him "that hath the steerage of my course," anticipating his later images of the ship and the voyage of life.

Classification #4

analysis

35

40

45

Also repeated in the play is the image of Death as the lover of Juliet. She herself uses it, her father uses it beside her bier, and Romeo uses it most effectively in the final scene. The effect of this repeated image is to suggest that Juliet is foredoomed to die, that Death, personified, has claimed her for his own. It thus strengthens the ominous note of fate which is felt throughout the play.

Classification #5

analysis

evaluation

50

55

That *Romeo and Juliet* is a tragedy of fate can hardly be doubted. Shakespeare says as much in the Prologue. The lovers are marked for death; their fortunes are

Classification #6

analysis

"crossed" by the stars. The reason for their doom is like- 60
wise given: only the shock of their deaths can force their
parents to end the senseless feud. At the end of the play
Capulet calls the lovers "poor sacrifices of our enmity,"
and the Prince describes their deaths as Heaven's punishment of their parents' hate. Romeo's premonition of death
before going to the party attributes it to "some conse- 65
quence yet hanging in the stars." The note of fate is struck
repeatedly during the play. "A greater power than we can
contradict / Hath thwarted our intents," says Friar Laurence to Juliet in the tomb. The numerous mischances

General
conclusion

experienced by the lovers are not fortuitous bad luck but 70
represent the working out of some hidden design. Critics
who attack the play for lacking inevitability have misun-
derstood Shakespeare's dramatic technique. Like Hamlet's adventure with the pirates, the sequence of mishaps
here is deliberately made so improbable that chance alone 75
cannot explain it. Only fate, or the will of Heaven, affords
a sufficient explanation.

1. What transitional devices does the writer use to lead the reader from one
   "central theme" to another?
2. What kinds of support does the writer give for the various interpretations of
   the central theme?
3. Check the etymology, denotation, and connotation of *hereditary, supplementing, imagery, apothecary, bark* (as used here), *steerage, bier, thwarted,
   fortuitous.*

16-C   Puns and Other Wordplay in *Romeo and Juliet*

M. M. Mahood

These paragraphs conclude the chapter on *Romeo and Juliet* in *Shakespeare's Wordplay*
(1957), a scholarly book devoted to a close analysis of a specific aspect of Shakespeare's
writing to determine what light it may shed on interpreting the plays.

Some of the most notorious puns in Shakespeare occur in this scene
between Juliet and her Nurse, when the Nurse's confusion misleads
Juliet into thinking Romeo has killed himself:

> Hath Romeo slaine himselfe? say thou but *I*,
> And that bare vowell *I* shall poyson more   5
> Then the death darting *eye* of Cockatrice,
> *I* am not *I*, if there be such an *I.*
> Or those *eyes* shut, that makes thee answer *I*:
> If he be slaine say *I*, or if not, no.
>
> (III.ii.45–50)   10

Excuses might be made for this. It does achieve a remarkable
sound-effect by setting Juliet's high-pitched keening of "I" against the

Nurse's moans of "O Romeo, Romeo." It also sustains the eye imagery of
Juliet's great speech at the opening of this scene: the runaways' eyes, the
blindness of love, Juliet hooded like a hawk, Romeo as the eye of heaven. 15
But excuses are scarcely needed since this is one of Shakespeare's first
attempts to reveal a profound disturbance of mind by the use of quibbles.
Romeo's puns in the next scene at Friar Laurence's cell are of the same
kind: flies may kiss Juliet, but he must fly from her; the Friar, though a
friend *professed,* will offer him no sudden means of death, though ne'er 20
so mean; he longs to know what his concealed lady says to their cancelled
love. This is technically crude, and perhaps we do well to omit it in
modern productions; but it represents a psychological discovery that
Shakespeare was to put to masterly use in later plays. Against this
feverish language of Romeo's, Shakespeare sets the Friar's sober knowl- 25
edge that lovers have suffered and survived these calamities since the
beginning of time. For the Friar, "the world is broad and wide," for
Romeo, "there is no world without Verona wall." When the Friar tries to
dispute with him of his "estate," the generalised, prayer-bookish word
suggests that Romeo's distress is the common human lot, and we believe 30
as much even while we join with Romeo in his protest: "Thou canst not
speak of that thou dost not feele." Tragedy continually restates the
paradox that "all cases are unique and very similar to others."

The lovers' parting at dawn sustains this contradiction. Lovers'
hours may be full eternity, but the sun must still rise. Their happiness 35
has placed them out of the reach of fate; but from now on, an accelerat-
ing series of misfortunes is to confound their triumph in disaster without
making it any less of a triumph. With Lady Capulet's arrival to announce the match with Paris, love's enemies begin to close in. Juliet
meets her mother with equivocations which suggest that Romeo's "snow- 40
ie Dove" has grown wise as serpents since the story began, and which
prepare us for her resolution in feigning death to remain loyal to
Romeo:

> Indeed I neuer shall be satisfied
> With Romeo, till I behold him. Dead   45
> Is my poore heart so for a kinsman vext.
>   (III.v.94–96)

This is a triple ambiguity, with one meaning for Juliet, another for
her mother and a third for us, the audience: Juliet will never in fact see
Romeo again until she wakes and finds him dead beside her. 50

A pun which has escaped most editors is made by Paris at the
beginning of Act IV. He tells the Friar he has talked little of love with
Juliet because "Venus smiles not in a house of teares." Here *house of
tears* means, beside the bereaved Capulet household, an inauspicious
section of the heavens—perhaps the eighth house or "house of death." 55
Spenser's line "When oblique Saturne sate in the house of agonyes"
shows that the image was familiar to the Elizabethans, and here it adds its
weight to the lovers' yoke of inauspicious stars. But this is one of very few

quibbles in the last two acts. The wordplay which, in the first part of the
play, served to point up the meaning of the action is no longer required. 60
What quibbles there are in the final scenes have, however, extraordinary
force. Those spoken by Romeo after he has drunk the poison reaffirm the
paradox of the play's experience at its most dramatic moment:

> O *true* Appothecary:
> Thy drugs are *quicke*. Thus with a kisse I die.   65
> (V.iii.119–20)

Like the Friar's herbs, the apothecary's poison both heals and destroys. He is *true* not only because he has spoken the truth to Romeo
in describing the poison's potency, but because he has been true to his
calling in finding the salve for Romeo's ills. His drugs are not only 70
speedy, but also *quick* in the sense of "life-giving." Romeo and Juliet
"cease to die, by dying."

It is the prerogative of poetry to give effect and value to incompatible meanings. In *Romeo and Juliet,* several poetic means contribute to
this end: the paradox, the recurrent image, the juxtaposition of old and 75
young in such a way that we are both absorbed by and aloof from the
lovers' feelings, and the sparkling wordplay. By such means Shakespeare ensures that our final emotion is neither the satisfaction we
should feel in the lovers' death if the play were a simple expression of
the *Liebestod* theme, nor the dismay of seeing two lives thwarted and 80
destroyed by vicious fates, but a tragic equilibrium which includes and
transcends both these feelings.

1. What generalizations does the writer give to guide us among the many
   specific examples he cites?
2. Check the etymology, denotation, and connotation of *notorious, keening,
   sustains, imagery, quibbles, confound, equivocations, feigning, inauspicious, yoke, paradox, apothecary, potency, salve, prerogative, juxtaposition,
   Liebestod, equilibrium, transcend.*

16-D   Juliet's Nurse

Susan Ross (student)

This essay was written for an open-book essay test. The assignment was to show how one
of the minor characters in the play helps us to understand one or more of the major
characters. Countless critics have written on Shakespeare's use of minor characters, and
students are unlikely to find anything fresh to say. This student, by concentrating firmly
on the nurse, makes a vigorous statement that avoids clichés and sweeping generalizations and that shows a close reading of the play.

The most important minor character in *Romeo and Juliet* is the
nurse. Her enthusiasm for sex and her lack of inhibitions are shown in
her constant joking references to sexual intercourse. She makes it easy
for us to understand Juliet's capacity for love and making love even
though she is so young—only fourteen. In one sense, Juliet has led a 5

sheltered life, but because she has been brought up by the nurse she is not an ignorant little girl who knows nothing of the facts of life. When she falls in love with Romeo she acts like a passionate woman, not a teenager with a crush.

The nurse also shows us how young Juliet is in many ways in most 10 of the play. She gives Juliet advice on all sorts of things, and Juliet turns to her constantly. She even trusts the nurse to keep the secret of her marriage to Romeo.

All of this makes us realize how much Juliet grows up in the few days covered by the action of the play. In her last scene with the nurse 15 Juliet is desperate because her father is insisting that she marry Paris or be thrown out of the house. Juliet again turns to the nurse for advice. The nurse knows all about Juliet's secret marriage to Romeo and up to this point has been full of praise for Romeo's good looks and charm, but now she tells Juliet to go ahead and marry Paris because Paris is rich 20 and handsome, Romeo is in exile, and a bird in the hand is worth two in the bush. The fact that this would be bigamy doesn't bother the nurse at all. Horrified by this treacherous immorality and insensitivity, Juliet calls the nurse "Ancient damnation! O most wicked fiend!" and swears never to trust her again. From there on, Juliet realizes that she must 25 solve her problems alone.

By using contrasting characters Shakespeare helps us to understand Romeo and Juliet and the picture of a beautiful young love. An essential contrast is the nurse. Her crude earthiness and materialism make her a perfect foil for Juliet's passionate idealism.   30

16-E   For Love or Money

John Porter (student)

This essay was written as homework on the assigned question: How important is money in *Romeo and Juliet?* Note how the writer examines carefully all the relevant lines to find their significance to the larger elements of the play and uses quotations and specific references to support his interpretations. In the last paragraph he shows how the quotation illustrates both his particular point about money and also the main theme of the play, the doom of the young lovers.

When most people think of *Romeo and Juliet* they think of the beauty of the balcony scene or the tragedy of the lovers' deaths in the tomb, but in the background there is a busy city where money talks. We notice this particularly with Juliet's father, Capulet.

In the first act one of his servants describes him as "the great rich 5 Capulet," and Juliet's nurse tells Romeo that the man who marries Juliet "shall have the chinks," meaning that he will get a wife with a big dowry. In the third act Capulet tells Juliet that she must marry Paris. When she refuses, he is furious and threatens her. He tells her to "beg, starve, die in the streets" if she won't obey him and says he will cut her off without a penny: "What is mine shall never do thee good." In the next act Juliet 10 takes the potion and goes into a coma. Capulet thinks she is dead and is overcome with grief, but even in his grief he thinks about his money:

> Death is my heir;
> My daughter he hath wedded. I will die
> And leave him all. Life, living, all is Death's.   15

At the end of the play he is still thinking of money. He meets Romeo's father when the dead bodies of Romeo and Juliet are discovered in the tomb and asks to shake hands with him, saying

> This is my daughter's jointure, for no more
> Can I demand.   20

When Romeo's father answers that he will have a pure gold statue of Juliet made in her honor, Capulet meets the bid and says that he will have a statue that is just "as rich" made of Romeo. In Capulet, Shakespeare shows us a very realistic picture of a rich businessman who is 25 used to bossing people around. All these references to money, particularly to Juliet's dowry and inheritance, help us to understand the pressures on Juliet to obey her father and make us appreciate all the more her courage in defying him.

There are other examples of the importance of money to some of 30 the characters. For instance, the nurse is pleased to take a tip from Romeo when she gives him a message from Juliet, and at the beginning of the last act Romeo gets some illegal poison by giving forty ducats to an apothecary who says he is too poor to refuse the bribe.

Throughout the play, Shakespeare combines realism and idealism, 35 and all these mentions of money make an ironic contrast to the attitudes of the lovers. It is very appropriate that when Romeo first sees Juliet he says that she

> hangs upon the cheek of night
> Like a rich jewel in an Ethiop's ear—   40
> Beauty too rich for use, for earth too dear!

The lovers' feelings are far above the world of money and business, and that is why they are such perfect symbols of young love.

16-F   The Holes in Black Holes

Martin Gardner

These paragraphs, from a review published in 1977 of seven recent books on astrophysics, exemplify sound critical principles and methods applied to new books. A reviewer of new books has a special duty to evaluate their merits as well as to describe their general nature.

Nigel Calder's big, handsome volume [*The Key to the Universe: A Report on the New Physics*] devotes only two chapters to black holes, but they are excellent nontechnical summaries, and the other chapters are a splendid introduction to the latest theories of matter. Calder is one

of the most reliable of British science writers. His book, based on a 5
popular BBC television show which he wrote and presented last January, is abundantly illustrated with diagrams and photographs, including
pictures of famous physicists whose faces the public seldom sees.

Calder is unusually skillful in explaining quark theory and why it
is rapidly outrunning its nearest rival, the "bootstrap" theory. The boot- 10
strap hypothesis is the "democratic" view that none of the particles that
make up matter is more fundamental than any other. Each is simply an
interaction of a set of other particles. The entire family thus supports
itself in midair like a man tugging on his bootstraps, or a transcendental
meditator in the lotus position, suspended a few feet above the floor. 15

Quark theory is the aristocratic view that particles are combinations of more elementary units which Murray Gell-Mann named quarks
after the line in *Finnegans Wake,* "Three quarks for Muster Mark!" At
first only three kinds of quarks were believed necessary; up, down, and
strange, together with their antiparticles. The three kinds are called 20
"flavors." There are now reasons for thinking there is a fourth flavor,
"charm." Each flavor comes in three "colors." In the U.S. the colors
naturally are red, white and blue. (Calder's plates use red, blue, and
green, with turquoise, mauve, and yellow for the anticolors.) This makes
twelve quarks in all, with their twelve antiquarks. 25

Color and charm are, of course, whimsical terms unrelated to their
usual meaning, although the mixing of quark colors does obligingly
correspond (as Calder shows) to the mixing of actual colors. Some theorists think there are still other quark properties such as truth, beauty,
and goodness. Abdus Salam, the noted Pakistani physicist, is now pro- 30
moting a "quark liberation movement" that regards quarks as made of
"prequarks" or "preons." In Peking a group of young physicists have a
similar view involving "stratons" that form an infinite nest like a set of
Chinese boxes.

The essences of these debates are skillfully outlined in Calder's 35
book. He even leads you to the brink of the new, exciting "gauge
theories" that may someday unify the strong, weak, and electromagnetic forces—perhaps even gravity—in one fundamental theory.

. . .

Our two remaining books, entirely about black holes and related 40
matters, plunge into unrestrained fantasy. Adrian Berry, science writer
of a London newspaper, makes only a feeble attempt to separate fact
from reasonable conjecture, or reasonable conjecture from eccentric
conjecture. His book [*The Iron Sun: Crossing the Universe Through
Black Holes*] is best read as you would an Asimov science-fiction novel. 45
Indeed, some of Asimov's novels anticipate much of what Berry has to
say.

Berry is concerned mostly with the conjecture that every black
hole is joined by a wormhole to a white hole in some other part of the
cosmos, or to a white hole in a completely different cosmos. Perhaps the 50
"other" world is made of antimatter, like the Antiterra of Nabokov's

novel *Ada.* Matter pours into our black holes to emerge as antimatter in the other world's white holes, while its antimatter pours into its black holes to emerge from our white holes.

Some recent calculations have suggested that a spaceship just 55 might be able to rocket into a black hole and avoid hitting the dreadful singularity. Berry imagines a future in which spaceships use black and white holes as entrances and exits for instantaneous travel across vast distances. When this becomes possible, he writes, mankind will be able to roam and colonize the entire universe. Science fiction heroes have 60 been doing this for decades, but Berry dresses it up in the latest jargon, and his book is fun to read if you don't take it seriously.

[The review continues with a discussion of the "unrestrained fantasy" of the final book.]

16-G   David Bowie Looks Back in Horror

Tom Carson

This review from the *Village Voice* (October 1980) of Bowie's 1980 album is almost complete. Notice how the writer tries to describe music—a nonverbal medium—through words.

If any one figure summed up the '70s—as music, *Zeitgeist*, pose, whatever—it was David Bowie. From the start he parodied every rock and roll ideal of the relation between performer and community, performance and feeling. . . . His abandonment, in the late '70s, of the role of new-age spokesman, and subsequent retreat into the avant-garde, 5 had the earmarks of his usual canny timing; but it was also, I think, a case of utopianism gone sour.

RCA, can't blame them for trying, are doing their best to treat *Scary Monsters* as Bowie's return to the commercial fold, and the album does address itself to the world outside with a concreteness the *Low* 10 trilogy determinedly shied away from. . . . The images Bowie advanced then as gambits, analogues, imaginative strategies, have been turned into lifestyles—it's one thing to feel disengaged and dehumanized, and another to love it—and that seems to haunt him: on *Scary Monsters,* he looks back in horror. Only an idiot could dance to this nightmare.   15

The album doesn't have the arctic grace of *Low* and *"Heroes,"* or *Lodger's* airborne sweep and watercolor washes of sound—instead, it's the musical equivalent of brutalist in architecture: dissonant, abrasive, deliberately unpretty, all the raw materials left sticking bluntly out. On the opening cut, "It's No Game," the music comes swaying and shud- 20 dering into a leaden caricature of a funk beat; Bowie's vocal is one wrenching, off-key howl, intercut with bursts of Japanese that sound like an interrogation scene from a war movie. At the end, the song falls apart, chunk by chunk, until all that's left are the maddening pushbut-

ton tones of a Frippertronics tape loop, before Bowie's shouts of "Shut 25
up!" abruptly abort the track. (Fripp's presence, and other evidence—
lockstep bass-and-drum dynamics that recall similar motifs on *"Heroes,"*
the fact that some of the topical references are slightly dated—suggest
that some of this material was cut before *Lodger.*)

Scary Monsters takes the dread that's been in all Bowie's work and 30
makes it, for the first time, the only theme. The characters that drift
through these songs are numb inside, bewildered and lost everywhere
else—blankly estranged from cause and effect. . . . and most of them
don't know it or are too far gone to care. On the title cut, the drums
come in at a panicky gallop, the guitar oscillates like a police siren 35
outside the window, and the telegraphic cut-up lyrics sound like they
could be about half the girls at Max's Kansas City—"She had a horror
of rooms she was tired you can't hide beat / When I looked in her eyes
they were blue but nobody home."

Bowie has created a cold, dense, jagged, sound of half-heard tex- 40
tures and freeze-frame discontinuity—as visceral and dankly frightening as anything since *Second Edition.* Fripp's guitar evokes a formal-
ized hysteria, while the synthesizer struggles to hold the tunes on
course; for all their rhythmic top-heaviness, these songs have no real
anchor, and Bowie's use of dissociated repetition—recycling one instru- 45
mental part while completely altering its context—mirrors the shell-
shocked disorientation at the album's center. And there are historical
references that throw the songs into sudden relief, like the disjointed
Bo Diddley riff that lurches "Up the Hill Backwards" into gear, or the
startling juxtaposition at the end of "Teenage Wildlife," when Bowie's 50
voice goes soaring off into a letter-perfect Four Seasons falsetto.

This record is just as self-referential as the trilogy, but now the
references are to Bowie-the-star. . . . most spectacularly on "Ashes to
Ashes," an answer to "Space Oddity." With its disembodied echoing
keyboard notes dropping like a drunken rain, it's a condemnation of the 55
anywhere-out-of-this-world escapism Bowie once made so attractive.
The shifting sensations of strung-out decay—abasement, pride, the attempts to impose the illusion of order on quicksand—are brilliantly
detailed and there's an epic finality in the song's last, deathly verdict
on the age: "Ashes to ashes, funk to funky / We know Major Tom's a 60
junky. . . ." The sleep of reason does bring forth monsters. . . .

Significantly, the LP's one hint of redemption is in someone else's
words, in Bowie's cover of Tom Verlaine's "Kingdom Come." Even
here, the hope is muted, choked back. The original gets its force from
a dynamic rhythm and the amazing fluidity of Verlaine's guitar; Bowie 65
reduces Verlaine's kinetic swirls to a static synthesizer riff, rigidifies the
beat, and staves off the title line until the coda. This way, salvation
seems even more distant, and it's no conclusion. After "Because You're
Young," a recap of "It's No Game"—not harrowing this time, just exhausted—fades the album to an unresolved end. 70

Scary Monsters has its failings: occasional cleverness, a few lapses into Bowie's old hypercharged imagist kitsch. But its larger problem, I'd guess, is that he's been so distanced and knowing in the past that people may not trust his claims on horror now. I think I do, but then I always suspected him of being more of a romantic—which is to say, a moralist 75 —than he ever let on. Is it really any wonder that when he finally lets his romanticism out of the bag, it comes out as a shriek of outrage?

1. Where and how does the writer use comparison and contrast, background information, specific examples, and generalizations to present his opinions?
2. To describe the album, where does the writer use concrete, specific words? figurative language? specialized terminology?
3. Check the etymology, denotation, and connotation of *Zeitgeist, canny, utopianism, gambits, analogues, watercolor washes, dissonant, abrasive, tape loop, lockstep, estranged, oscillates, freeze-frame, visceral, dankly, riff, falsetto, referential, disembodied, abasement, quicksand, kinetic, staves off, coda, imagist, kitsch, romanticism.*

16-H   The Prestige of PRAL

Simon Hoggart

This essay, here complete, appeared first in *New Society* in 1983. Notice the writer's use of examples, real and hypothetical, to support his claims. Do the humorous tone and satiric touches make his criticisms less sharp?

I suppose it's because all international airlines are much the same that their advertising tends to have an air of desperation. One of my past favourites depicted an earnest travel agent advising an anxious-looking client. "Better fly GULF AIR," he was saying, "they know the way!" 5

Knowing the way is something you rather take for granted when you get on a plane. The pilot isn't likely to come over the loudspeaker saying: "Good morning, ladies and gentlemen, our flight to Bahrain will take just six hours, if and when the so-called navigator sitting next to me can get his map the right way up." Nor do you expect to see the pilot 10 hanging out of the cockpit like the early aviators following the N1 [highway] down to Paris.

The same faintly demented air clung to another "advert" which stuck vividly in my mind during the early sixties. It showed a young woman being comforted by her mother, who was saying: "Don't worry 15 darling, I used to think there must be someone in Brussels, till I learned about SABENA service across the Atlantic." It seemed to me that a woman sufficiently cretinous to believe anyone would fly hundreds of miles in the wrong direction in order to travel with another airline deserved to have an unfaithful husband. 20

Even today, when every newspaper and magazine is stuffed with airline ads, there is still the same sense of desperation as each tries to prove itself unique. The styles are painfully familiar. "Your holiday in Bulgaria begins the moment you step aboard one of our prop-jets . . ." "Two tickets to Addis Ababa, please. And make sure they're 25 with FLUGLINE!"

The heaviest investment is in something which, for want of a snap-pier acronym, I have called PRAL. This stands for Pointless, Re-Assur-ing Luxury. *PRAL* has now extended to every corner of the travel trade, though it is most rampant in the hotel and airline business. Like 30 real luxury, it isn't essential. Unlike real luxury, PRAL isn't even desir-able. It exists for the sole purpose of comforting and reassuring its recipient by telling him how important he is.

For example, on a long air journey it would be genuinely luxurious to have a sleeper seat, so that you could stretch out to sleep as if at home 35 in bed. By contrast, many airlines make an elaborate point of serving drinks to business class passengers in real glassware. This is of course PRAL since it couldn't possibly make any real difference to anyone whether they drank out of glass or plastic; certainly not enough to justify the extra fare. 40

Business class is a particularly interesting example of PRAL. It is usually given some other sobriquet, such as "Executive Class" or "Silver Service," the name itself also a meaningless offer of status. Some busi-ness classes are just a rip-off. For example, on the London to Dublin route it costs about £70 more than an ordinary economy return [round 45 trip]. The seat is identical to the ones in the back of the plane, there is no more leg room, no in-flight entertainment, and the cabin is some-times more crowded than the back.

You'll probably get a plastic snack, and of course drinks are "free," though you would need to gulp down a large gin-and-tonic every two 50 minutes from take-off to landing in order to match the increased cost.

On longer routes the airlines have to provide something which at least looks like a difference. And how they exploit it. The ads all have a shrill sameness:

"Prang! That's the traditional Adelphian greeting which wel- 55 comes you to three centuries of our world-famed hospitality. And what an honoured guest you'll be when you step into the quiet luxury of the Golden Buzzard cabin on board one of AIR ADELPHIA'S fleet of modern Boeings! First you'll notice the elegant calm of designer-styled interior. Air Adelphia's own team of ergonomic engineers 60 ripped out the old seating and replaced it with our exclusive 'Comfort Contour' fauteuil. You'll purr with pleasure when you settle into its generous 2.7 cm extra width—and you're never more than two seats away from window or aisle. See what else you'll enjoy flying Golden Buzzard class: 65

—Gourmet meals served on real china, and featuring a choice of entrée from recipes prepared under the personal supervision of Maxim de Paris.

—Cheers! Cocktails are complimentary when you fly the Golden Buzzard! 70

—'Luxu-pad' earphones for your choice of listening on Air Adelphia's famed 'Music Hall in the Sky,' featuring Adelphian folk music under the direction of internationally celebrated Adelphian conductor, Elvig Spath.

—Slipperettes to cosset your feet." 75

In other words, nothing you could possibly want or couldn't provide for yourself at a tiny fraction of the cost. What's being offered is pure PRAL, phoney prestige, valueless tokens of esteem.

Oddly enough, all this nonsense co-exists with the growth in cheaper, no-frills air travel. At the very time the People Express is 80 offering half-price trips across the Atlantic, other airlines are offering, at enormous cost, nylon slipperettes and vinyl-padded earphones.

The habit is spreading fast to hotels. Many American hotels now offer what are generally called Executive Apartments. (They can't call them "suites" because they've only got one room; on the other hand, 85 a mere "room" sounds far too plain.) These lodgements can cost $50 or $60 a night more than ordinary rooms in the same hotel. Naturally the management have to provide something which makes the place at least look different, so what they do is fill it up with PRAL.

There will be a toilet bag packed with unwanted rubbish in the 90 bathroom, an absurd little sewing kit which wouldn't darn a torn handkerchief, still less the ripped seam in one's only suit, and a bowl of fresh fruit. (Who on earth is going to sit down and scoff [gobble] an entire pineapple?)

The only perk [perquisite] worth having is the shared Executive 95 Lounge, where tired businessmen may drink themselves silly between 10:30 AM and midnight. But again, you would need to guzzle an awful lot of Remy Martin to match the extra cost of your room.

Many items of PRAL are positively annoying. For instance, there's no point in being lent a Cosilux ankle-length white bathrobe with dis- 100 tinctive monogram if you've already brought your Marks and Spencer dressing gown from home. In my experience the kind of man who uses after-shave will have already packed it, rather than trust that the hotel will furnish a tiny phial of some vile chemical marked with the name of an elderly French couturier. 105

So I wasn't terribly pleased to see PRAL, like industrial smog, floating across to Britain. I was in northern Scotland the other day, staying in a large and unpleasant "motor lodge," a term which only indicates that the hotel has its own car park. Plastered around the reception area were signs inviting guests to try the hotel's new "Gold 110

Star" executive rooms. I imagine the scheme applies to all the establishments in the same chain.

Out of curiosity I sought out another notice which explained what you got in a Gold Star room. There was "use of trouser press," one of those devices which employs heat to weld a crease in your pants almost 115 exactly parallel to the one already in them, "sachet of drinking chocolate mix," "foam bath capsule," "free shower cap," "fresh apple and orange" and "after-dinner mint on your pillow at bedtime." What sad mind could devise such offers, and what even sadder person could possibly need the comfort and reassurance which they offer?   120

1. Examine recent advertisements for airlines and hotels. Do they provide examples of "PRAL"? If they do, analyze them in detail to determine how the advertisers are trying to influence readers. If they do not contain examples of "PRAL," on what basis are they trying to appeal to readers?
2. To what extent would Bolinger (4-E) be likely to agree with Hoggart?
3. Check the etymology, denotation, and connotation of *demented, cretinous, acronym, rampant, sobriquet, ergonomic, cosset, phial.*

16-I   How to Write like a Social Scientist

Samuel T. Williamson

These paragraphs form half of an essay from the *Saturday Review* (1947). To satirize long-winded writing, the author reverses his real meaning.

There once was a time when everyday folk spoke one language, and learned men wrote another. It was called the Dark Ages. The world is in such a state that we may return to the Dark Ages if we do not acquire wisdom. If social scientists have answers to our problems yet feel under no obligation to make themselves understood, then we lay- 5 men must learn their language. This may take some practice, but practice should become perfect by following six simple rules of the guild of social science writers. Examples which I give are sound and well tested; they come from manuscripts I edited.

Rule 1. Never use a short word when you can think of a long one. 10 Never say "now," but "currently." It is not "soon" but "presently." You did not have "enough" but a "sufficiency." Never do you come to the "end" but to the "termination." This rule is basic.

Rule 2. Never use one word when you can use two or more. Eschew "probably." Write, "it is probable," and raise this to "it is not improba- 15 ble." Then you'll be able to parlay "probably" into "available evidence would tend to indicate that it is not unreasonable to suppose."

Rule 3. Put one-syllable thoughts into polysyllabic terms. Instead of observing that a work force might be bigger and better, write, "In addition to quantitative enlargement, it is not improbable that there is 20

need also for qualitative improvement in the personnel of the service."
If you have discovered that musicians out of practice can't hold jobs,
report that "the fact of rapid deterioration of musical skill when not in
use soon converts the unemployed into the unemployable." Resist the
impulse to say that much men's clothing is machine made. Put it thus: 25
"Nearly all operations in the industry lend themselves to performance
by machine, and all grades of men's clothing sold in significant quantity
involve a very substantial amount of machine work."

Rule 4. Put the obvious in terms of the unintelligible. When you
write that "the product of the activity of janitors is expended in the 30
identical locality in which that activity takes place," your lay reader is
in for a time of it. After an hour's puzzlement, he may conclude that
janitors' sweepings are thrown on the town dump. See what you can do
with this: "Each article sent to the cleaner is handled separately." You
become a member of the guild in good standing if you put it like this: 35
"Within the cleaning plant proper the business of the industry involves
several well-defined processes, which, from the economic point of view,
may be characterized simply by saying that most of them require separate handling of each individual garment or piece of material to be
cleaned."
40

Rule 5. Announce what you are going to say before you say it. This
pitcher's wind-up technique before hurling towards—not at—home
plate has two varieties. First is the quick windup: "In the following
section the policies of the administration will be considered." Then you
become strong enough for the contortionist wind-up: "Perhaps more 45
important, therefore, than the question of what standards are in a
particular case, there are the questions of the extent of observance of
these standards and the methods of their enforcement." Also you can
play with reversing Rule 5 and *say what you have said after you have
said it.*
50

Rule 6. Defend your style as "scientific." Look down on—not up
to—clear simple English. Sneer at it as "popular." Scorn it as "journalistic." Explain your failure to put more mental sweat into your writing
on the ground that "the social scientists who want to be scientific believe that we can have scientific description of human behavior and 55
trustworthy predictions in the scientific sense only as we build adequate
taxonomic systems for observable phenomena and symbolic systems for
the manipulation of ideal and abstract entities."

1. Briefly rewrite the six rules under the heading "How *Not* to Write like a
   Social Scientist." What is lost in the probable effect on the reader?
2. Williamson's main points are much the same as Zinsser's in "Clutter" (Unit
   6-D). Which presentation is more likely to influence a reader?
3. Check the etymology, denotation, and connotation of *eschew, taxonomic,
   phenomena, entities.* When and what were the Dark Ages in European
   history?

16-J Virtuous Sin

The New York Times

This short satire, here complete, makes its point by a transfer of the real object of the criticism—the use of gambling and pornography—to other areas.

By sponsoring weekly bingo games, churches and synagogues across the land have long enjoyed the tribute that vice can be made to pay to virtue. Their example has led to "Las Vegas Nights," on which such pastimes as blackjack, roulette and even craps are turned to worthy purposes. And now we learn from *Variety* of senior citizens in Bemidji, Minn., who arranged for showings of an X-rated film, "Erotic Adventures of Zorro," to raise money for a new senior citizens center. It brought $825. Clearly, the vistas of vice are vast: pot parties for the benefit of the American Cancer Society perhaps; after-hours clubs run by Alcoholics Anonymous; massage parlors to finance Planned Parenthood. Since the goods would no doubt be exemplary, the prices fair and the advertising honest, the cause of moral uplift would be well served.

1. How appropriate are the other areas to which the satire is transferred?
2. Check the full dictionary entry for *exemplary.*

Assignments

In each of these assignments, try to persuade your readers to accept your point of view. Remember to support your criticism with specific details about your subject and to make use of the aids to exposition, organizing, and reasoning discussed in earlier units.

1. Write a critical review of a movie, TV drama, book, or play that you saw or read recently.
2. Which one of the essays you have read so far in this book has interested you most? Write a critical analysis of its good points—and of its bad points, if you find any—and explain why you think other readers might like it.
3. Which TV commercials do you think are the best? the worst? Write a critical analysis, contrasting one or two commercials that you like with one or two you dislike.
4. Who is your favorite singer, composer, music group? Write a critical analysis of the qualities you admire. Include discussion of any weaknesses.
5. What recent record album do you think shows decided talent or lack of talent? Write a critical analysis explaining exactly what you think is right or wrong in it.
6. Write a critical analysis of the performance of the best and poorest players on the athletic team you watch most often.
7. Rewrite one of your essays as a satire.

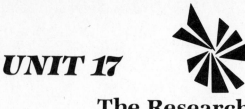

UNIT 17

The Research Paper

The label "research paper" is applied to a considerable range of writing and is frequently used interchangeably with "report," but the further you go in scholarly work the more you will see the difference between a report and a true research paper. Both are based on information the writers have gathered from various sources, and for both this process of gathering information from assorted facts and opinions is "research." There the similarity ends.

Report writers do not try to find facts unknown before or to make new interpretations of known facts. Although they may include many of their own opinions, they make no claim that these opinions have never been expressed before. Many magazine and newspaper writers perform this kind of research. The information they present may be new to their readers, but it is already available in books or other publications and was not first discovered by the writers. Writing such a paper can be a very rewarding activity for you: you learn something new to you, and your paper will inform others. However, you are not adding anything new to the existing body of facts and opinions.

The writer of the true research paper, on the other hand, has as a primary purpose casting a wholly new light on a subject, either by finding new facts and forming new opinions or by reevaluating known facts and opinions, or by using both methods. The writer of a true research paper not only gives a clear, orderly report on information gathered from various sources but also uses that information to say something original. As you go on in scholarly work, you will be increasingly expected to perform research of this kind.

As an undergraduate you are unlikely to have a chance to discover something that is both new and important, such as a cure for cancer or evidence proving absolutely that Egyptians visited Mexico four thousand years ago. But this does not mean that you cannot do original research that will be interesting and valuable. Two general approaches are open to you:

320

a. You can gather information on a relatively small subject that no one has examined before or that no one has examined thoroughly. For example, you can collect all the available facts on a local political situation or environmental problem, or use newspaper files to put together the story of an unsolved crime and work out your own suggestions for the solution, or interview an elderly person and, with the help of background reading in appropriate historical material, write a chapter in a projected biography of that person. There are thousands of such subjects, full of facts that have not yet been sorted out and interpreted.

b. You can examine a well-known subject in a new light. For example, new theories continue to appear on the assassination of President Kennedy, and a good researcher will examine each new theory, comparing and contrasting it with earlier ones and also reexamining the earlier ones in the light of the new one, so that with each new theory a reevaluation must be made of all previous theories, if only to conclude, with supporting evidence, that the new one does not change anything.

Whichever general approach you choose, you may gather information from printed sources of all kinds, from laboratory experiments, from opinion surveys, or from a combination of all of these. The more information you have, the more authoritative you will be on your subject and the better able to say something significant.

Writing a research paper is hard and exacting work, and most of that work takes place before the actual writing of the paper. You will spend many hours searching for, selecting, and using source materials. You will go down blind alleys and will have to try to reconcile conflicting opinions or contradictory evidence. The process is often like detective work, and sometimes an answer you are hunting down will escape you, but the hunt itself can be exciting, and each new piece of evidence that you discover will make you feel triumphant.

To write a research paper you must complete five major actions: (1) choose a subject; (2) build a bibliography; (3) gather information from reading and whatever other sources are appropriate, such as opinion surveys, interviews, and laboratory experiments; (4) sort out and organize the information until you have defined your specific topic and determined your main point; (5) write and document the paper.

* * *   * * *   * * *

Begin narrowing your subject to a specific, manageable topic and then forming an opinion—or main point—on that topic. This will be a continuing process. The more you learn about your subject in general and your topic in particular, the more precisely you will define what you wish to cover and what main point you want your readers to see in it.

1. Your subject should be one that interests you. A research paper, compared to the other assignments in this book, is a long, drawn-out affair, and you will have to live with your subject for several weeks. What are you interested in? What would you like to know more about? If you are a business major, you might examine the economic forecasts published in newspapers and business journals in a particular month in the recent past and then determine their accuracy by finding out about the present state of the economy. If you are a science major, you might examine the published opinions on the value of a new drug or on a new cancer threat, find out its history and that of others similar to it, ask physicians for their opinions, and arrive at your own conclusions. If you are a sports fan, you might analyze your favorite team's performance in the last year, the opinions of sports writers and of the coach and players themselves. If you are interested in history, you have an irreplaceable resource in any elderly person you know, and you can write a biographical study by setting the facts on an interesting part of his or her life in the appropriate historical context. If you are curious about human behavior you can devise a questionnaire on a controversial topic, make an opinion survey of the students on your campus, and use the results along with your reading on the subject as the basis for an analysis of the psychological and social significance of the students' answers. And so on—the opportunities are as wide as your interests.

Whatever subject you choose, be sure to *limit* it so that you can cover it thoroughly. The broader the subject is, the less likely you will be to find anything new to say. If you are writing a biography of one of your grandparents, concentrate on a few years or even on a few months or weeks and give those in full detail, with at most only a summary of the rest of his or her life as a frame for the most interesting part of it.

2. The reference collections in your college and local libraries will almost certainly be essential to your research. They will be your chief means of finding material on any subject. Familiarize yourself with what they contain. Walk beside the shelves, reading titles and leafing through any work that seems promising. Knowing how to take full advantage of a reference collection is as necessary for a researcher as knowing how to use the telephone is for most Americans.

Begin with a bird's-eye view of what is known on your subject by looking it up in several sources of general information. Encyclopedias are most likely to be helpful. These include not only the *Britannica, Americana,* and *New International,* but others specializing in a single field, such as religion, education, or sociology; collections of brief biographies, such as the international *Who's Who,* the *Dictionary of National Biography* for the British, and *Who's Who in America* for Americans; and collections of facts and statistics, such as the *World Almanac* and other yearbooks. *Winchell's Guide to Reference Books,* kept up to date by occasional supplements, classifies by type and subject matter all kinds of reference works besides the famous ones just mentioned.

Make notes on ruled index cards (3″ × 5″ or 4″ × 6″) as you look through the reference books, recording the names and facts they emphasize. Write only one note on each card so that you will be able to arrange and rearrange them later as you explore their relationships. Record with each the title and page number of the work from which you took it. These notes will help you to keep the main outlines of your subject straight so that you will see the significance and relationships of the parts. If an encyclopedia article mentions important books on your subject, make notes of these by author and title on separate cards so that you can check later on their availability in your library.

3. The library catalog and the appropriate periodical indexes will be the two big sources of information on the material printed on your subject.

The **catalog,** whether it is in card or book form or computerized, lists every book in the library alphabetically by both author and title and usually also under several headings for the subjects with which the book deals. For example, you will probably find *The Uses of Enchantment* by Bruno Bettelheim listed not only under *B* by the author's name and under *U* by its title, but also in several subject categories, such as "Fairy Tales—History and Criticism," "Psychoanalysis," "Folk-lore and Children," and "Child Psychology."

The **periodical indexes,** probably shelved in the reference room of the library, will help you find articles in periodicals—newspapers, magazines, and journals of all kinds.

The *Reader's Guide to Periodical Literature* is issued monthly in magazine form and at intervals cumulated into volumes covering several years. It indexes, under both author and subject headings, the contents of the better-known American (and a few British) periodicals on general subjects since 1900.

Poole's Index covers British and American periodicals from 1802 to 1906.

The International Index covers a selected list of American and European periodicals in the humanities, social sciences, and sciences, from 1916 to 1965. The *Social Science and Humanities Index* covers about 175 American and British periodicals from 1965 to 1974. Two separate publications continue the listing, the *Social Sciences Index* and the *Humanities Index.*

There are many specialized indexes for particular fields, such as agriculture, engineering, psychology, industrial art, literature, dentistry, medicine, and law. Some of these list books and bulletins as well as articles and periodicals.

The *New York Times Index,* published annually, covers all that newspaper's stories and articles. Since most major news is handled on the same or the following day by all the principal newspapers, this index can help you locate material in other papers as well.

Check the catalog to determine which periodicals related to your subject are in your library; ask a reference librarian what others are available at nearby libraries and how to arrange for photocopies of articles in periodicals held by libraries you cannot visit. (Probably, the reference librarians are the most valuable of all sources of information in any library. They are specially trained in information retrieval. Turn to them when you find yourself in a blind alley, but always first try to solve problems yourself—the more practice you have, the more efficient a researcher you will be.)

Important: In your preliminary survey of resources, do not try to make a thorough search or you will be overwhelmed by the quantity available. Instead, just make sure that there is plenty of material on your general subject and that it includes up-to-date items—check publication dates. Also, all the time you are looking over the catalog and the indexes, be alert for clues that will help you to narrow your subject to a manageable topic. The titles of books and articles will give you an overall impression of what others have said and may suggest a topic appropriate for your purposes. Keep your mind open for such possibilities and jot them down as they occur to you.

4. You are now ready to decide on a specific topic. First, make a quick review of the available material. Then, think over what you now know of your subject. Keep in mind the constraints of the length and deadline for the paper and of the importance of giving your readers something on your subject—facts, opinions, or both—that they will not find elsewhere. Choose a specific topic that will fit your needs and theirs, but remember that you may revise it more than once as you continue your research and think over it longer.

This topic will be the basis for your next step, building a bibliography.

*   *   *   *   *   *   *   *   *

Begin to build a working bibliography, a list of every printed item you find mentioned that seems worth at least a glance. Eventually, this will be the basis for your final bibliography, a list of all the printed materials you actually use, placed at the end of your paper.

With a supply of 3" × 5" index cards in hand, go back to the library catalog and the periodical indexes. For every work listed that looks at all promising, take down the information you need to find it in the library, using one card for each book or article. The general information that you have already gathered from reading the encyclopedias and surveying the library resources will help you to recognize what may prove useful, as may the titles of the works. If in doubt about the value of something, fill out a card on it anyway. It is better to have to discard items later than to miss a good one.

For each book, record the full name of the author (last name first, for convenience in alphabetizing), the title (underlined to indicate a book), and the library call number for your later convenience in locating the book in the stacks. You should also record the place of publication, the name of the publisher, the date of publication, and any special information that the library catalog gives as to an editor, translator, or edition other than the first. All this will be required for your final bibliography. A typical example of a completed card looks like this:

> GV
> 706
> .E37
>
> *Edwards, Harry*
> *The Sociology of Sport*
> *Homewood, Ill.: Dorsey*
> *Press, 1973*

The information needed for periodical articles is slightly different. For each, give the author, with last name first, as before (if the article is anonymous, leave blank the line where the author's name would regularly go and alphabetize the cards by the article title instead); the title (in quotation marks to indicate that it is only part of something); the title of the periodical (underlined); the volume and issue numbers (if it is not a weekly or monthly periodical) and full date of the copy that contains the article; and the inclusive page numbers within which it appears.

There are *two kinds of source material: primary and secondary.* If your topic is a particular company's chance for future success, then any information issued by the company and any statements made by its officials, either oral or written, are primary sources. Information and opinions of writers discussing the company in books and periodical articles are secondary. But if your topic is an evaluation of the accuracy of the forecasts about the company made by financial analysts, then their opinions become primary sources, and secondary sources for such a study would be other analysts' opinions of their opinions.

Base your opinions on primary sources whenever possible—information "straight from the horse's mouth." Use secondary sources to show the extent to which you agree or disagree with others who have written on the subject and to give general background information. If your topic is a biographical study of your grandfather and his struggles as a farmer in the Depression of the 1930s, your chief source of information will be what he and any of his contemporaries can tell you (primary) and economic reports published at that time (primary). For background material you should rely on facts and opinions about the period given in books and articles by respected authorities (secondary), especially the more recent ones, since those writers will have the benefit of greater perspective.

Examine all your sources with a sharply critical eye.

When you begin your project you may not know which writers are respected, well-known authorities, which are respectable though little known, and which are questionable. Your ability to judge will grow as your familiarity with the subject grows. But even at the start, watch out in your secondary sources for any signs of biased opinions, illogical deductions, unsupported claims, and sweeping generalizations. What sources do they use? What other writers on the subject do they refer to as authoritative? If you are in doubt about a book, see if it is mentioned in the *Book Review Digest* or reviews in appropriate scholarly journals and, of course, ask your instructor's advice.

Note: Remember that articles in newspapers and popular magazines are intended as introductions to a subject. They are very useful for up-to-the-minute information, but for a more thorough analysis you must go to specialized magazines, scholarly journals, and books. Always check the most recent publications as well as the famous and basic ones.

*   *   *   *   *   *   *   *   *

Begin serious reading and note-taking when you have listed on your index cards all the promising materials on your subject that are available in the library.

1. Skim through all the available material to select what you will look at carefully later. Remember that the preface of a book may often indicate whether it is likely to include anything for your purpose. The table of contents is even more useful; a glance at chapter headings may save you from going further or direct you quickly to the one section that may be all that will be useful. Learn to "skim"—to glance rapidly through material in search of the significant. By these means, eliminate items that now seem unsuitable. Then you can settle down to a thorough reading of what seems really worthwhile.

2. Take accurate notes, while reading, of any facts and opinions that you may later wish to quote or refer to in your paper. Good notes will not only form the basis of your paper but will also help you to organize it. As you form a general picture of your subject, decide on its main divisions and subdivisions and use these as headings for the note cards, always remembering that you can at any time make further subdivisions or change a note from one subdivision to another as your knowledge of the subject grows. For example, for a biographical study of your grandfather you may want to subdivide a preliminary heading "education" into "education—elementary school" and "education—high school" or into "education—formal" and "education—practical."

3. Write your reading notes on cards. (Convenient sizes are 4″ × 6″ and 5″ × 8″; be sure to stick to one size for convenience in handling and filing.) Limit each card to a single note on a single topic taken from a single source and give each a classifying heading. Then, instead of a hodgepodge, you will eventually have a mass of material that you can arrange easily under common headings and will be able to rearrange and discard items without disturbing the rest. The flexibility of such notes makes selecting and organizing the material relatively simple.

(**Note:** Make your work easier for yourself by writing on only one side of each card so that you can see the whole note at a glance. If a note is too long for one card, continue it on a second card, marking it at the top with the source and "cont.—p. 2" so that if it is ever separated from the first you will know instantly where it belongs.)

4. Record the exact source of the borrowed material on each note card. Your finished work must show not only the book or article from which the words or idea came but also the page number (and with newspaper articles, the column number as well). After each note you take, jot down the page number or numbers on which you found the information. In the upper right-hand corner identify the source by giving the author's last name or a short form of the title of the work or both, as briefly as possible but with enough information to avoid any chance of confusion with another author or work with a similar name.

5. Copy accurately any material you may wish to quote in your paper. Most of your notes will be summaries; they will give in your words the gist of the material you read. But in your paper you may often wish to support important points with the exact words of your source. Be sure to copy these precisely as they appear in the original, with all the grammar and punctuation intact and even with any errors in facts or writing that they may contain. Set each one off with a pair of double quotation marks so that later you will be able to see at a glance that they are quotations. You may eventually use only a few of these, but remember that although you can easily summarize a direct quotation when writing your paper, you cannot turn your summary back into a quotation unless you have the exact words before you.

6. Learn to combine reading and note-taking. Reading a long article without jotting down notes will certainly result in many rereadings, but taking notes at frequent intervals may result in many repetitions. How much to read before taking notes depends on the nature of the material and the strength of your memory. **Important:** Be prepared to add to your bibliography as you go along. You may discover some of your best material through references made in your reading and the bibliographies that most scholarly works include.

* * *   * * *   * * *

Begin composing your paper when you have gathered most of what you think will be your important material—by reading, interviewing, conducting a survey, performing an experiment, and doing whatever else is necessary for your project. For detailed advice on composing, review Unit 1, pages 4–14. Remember that at this point your insights and plans are still tentative. In any research project there is always the possibility of turning up some fact or having some new insight that will make you recast part of your work, perhaps all of it. Keep your mind open for new thoughts and for reseeing earlier thoughts.

1. Glance over all your material, jotting down any new ideas that occur to you and looking for other ways to divide and subdivide it that may show new relationships. Then, with your specific topic in mind, **draft a tentative statement of your main point and make a rough outline** for your own use. These steps will help you to determine how much more research is needed and in exactly what areas. If your instructor requires a formal outline of your paper, these steps will be the basis for it.

2. When you have finished whatever additional research you find necessary, **make your rough outline definite.** Imagine that your readers know something about your subject but that their opinions differ from yours, and compose a rough draft for a **tentative ending** of your paper —what you want those readers to have in mind when they finish reading. Glance rapidly over your outline and your ending, looking for ways to make them stronger and clearer. Next, with the same imagined readers in mind, compose a rough draft of your beginning—what your readers will need so that they can easily follow what you say in the main body of the paper.

3. You are now ready to **write a rough draft**—perhaps the first of several—of the whole paper. Remember that all the basic principles of clear, logical writing discussed in the earlier units apply to writing a research paper. Review the advice in Units 11 through 15 on the chief ways to develop and support the main point and to present evidence coherently and logically, and also review Unit 7 on how to quote, paraphrase, and summarize effectively.

4. Remember that **revision is a continuous process** throughout the composition of any paper, particularly longer ones. Each new fact and opinion gathered may make you resee and therefore revise your ideas. Each time you review your work you may see new relationships among the parts. Certainly, when your first rough draft is complete and you can see the paper as a whole, you will want to make changes to unify and strengthen it. You may even want to make drastic changes in the organization and content. Professional writers often find that their final draft bears little resemblance to their first draft.

5. In making the **final copy** and **proofreading** it, review the directions in Unit 1, pages 14–19, and also follow the directions in the next section of this unit on documenting the sources of your material.

* * *   * * *   * * *

You must document all your sources for your research paper. The chief support for your opinions will, of course, be the facts you have gathered and the opinions of others that you quote, paraphrase, or summarize. Whenever you use facts or opinions that can in any way be considered the property of someone else and whenever you quote the words written or spoken by someone else, you must give full credit to your sources by documenting them. Failure to do so is plagiarism—a form of theft and therefore a legally punishable crime. You do not need to give sources for well-known facts mentioned by many writers or for widely held opinions, but if you use another writer's words to present them you should acknowledge that writer as your source, no matter how familiar the facts or opinions may be. Conversely, if you present a little-known fact or opinion, even in wording that is entirely your own, you should give your sources. Notice how Jill Taylor, the student who wrote the sample research paper presented later in this unit, supports her opinions by drawing on other writers and how she documents her sources. Any reader who wishes to check on her accuracy or read more about the topic can quickly learn not only exactly which books and essays she consulted but also the precise numbers of the pages on which she found the material.

Two systems for documenting the printed sources of scholarly writing are widely used: that of the **Modern Language Association, or MLA,** and that of the **American Psychological Association, or APA.** The MLA system was devised primarily for use in scholarly writing on literature, history, and biography but has traditionally been used in works, regardless of subject matter, directed to the general reader. In its latest version (1982), the MLA system is very similar to the APA system, which is used, with minor variations, in scholarly writing in the social and laboratory sciences. Ask your instructor which system you should use.

Both systems require that you make an alphabetized list of all the sources you mention in your paper, whether in quotations, paraphrases, summaries, or direct references. This is called a **bibliography,** a **source list,** or a **reference list.** Many writers, to show the thoroughness of their research and to help their readers, also list other works they consulted even though they did not quote or in other ways refer directly to them. Writers using a large number of sources—roughly thirty or more—often divide them into groups according to whatever classifications are appropriate to the material.

The **following bibliography in the MLA style,** as revised in 1982, gives examples of the kinds of printed material you are most likely to use in research. Study closely the kinds of information given and the arrangement, punctuation, and use of abbreviations. Since the bibliography is alphabetized, the author's last name appears first in each entry, followed by a comma and whatever form of first name or initials the author uses. Unsigned works are alphabetized by title, always omitting *A, An,* and *The* from consideration. Use a period after each of the three main divisions of each entry—the author's name, the title of the work, and the publication data, which is composed of the place of publication, the name of the publisher, and the date of publication. Use a period also after any additional information, such as the edition or number of volumes, that comes between the title and the publication data. Use parentheses only around a year that is preceded by a volume number in an entry for a periodical. Underline the title of each book and periodical—this indicates that it should be printed in italics; set off the title of each shorter work with a pair of double quotation marks, and end the entry for it with inclusive page numbers to show all the pages it occupies in the larger work.

Use reverse paragraph indentation for each entry to make the alphabetized word stand out clearly. Begin the first word of each entry at the left margin; if the entry requires more than one line, begin all other lines about five spaces to the right of the left margin.

The first edition of a book by a single author (this requires only the most basic information—the author's name, the title of the book, and the publication data):

Ardrey, Robert. <u>African Genesis</u>. New York: Atheneum Press,
    1961.

Another book by the same writer (instead of repeating his or her name, type hyphens or draw a line of equivalent length; you may arrange works by the same author either chronologically by publication date, or alphabetically by title; whichever method you choose, use the same one throughout your bibliography):

----------. <u>The Territorial Imperative</u>. New York: Atheneum Press,
    1966.

A book by two or more authors (only the first author's name is in reverse order because the book is alphabetized by that, no matter how many other authors' names are listed):

Bosworth, Joseph, and T. Northcoate Toller. <u>An Anglo-Saxon
    Dictionary</u>. Oxford: Oxford Univ. Press, 1898.

A book composed of more than one volume:

Davison, Frank Dalby. <u>The White Thorntree</u>. 2 vols. Sydney: Ure
    Smith, 1970.

A book that has been reprinted (give the year of the first edition immediately after the title):

Durrell, Gerald. <u>My Family and Other Animals</u>. 1956; rpt. New
    York: Viking Press, 1963.

A later edition revised by the author (always try to use the latest edition of any book unless an earlier version is significant in some way to your research):

Empson, William. <u>Milton's God</u>. Rev. ed. London: Chatto and
    Windus, 1965.

A specially edited edition (the name of the country is included because the town is not well known):

Eliot, George. <u>Daniel Deronda</u>. Ed. Barbara Hardy. Harmonds-
    worth, England: Penguin, 1967.

A translation:

Gadamer, Hans-Georg. <u>Dialogue and Dialectic</u>. Trans. P. Christopher Smith. New Haven: Yale Univ. Press, 1980.

An essay, poem, or other short work, published in a book:

Miller, J. Hillis. "Optic and Semiotic in Middlemarch." In <u>The
Worlds of Victorian Fictio</u>n. Ed. Jerome Buckley. Cambridge: Harvard Univ. Press, 1975, 125-145.

An introduction or preface by an editor or another writer (the
inclusive page numbers of the introduction are in lower-case Roman
numerals because these were used in the original):

Murry, J. Middleton, ed. "Introduction." In <u>Journal of Katherine Mansfield</u>. New York: Alfred A. Knopf, 1936, vii–xvii.

An article in an encyclopedia (some encyclopedias give only the
author's initials at the end of each article, but an index elsewhere in the
set translates the initials into names; with well-known encyclopedias,
and also with dictionaries, you need not give the place of publication,
the name of the publisher, or the volume and page numbers since the
articles are arranged alphabetically, but you must give either the number of the edition or the date of publication because other editions may
not contain the same article):

Onati, Oscar. "Migrant Labour." <u>Encyclopedia Britannica</u>:
Macropedia, 15th ed.

An article in a monthly or weekly periodical in which the pages are
numbered separately for each issue (give the full date of the issue):

Powers, Thomas. "What Is It About?" <u>The Atlantic Monthly</u>, January 1984: 35-55.

An article in a periodical in which the pages are numbered con-
secutively through all the issues of each year (this periodical, like many
scholarly journals, is known by the initials of its title; the volume number follows the title):

Sudrann, Jean. "<u>Daniel Deronda</u> and the Landscape of Exile."
<u>ELH</u> 37 (1970): 433-55.

An article in a newspaper (give the edition, section number, date,
and page number; column numbers are not required but are a convenience for readers who wish to consult the article; "sec.," "p." and "col."
are necessary to distinguish among the numbers):

Treaster, Joseph B. "Artillery Battles Erupt in Lebanon as
Talks Proceed." <u>The New York Times</u>, 8 January 1984, late
edition, sec. 1, p. 1, col. 6, and p. 33, cols. 1-3.

An unsigned article of any kind:

"Watergate Sequel." <u>The New York Times</u>, 8 January 1984, late
edition, sec. 1, p. 33, cols. 1-3.

Use notes within the text of your paper to identify the source of
each quotation, paraphrase, summary, or direct reference to the opinions of someone else or to a little-known fact. Each note, set off in

parentheses, should direct your reader to the relevant entry in your bibliography and give the page number where the material can be found. The MLA recommends the style exemplified in these notes referring to works listed earlier in the bibliography.

A book—the note gives the author's surname, a short form of the title, and the page number:

(Ardrey, Genesis, 62)

A book with more than one volume:

(Dalby, Thorntree, 2:54)

An essay or other short work:

(Miller, "Optic and Semiotic," 127)

An unsigned work of any kind—give as much of the title as your readers will need to find the entry for the work in your bibliography:

("Watergate," 33)

If a work has three or more authors, you may shorten the note by giving the surname only of the first and then writing "et al.," an abbreviation of the Latin phrase meaning "and others." If two authors have the same surname, distinguish between them in your notes by giving their first initials as well.

If you have just mentioned an author and readers will easily see that a note refers to that author, you may omit his or her name in the note:

Ardrey describes his discovery of a murder (*Genesis,* 203).

Similarly, you may omit the title of a work that you have just mentioned:

In African Genesis, Ardrey describes his discovery of a murder (203).

Note: In the revised MLA system, use Arabic numerals, separated by periods, to refer to acts and scenes in plays, to the sections of a long poem, and the chapters and verses in the Bible. For example, a quotation of the opening of Mark Antony's speech at Caesar's funeral in *Julius Caesar* by Shakespeare should have this note to indicate the act, scene, and lines: (3.2.73–77). A reference to the closing sentence of the ninth book of Milton's *Paradise Lost,* a poem of over 10,000 lines divided into twelve "books," should have this note: (9.1187–89). A specific reference to the story of Samson and the lion in the Bible would have this note giving the name of the book, the number of the chapter, and the inclusive verse numbers: (Judges 14.5–9).

* * *   * * *   * * *

In the **APA system,** the final bibliography is called the reference list and includes only sources referred to in the paper, not those read for general background information. The information given on each source and the method of presentation are almost exactly the same as that recommended by the MLA, with these small differences:

1. Give only the initials of authors' first names.
2. Capitalize the first letter of the first word in titles of articles, books, and chapters of books (the first letters of all proper names, including those of periodicals, are, however, capitalized in conventional

fashion). Italicize (underline) not only book and periodical titles but also volume numbers of periodicals, but do not set off article titles in quotation marks.

3. For two or more works by the same author, **repeat the author's surname and initials for each and arrange them chronologically, starting with the earliest.** If an author published two or more works in one year, alphabetize them within that year by title and differentiate among them with a small letter in parentheses—(a), (b), and so on—at the end of each entry.

In the APA system each note documenting a printed source gives the author's surname, the year the work was published but not the title, and, if the reference is to a specific page, the page number. Place this information in parentheses in the text of your paper immediately after the words you wish to document. If the author's name or the date appears nearby in the same sentence, you need not repeat them in the note. Document material from an unsigned article with a short form of the title, followed by the date.

*   *   *   *   *   *   *   *   *

To document unprinted sources—lectures, concerts, television shows, theatrical performances, paintings, and so on—follow the same general methods with both the APA and MLA systems. Begin with the name of the lecturer, conductor, director, or whoever was most responsible for the content and style of the performance. Then give the title and author of the work and the place and date of the performance. In capitalizing letters in titles, each system follows its practices for referring to printed sources.

With unpublished written material of any kind, such as honors papers, M.A. theses, letters, and answers to surveys, identify the persons concerned, give the dates and whatever other information your readers will need if they wish to try to see the material.

Since all these sources are not printed, they do not belong in the final bibliography (MLA) or the reference list (APA). If you are using the MLA system, make a separate list of the information following the final bibliography and head it "Other Sources Consulted." Arrange the material in appropriate categories, alphabetizing the entries within each category. If you refer to such a source in the text of your paper, follow the full MLA procedure for a note, presenting the same information to identify the source at the appropriate spot in the text of your paper.

If you are using the APA system, make a separate list, following the text of your paper but preceding your reference list and headed "Reference Notes." Number and arrange the notes in sequence according to the order of the material they document; the result will be almost identical with MLA notes for similar material. In the text of the paper, immediately after the documented material, insert "(Note 1)," "(Note 2)," and so on. A sentence would look like this:

James Bridges' film, *The China Syndrome* (Note 1), dramatizes the risks of nuclear fuel.

For help in documenting any sources that create special problems, consult the *MLA Handbook* or the APA *Publications Manual.*

* * * * * * * * *

Information notes serve a different purpose and are not like notes documenting sources. Use an information note to tell your readers something that would not fit smoothly into the general style of your paper, such as a critical comment, an explanation, a definition, or an illustrative anecdote. You may treat each as a footnote, placing it at the bottom of the page on which the material it refers to is located, number-ing it, and placing a matching number in the text of your paper immedi-ately after the material to which it refers. You may, instead, treat each as an endnote, placing all such notes together at the end of your paper, just before your bibliography. In either case, number the notes consecu-tively and place matching numbers in the text of your paper after the material to which the notes refer.

If you have only a few information notes, not more than one on any page of your manuscript, and if you present them as footnotes, you need not number them. Instead, place an asterisk at the beginning of the note and another in the text of your paper immediately after the mate-rial to which the note refers. If such a note requires documentation of its own, give it in parentheses at the end of the note, applying which-ever system you use for your bibliography.

Example

The following essay was written as a research paper in an introduc-tory college course, but many other selections in this book show how the writers drew on research, their own and that of others, to support their opinions.

For the use of quotation, paraphrase, summary, and historical ref-erence, see particularly Bennett's "Benjamin Banneker" (2-H), Daven-port's " 'Trees' " (7-A), and Tysoe's "And If We Hanged the Wrong Man?" (11-D). For the use of statistics, see particularly Gould's "Left Holding the Bat" (12-F), Cohen's "The Language of Uncertainty" (13-B), and Ketchum's "The Farmer—an Endangered Species?" (15-E). For the logical investigation of raw material, see Hillary's "Epitaph to the Elusive Abominable Snowman" (13-J) and Ardrey's "Light from an Ape's Jaw" (13-K). For references to literary sources, see Mahood's "Puns and Other Wordplay in *Romeo and Juliet*" (16-C), Ross's "Juliet's Nurse" (16-D), and Porter's "For Love or Money" (16-E). For reporting on the research of others, see Johmann's "Sex and the Split Brain" (7-B),

Brody's "Mental Depression" (10-C), Gardner's "Are Television's Effects Due to Television?" (12-E), and Tysoe's two essays "Do You Inherit Your Personality?" (4-F) and "And If We Hanged the Wrong Man?" (11-D).

In the research paper that follows, notice how the student used the opinions of others to try to reach conclusions of her own. Although she confesses somewhat sadly at the end that she has not arrived at many firm answers, her research has helped her to define her questions on her topic more precisely so that eventually she may reach the answers she seeks.

Notice her punctuation and different ways of fitting material from other writers into her sentences and paragraphs:

1. quotations incorporated completely into her sentences—see those documented by notes in lines 44, 89, 105, 128, and 189;
2. paraphrases and summaries—see those documented by notes in lines 52–53, 67, 79, 117, 123, and 146;
3. omissions of unnecessary parts of quotations—see those documented by notes in lines 44, 128, and 139;
4. a long quotation—see the one in lines 133–139;
5. introductory remarks and insertions within quotations, paraphrases, and summaries to identify authors—see particularly those for material documented by notes in lines 6, 11, 104, 143, and 147.

Notice also how she handles a rather common problem in giving sources. In lines 40–41 she names an article by another writer as the source of the writer she is quoting. When you cannot determine where a quoted remark was first published, give the full information for the work in which you found it so that your reader will have the same information on it that you have.

On her instructor's recommendation, the student followed the MLA system then in effect for documentation. She has since updated it to conform with current MLA practice.

Sociology and the Sports Spectator: Some Questions

Jill Taylor (student)

Although sports have always formed an important part of popular culture, "spectatorism," the watching of sporting events directly or on TV, has not received much attention as a subject for serious social research. As Harry Edwards remarked in 1973 in *The Sociology of Sport,* "Perhaps the least studied and understood role in the institution 5 of sport is that of the 'fan' " (238). A. S. Daniels raised the question a few years earlier when he noted in the "Study of Sport" that "We can offer no scientific explanation why football in some American universities will draw 85,000 spectators into the stadium six times in the span of ten

weeks, while no university program in music, art, or even education 10
and science can approach this" (21).

I have chosen to try to investigate this subject because I have had
a long familiarity with fanatic (from which word, incidentally, we derive
the word "fan") TV and live-sports spectators. The chief example for me
has been my father. For years, I have been amazed at the behavior he 15
exhibits while spending innumerable hours in front of sports programs
on TV. From my earliest childhood on, I have never dared to interrupt
him at any point from the time the "Star Spangled Banner" has ended
and a game is about to start until the time when the last whistle has been
blown and the winners have been announced. I am quite overwhelmed 20
by the extensive sports knowledge displayed by this man who has never
actually participated in any athletic endeavor. The vicarious identification with certain teams and players, the emotional outbursts emitted
into the late hours of the night, even including wild screams by a man
who at all other times is the personification of quiet gentleness, make 25
me feel that sports-watching as a leisure activity and as a mass entertainment is truly a fascinating behavioral phenomenon.

The history of sports-watching is long. In ancient Greece the various games began as a means of celebrating individual competition,
honoring the gods, and entertaining the "fans." Organizing athletes 30
into groups to represent their home towns began at the most famous
of the ancient games, the ones held at Olympia, and athletic achievement was celebrated by the greatest sculptors and poets of the day. The
Romans continued the idea of individual competition, and during the
Middle Ages in Europe the aristocracy enjoyed knightly jousting in 35
tournaments and ordinary people organized village and parish teams to
compete in various athletic contests. The custom spread to America and
by the nineteenth century town-versus-town baseball games were common, and spectatorism flourished as a shared experience among enthu-
siastic supporters. Tristram P. Coffin, the folklore scholar, is quoted by 40
Michael Roberts in "The Vicarious Heroism of the Sports Spectator" as
remarking that "most of the games . . . ended up in brawls" but that
the games represented "some semi-civilized replacement for village-to-
village wars. And this is an aspect of the game that has never left it" (18).

In a sociological analysis it can be seen that today, as in the past, 45
spectatorism as a form of mass enjoyment is based on a unifying association of people. Individual "fans" are united by their identification with
a team or athlete who represents some kind of community to which
they themselves belong, such as a school, city, nation, race, or religion.
There are countless examples of this. Coffin cites the American League 50
pennant race in 1967 which brought work to a virtual standstill in four
large American cities, while everyone listened to the games (Roberts
19).

The spread of spectatorism as a leisure activity is probably the
result of the increase in the accessibility of all sports. Before World War 55
II, newspapers disseminated facts about sports to a wide audience. After

World War II, television programs on sports, with close-up shots, instant replays, slow motion, and explanatory commentaries, helped to bring sports into practically every home in America and made them much more understandable to the audience. Television has been the chief 60 cause of the increase in the number of "passive fans," the spectators who find enjoyment within the privacy of their own homes. However, the great response of "active fans," who attend sports events by the thousands, is also a noticeable part of spectatorism, and there is some evidence that this response is growing more intense. The Burns Secu- 65 rity Institute points to increasing destructiveness by fans of both the winning and losing teams after a big game (Roberts 19).

Because spectatorism has not received widespread attention from scholars in social research, there have not been many empirical studies to give verifiable conclusions about it. But various sociologists have 70 discussed the spectator role in terms of its functions and purposes. Although I cannot make generalizations on the subject, I can provide some analysis of these views on spectatorism within a sociological perspective. The reader must remember, however, that these statements are hypotheses, not generalizations based on empirical studies.   75

Arnold Beisser, a psychiatrist, offers the psychosocial view that spectatorism serves a social function. In a mass society it satisfies the alienated individual's need for identity and a feeling of belonging to a group (*Madness* 129). This concept brings to mind the faithful college alumni who support their teams long after graduation. At almost any 80 college game, and certainly at all the big ones, middle-aged and elderly fans can be seen—and heard—rooting with all their might for their old alma mater. Another social function of spectatorism, according to Beisser, is social communication. Viewing live sports and even sports programs on TV gives fans a way to share their feelings and opinions 85 with a large number of others who are participating in the same experience. Nothing else gives such a chance to be "at one with a sympathetic crowd," knowing that we do not stand alone in our intense feelings but "that such feelings are shared by a host of others" (130). Total strangers will exchange remarks with no signs of inhibition, and in moments of 90 great enthusiasm over a touchdown or a home run they may slap each other on the back or even hug each other and dance up and down.

A psychological function of spectatorism is giving socially acceptable outlets to forms of behavior that are not otherwise acceptable or approved by society. It releases suppressed tensions. Watching any 95 baseball or football game makes this clear. The screaming, yelling, cheering, and booing which are a characteristic part of these games are wholly acceptable and even expected. Some social scientists see this psychological function as related to the social function of identification mentioned above. "The public seems to need a permissible outlet for 100 certain barbaric impulses," Michael Roberts remarks. "Behavior such as assault and battery and indecent exposure are considered quite correct under the etiquette prevailing at, say, the Texas-Oklahoma football game" (19). Beisser, making the same point, mentions the standard cry "Kill the bums!" (130). Sociologists suggest that the violent and emotional outbursts are the result of a fanatical level of identification with the athletes. In recent years there have been many news stories from Latin America and European countries describing murders and suicides that have resulted from soccer scores.

Perhaps these emotional outbursts, acts of violence, and verbal assaults on players, coaches and judges are the result of the frustrations felt by the fans in their everyday lives. Violent fans, Harry Edwards suggests, may be unconsciously directing against the players and coaches the anger they cannot express against their employers, their families, and whatever other persons they may see as obstacles in their efforts to achieve the goals and the social and psychological security they want (243).

In a related hypothesis, Gregory Stone suggests in "American Sports: Play and Display" that spectators have destroyed the "play" aspect of sports and turned them into a spectacle or "display," played for the spectators, not for the players. He thinks that sports have lost many of their original qualities and are being turned into a type of ritual, a predetermined and therefore predictable activity (46). If Stone is right, then perhaps the violence will gradually decrease as the activity becomes more ritualized. Walter E. Schafer, in "Some Social Sources and Consequences of Interscholastic Athletics," sees the identification of the fans with the players as the result of feeling that "it is the *thing* to support your school's football, basketball, and . . . track team" (33), and that fans are merely conforming to what they see as "normal" behavior.

If we lose the sense of play, of enjoying games for their own sake, we may suffer as a society. In "Games: The Extensions of Man," Marshall McLuhan says:

> Games . . . are contrived and controlled situations, extensions of group awareness that permit a respite from customary patterns. They are a kind of talking to itself on the part of society as a whole. And talking to oneself is a recognizable form of play that is indispensable to any growth of self-confidence. . . . To take mere worldly things in dead earnest betokens a defect of awareness that is pitiable. . . . Play goes with an awareness of huge disproportion between the ostensible situation and the real stakes. (215)

Johan Huizinga makes the same point when he says in "The Play Element in Contemporary Civilization" that "real civilization cannot exist in the absence of a certain play-element, for civilization presupposes limitation and mastery of the self" (19). This is in agreement with Harry Edwards' claim that the most important function of sports is the reaffirmation of established values and beliefs and through them of the spectators' sense of their own worth (243). To Huizinga, "the cheat or spoilsport shatters civilization itself" (19).

All these views are hypotheses, calling for a great deal of further research. Many of these views fit with what I have observed as a specta-

tor. The identification with a team, the reinforcement of membership 150
in a larger social unit, the release of pent-up emotions and frustrations,
all match my own experiences as a spectator and as an observer of other
spectators. I also see the role of the fan as a means of reinforcing the
values of "the American Way," our belief that competition, hard work,
ambition, and determination are the qualities needed for individual 155
success and for a strong America, qualities that are embodied in the
"Horatio Alger" myth.

As I look back on what I have written, my training in social science
makes me recognize that I have not provided many answers, but I think
I have raised questions worth examining. Statistical reports and re- 160
search studies on spectatorism are definitely needed to answer them.
This is good, because new research in social science depends on propos-
ing new questions.

The questions I would like to see answered include the following:
Among TV spectators, are feelings shared with others and is a sense of 165
unification evident? If they are, then what differences, if any, exist
between the feelings and behavior of TV spectators and spectators
actually present at an event? Why do spectators choose to follow a
particular sport? What are the characteristics and causes of "fanatical
behavior"? What differences, if any, are there between the behavior 170
and feelings of spectators at an amateur event and ones at a professional
event? Although I do not agree with Gregory Stone's claim that all
sports are spectacles put on by the players for the benefit of the audience, I think that his idea is provocative, especially in the light of the
growing commercialism of our product-consumption oriented society. 175
This brings up the question of the role of economics in the "sports
industry," the attitudes of spectator toward the high cost of some tickets, the high salaries of some players, the "scholarships" for college
athletes, and the heavy betting on some games.

Other questions that should be explored empirically include the 180
class inequalities in spectator sports. Many sociologists have remarked
on the fact that the members of the lower economic class tend to
identify with baseball, perhaps because, as George Vecsey suggests,
during the Depression it was a sport for "hooky players, unemployed,
or anybody else with a clear mind and lots of time," while football, 185
"packaged like white bread and Detroit cars, has been accepted by
many upper class people" as "our game" ("Fans" 155). A particularly
important and complex question deserving research is why the great
majority of spectators for all sports are male.

After raising so many questions, I feel somewhat discouraged that 190
I have not made any conclusive findings. Yet I also feel that an important part of sociological thinking is to go on critically examining and
raising questions. Many of the questions I have raised will, I hope, be
answered in the future by the continued development of organized
research in the sociology of sport. The books and articles that I read 195
show that the research is beginning.

Bibliography

Beisser, Arnold. *The Madness in Sports.* New York: Meredith, 1967.

Daniels, A. S. "The Study of Sport as an Element of Culture," in *Sport, Culture and Society.* Ed. John W. Loy and Gerald S. Kenyon. London: Collier-Macmillan, 1969, 21–32.

Edwards, Harry. *The Sociology of Sport.* Homewood, Illinois: Dorsey, 1973.

Huizinga, Johan. "The Play Element in Contemporary Civilization." *Homo Ludens: A Study of the Play Element in Culture.* Boston: The Beacon Press, 1950. Rpt. in *Sport, Culture, and Society.* Ed. John W. Loy and Gerald S. Kenyon, London: Collier-Macmillan, 1969, 5–20.

McLuhan, Marshall. "Games: The Extensions of Man," *Understanding Media* (1964; rpt. New York, New American Library, n.d.), 207–216.

Roberts, Michael. "The Vicarious Heroism of the Sports Spectator." *The New Republic,* 23 Nov. 1974, 17–19.

Schafer, Walter E. "Some Social Sources and Consequences of Interscholastic Athletics." *Proceedings of the C. I. C. Symposium on the Sociology of Sport.* Ed. Gerald Kenyon. Chicago: The Athletic Institute, 1969, 33–34.

Stone, Gregory. "American Sports: Play and Display." *The Sociology of Sports: A Selection of Readings.* Ed. Eric Dunning. London: Cass, 1971, 42–49.

Vecsey, George. "Fans." *Esquire,* Oct. 1974, 151–155.

Assignments

Besides the suggestions made earlier in "Choosing a Subject," here are others that may appeal to you:

1. A critical history of a particular music group set in the context of trends in contemporary music.
2. What was happening in the world on the day you or one of your parents was born and what has been the outcome of some of the problems and events described in newspapers covering that day.
3. A critical analysis of the coverage of a particular event by a variety of periodicals.
4. An analysis of changes in advertising for women's fashions—has the women's liberation movement had an effect on what the advertisements say and on the pictures used?
5. The history of your hometown in the context of the history of the country, the region, or the state.
6. An examination of the special words and phrases used by any particular group or in any specialized activity with which you are familiar, such as slang used by children and teenagers, the combinations of slang and professional terminology of plumbers, jazz musicians, or the fans of any particular sport, or an analysis, comparison and contrast of the slang used by U.S. soldiers in World War I, World War II, and the Vietnam War.

UNIT 18

Essay Examinations

"What do you mean—'two questions out of three'? Didn't we have to write on all of them?" "When the bell rang, I was only halfway through the second question." "Ye gods! I just realized that I left out the most important example!" "When I saw everybody else still writing like crazy, I got scared and added a lot of junk the professor won't like." "When I got to the ending I realized I should have started differently, but it was too late to change things." "I thought I had an easy A for that course, but I think I've blown the final."

Some of your most important writing in college will be on examinations. Many good students, who have been conscientious about their work all term, do not get the final grade they expected because they give too little thought to their writing on the final examination and produce essays that are a confusing jumble. You may know a great deal about a subject, but unless you present your knowledge in a clear, well-organized form, your readers will not be able to evaluate it. In composing an effective essay for an examination, apply all the advice and suggestions given earlier in this book, especially those in Unit 1.

Take time to plan. For each question, jot down notes on scrap paper and make a rough outline. Then you will not risk forgetting an important point or losing track of your overall organization. Do not give in to your impatience or let the sight of your classmates writing away feverishly make you begin before you are ready.

First, read all the directions carefully. The student who handed in an unfinished paper late and complained that there was not enough time to answer ten questions got little sympathy from the instructor, who pointed out that the directions called for answering only seven of the ten.

Read through all the questions. Every set of questions represents an instructor's estimate of what most of the students in the class should be able to do in the time allowed. If you spend too much time on the first question, you will be rushed on the last ones. Also, by reading through all the questions before starting to write, you can discover the ones you are best prepared to answer. An exceptionally good and complete discussion of some questions may compensate for a brief treatment of those about which you know less. Moreover, if you find that some questions overlap, you can decide in advance what to include in each answer and save time and effort later.

Pay close attention to directions on the manner in which each question is to be answered. For example, among the questions that call for true essays there may be factual questions that you can answer in a few words. If you are asked to "list six reasons" or "enumerate eight causes," do not write a long discussion of reasons and causes. You cannot expect your instructor to take time to dig the vital points out of your discussion. If you are asked to state something in a single sentence, use no more and no less; but when you are told "discuss at length" or "explain fully," you should write at least a paragraph.

Determine the length of your answers on the basis of three factors: the number of questions, the time allowed, and your knowledge of your own speed of thinking and writing. When instructors give a single question as a three-hour final, they naturally expect a wealth of detail that they definitely do not expect when they give five questions to be answered in an hour. The more comprehensive your answer is supposed to be, the more pains you should take in planning it.

Remember that there is no special value in mere length. Your instructor, who must read dozens of examination papers every time you write one, is likely to be more favorably impressed by a concise answer that drives straight to the point than by a long and flowery piece of rhetoric. A brief generalization supported by a few well-chosen examples is always worth pages of vague abstraction.

In answering discussion questions, you will find a use for the types of writing analyzed in this book. You may be asked to describe a battle or the characteristics of a political leader (Unit 2); to narrate the chief events in the life of a literary or historical figure (Unit 3); to give specific examples of a general concept (Unit 4); to outline or summarize the main points of an argument, event, or theory (Units 6 and 7); to tell how to make a piece of laboratory equipment or carry on an industrial process (Unit 8); to compare two characters in a book of fiction or the circumstances leading up to two events (Unit 9); to classify people, poems, or natural phenomena (Unit 10); to name and explain the parts of a flower or a piece of machinery, or to analyze a social problem (Unit 11); to discuss causes and effects, such as the reasons for the Depression or the results of Prohibition (Unit 12); to report the results of an experiment, to draw conclusions from evidence, or to apply general laws of science or principles of economics to specific cases (Unit 13); to define terms from the new vocabulary that almost every course forces you to learn (Unit 14); to defend an opinion or theory (Unit 15); to make a critical analysis of your outside reading (Unit 16); or to correlate various reading materials, as in a research paper (Unit 17). In fact, the fields you are studying are so varied and the possibilities for kinds of essay examinations are so numerous that there is no limit to the methods of thinking and writing that you may be called on to use.

Always reserve a few moments at the end to reread your work, to catch errors in spelling, grammar, and punctuation as well as in content. Remember that a single slip of the pen may change the meaning of a whole paragraph. Your instructors may not consciously lower grades for inaccuracies in composition, but they cannot avoid being at least subconsciously put off by careless errors and impressed by careful writing. No one will object to corrections and deletions or to additions placed between the lines on the examination paper, but the more easily your instructors can read your papers, the better. Write legibly in ink—it is wise to take a spare pen with you—and leave reasonable margins. This is not to imply that college instructors place a "grade school" premium on neatness, but they can appreciate the good points of a paper more easily if they can read it easily.

Another mechanical but important aspect of examination writing is the numbering of your answers. Your replies should not only appear in the order of the questions but should be carefully labeled to match them. Questions labeled with Roman numerals may be subdivided into parts labeled with capital letters, and ones with Arabic numerals may have parts marked "a," "b," and so on. Be sure to label your corresponding answers with both designations, clearly and in order, and place them at or in the margin where they can be seen immediately, not buried within a paragraph. If there is a question that you cannot answer, include its number and leave a space so that you can return to it later if something suitable occurs to you. This method will also prevent your instructor from suspecting that you left out the number deliberately.

Much of this advice applies to objective examinations of all kinds —true-false, filling-in-blanks, multiple-choice, matching. Read each question carefully and follow all the directions exactly. If you read hastily through true-false statements and jump to conclusions, if you use plus and minus signs when "T" and "F" were asked for, if you write your answers at the sentence ends instead of in the designated places, or if you use ink when a No. 2 pencil is required, you may fail even though you know all the answers. Correction keys and computers make no allowances for personal idiosyncracies and give no credit for good intentions.

The objective examination is frequently a time test as well as an information test, designed to check your speed as well as your knowledge. Consequently, you should first read through it rapidly, answering only those questions whose answers occur to you immediately. Then you can return and spend the necessary time on the troublesome ones, without worrying that you will be caught at the end of the period with some obvious ones unanswered.

Note: You have probably been told many times that cramming is a vicious habit—and every word you were told is true. Have the good sense and willpower to make reviewing a simple everyday matter instead of cramming all night before an examination. You will be rewarded not only with higher grades, which, after all, are only an immediate, temporary concern, but with a far better and more lasting knowledge of the subject. If you do your reviewing the day before, get a good night's sleep, and go to the examination without further study, you will gain far more from your resulting clear-headed perspective on the whole subject than from frantically cramming your mind with jumbled details up to the last minute.

This may sound like an impossible ideal—but you can achieve it.

Examples

18-A   Freedom of Speech

Richard Peterson (student)

This essay was written for the final examination in an introductory course in American government. The question was "What rights are guaranteed by the First Amendment and what limitations are placed on them in ordinary practice?" The instructor recommended that the students spend one hour on the question. The information in this student's essay is accurate, the examples are appropriate, and the overall organization is firm and clear. The result, although not brilliant, is satisfactory.

The most important "right" defined by the Bill of Rights is freedom of speech. It is essential in a democracy, and all our other rights and freedoms depend on it. That is why it was the first amendment made to the Constitution.

If we want to decide any question intelligently, we should hear the 5 arguments on all sides. An argument may seem very strong and good, but we cannot be sure that it is completely right until we have heard the opposing views. They may show us something that we have overlooked. If we think the opposing views are wrong or foolish or even immoral, we should remember that listening to them doesn't mean 10 accepting them. I think the students should have listened last June instead of shouting down Jeane Kirkpatrick when she tried to give a speech at their college. So what if they didn't like her foreign policy? They didn't have to agree with it, but she had a right to present her ideas.   15

The only danger in giving everyone freedom of speech is that someone may use that right for the wrong purpose, just to make trouble. The standard example is the maniac who shouts "Fire!" in a crowded theater just to see the panic and the stampede to the exits. Even when there really is a fire, we shouldn't use that way to alert 20 people. It's an abuse of free speech. A more common abuse of free speech occurs when a speaker deliberately stirs people up to make them riot and turn to violence, doing such things as overturning cars, setting fire to buildings, and beating up other people.

Earlier in this century two Supreme Court Justices, Oliver Wendell 25
Holmes and Louis Brandeis, ruled that anyone who used the right to
free speech to stir up trouble was wrong and should be punished. This
ruling is known as the "clear and present danger test." A related ruling
by the Supreme Court says that the government can limit someone's
right to free speech if that person's remarks *might* lead others to do 30
illegal things. This ruling is much more difficult to interpret, and it was
a key point in the court case that developed over the American Nazi
Party's plan to march through Skokie, Illinois, a town where many
Jewish people lived who had been refugees from the Nazi Holocaust of
World War II. The American Nazis claimed that they just wanted to 35
have a peaceful parade and that they had a right to express their opinions that way, but the Skokie residents claimed that what the Nazis
really wanted was to stir up a violent reaction by the Jews so that they
could have a fight.

Cases involving freedom of speech are usually very hard to decide 40
and are likely to cause a lot of bad feelings on both sides, but the right
involved is well worth the trouble because it is so important to a democratic way of life.

1. Notice the short introductory and concluding paragraphs giving the writer's
   subject and general opinion and acting as a frame for the essay.
2. Why does the writer give two paragraphs to the dangers of free speech but
   only one to explaining why he thinks it is important?

18-B   The Greenhouse Effect

Lisa Weber (student)

This essay was written for the final examination in an introductory course in natural
science. The question was "What is the 'greenhouse effect' and why do many scientists
think we may be endangered by it?" The instructor recommended that the students
spend thirty minutes on it. The student has given accurate information and organized it
in a clear, simple pattern.

The "greenhouse effect" is the name that scientists have given to
what may result from having more carbon dioxide in the earth's atmosphere than we used to have.

Scientific measurements have shown that the amount of carbon
dioxide in the atmosphere of the earth is increasing rapidly. This is 5
happening because coal, oil, natural gas, and wood all give off carbon
dioxide when they burn, and we are using more and more fuel for
energy. Also, many forests in the world are being destroyed or at least
reduced in size because of the expansions in farms and cities as the
population of the world increases. Trees convert carbon dioxide into 10
oxygen, and so the more trees we cut down, the fewer converters of

carbon dioxide will be here to help us, the more carbon dioxide there will be in the atmosphere, and the less oxygen for us to breathe.

Another result creates a more immediate danger. The visible rays of the sun can go through carbon dioxide and reach the earth, warming 15 it up. The warmth makes the earth give off infrared rays. These rays are absorbed by the carbon dioxide instead of escaping into space, as they would if there were less carbon dioxide. The earth will work like a huge greenhouse, growing warmer and warmer from these combined effects.   20

If the warming process continues, there will be many major changes in ecology. The polar icecaps would melt, gradually raising the sea level all over the world and flooding low-lying coastal areas. Cities like Boston, New York, Miami, New Orleans, and Los Angeles would disappear. Also, the desert areas all over the world would grow larger 25 because many kinds of plants will not grow in a warmer climate and the heat in the air would dry up small rivers. These results would mean not only major changes in the way we live but would also create worldwide hunger.

If the scientists are right in their predictions, we should be taking 30 action now to reduce the greenhouse effect as quickly as possible.

1. In what ways is the overall organization of this example similar to that of 18-A?
2. How and where does the student use cause-and-effect relationships and deductive reasoning to arrive at conclusions?

Assignments

1. If you have access to files of old examination questions, look through them to discover the type of writing that is required in the answers. If among them are questions covering the work of courses you are now taking, try writing answers to any with which you are already familiar.
2. Save your own examination questions and compare them with your answers after your paper has been returned. If your grade was lower than you expected, try to discover whether you were penalized for lack of preparation or poor presentation. (If in doubt, ask the instructor to go over the paper with you.) Practice rewriting some of your answers, after referring to the suggestions given in the preceding units for the types of writing they require.

One of the most important results of your college training in composition should be that through leisurely and painstaking writing, like that in the themes you prepare outside of class, you gradually learn to write papers of acceptable quality while working rapidly and under pressure, as you are obliged to do in writing examinations and themes in class.

UNIT 19

The Business Letter

Many books and whole courses are devoted to business English, but here we shall consider only the kinds of letters that you as an individual are likely to write. "Business English" requires as much clearness and correctness as does all your other writing. But, because it has the practical purpose of getting something done rather than only informing or entertaining, it tends to be simpler and more direct. The modern trend is in sharp contrast to the past, when letters were often only collections of elaborate set expressions. A publisher, promoting better business letters, writes:

> If we're not careful, the standard terminology of business letters can be pretty silly. Used thoughtlessly, it can be downright insulting. Here are some common expressions—with the possible reactions of a modern reader:
>
> I have before me your letter . . . . Okay, answer it!
> In due course of time . . . . After the usual boondoggling.
> I wish to state . . . . Why wish? Just say it!
> We are this day in receipt of . . . . By George, they got it!
> Kindly advise the undersigned . . Who's writing the letter, anyhow?
> Please accept our order . . . . Any time!
> Thank you for your patronage . . Patrons went out of style long ago.
> And so did these expressions. (The Economics Press, Inc., Fairfield, NJ)

Such time-wasting patterns are being dropped in favor of a direct, simple reply. Beginnings such as "Replying to your letter of March 6" and endings such as "Hoping to hear from you soon, we remain" now sound old-fashioned. Simplicity may go to an extreme, however. In the telegraphic style, the writer lops off words as if they cost a dollar each:

> Received your letter. Adjustment suggested is satisfactory. Will return goods at once and await immediate refund.

Make your business English the language of natural speech, but remember that complete sentences are usually more understandable, even in speaking.

* * *   * , * *   * * *

The conventional business letter has five parts, besides the message itself. Before the message are the heading, the inside address, and the salutation; after the message are the complimentary close and the signature. See the model letters on pages 349–350 for illustrations.

1. The **heading** includes your address and the date on which you are writing. It usually occupies three lines in the upper right corner, far enough to the left to allow the longest line to end at the right-hand margin. Business firms use stationery with letterheads giving their names and addresses; if you have stationery with a letterhead, you need only add the date below it, either near the right margin or centered under the letterhead. (Include the correct zip code numbers in all addresses—heading, inside address, envelope—always after the state and with no punctuation.)

2. The **inside address** contains the name and address of the person or firm to whom you are writing, just as it will appear on the envelope. Although its use is essentially a matter of office procedure for convenience in filing, it has become conventional for all business letters. Begin it at the left margin at least two spaces below the date. (More space is allowable here, if you are arranging a short letter on a large page.)

If your letter is addressed to a firm but you wish it to come to the attention of a particular person or officer, you may include an "attention note" (see page 350) beginning at the margin between the inside address and the salutation, with a space above and below.

3. The **salutation** appears at the left margin, two spaces below the inside address, and consists of the words with which you greet the person to whom you are writing. Whatever the occasion, follow these rules:

a. Choose a salutation that matches the inside address in number and gender disregarding any intervening attention note.

b. Choose one expressing the degree of formality suited to the occasion.

c. Capitalize the first word and all nouns.

d. Punctuate with a colon always—nothing more.

For a formal salutation when you do not know whether you are addressing men or women, or when you know that you are addressing both, use one that includes both sexes.

To more than one recipient:	*To one recipient:*
Dear Sirs and Mesdames:	Dear Sir or Madam:
Ladies and Gentlemen:	Dear Committee Member:
Dear Committee Members:	Dear Classmate:
Dear Classmates:	

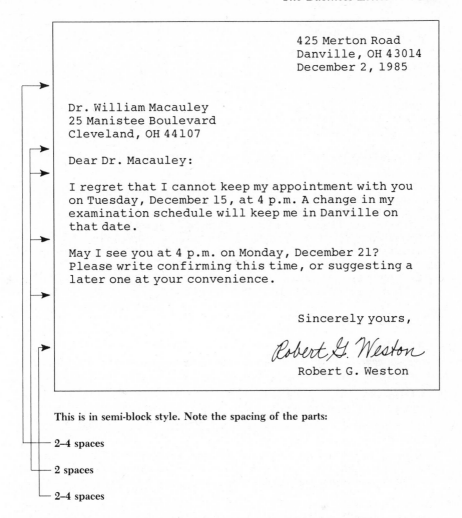

425 Merton Road
Danville, OH 43014
December 2, 1985

Dr. William Macauley
25 Manistee Boulevard
Cleveland, OH 44107

Dear Dr. Macauley:

I regret that I cannot keep my appointment with you on Tuesday, December 15, at 4 p.m. A change in my examination schedule will keep me in Danville on that date.

May I see you at 4 p.m. on Monday, December 21? Please write confirming this time, or suggesting a later one at your convenience.

Sincerely yours,

Robert G. Weston

Robert G. Weston

This is in semi-block style. Note the spacing of the parts:

2–4 spaces

2 spaces

2–4 spaces

If you know the sex but nothing else, use "Gentlemen" or "Sirs" for men and "Mesdames" for women.

When you know the name and sex of the recipient, choose among these conventional phrases:

To a male recipient:	*To a female recipient:*
Dear Sir:	Dear Madam:
My dear Mr. Blank:	My dear Miss (*or* Ms. *or* Mrs., as appropriate)
Dear Mr. Blank:	Blank:
	Dear Miss (*or* Ms. *or* Mrs., as appropriate) Blank:

Plurals: For "Mr." use "Messrs."; for "Mrs." and "Madam" use "Mmes."; for "Miss" use "Misses"; "Ms." may be either singular or plural.

"My dear Mr. Blank, "My dear Miss Blank," and so on, are generally considered slightly more formal than "Dear Mr. Blank," "Dear Miss Blank," and so on. (This is the reverse of British usage.) "Dear Sir" and

```
Route 3, Box 61
Naylorton, TN 37836
January 19, 1985


The Acme Photo Company
1018 East Moore Street
Detroit, MI 48200

Attention: Mr. H. A. Green, Framing Department

Gentlemen:

The price you quote in your letter of January 11 for
enlarging and framing the photograph of my two sons,
about which I wrote you in December, is entirely
satisfactory.

I am therefore enclosing the negative and the folder
with mat samples on which I have marked my preference. I
look forward to receiving the completed picture in about
ten days, as you have indicated.

Very truly yours,

Linda Williams

Linda Williams
(Mrs. Arthur Williams)
```

This is in full-block style. Note that the spacing of the parts is the same as in semi-block. Note, also, the "attention" line and writer's married name in parentheses to indicate how she wishes to be addressed.

"Dear Madam" remain the most formal salutations of all. *Never* write "Dear Gentlemen" or "Dear Ladies." For a less formal salutation that avoids the problem of a title for the recipient, simply use his or her full name: "Dear John Blank" or "Dear Jane Blank."

4. The **complimentary close,** the words by which you take your leave, should begin far enough from the right margin for your name and title, if any, to end before the right margin. Place them at least two spaces below the last line of your letter. (This space, like that between the heading and the inside address, can be increased for arrangement's sake.) Like the salutation, the complimentary close has become conventionalized into a few acceptable phrases, of which these are the most popular:

   a. Very truly yours, Yours very truly, Yours truly,
   b. Sincerely yours, Yours sincerely, Yours very sincerely, Sincerely,
   c. Cordially yours, Yours cordially, Cordially,

The first group is very impersonal, the second friendlier, the third the warmest. Words like "faithfully" and "respectfully" have gone out of general business use in America.

a. Choose a close that will match the degree of formality expressed in your salutation.

b. Capitalize the first word only.

c. Punctuate with a comma.

5. Directly under the complimentary close, **sign your name** as you are in the habit of writing it. Be sure that it can be easily read; do not pride yourself on one of those highly distinctive signatures that look more like a careless drawing than a row of letters (experts say they are more easily forged than are decipherable ones). If you type your letter, type your name also, to make certain of its legibility, but leave room (four lines will do it) between the complimentary close and the typed name for your handwritten signature, to certify the letter as your own. If you are writing in any official capacity, your title should appear below your name:

> Jane Blank
> President
> Pre-Med Society

As for social titles, a man never signs himself "Mr.," since that title is taken for granted. But a woman may wish to indicate her marital status with "Miss," "Ms." or "Mrs." for the convenience of the person replying. Those titles are not part of her legal signature, however, just as "Mr." is not part of a man's, and they should therefore be enclosed in parentheses:

(Miss) Jane Blank	for an unmarried woman
(Mrs.) John R. Blank	for a married woman
(Mrs.) Jane Blank	for a married woman with a career or for a formerly married woman
(Ms.) Jane Blank	for any of the above

Two pairs of initials that usually appear at the left margin of a business letter opposite or slightly below the signature are those of the person sending the letter and of the secretary who typed it, for purposes of record. As an individual writing your own business letters, you do not need to add initials in this spot.

Abbreviations. You must use the abbreviations "Mr.," "Mrs.," and "Ms." since these forms are never written out. Other abbreviations in common use include "Dr." and (after names) "Jr.," "D.D.S.," "M.D.," and so on. You may abbreviate first names to initials (especially if the owners do so themselves), terms describing businesses if the business itself does (Sears, Roebuck and Co., Mumford & Jones), and directions (1014 E. Morton Street, 444 Vermont Street N.W.—designating a section of a city). Names of countries are not abbreviated except "U.S.A."

and "U.S.S.R.," but those of states usually are when they are part of a written address. Use the two-letter abbreviations of the states authorized by the U.S. Postal Department.

Other abbreviations (of months, street names, etc.) are generally frowned on in business letters; the slight saving of time is not enough to offset the appearance of haste or lack of effort.

* * *   * * *   * * *

In the general format for your letter, observe these six conventions.

1. Type your letter or write neatly and legibly in blue or black ink—never use pencil or ink of any other color. Make a carbon or photocopy for your own records; it may prevent many problems later.

2. For **stationery,** use a good grade of white paper of standard "typewriter size" (8½ × 11 inches). It should always be unruled (use a ruled guide under a handwritten letter to keep lines reasonably straight). For very brief letters you may use the half-sheet size of paper (8½ × 5½). On this size you may write either the long way, producing a short letter of standard width (this is generally preferred, for convenience in handling and filing), or the short way, producing a miniature letter of standard proportions (this is chosen by some for its appearance).

3. Arrange your whole letter carefully on the page. Whatever size paper you use, the letter should look like a well-framed picture.

a. Make the spacing of the parts and the width of the margins appropriate to the length of the letter as a whole.

b. All four margins should be approximately equal; each should be at least 1½ inches wide, with the bottom one slightly wider than the others.

c. Use single-spacing, with double-spacing between paragraphs for typed letters of three or more lines. For a very brief letter, use double-spacing and a half-sheet of paper to avoid the lonely look of a single line or two of message.

d. Hyphenate very long words at the ends of the lines to keep the right-hand margin roughly in line. (Check the dictionary to determine where to divide words.)

e. Be concise; try to keep to one page. If your letter must be longer, keep the margins at least 1½ inches wide and make sure that you have at least three lines of the message on the last page. Number each page after the first.

f. *Never* write on the back of a sheet.

4. Arrange the parts of the letter in **semiblock** or **full-block** style.

a. In semi-block (see the example on page 349), all the lines of the inside address begin at the left margin, as does the salutation; all the lines of the heading begin at one inside margin, and the complimentary close and signature begin at another. In typed letters, the paragraphs may begin at the left margin because double-spacing between them will be enough to show paragraph divisions. In handwritten letters, indented paragraphs are advisable.

b. In full-block (see page 350), all the lines of the heading, salutation, complimentary close, and signature begin at the left margin.

c. The only punctuation *ending* these parts is a colon after the salutation (a comma is conventional in a social letter) and a comma after the complimentary close.

d. The only punctuation *within* these parts is a comma in the traditional style of date, separating the day and year, and in the address, separating the name of the town or city from that of the state.

5. Use a **white envelope** of the same quality and finish as your paper. The standard small size (3¾ × 6½) will take a half-sheet letter or a full-sheet one of one page. For a longer letter, use the official size (4¼ × 9½).

a. Make the outside address identical with the inside, beginning it at the approximate center of the envelope so that it will occupy roughly the lower right quarter of the envelope face.

b. Put your name and complete address in the extreme upper left corner.

c. Place any special directions such as an attention note, "Personal," or "Please Forward" in the lower left corner.

d. Attach the stamp—right side up—well inside the upper right corner of the envelope. It will look better and be protected from accidental tearing.

6. Fold the letter so that the recipient can withdraw it easily.

a. Fold a half-sheet letter in three parts. The two wings should be slightly narrower than the center section.

b. Fold a one-sheet letter into six parts. Bring the bottom up to within half an inch of the top, and crease; then fold it as you would a half-sheet letter.

c. Fold a longer letter into three parts, bringing the bottom up about two-thirds of the way to the top and the top down to about half an inch from the resulting crease.

* * *   * * *   * * *

1. Identify the conventional letter parts before and after the messages in the model letters on pages 349 and 350.
2. Name the arrangement used in each.
3. In what respects is the form of the two letters identical? in what different?
4. Which form is the more commonly used? What are the advantages and disadvantages of each? Which do you prefer?
5. Do the choices of salutation and complimentary close correctly indicate in each letter the degree of formality that seems to be intended?
6. Address an envelope (an appropriately sized rectangle will serve for practice) for the letter in semi-block style, including your return address.

7. Practice folding an 8½-×-11-inch sheet and inserting it properly into a commercial-size envelope; into an official-size envelope. Repeat with a half-sheet and a commercial-size envelope. Practice until you can perform the required operations smoothly and correctly, without pausing to think.

8. How many errors can you discover in the letter form that follows:

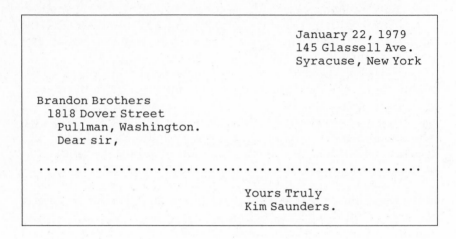

                                              January 22, 1979
                                              145 Glassell Ave.
                                              Syracuse, New York

Brandon Brothers
  1818 Dover Street
    Pullman, Washington.
    Dear sir,

. . . .

                                        Yours Truly
                                        Kim Saunders.

FOUR TYPES OF LETTERS

1. For a letter making an inquiry—one asking for prices, catalogs, accommodations, general information—use the basic form already described and also follow these directions:

a. Be explicit. Include enough details to make a definite reply possible. A letter asking a hotel if rooms are available is pointless if you omit the date for which you want them, the number of people concerned, and the type of accommodations preferred. Make your inquiry so clear that the reply can be an answer instead of a request for more specific information.

b. Be brief. Include all the necessary details but nothing that is beside the point. A request for information about a company's product may appropriately include the use to which you plan to put it, but an inquiry about theater tickets need not include your reasons for seeing the play.

c. Be courteous. Even though your inquiry may lead to a sale that the firm will be glad to make, remember that you are asking a favor. "Send me your catalog" will doubtless get results, but "please" and "thank you" are still welcome oil in the gears.

Notice how the two letters that follow meet these requirements.

(1) Will you please send me a copy of your current "Gardener's Guide" advertised in the May issue of *Flower and Garden*.

(A question like this—really a politely worded command—is usually punctuated with a period instead of a question mark. Mentioning where you learned of the literature requested is an added courtesy; it helps the company to know exactly what you wish and also to check on the effectiveness of its advertising.)

> (2) I own a four-quart pressure cooker, model 2K64B, that my parents bought about thirty years ago. The gasket on the cover has begun to leak steam, reducing the pressure inside. Except for this difficulty, the cooker works well, and I would like to continue to use it, but my local hardware store has no gaskets the right size.
> Do you still have gaskets for this model in stock? If you do, please let me know the types and prices. If you do not, can you suggest a substitute?

(This gives all the details that the company will need to make a reply. The letter could have been treated as one paragraph because it is brief and all on one subject, but the short final paragraph emphasizes the writer's inquiry. Notice that the first and last sentences in that paragraph are real questions, unlike the polite command in the first letter, and therefore have question marks.)

2. For **a letter making an order** from a catalog or advertisement, use the general form already discussed and also observe the following directions:

a. Give an exact description of the article desired—quantity, size, color, price, and catalog or order number, if there is one.

b. Give the method of shipment: air, parcel post, express, freight; the "fastest" or "cheapest" way; special delivery; prepaid or collect.

c. Give the arrangement for payment: C.O.D.; cash, stamps, check, money order; a charge to your account or credit card, with the name and number.

> Please send me one (1) pair of your new line of stereo headphones with the SM-700 "Studio Master," using 2¾-inch Mylar diaphragm drivers.
> I enclose my check for $65.00, the advertised price, and understand that you will send it postage paid.

(This letter is both brief and explicit. It makes clear the item desired, the method of shipment, and the arrangement for paying.)

3. In **a letter making a complaint,** tact is important. Remember that courtesy is not only pleasing but profitable—as the old saying goes, more flies are caught with honey than vinegar. Any business firm finds it easier to say "The customer is always right" if he or she is also reasonable.

a. Be sure that you have real cause to complain. Better to wait a day or two, for instance, than to send a complaint of nonarrival that crosses the shipment in the mail.

b. Be sure that your complaint is just. Check your order to make sure that you wrote the size correctly and legibly, before blaming the store because your new boots do not fit.

c. Write reasonably and courteously. Be exact and clear in explaining the cause for your dissatisfaction, and suggest what you regard as a suitable adjustment.

Consider the probable effects of the two letters that follow.

> (1) Last week I spent good money to go clear into Centerville to buy a sweater at your Sports Bar. I got one, but your salesclerk was careful not to tell me that it was soiled from lying around too long on your shelves waiting for a sucker like me, and I didn't see the soil marks until I got home. I think that any store that does that kind of trick ought to be ashamed of itself, and I can promise you that you won't get any more trade from me or any of my friends.

(The writer now probably feels much better for the time being, but the store has been given no suggestion for a suitable adjustment and no opening to make one. If the writer is wise, he or she will follow Mark Twain's practice and tear up this caustic masterpiece and start again.)

> (2) When I was in Centerville last week I bought a beige wool pullover sweater at your Sports Bar for $45.98. Not until I got home did I see that there were two badly soiled areas on the back caused by lying folded on the shelf.
>
> Do you wish me to return it in exchange for another, or would you prefer to pay me for having it cleaned locally? (The cost would be $8.00.) I would prefer to have it cleaned, because I did not see another one in your stock of just this style and color.

(The lack of recrimination is not only courteous but fair, since no one seems particularly at fault. Customers can scarcely blame the salesclerk for not noticing what they themselves overlooked. The psychology of taking for granted that an adjustment will be made is particularly good, far superior to merely asking if the firm will make one. Also, the suggestion of specific adjustment possibilities, with a statement of the customer's preference, simplifies the whole transaction.)

4. Letters of application may be the most important letters that you ever write. If you are applying for an award, for admission to a special program, or for a job, your letter may change your life.

a. Make the letter appealing. Courtesy and clearness are all you need for inquiries, orders, and complaints, but the application letter is essentially a sales letter.

(1) Think first of the viewpoint of your prospective readers. They will be interested in what you may be able to contribute to the field, not in your purely personal considerations. You are "selling" your skills, not yourself. "Because of my long interest in popular music and because I have been taking piano lessons for the past three years, I believe I can be useful in your record store" is more likely to appeal to the store owner than "I want to work for you because I would like a discount on buying records" or "because my best friend works in the coffee shop across the street and can give me a ride."

(2) **Do not be too modest.** The door-to-door salesman who asked "You don't want to buy some magazines, do you?" may have gotten a few orders out of pity, but he didn't get fat on commissions. Never begin with such expressions as "I don't know whether I can do this work" or "I know nothing about your program." In an application letter, put your best foot foremost and keep the other safely out of sight.

(3) **Do not be boastful.** A statement like "I have always been a super salesman ever since I was a child," or "I have always outranked every other student in my class" may be perfectly true, but it is likely to antagonize. Leave such information for others to supply in the letters of recommendation they write for you.

(4) **Do not sound superior** to whatever you are applying for. No reader was ever won by such remarks as "I am willing to work in your program until I can find one that suits me better," "My experience has been in colleges with more prestige than yours," or "I am looking for a job only because of recent financial problems in my family."

(5) **State honestly the achievements that are relevant** to whatever you are applying for. What may be an important asset for some applications may be irrelevant boasting for others. "All through high school I spent my spare time helping in a sports program for neighborhood children" would be valuable if you were applying for work as a camp counselor or for admission to a child psychology program but not for work in accounting.

(6) **Try to make your letter stand out favorably** from others. Your prospective readers may receive dozens or even hundreds of letters from qualified persons, and you must try to make them notice yours. But do not mistake mere freakishness for individuality. Your letter of application should be serious and dignified, without any of the extra devices often used in other types of sales letters.

b. **The content of your letter of application** will normally fall into five main sections: introduction, personal data, qualifications, list of references, and conclusion.

(1) Your introduction will depend on your particular situation. If you are answering an advertisement or announcement, begin with a reference to it. If you learned indirectly of the award, program, or job opening, mention how you learned of it. If you have no definite knowledge of an opening but are hopeful that one may develop, begin with some mention of your reasons for applying to the particular awards committee, college, or firm to whom you are writing.

(2) Give the personal data relevant to the situation—a list of objective facts about yourself, such as your age, sex, marital status, and any other items, such as health, citizenship, or religion, that may be pertinent.

(3) Give the qualifications that fit you for whatever you are applying for: your education, experience, interest, aptitudes.

(4) List your references—the names, official positions, and addresses of the people best qualified to recommend you, as to both character and ability. (You will, of course, have already gotten their permission to name them as references, and later you will thank them for recommending you.)

(5) Conclude your letter of application with something to ensure a reply: a request for an interview; a reminder that you have enclosed a stamped, self-addressed envelope for your reader's convenience; an indication that you hope for an early reply.

(Which of these many items to stress and which to omit will depend, of course, on the nature of what you are seeking. Religious education, for instance, may be important in becoming a counselor in a church-supported summer camp but not for admission to an intensive foreign language program. Experience and references from previous employers are always important. Since you are a student, your education, with specific references to relevant courses, and recommendations from faculty members who know you well will probably be your chief assets.)

c. Compose a resumé (data sheet) if the material that you wish to include covers half a typed page or more. This is a separate unit listing the objective, or factual, information (personal data, qualifications, references). Here the information can be neatly and clearly arranged under suitable headings and subheadings that readers can consult easily and quickly. A big advantage of the resumé is that you can photocopy it, thus saving time. The actual letters of application must, of course, be written individually. Another advantage is that you can make the letter itself shorter and more readable, more like a little essay on your interest in the field, your general aptitude and inclination for it, and your hopes for future accomplishment. Remember that the letter of application is essentially a sales letter.

d. Notice the organization, content, and effort to appeal to readers in the following examples of letters of application. The heading, inside address, and complimentary close are omitted to save space. The first is an answer to a newspaper advertisement with only a box number to which to reply: "Wanted—college student to read to invalid, afternoons or evenings. Box 41, Sheldon *Post.*"

Dear Sir or Madam:

In answer to your advertisement in today's *Post* for a college student to read to an invalid, I would like to be considered for the position.

I have already had some experience as a reader because my grandmother, who had lost her eyesight, lived in our home while I was in high school. Now I am a sophomore in the university, where I am majoring in speech, and I am particularly interested in interpretive reading.

Professor John Secord of the Speech Department has kindly agreed to write a recommendation about my ability to read aloud, and Mrs. Elizabeth Davis, director of volunteer services at Northside Hospital, where I worked as a candy-striper last summer, may be consulted about my personality and character.

My present schedule leaves me free on Monday, Wednesday, and Friday afternoons and most weekday evenings. I would very much like to have several hours a week of such congenial part-time work. May I have an interview? My telephone number is 586-6774.

The second is an application for a known opening in a program for special study.

Dear Professor Hamilton:

Dr. R. M. Baker, head of the Biology Department here at Sheffield College, has told me that your institute offers an intensive summer program in biology for undergraduates with special abilities. I would like to apply for admission to the program this summer.

I expect to complete my work at Sheffield for the B.A. with a major in biology in June of next year and hope to go on immediately to graduate school. My goals are a Ph.D. and a position in a research laboratory.

At the end of this semester I shall have 36 hours of credit in biology at Sheffield. My average for all my undergraduate work to date is B, and in biology it is A-. My special interest is in enzymes, and last summer I helped in measuring enzymes in the umbilical cord as part of a study at Memorial Hospital of the effects on the newborn of their mothers' having smoked during pregnancy.

Throughout the current year I have worked as an undergraduate laboratory assistant for Dr. Baker in the introductory biology course. He has offered to write to you about me, at your request, and so has Dr. Jane Allen, director of my junior thesis, and Dean John Davis of the Liberal Arts College. If I am considered for admission to your program, I shall be glad to send my complete transcript for your evaluation and to supply any additional information you may need about me, my work, or my plans.

The third letter is written in the hope of an opening in a company for which the student particularly wants to work, as her letter indicates. She addresses it to the chief personnel officer, whose name she learned by telephoning the company's head office, and includes a resumé on a separate sheet of paper.

Dear Mr. Robinson:

My chief ambition has always been to become a flight attendant, and because I also have a special interest in South America, I would particularly like to work for Panagra. Since your main flights are to South American cities, and since I speak fairly good Spanish and some Portuguese, I think I can be particularly useful to your company.

At present I am a senior at Flanham College, where I am majoring in psychology with special emphasis on personnel work. I am also active in a number of campus organizations and so am gaining experience in working with people. My college minor is in Spanish and Portuguese. Also, I have always been much interested in all phases of aviation and am learning to fly at Hoadley Airport nearby. I now have twelve hours of flying time to my credit.

The accompanying resumé will give you more details on my preparation and experience and includes a list of persons to whom you may write for further information about me. I do not know whether you accept beginners for your special training course, but if you do I shall be happy to come to Chicago for an interview any time this spring (preferably on Saturday, when I have no classes). If you have no openings at present but anticipate some in the near future, I hope that you will keep my application on file.

Resumé

Personal
  Name: Linda Katherine Harris
  College address: Sarah Black Residence Hall, Flanham
                   College, Danvers, Iowa 51091
  Home address: 286 Oak Street, Moulton, Ohio 43786

  Age: 22   Nationality: American
  Height: 5'5"   Marital status: single
  Weight: 120 lbs.   Health: excellent

Education
  Moulton High School graduate, February, 1981
  6 months in Wahl Business College, Moulton, 1981
  B.S., Flanham College (expected in June, 1985)
  Major in psychology
  Minor in languages
  General courses: English, history, mathematics,
                   physics, chemistry, psychology,
                   sociology
  Special courses: Meteorology, navigation,
                   engineering, drawing, service and
                   operation of aircraft

Activities
  Airways Club (vice-president)
  Dramatic Society (parts in three major productions)
  Science Club (program chairman, 1 year)

Experience
  Secretary to director of personnel, Ames Aircraft
    Corporation, Benzie, Illinois (1 year)
  Student assistant to head of Sarah Black Residence
    Hall, Flanham College (2 years, part-time)

References
  Dr. Ernest Beers, Head of Psychology Department,
    Flanham College
  Ms. Edna Markham, Director of Personnel, Ames Aircraft
    Corporation, Benzie, Illinois 61572
  Mr. Ted Houston, Manager, Hoadley Airport, Danvers,
    Iowa 51092

Assignments

The following requirements are stated generally, instead of being given in the form of specific problems, so that you can choose subjects that interest you, real-life situations for which you can write actual letters instead of merely going through the motions of a classroom exercise.

1. Write an inquiry about vacation tours, resort accommodations, services offered, goods for sale, to any actual business firm from whom you would really be interested in getting information. (Look through the current issue of a popular magazine for suggestions.)
2. Write a letter ordering merchandise, repairs, tickets—anything that you would really like to have from a real firm with a real address.
3. Write a letter complaining about any unsatisfactory goods or services (repairs, transportation, and the like) that you have recently had the misfortune to encounter.
4. Write a letter replying to a classified ad in your local paper, in which you apply for a position that you are qualified to fill.
5. Write a letter applying for summer work at some place where you know there is an opening in some line of work for which you are qualified.
6. Write a letter of application, accompanied by a data sheet, applying for the position that you think you would like when you graduate. Direct it to an actual firm, institution, or person by whom you would like to be employed.

UNIT 20

Essays for Further Reading

The seven essays that follow are arranged chronologically and span three centuries. The writers are as different in style and personality as are the events that inspired them, yet each is recognized as an important influence on contemporary writing and thought.

Four of the essays were first delivered as speeches. A good speech is, by nature, always a good essay. Rhetorical theory began with the orators of ancient Greece, and good writers ever since have used their methods. In all these essays you will find examples of the patterns of organization and the devices for effective writing discussed in the other units of this book.

Notice particularly the description of the early stages of President Kennedy's inaugural address, which includes a comparison of the rough drafts of several sentences. The principles shown there apply to effective writing of all kinds.

20-A   A Modest Proposal

Jonathan Swift (1667–1745)

Although Swift had little love for Ireland and felt the years he lived there were an exile, his devotion to justice made him a passionate fighter for Irish rights and humane treatment of the Irish poor. "A Modest Proposal" is the bitterest and most forceful attack in the English language on the exploitation of the weak by the powerful. Swift wrote it in 1729 when, after three years of poor harvests, thousands of homeless people were begging on the roads in Ireland—whole families, unable to pay rent on their farms, had been evicted by callous landlords, most of whom lived abroad to avoid paying taxes.

In this essay Swift assumes a "persona": he pretends to be completely unimaginative and concerned only with statistics and ways to save the government money. By writing of people as if they were animals and by seeming blind to the horror of his suggestions, he satirizes the attitudes of the government and the landlords and shocks the reader into seeing their inhumanity.

It is a melancholy object to those who walk through this great town[1] or travel in the country, when they see the streets, the roads, and cabin doors, crowded with beggars of the female sex, followed by three, four, or six children, all in rags and importuning every passenger for an alms. These mothers, instead of being able to work for their honest livelihood, are forced to employ all their time in strolling to beg sustenance for their helpless infants, who, as they grow up, either turn thieves for want of work, or leave their dear native country to fight for the Pretender in Spain, or sell themselves to the Barbadoes.[2]

I think it is agreed by all parties that this prodigious number of children in the arms, or on the backs, or at the heels of their mothers, and frequently of their fathers, is in the present deplorable state of the kingdom a very great additional grievance; and therefore whoever could find out a fair, cheap, and easy method of making these children sound, useful members of the commonwealth would deserve so well of the public as to have his statue set up for a preserver of the nation.

But my intention is very far from being confined to provide only for the children of professed beggars; it is of a much greater extent, and shall take in the whole number of infants at a certain age who are born of parents in effect as little able to support them as those who demand our charity in the streets.

As to my own part, having turned my thoughts for many years upon this important subject, and maturely weighed the several schemes of other projectors, I have always found them grossly mistaken in their computation. It is true, a child just dropped from its dam may be supported by her milk for a solar year, with little other nourishment; at most not above the value of two shillings,[3] which the mother may certainly get, or the value in scraps, by her lawful occupation of begging; and it is exactly at one year old that I propose to provide for them in such a manner as instead of being a charge upon their parents or the parish, or wanting food and raiment for the rest of their lives, they shall on the contrary contribute to the feeding, and partly to the clothing, of many thousands.

There is likewise another great advantage in my scheme, that it will prevent those voluntary abortions, and that horrid practice of women murdering their bastard children, alas, too frequent among us, sacrificing the poor innocent babes, I doubt, more to avoid the expense than the shame, which would move tears and pity in the most savage and inhuman breast.

---

[1]Dublin.

[2]The pretender to the throne of England was James Stuart (1688–1766), son of James II, who was living in exile in Spain. Many Irishmen, sympathetic to his cause, had joined him there; others had gone as indentured servants to Barbados and other British colonies in the West Indies.

[3]The British pound sterling was subdivided into twenty shillings; a crown equalled five shillings.

The number of souls in this kingdom being usually reckoned one 40
million and a half, of these I calculate there may be about two hundred
thousand couple whose wives are breeders; from which number I subtract thirty thousand couples who are able to maintain their own children, although I apprehend there cannot be so many under the present
distress of the kingdom; but this being granted, there will remain an 45
hundred and seventy thousand breeders. I again subtract fifty thousand
for those women who miscarry, or whose children die by accident or
disease within the year. There only remain an hundred and twenty
thousand children of poor parents annually born. The question therefore is, how this number shall be reared and provided for, which, as I 50
have already said, under the present situation of affairs, is utterly impossible by all the methods hitherto proposed. For we can neither employ
them in handicraft or agriculture; we neither build houses (I mean in
the country) nor cultivate land. They can very seldom pick up a livelihood by stealing till they arrive at six years old, except where they are 55
of towardly parts;[4] although I confess they learn the rudiments much
earlier, during which time they can however be looked upon only as
probationers, as I have been informed by a principal gentleman in the
county of Cavan, who protested to me that he never knew above one
or two instances under the age of six, even in a part of the kingdom so 60
renowned for the quickest proficiency in that art.

I am assured by our merchants that a boy or a girl before twelve
years old is no salable commodity; and even when they come to this age
they will not yield above three pounds, or three pounds and half a
crown at most on the Exchange; which cannot turn to account either 65
to the parents or the kingdom, the charge of nutriment and rags having
been at least four times that value.

I shall now therefore humbly propose my own thoughts, which I
hope will not be liable to the least objection.

I have been assured by a very knowing American of my acquaint- 70
ance in London, that a young healthy child well nursed is at a year old
a most delicious, nourishing, and wholesome food, whether stewed,
roasted, baked, or boiled; and I make no doubt that it will equally serve
in a fricassee or a ragout.

I do therefore humbly offer it to public consideration that of the 75
hundred and twenty thousand children, already computed, twenty
thousand may be reserved for breed, whereof only one fourth part to
be males, which is more than we allow to sheep, black cattle, or swine;
and my reason is that these children are seldom the fruits of marriage,
a circumstance not much regarded by our savages, therefore one male 80
will be sufficient to serve four females. That the remaining hundred

---

[4]Smart for their age.

thousand may at a year old be offered in sale to the persons of quality and fortune through the kingdom, always advising the mother to let them suck plentifully in the last month, so as to render them plump and fat for a good table. A child will make two dishes at an entertainment 85 for friends; and when the family dines alone, the fore or hind quarter will make a reasonable dish, and seasoned with a little pepper or salt will be very good boiled on the fourth day, especially in winter.

I have reckoned upon a medium that a child just born will weigh twelve pounds, and in a solar year if tolerably nursed increaseth to 90 twenty-eight pounds.

I grant this food will be somewhat dear, and therefore very proper for landlords, who, as they have already devoured most of the parents, seem to have the best title to the children.

Infant's flesh will be in season throughout the year, but more plenti- 95 ful in March, and a little before and after. For we are told by a grave author, an eminent French physician,[5] that fish being a prolific diet, there are more children born in Roman Catholic countries about nine months after Lent than at any other season; therefore, reckoning a year after Lent, the markets will be more glutted than usual, because the 100 number of popish infants is at least three to one in this kingdom; and therefore it will have one other collateral advantage, by lessening the number of Papists among us.

I have already computed the charge of nursing a beggar's child (in which list I reckon all cottagers, laborers, and four fifths of the farmers) 105 to be about two shillings per annum, rags included; and I believe no gentleman would repine to give ten shillings for the carcass of a good fat child, which, as I have said, will make four dishes of excellent nutritive meat, when he hath only some particular friend or his own family to dine with him. Thus the squire will learn to be a good landlord, and 110 grow popular among the tenants; the mother will have eight shillings net profit, and be fit for work till she produces another child.

Those who are more thrifty (as I must confess the times require) may flay the carcass; the skin of which artificially dressed will make admirable gloves for ladies, and summer boots for fine gentlemen.   115

As to our city of Dublin, shambles[6] may be appointed for this purpose in the most convenient parts of it, and butchers we may be assured will not be wanting; although I rather recommend buying the children alive, and dressing them hot from the knife as we do roasting pigs.   120

A very worthy person, a true lover of his country, and whose virtues

---

[5]François Rabelais, the sixteenth-century French satirist, who suggested as a joke that a diet of fish stimulated human fertility.
[6]Slaughterhouses.

I highly esteem, was lately pleased in discoursing on this matter to offer a refinement upon my scheme. He said that many gentlemen of this kingdom, having of late destroyed their deer, he conceived that the want of venison might be well supplied by the bodies of young lads and 125 maidens, not exceeding fourteen years of age nor under twelve, so great a number of both sexes in every country being now ready to starve for want of work and service; and these to be disposed of by their parents, if alive, or otherwise by their nearest relations. But with due deference to so excellent a friend and so deserving a patriot, I cannot be altogether 130 in his sentiments; for as to the males, my American acquaintance assured me from frequent experience that their flesh was generally tough and lean, like that of our schoolboys, by continual exercise, and their taste disagreeable; and to fatten them would not answer the charge. Then as to the females, it would, I think with humble submission, be a 135 loss to the public, because they soon would become breeders themselves: and besides, it is not improbable that some scrupulous people might be apt to censure such a practice (although indeed very unjustly) as a little bordering upon cruelty; which, I confess, hath always been with me the strongest objection against any project, how well soever 140 intended.

But in order to justify my friend, he confessed that this expedient was put into his head by the famous Psalmanazar,[7] a native of the island Formosa, who came from thence to London above twenty years ago, and in conversation told my friend that in his country when any young 145 person happened to be put to death, the executioner sold the carcass to persons of quality as a prime dainty; and that in his time the body of a plump girl of fifteen, who was crucified for an attempt to poison the emperor, was sold to his Imperial Majesty's prime minister of state, and other great mandarins of the court, in joints from the gibbet, at four 150 hundred crowns. Neither indeed can I deny that if the same use were made of several plump young girls in this town, who without one single groat to their fortunes cannot stir abroad without a chair, and appear at the playhouse and assemblies in foreign fineries which they never will pay for, the kingdom would not be the worse. 155

Some persons of a desponding spirit are in great concern about that vast number of poor people who are aged, diseased, or maimed, and I have been desired to employ my thoughts what course may be taken to ease the nation of so grievous an encumbrance. But I am not in the least pain upon that matter, because it is very well known that they are 160 every day dying and rotting by cold and famine, and filth and vermin, as fast as can be reasonably expected. And as to the younger laborers,

---

[7]A French contemporary of Swift's who became a celebrity in London by passing himself off as a native of Taiwan—or Formosa, as the Portuguese explorers called it.

they are now in almost as hopeful a condition. They cannot get work, and consequently pine away for want of nourishment to a degree that if at any time they are accidentally hired to common labor, they have not strength to perform it; and thus the country and themselves are happily delivered from the evils to come. 165

I have too long digressed, and therefore shall return to my subject. I think the advantages by the proposal which I have made are obvious and many, as well as of the highest importance. 170

For first, as I have already observed, it would greatly lessen the number of Papists,[8] with whom we are yearly overrun, being the principal breeders of the nation as well as our most dangerous enemies; and who stay at home on purpose to deliver the kingdom to the Pretender, hoping to take their advantage by the absence of so many good Protes- 175 tants, who have chosen rather to leave their country than stay at home and pay tithes against their conscience to an Episcopal curate.

Secondly, the poorer tenants will have something valuable of their own, which by law may be made liable to distress, and help to pay their landlord's rent, their corn and cattle being already seized and money 180 a thing unknown.

Thirdly, whereas the maintenance of an hundred thousand children, from two years old and upward, cannot be computed at less than ten shillings a piece per annum, the nation's stock will be thereby increased fifty thousand pounds per annum, besides the profit of a new 185 dish introduced to the tables of all gentlemen of fortune in the kingdom who have any refinement in taste. And the money will circulate among ourselves, the goods being entirely of our own growth and manufacture.

Fourthly, the constant breeders, besides the gain of eight shillings sterling per annum by the sale of their children, will be rid of the charge 190 of maintaining them after the first year.

Fifthly, this food would likewise bring great custom to taverns, where the vintners will certainly be so prudent as to procure the best receipts for dressing it to perfection, and consequently have their houses frequented by all the fine gentlemen, who justly value them- 195 selves upon their knowledge in good eating; and a skillful cook, who understands how to oblige his guests, will contrive to make it as expensive as they please.

Sixthly, this would be a great inducement to marriage, which all wise nations have either encouraged by rewards or enforced by laws 200 and penalties. It would increase the care and tenderness of mothers toward their children, when they were sure of a settlement for life to the poor babes, provided in some sort by the public, to their annual profit instead of expense. We should see an honest emulation among the

---

[8]Roman Catholics.

married women, which of them could bring the fattest child to the 205
market. Men would become as fond of their wives during the time of
their pregnancy as they are now of their mares in foal, their cows in calf,
or sows when they are ready to farrow; nor offer to beat or kick them
(as is too frequent a practice) for fear of a miscarriage.

Many other advantages might be enumerated. For instance, the 210
addition of some thousand carcasses in our exportation of barreled beef,
the propagation of swine's flesh, and improvement in the art of making
good bacon, so much wanted among us by the great destruction of pigs,
too frequent at our tables, which are no way comparable in taste or
magnificence to a well-grown, fat, yearling child, which roasted whole 215
will make a considerable figure at a lord mayor's feast or any other
public entertainment. But this and many others I omit, being studious
of brevity.

Supposing that one thousand families in this city would be constant
customers for infants' flesh, besides others who might have it at merry 220
meetings, particularly weddings and christenings, I compute that Dublin would take off annually about twenty thousand carcasses, and the
rest of the kingdom (where probably they will be sold somewhat
cheaper) the remaining eighty thousand.

I can think of no one objection that will possibly be raised against 225
this proposal, unless it should be urged that the number of people will
be thereby much lessened in the kingdom. This I freely own, and it was
indeed one principal design in offering it to the world. I desire the
reader will observe, that I calculate my remedy for this one individual
kingdom of Ireland and for no other that ever was, is, or I think ever 230
can be upon earth. Therefore let no man talk to me of other expedients:[9]
of taxing our absentees at five shillings a pound: of using neither clothes
nor household furniture except what is of our own growth and manufacture: of utterly rejecting the materials and instruments that promote
foreign luxury: of curing the expensiveness of pride, vanity, idleness,
and gaming in our women: of introducing a vein of parsimony, pru- 235
dence, and temperance: of learning to love our country, in the want of
which we differ even from Laplanders and the inhabitants of Topinam-
boo:[10] of quitting our animosities and factions, nor acting any longer like
the Jews, who were murdering one another at the very moment their
city was taken: of being a little cautious not to sell our country and 240
conscience for nothing: of teaching landlords to have at least one degree of mercy toward their tenants: lastly, of putting a spirit of honesty,
industry, and skill into our shopkeepers; who, if a resolution could now
be taken to buy only our native goods, would immediately unite to
cheat and exact upon us in the price, the measure, and the goodness, 245

---

[9]What follows are serious suggestions that Swift had made in earlier pamphlets.
[10]A remote part of the Brazilian jungle.

nor could ever yet be brought to make one fair proposal of just dealing, though often and earnestly invited to it.

Therefore I repeat, let no man talk to me of these and the like expedients, till he hath at least some glimpse of hope that there will ever be some hearty and sincere attempt to put them in practice.   250

But as to myself, having been wearied out for many years with offering vain, idle, visionary thoughts, and at length utterly despairing of success, I fortunately fell upon this proposal, which, as it is wholly new, so it hath something solid and real, of no expense and little trouble, full in our own power, and whereby we can incur no danger in disoblig-   255 ing England. For this kind of commodity will not bear exportation, the flesh being of too tender a consistence to admit a long continuance in salt, although perhaps I could name a country[11] which would be glad to eat up our whole nation without it.

After all, I am not so violently bent upon my own opinion as to   260 reject any offer proposed by wise men, which shall be found equally innocent, cheap, easy, and effectual. But before something of that kind shall be advanced in contradiction to my scheme, and offering a better, I desire the author or authors will be pleased maturely to consider two points. First, as things now stand, how they will be able to find food and   265 raiment for an hundred thousand useless mouths and backs. And secondly, there being a round million of creatures in human figure throughout this kingdom, whose sole subsistence put into a common stock would leave them in debt two millions of pounds sterling, adding those who are beggars by profession to the bulk of farmers, cottagers,   270 and laborers, with their wives and children who are beggars in effect; I desire those politicians who dislike my overture, and may perhaps be so bold to attempt an answer, that they will first ask the parents of these mortals whether they would not at this day think it a great happiness to have been sold for food at a year old in the manner I prescribe, and   275 thereby have avoided such a perpetual scene of misfortunes as they have since gone through by the oppression of landlords, the impossibility of paying rent without money or trade, the want of common sustenance, with neither house nor clothes to cover them from the inclemencies of the weather, and the most inevitable prospect of entailing the   280 like or greater miseries upon their breed forever.

I profess, in the sincerity of my heart, that I have not the least personal interest in endeavoring to promote this necessary work, having no other motive than the public good of my country, by advancing our trade, providing for infants, relieving the poor, and giving some   285 pleasure to the rich. I have no children by which I can propose to get a single penny; the youngest being nine years old, and my wife past childbearing.

---

[11]England.

20-B   A Plea for Free Speech in Boston

Frederick Douglass (1817–1895)

Born into slavery in Maryland, Douglass escaped to Massachusetts and became a leader
in the antislavery movement. He described his early years in *Narrative of the Life of
Frederick Douglass* (1845). In late November of 1860 an antislavery meeting in Boston
was broken up by a crowd of prominent Bostonians who opposed the antislavery movement. A few days later, Douglass delivered this speech in the Boston Music Hall. Notice
how he appeals to his audience's local pride by reminding them of Boston's traditional
respect for individual freedom. Notice also his use of inductive and deductive reasoning,
repetition, short sentences, balanced structures, and questions to emphasize important
points.

Boston is a great city—and Music Hall has a fame almost as extensive as that of Boston. Nowhere more than here have the principles of
human freedom been expounded. But for the circumstances already
mentioned, it would seem almost presumption for me to say anything
here about those principles. And yet, even here, in Boston, the moral 5
atmosphere is dark and heavy. The principles of human liberty, even
if correctly apprehended, find but limited support in this hour of trial.
The world moves slowly, and Boston is much like the world. We thought
the principle of free speech was an accomplished fact. Here, if nowhere
else, we thought the right of the people to assemble and to express their 10
opinion was secure. Dr. Channing had defended the right, Mr. Garrison
had practically asserted the right, and Theodore Parker had maintained
it with steadiness and fidelity to the last.*

But here we are to-day contending for what we thought was gained
years ago. The mortifying and disgraceful fact stares us in the face, that 15
though Faneuil Hall and Bunker Hill Monument stand, freedom of
speech is struck down. No lengthy detail of facts is needed. They are
already notorious; far more so than will be wished ten years hence.

The world knows that last Monday a meeting assembled to discuss
the question: "How Shall Slavery Be Abolished?" The world also knows 20
that that meeting was invaded, insulted, captured, by a mob of gentlemen, and thereafter broken up and dispersed by the order of the
mayor, who refused to protect it, though called upon to do so. If this had
been a mere outbreak of passion and prejudice among the baser sort,
maddened by rum and hounded on by some wily politician to serve 25
some immediate purpose,—a mere exceptional affair,—it might be allowed to rest with what has already been said. But the leaders of the
mob were gentlemen. They were men who pride themselves upon
their respect for law and order.

───────────

*Three prominent and widely respected New Englanders who had been active in
the antislavery movement.

These gentlemen brought their respect for the law with them and 30
proclaimed it loudly while in the very act of breaking the law. Theirs
was the law of slavery. The law of free speech and the law for the
protection of public meetings they trampled under foot, while they
greatly magnified the law of slavery.

The scene was an instructive one. Men seldom see such a blending 35
of the gentleman with the rowdy, as was shown on that occasion. It
proved that human nature is very much the same, whether in tarpaulin
or broadcloth. Nevertheless, when gentlemen approach us in the character of lawless and abandoned loafers,—assuming for the moment
their manners and tempers,—they have themselves to blame if they are 40
estimated below their quality.

No right was deemed by the fathers of the Government more
sacred than the right of speech. It was in their eyes, as in the eyes of
all thoughtful men, the great moral renovator of society and government. Daniel Webster called it a homebred right, a fireside privilege. 45
Liberty is meaningless where the right to utter one's thoughts and
opinions has ceased to exist. That, of all rights, is the dread of tyrants.
It is the right which they first of all strike down. They know its power.
Thrones, dominions, principalities, and powers, founded in injustice
and wrong, are sure to tremble, if men are allowed to reason of righ- 50
teousness, temperance, and of a judgment to come in their presence.
Slavery cannot tolerate free speech. Five years of its exercise would
banish the auction block and break every chain in the South. They will
have none of it there, for they have the power. But shall it be so here?

Even here in Boston, and among the friends of freedom, we hear 55
two voices: one denouncing the mob that broke up our meeting on
Monday as a base and cowardly outrage; and another, deprecating and
regretting the holding of such a meeting, by such men, at such a time.
We are told that the meeting was ill-timed, and the parties to it unwise.

Why, what is the matter with us? Are we going to palliate and 60
excuse a palpable and flagrant outrage on the right of speech, by implying that only a particular description of persons should exercise that
right? Are we, at such a time, when a great principle has been struck
down, to quench the moral indignation which the deed excites, by
casting reflections upon those on whose persons the outrage has been 65
committed? After all the arguments for liberty to which Boston has
listened for more than a quarter of a century, has she yet to learn that
the time to assert a right is the time when the right itself is called in
question, and that the men of all others to assert it are the men to whom
the right has been denied? 70

It would be no vindication of the right of speech to prove that
certain gentlemen of great distinction, eminent for their learning and
ability, are allowed to freely express their opinions on all subjects—

including the subject of slavery. Such a vindication would need, itself, to be vindicated. It would add insult to injury. Not even an old-fash- 75 ioned abolition meeting could vindicate that right in Boston just now. There can be no right of speech where any man, however lifted up, or however humble, however young, or however old, is overawed by force, and compelled to suppress his honest sentiments.

Equally clear is the right to hear. To suppress free speech is a 80 double wrong. It violates the rights of the hearer as well as those of the speaker. It is just as criminal to rob a man of his right to speak and hear as it would be to rob him of his money. I have no doubt that Boston will vindicate this right. But in order to do so, there must be no concessions to the enemy. When a man is allowed to speak because he is rich and 85 powerful, it aggravates the crime of denying the right to the poor and humble.

The principle must rest upon its own proper basis. And until the right is accorded to the humblest as freely as to the most exalted citizen, the government of Boston is but an empty name, and its freedom a 90 mockery. A man's right to speak does not depend upon where he was born or upon his color. The simple quality of manhood is the solid basis of the right—and there let it rest forever.

20-C   The Second Inaugural Address

Abraham Lincoln (1809–1865)

When Lincoln delivered his second inaugural address in March 1865, the Civil War was still dragging on. Although he had reason to hope that it would end soon, he could not be sure. His address shows this mixture of hope and doubt. Notice the organization: one very long paragraph reviewing the events and emotions of the past four years, and one short paragraph, composed of a single sentence, looking forward. Notice also his use of comparison and contrast, inductive and deductive reasoning, balanced sentence structures, questions, varied sentence length, and repetition to make his points clear and to emphasize them.

At this second appearing to take the oath of the presidential office, there is less occasion for an extended address than at the first. Then a statement somewhat in detail of the course to be pursued seemed very fitting and proper; now, at the expiration of four years, during which public declarations have constantly been called forth 5 concerning every point and place of the great contest which still absorbs attention and engrosses the energies of the nation, little that is new could be presented. The progress of our arms, upon which all else chiefly depends, is as well known to the public as to myself. It is, I trust, reasonably satisfactory and encouraging to all. With a high 10 hope for the future, no prediction in that regard is ventured. On the

occasion corresponding to this four years ago, all thoughts were anxiously directed to an impending civil war. All dreaded it. All sought to
avoid it. While the Inaugural Address was being delivered from this
place, devoted altogether to saving the Union without war, the insur-
gent agents were in the city seeking to destroy it without war,—seek- 15
ing to dissolve the Union, and divide the effects by negotiating. Both
parties deprecated war, but one of them would make war rather than
let it perish, and war came. One-eighth of the whole population were
colored slaves, not distributed generally over the Union, but located
in the southern part. These slaves contributed a peculiar and powerful 20
interest. All knew the interest would somehow cause war. To
strengthen, perpetuate, and extend this interest was the object for
which the insurgents would rend the Union by war, while the Government claimed no right to do more than restrict the territorial enlargement of it. Neither party expected the magnitude or duration 25
which it has already attained; neither anticipated that the cause of the
conflict might cease even before the conflict itself should cease. Each
looked for an easier triumph and a result less fundamental and aston-
ishing. Both read the same Bible and pray to the same God. Each
invokes his aid against the other. It may seem strange that any man 30
should dare to ask a just God's assistance in wringing bread from the
sweat of other men's faces; but let us judge not, that we be not
judged. The prayer of both should not be answered; that of neither
has been answered fully, for the Almighty has his own purposes. "Woe
unto the world because of offenses, for it must needs be that offense 35
come; but woe unto that man by whom the offense cometh." If we
shall suppose American slavery one of those offenses which, in the
providence of God, must needs come, but which, having continued
through his appointed time, he now wills to remove, and that he gives
to both North and South this terrible war, as was due to those by 40
whom the offense came, shall we discern that there is any departure
from those divine attributes which believers in the living God always
ascribe to him? Fondly do we hope, fervently do we pray, that this
mighty scourge of war may speedily pass away; yet if it be God's will
that it continue until the wealth piled by bondsmen by two hundred 45
and fifty years' unrequited toil shall be sunk, and until every drop of
blood drawn with the lash shall be paid by another drawn with the
sword, as was said three thousand years ago, so still it must be said that
the judgments of the Lord are true and righteous altogether.

With malice towards none, with charity for all, with firmness in the 50
right, as God gives us to see the right, let us strive on to finish the work
we are in, to bind up the nation's wounds, to care for him who shall have
borne the battle, and for his widow and orphans; to do all which may
achieve and cherish a just and a lasting peace among ourselves and with
all nations.   55

20-D   The Patron and the Crocus

Virginia Woolf (1882–1941)

Virginia Woolf helped to shape the style of the novel in the twentieth century. Notably
in *Mrs. Dalloway* (1925), *To the Lighthouse* (1927), and *The Waves* (1931), she brought
a new sensitivity to the analysis of human psychology. Raised in a family active in the
intellectual life of London, she became one of the central figures in the "Bloomsbury
group" of writers and artists and called special attention to the struggles of creative
people, particularly women, to develop their talents. In this essay she analyzes the complexities of the relationship between writers and the readers who are in effect their
patrons. She uses a crocus first as the subject of an imagined literary work and then as
a symbol of the work itself. Every writer, she says, needs a reader—patron—who will be
both sympathetic and discriminating, and "the fate of literature depends on their happy
alliance." In the course of describing what a good "patron" should do and be, she gives
useful advice on writing.

Young men and women beginning to write are generally given the
plausible but utterly impracticable advice to write what they have to
write as shortly as possible, as clearly as possible, and without other
thought in their minds except to say exactly what is in them. Nobody
ever adds on these occasions the one thing needful: "And be sure you 5
choose your patron wisely," though that is the gist of the whole matter.
For a book is always written for somebody to read, and, since the patron
is not merely the paymaster, but also in a very subtle and insidious way
the instigator and inspirer of what is written, it is of the utmost importance that he should be a desirable man.   10
But who, then, is the desirable man—the patron who will cajole the
best out of the writer's brain and bring to birth the most varied and
vigorous progeny of which he is capable? Different ages have answered
the question differently. The Elizabethans, to speak roughly, chose the
aristocracy to write for and the playhouse public. The eighteenth-cen- 15
tury patron was a combination of coffee-house wit and Grub Street
bookseller. In the nineteenth century the great writers wrote for the
half-crown magazines and the leisured classes. And looking back and
applauding the splendid results of these different alliances, it all seems
enviably simple, and plain as a pikestaff compared with our own predic- 20
ament—for whom should we write? For the present supply of patrons
is of unexampled and bewildering variety. There is the daily Press, the
weekly Press, the monthly Press; the English public and the American
public; the best-seller public and the worst-seller public; the high-brow
public and the red-blood public; all now organised self-conscious enti- 25
ties capable through their various mouthpieces of making their needs
known and their approval or displeasure felt. Thus the writer who has
been moved by the sight of the first crocus in Kensington Gardens has,
before he sets pen to paper, to choose from a crowd of competitors the
particular patron who suits him best. It is futile to say, "Dismiss them 30

all; think only of your crocus," because writing is a method of communication; and the crocus is an imperfect crocus until it has been shared.
The first man or the last may write for himself alone, but he is an
exception and an unenviable one at that, and the gulls are welcome to
his works if the gulls can read them.   35

Granted, then, that every writer has some public or other at the
end of his pen, the high-minded will say that it should be a submissive
public, accepting obediently whatever he likes to give it. Plausible as
the theory sounds, great risks are attached to it. For in that case the
writer remains conscious of his public, yet is superior to it—an uncom-   40
fortable and unfortunate combination, as the works of Samuel Butler,
George Meredith, and Henry James may be taken to prove. Each de-
spised the public; each desired a public; each failed to attain a public;
and each wreaked his failure upon the public by a succession, gradually increasing in intensity, of angularities, obscurities, and affectations   45
which no writer whose patron was his equal and friend would have
thought it necessary to inflict. Their crocuses in consequence are tor-
tured plants, beautiful and bright, but with something wry-necked
about them, malformed, shrivelled on the one side, overblown on the
other. A touch of the sun would have done them a world of good.   50
Shall we then rush to the opposite extreme and accept (if in fancy
alone) the flattering proposals which the editors of the *Times* and the
Daily News may be supposed to make us—"Twenty pounds down for
your crocus in precisely fifteen hundred words, which shall blossom
upon every breakfast table from John o' Groats to the Land's End   55
before nine o'clock to-morrow morning with the writer's name attached"?

But will one crocus be enough, and must it not be a very brilliant
yellow to shine so far, to cost so much, and to have one's name attached
to it? The Press is undoubtedly a great multiplier of crocuses. But if we 60
look at some of these plants, we shall find that they are only very
distantly related to the original little yellow or purple flower which
pokes up through the grass in Kensington Gardens about this time of
year. The newspaper crocus is amazing but still a very different plant.
It fills precisely the space allotted to it. It radiates a golden glow. It is   65
genial, affable, warmhearted. It is beautifully finished, too, for let nobody think that the art of "our dramatic critic" of the *Times* or of Mr.
Lynd of the *Daily News* is an easy one. It is no despicable feat to start
a million brains running at nine o'clock in the morning, to give two
million eyes something bright and brisk and amusing to look at. But the 70
night comes and these flowers fade. So little bits of glass lose their lustre
if you take them out of the sea; great prima donnas howl like hyenas
if you shut them up in telephone boxes; and the most brilliant of articles
when removed from its element is dust and sand and the husks of straw.
Journalism embalmed in a book is unreadable.   75

The patron we want, then, is one who will help us to preserve our flowers from decay. But as his qualities change from age to age, and it needs considerable integrity and conviction not to be dazzled by the pretensions or bamboozled by the persuasions of the competing crowd, this business of patron-finding is one of the tests and trials of 80 authorship. To know whom to write for is to know how to write. Some of the modern patron's qualities are, however, fairly plain. The writer will require at this moment, it is obvious, a patron with the book-reading habit rather than the play-going habit. Nowadays, too, he must be instructed in the literature of other times and races. But 85 there are other qualities which our special weaknesses and tendencies demand in him. There is the question of indecency, for instance, which plagues us and puzzles us much more than it did the Elizabethans. The twentieth-century patron must be immune from shock. He must distinguish infallibly between the little clod of manure which 90 sticks to the crocus of necessity, and that which is plastered to it out of bravado. He must be a judge, too, of those social influences which inevitably play so large a part in modern literature, and able to say which matures and fortifies, which inhibits and makes sterile. Further, there is emotion for him to pronounce on, and in no department can 95 he do more useful work than in bracing a writer against sentimentality on the one hand and a craven fear of expressing his feeling on the other. It is worse, he will say, and perhaps more common, to be afraid of feeling than to feel too much. He will add, perhaps, something about language, and point out how many words Shakespeare used and 100 how much grammar Shakespeare violated, while we, though we keep our fingers so demurely to the black notes on the piano, have not appreciably improved upon *Antony and Cleopatra*. And if you can forget your sex altogether, he will say, so much the better; a writer has none. But all this is by the way—elementary and disputable. The 105 patron's prime quality is something different, only to be expressed perhaps by the use of that convenient word which cloaks so much— atmosphere. It is necessary that the patron should shed and envelop the crocus in an atmosphere which makes it appear a plant of the very highest importance, so that to misrepresent it is the one outrage 110 not to be forgiven this side of the grave. He must make us feel that a single crocus, if it be a real crocus, is enough for him; that he does not want to be lectured, elevated, instructed, or improved; that he is sorry that he bullied Carlyle into vociferation, Tennyson into idyllics, and Ruskin into insanity; that he is now ready to efface himself or assert 115 himself as his writers require; that he is bound to them by a more than maternal tie; that they are twins indeed, one dying if the other dies, one flourishing if the other flourishes; that the fate of literature depends upon their happy alliance—all of which proves, as we began by saying, that the choice of a patron is of the highest importance. But 120 how to choose rightly? How to write well? Those are the questions.

20-E   A Hanging

George Orwell (1903–1950)

Orwell, whose real name was Eric Blair, was born in Bengal, India, attended school in
England, and then, between the ages of nineteen and twenty-four, served in the British
police force in Burma. He returned to England and became an essayist and fiction writer.
His satire *Animal Farm* (1946) and his novel *1984* (1949) have become modern classics.
This essay records an intense personal experience that has universal applications. Notice
throughout how Orwell's use of concrete details makes the experience come alive for the
reader. Examine particularly the brilliantly compact paragraph (lines 69–82) summing up
the moral dilemma posed by capital punishment and the brief, objectively presented
scene at the end implying a criticism of human behavior.

It was in Burma, a sodden morning of the rains. A sickly light, like
yellow tinfoil, was slanting over the high walls into the jail yard. We
were waiting outside the condemned cells, a row of sheds fronted
with double bars, like small animal cages. Each cell measured about
ten feet by ten and was quite bare within except for a plank bed and 5
a pot for drinking water. In some of them brown, silent men were
squatting at the inner bars, with their blankets draped round them.
These were the condemned men, due to be hanged within the next
week or two.

One prisoner had been brought out of his cell. He was a Hindu, a 10
puny wisp of a man, with a shaven head and vague liquid eyes. He had
a thick, sprouting moustache, absurdly too big for his body, rather like
the moustache of a comic man on the films. Six tall Indian warders were
guarding him and getting him ready for the gallows. Two of them stood
by with rifles and fixed bayonets, while the others handcuffed him, 15
passed a chain through his handcuffs and fixed it to their belts, and
lashed his arms tight to his sides. They crowded very close about him,
with their hands always on him in a careful, caressing grip, as though
all the while feeling him to make sure he was there. It was like men
handling a fish which is still alive and may jump back into the water. 20
But he stood quite unresisting, yielding his arms limply to the ropes, as
though he hardly noticed what was happening.

Eight o'clock struck and a bugle call, desolately thin in the wet air,
floated from the distant barracks. The superintendent of the jail, who
was standing apart from the rest of us, moodily prodding the gravel 25
with his stick, raised his head at the sound. He was an army doctor, with
a grey toothbrush moustache and a gruff voice. "For God's sake hurry
up, Francis," he said irritably. "The man ought to have been dead by
this time. Aren't you ready yet?"

Francis, the head jailer, a fat Dravidian in a white drill suit and gold 30
spectacles, waved his black hand. "Yes sir, yes sir," he bubbled. "All iss
satisfactorily prepared. The hangman iss waiting. We shall proceed."[4]

"Well, quick march, then. The prisoners can't get their breakfast
till this job's over."

We set out for the gallows. Two warders marched on either side of 35
the prisoner, with their rifles at the slope; two others marched close
against him, gripping him by arm and shoulder, as though at once
pushing and supporting him. The rest of us, magistrates and the like,
followed behind. Suddenly, when we had gone ten yards, the proces-
sion stopped short without any order or warning. A dreadful thing had 40
happened—a dog, come goodness knows whence, had appeared in the
yard. It came bounding among us with a loud volley of barks and leapt
round us wagging its whole body, wild with glee at finding so many
human beings together. It was a large woolly dog, half Airedale, half
pariah. For a moment it pranced round us, and then, before anyone 45
could stop it, it had made a dash for the prisoner, and jumping up tried
to lick his face. Everybody stood aghast, too taken aback even to grab
the dog.

"Who let that bloody brute in here?" said the superintendent an-
grily. "Catch it, someone!"   50

A warder detached from the escort, charged clumsily after the dog,
but it danced and gambolled just out of his reach, taking everything as
part of the game. A young Eurasian jailer picked up a handful of gravel
and tried to stone the dog away, but it dodged the stones and came after
us again. Its taps echoed from the jail walls. The prisoner, in the grasp 55
of the two wardens, looked on incuriously, as though this was another
formality of the hanging. It was several minutes before someone
managed to catch the dog. Then we put my handkerchief through its
collar and moved off once more, with the dog still straining and whimp-
ering.   60

It was about forty yards to the gallows. I watched the bare brown
back of the prisoner marching in front of me. He walked clumsily with
his bound arms, but quite steadily, with that bobbing gait of the Indian
who never straightens his knees. At each step his muscles slid neatly
into place, the lock of hair on his scalp danced up and down, his feet 65
printed themselves on the wet gravel. And once, in spite of the men
who gripped him by each shoulder, he stepped lightly aside to avoid a
puddle on the path.

It is curious, but till that moment I had never realized what it
means to destroy a healthy, conscious man. When I saw the prisoner 70
step aside to avoid the puddle I saw the mystery, the unspeakable
wrongness, of cutting a life short when it is in full tide. This man was
not dying, he was alive just as we are alive. All the organs of his body
were working—bowels digesting food, skin renewing itself, nails growing, tissues forming—all toiling away in solemn foolery. His nails would 75
still be growing when he stood on the drop, when he was falling through
the air with a tenth-of-a-second to live. His eyes saw the yellow gravel
and the grey walls, and his brain still remembered, foresaw, reasoned
—even about puddles. He and we were a party of men walking to-

gether, seeing, hearing, feeling, understanding the same world; and in 80
two minutes, with a sudden snap, one of us would be gone—one mind
less, one world less.

The gallows stood in a small yard, separate from the main grounds
of the prison, and overgrown with tall prickly weeds. It was a brick
erection like three sides of a shed, with planking on top, and above that 85
two beams and a crossbar with the rope dangling. The hangman, a
grey-haired convict in the white uniform of the prison, was waiting
beside his machine. He greeted us with a servile crouch as we entered.
At a word from Francis the two warders, gripping the prisoner more
closely than ever, half led, half pushed him to the gallows and helped 90
him clumsily up the ladder. Then the hangman climbed up and fixed
the rope round the prisoner's neck.

We stood waiting, five yards away. The warders had formed in a
rough circle round the gallows. And then, when the noose was fixed,
the prisoner began crying to his god. It was a high, reiterated cry of 95
"Ram! Ram! Ram! Ram!" not urgent and fearful like a prayer or cry
for help, but steady, rhythmical, almost like the tolling of a bell. The
dog answered the sound with a whine. The hangman, still standing
on the gallows, produced a small cotton bag like a flour bag and
drew it down over the prisoner's face. But the sound, muffled by the 100
cloth, still persisted, over and over again: "Ram! Ram! Ram! Ram!
Ram!"

The hangman climbed down and stood ready, holding the lever.
Minutes seemed to pass. The steady, muffled crying from the prisoner
went on and on, "Ram! Ram! Ram!" never faltering for an instant. The 105
superintendent, his head on his chest, was slowly poking the ground
with his stick; perhaps he was counting the cries, allowing the prisoner
a fixed number—fifty, perhaps, or a hundred. Everyone had changed
colour. The Indians had gone grey like bad coffee, and one or two of the
bayonets were wavering. We looked at the lashed, hooded man on the 110
drop, and listened to his cries—each cry another second of life; the same
thought was in all our minds: oh, kill him quickly, get it over, stop that
abominable noise!

Suddenly the superintendent made up his mind. Throwing up his
head he made a swift motion with his stick. "Chalo!" he shouted almost 115
fiercely.

There was a clanking noise, and then dead silence. The prisoner
had vanished, and the rope was twisting on itself. I let go of the dog,
and it galloped immediately to the back of the gallows; but when it got
there it stopped short, barked, and then retreated into a corner of the 120
yard, where it stood among the weeds, looking timorously out at us. We
went round the gallows to inspect the prisoner's body. He was dangling
with his toes pointed straight downwards, very slowly revolving, as
dead as a stone.

The superintendent reached out with his stick and poked the bare 125
brown body; it oscillated slightly. "*He's* all right," said the superintendent. He backed out from under the gallows, and blew out a deep
breath. The moody look had gone out of his face quite suddenly. He
glanced at his wrist-watch. "Eight minutes past eight. Well, that's all for
this morning, thank God."   130

The warders unfixed bayonets and marched away. The dog, so-
bered and conscious of having misbehaved itself, slipped after them.
We walked out of the gallows yard, past the condemned cells with their
waiting prisoners, into the big central yard of the prison. The convicts,
under the command of warders armed with lathis, were already receiv- 135
ing their breakfast. They squatted in long rows, each man holding a tin
pannikin, while two warders with buckets marched round ladling out
rice; it seemed quite a homely, jolly scene, after the hanging. An enormous relief had come upon us now that the job was done. One felt an
impulse to sing, to break into a run, to snigger. All at once everyone 140
began chattering gaily.

The Eurasian boy walking beside me nodded towards the way we
had come, with a knowing smile: "Do you know, sir, our friend (he
meant the dead man) when he heard his appeal had been dismissed, he
pissed on the floor of his cell. From fright. Kindly take one of my 145
cigarettes, sir. Do you not admire my new silver case, sir? From the
boxwallah, two rupees eight annas. Classy European style."

Several people laughed—at what, nobody seemed certain.

Francis was walking by the superintendent, talking garrulously:
"Well, sir, all has passed off with the utmost satisfactoriness. It was all 150
finished—flick! like that. It iss not always so—oah, no! I have known
cases where the doctor wass obliged to go beneath the gallows and pull
the prissoner's legs to ensure decease. Most disagreeable!"

"Wriggling about, eh? That's bad," said the superintendent.

"Ach, sir, it iss worse when they become refractory! One man, I 155
recall, clung to the bars of hiss cage when we went to take him out. You
will scarcely credit, sir, that it took six warders to dislodge him, three
pulling at each leg. We reasoned with him. 'My dear fellow,' we said,
'think of all the pain and trouble you are causing to us!' But no, he would
not listen! Ach, he wass very troublesome!"   160

I found that I was laughing quite loudly. Everyone was laughing.
Even the superintendent grinned in a tolerant way. "You'd better all
come out and have a drink," he said quite genially. "I've got a bottle
of whisky in the car. We could do with it."

We went through the big double gates of the prison into the road. 165
"Pulling at his legs!" exclaimed a Burmese magistrate suddenly, and
burst into a loud chuckling. We all began laughing again. At the moment Francis' anecdote seemed extraordinarily funny. We all had a
drink together, native and European alike, quite amicably. The dead
man was a hundred yards away.   170

20-F Inaugural Address

John F. Kennedy (1917–1963)

A clear, simple writing style is usually the result of much hard work and many revisions. Study the samples of Kennedy's rough drafts and, in his final version, notice his use of short sentences and balanced structures to emphasize important points. His biographer, Theodore Sorensen, tells us that Kennedy first mentioned the inaugural address soon after his election in November:

He wanted suggestions from everyone. He wanted it short. He wanted it focused on foreign policy. He did not want to sound partisan, pessimistic, or critical of his predecessor. He wanted neither the customary cold war rhetoric about the Communist menace nor any weasel words that Khrushchev might misinterpret. And he wanted it to set a tone for the era about to begin.

He asked me to read all the past Inaugural Addresses. . . . He asked me to study the secret of Lincoln's Gettysburg Address (my conclusion, which his Inaugural applied, was that Lincoln never used a two- or three-syllable word where a one-syllable word would do, and never used two or three words where one would do).

Actual drafting did not get under way until the week before it was due. As had been true of his acceptance speech at Los Angeles, pages, paragraphs, and complete drafts had poured in, solicited . . . and unsolicited. . . .

The final text included several phrases, sentences and themes suggested by these sources. . . . Credit should also go to other Kennedy advisers who reviewed the early drafts and offered suggestions or encouragement.

But however numerous the assistant artisans, the principal architect of the Inaugural Address was John Fitzgerald Kennedy. Many of the most memorable passages can be traced to earlier Kennedy speeches and writings. For example:

Inaugural Address	Other Addresses
For man holds in his mortal hands the power to abolish all forms of human poverty and all forms of human life.	. . . man . . . has taken into his mortal hands the power to exterminate the entire species some seven times over. —Acceptance speech at Los Angeles
. . . the torch has been passed to a new generation of Americans. . . .	It is time, in short, for a new generation of Americans. —Acceptance speech and several campaign speeches
And so, my fellow Americans, ask not what your country can do for you; ask what you can do for your country.	We do not campaign stressing what our country is going to do for us as a people. We stress what we can do for the country, all of us. —Televised campaign address from Washington, September 20, 1960

No Kennedy speech ever underwent so many drafts. Each paragraph was reworded, reworked and reduced. The following table illustrates the attention paid to detailed changes:

First Draft	Next-to-Last Draft	Final Text
We celebrate today not a victory of party but the sacrament of democracy.	We celebrate today not a victory of party but a convention of freedom.	We observe today not a victory of party but a celebration of freedom.

Each of us, whether we hold office or not, shares the responsibility for guiding this most difficult of all societies along the path of self-discipline and self-government.	In your hands, my fellow citizens, more than in mine, will be determined the success or failure of our course.	In your hands, my fellow citizens, more than mine, will rest the final success or failure of our course.
Nor can two great and powerful nations forever continue on this reckless course, both overburdened by the staggering cost of modern weapons . . .	. . . neither can two great and powerful nations long endure their present reckless course, both overburdened by the staggering cost of modern weapons . . .	. . . neither can two great and powerful groups of nations take comfort from our present course—both sides overburdened by the cost of modern weapons . . .
And if the fruits of cooperation prove sweeter than the dregs of suspicion, let both sides join ultimately in creating a true world order—neither a Pax Americana, nor a Pax Russiana, nor even a balance of power—but a community of power.	And if a beachhead of cooperation can be made in the jungles of suspicion, let both sides join some day in creating, not a new balance of power but a new world of law . . .	And if a beachhead of cooperation can push back the jungle of suspicion, let both sides join in creating a new endeavor, not a new balance of power, but a new world of law . . .

He [Kennedy] wanted it to be the shortest in the twentieth century, he said. "It's more effective that way and I don't want people to think I'm a windbag." He couldn't beat FDR's abbreviated wartime remarks in 1944, I said—and he settled for the [second] shortest (less than nineteen hundred words) since 1905. . . . He reworked it further. "Let's eliminate all the 'I's,' " he said. "Just say what 'we' will do. You'll have to leave it in about the oath and the responsibility, but let's cut it everywhere else." The ending, he said, "sounds an awful lot like the ending of the Massachusetts legislature speech, but I guess it's OK." He worked and reworked the "ask not" sentence, with the three campaign speeches containing a similar phrase (Anchorage, Detroit, Washington) spread out on a low glass coffee table beside him.

Later that day—January 17—as we flew back to Washington from Palm Beach, working in his cabin on the *Caroline,* the final phrasing was emerging. A Biblical quotation that was later used in his American University speech was deleted. The opening paragraphs were redictated. . . .

Arriving back in Washington, the work went on at his house and in our Senate offices. Kenneth Galbraith suggested "cooperative ventures" with our allies in places of "joint ventures," which sounded like a mining partnership. Dean Rusk suggested that the other peoples of the world be challenged to ask "what together we can do for freedom" instead of "what you can do for freedom." Walter Lippmann suggested that references to the Communist bloc be changed from "enemy" to "adversary." The President-elect inserted a phrase he had used in a campaign speech on Latin America—"a new alliance for progress." At the last moment, concerned that his emphasis on foreign affairs would be interpreted as an evasion on civil rights, he added to his commitment on human rights the words "at home and around the world."

On January 19, one day before inauguration, it was finished.

We observe today not a victory of party but a celebration of freedom, symbolizing an end as well as a beginning, signifying renewal as well as change. For I have sworn before you and Almighty God the same solemn oath our forebears prescribed nearly a century and three-quarters ago.   5

The world is very different now. For man holds in his mortal hands the power to abolish all forms of human poverty and all forms of human life. And yet the same revolutionary belief for which our forebears fought is still at issue around the globe, the belief that the rights of man come not from the generosity of the state but from the 10 hand of God.

We dare not forget today that we are the heirs of that first revolution. Let the word go forth from this time and place, to friend and foe alike, that the torch has been passed to a new generation of Americans, born in this century, tempered by war, disciplined by a hard and bitter 15 peace, proud of our ancient heritage, and unwilling to witness or permit the slow undoing of those human rights to which this nation has always been committed, and to which we are committed today at home and around the world.

Let every nation know, whether it wishes us well or ill, that we shall 20 pay any price, bear any burden, meet any hardship, support any friend, oppose any foe to assure the survival and the success of liberty.

This much we pledge—and more.

To those old allies whose cultural and spiritual origins we share, we pledge the loyalty of faithful friends. United, there is little we cannot 25 do in a host of cooperative ventures. Divided, there is little we can do, for we dare not meet a powerful challenge at odds and split asunder.

To those new states whom we welcome to the ranks of the free, we pledge our word that one form of colonial control shall not have passed away merely to be replaced by a far more iron tyranny. We shall not 30 always expect to find them supporting our view. But we shall always hope to find them strongly supporting their own freedom, and to remember that, in the past, those who foolishly sought power by riding the back of the tiger ended up inside.

To those peoples in the huts and villages of half the globe struggling 35 to break the bonds of mass misery, we pledge our best efforts to help them help themselves, for whatever period is required, not because the Communists may be doing it, not because we seek their votes, but because it is right. If a free society cannot help the many who are poor, it cannot save the few who are rich.   40

To our sister republics south of our border, we offer a special pledge: to convert our good words into good deeds, in a new alliance for progress, to assist free men and free governments in casting off the chains of poverty. But this peaceful revolution of hope cannot become the prey of hostile powers. Let all our neighbors know that we shall join 45 with them to oppose aggression or subversion anywhere in the Americas. And let every other power know that this hemisphere intends to remain the master of its own house.

To that world assembly of sovereign states, the United Nations, our last best hope in an age where the instruments of war have far outpaced the instruments of peace, we renew our pledge of support: to prevent it from becoming merely a forum for invective, to strengthen its shield of the new and the weak, and to enlarge the area in which its writ may run.

Finally, to those nations who would make themselves our adversary, we offer not a pledge but a request: that both sides begin anew the quest for peace, before the dark powers of destruction unleashed by science engulf all humanity in planned or accidental self-destruction.

We dare not tempt them with weakness. For only when our arms are sufficient beyond doubt can we be certain beyond doubt that they will never be employed.

But neither can two great and powerful groups of nations take comfort from our present course—both sides overburdened by the cost of modern weapons, both rightly alarmed by the steady spread of the deadly atom, yet both racing to alter that uncertain balance of terror that stays the hand of mankind's final war.

So let us begin anew, remembering on both sides that civility is not a sign of weakness, and sincerity is always subject to proof. Let us never negotiate out of fear, but let us never fear to negotiate.

Let both sides explore what problems unite us instead of belaboring those problems which divide us.

Let both sides, for the first time, formulate serious and precise proposals for the inspection and control of arms, and bring the absolute power to destroy other nations under the absolute control of all nations.

Let both sides seek to invoke the wonders of science instead of its terrors. Together let us explore the stars, conquer the deserts, eradicate disease, tap the ocean depths and encourage the arts and commerce.

Let both sides unite to heed in all corners of the earth the command of Isaiah to "undo the heavy burdens . . . [and] let the oppressed go free."

And if a beachhead of cooperation may push back the jungle of suspicion, let both sides join in creating a new endeavor, not a new balance of power, but a new world of law, where the strong are just and the weak secure and the peace preserved.

All this will not be finished in the first one hundred days. Nor will it be finished in the first one thousand days, nor in the life of this Administration, nor even perhaps in our lifetime on this planet. But let us begin.

In your hands, my fellow citizens, more than mine, will rest the final success or failure of our course. Since this country was founded, each generation of Americans has been summoned to give testimony to its national loyalty. The graves of young Americans who answered the call to service surround the globe.

Now the trumpet summons us again—not as a call to bear arms, though arms we need; not as a call to battle, though embattled we are; but a call to bear the burden of a long twilight struggle, year in and year out, "rejoicing in hope, patient in tribulation," a struggle against the common enemies of man: tyranny, poverty, disease and war itself.

Can we forge against these enemies a grand and global alliance, North and South, East and West, that can assure a more fruitful life for all mankind? Will you join in that historic effort?

In the long history of the world, only a few generations have been granted the role of defending freedom in its hour of maximum danger. I do not shrink from this responsibility; I welcome it. I do not believe that any of us would exchange places with any other people or any other generation. The energy, the faith, the devotion which we bring to this endeavor will light our country and all who serve it, and the glow from that fire can truly light the world.

And so, my fellow Americans, ask not what your country can do for you; ask what you can do for your country.

My fellow citizens of the world, ask not what America will do for you, but what together we can do for the freedom of man.

Finally, whether you are citizens of America or citizens of the world, ask of us here the same high standards of strength and sacrifice which we ask of you. With a good conscience our only sure reward, with history the final judge of our deeds, let us go forth to lead the land we love, asking His blessing and His help, but knowing that here on earth God's work must truly be our own.

20-G   The Nobel Peace Prize Acceptance Speech

Martin Luther King, Jr. (1929–1968)

In 1964 Dr. King was awarded the Nobel peace prize. At the ceremonies in Oslo he made the following speech. Notice his use of inductive and deductive reasoning, exemplification, figurative language, and analogy to make his thoughts clear. Notice also his use of repetition and balanced sentence structures to emphasize important points.

Your Majesty, your Royal Highness, Mr. President, excellencies, ladies and gentlemen:

I accept the Nobel prize for peace at a moment when twenty-two million Negroes of the United States of America are engaged in a creative battle to end the long night of racial injustice. I accept this award in behalf of a civil rights movement which is moving with determination and a majestic scorn for risk and danger to establish a reign of freedom and a rule of justice.

I am mindful that only yesterday in Birmingham, Alabama, our children, crying out for brotherhood, were answered with fire hoses, snarling dogs, and even death. I am mindful that only yesterday in

Philadelphia, Mississippi, young people seeking to secure the right to vote were brutalized and murdered.

I am mindful that debilitating and grinding poverty afflicts my people and chains them to the lowest rung of the economic ladder.   15

Therefore, I must ask why this prize is awarded to a movement which is beleaguered and committed to unrelenting struggle: to a movement which has not won the very peace and brotherhood which is the essence of the Nobel prize.

After contemplation, I conclude that this award which I received   20 on behalf of that movement is profound recognition that nonviolence is the answer to the crucial political and moral questions of our time— the need for man to overcome oppression and violence without resorting to violence and oppression.

Civilization and violence are antithetical concepts. Negroes of the   25 United States, following the people of India, have demonstrated that nonviolence is not sterile passivity, but a powerful moral force which makes for social transformation. Sooner or later, all the people of the world will have to discover a way to live together in peace, and thereby transform this pending cosmic energy into a creative psalm of brother-   30 hood.

If this is to be achieved, man must evolve for all human conflict a method which rejects revenge, aggression and retaliation. The foundation of such a method is love.

The tortuous road which has led from Montgomery, Alabama, to   35 Oslo bears witness to this truth. This is a road over which millions of Negroes are travelling to find a new sense of dignity. This same road has opened for all Americans a new era of progress and hope. It has led to a new civil rights bill, and it will, I am convinced, be widened and lengthened into a superhighway of justice as Negro and white men in   40 increasing numbers create alliances to overcome their common problems.

I accept this award today with an abiding faith in the future of mankind. I refuse to accept the idea that the "isness" of man's present nature makes him morally incapable of reaching up for the eternal   45 "oughtness" that forever confronts him.

I refuse to accept the idea that man is mere flotsam and jetsam in the river of life which surrounds him. I refuse to accept the view that mankind is so tragically bound to the starless midnight of racism and war that the bright daybreak of peace and brotherhood can never   50 become a reality.

I refuse to accept the cynical notion that nation after nation must spiral down a militaristic stairway into the hell of thermonuclear destruction. I believe that unarmed truth and unconditional love will have the final word in reality. This is why right temporarily defeated is   55 stronger than evil triumphant.

I believe that even amid today's mortar bursts and whining bullets, there is still hope for a brighter tomorrow. I believe that wounded justice, lying prostrate on the blood-flowing streets of our nations, can be lifted from this dust of shame to reign supreme among the children 60 of men.

I have the audacity to believe that people everywhere can have three meals a day for their bodies, education and culture for their minds, and dignity, equality and freedom for their spirits. I believe that what self-centered men have torn down men other-centered can build 65 up. I still believe that one day mankind will bow before the altars of God and be crowned triumphant over war and bloodshed, and nonviolent redemptive goodwill will proclaim the rule of the land, "And the lion and the lamb shall lie down together and every man shall sit under his own vine and fig tree and none shall be afraid." I still believe that we 70 shall overcome.

This faith can give us courage to face the uncertainties of the future. It will give our tired feet new strength as we continue our forward stride toward the city of freedom. When our days become dreary low-hovering clouds and our nights become darker than a thou- 75 sand midnights, we will know that we are living in the creative turmoil of a genuine civilization struggling to be born.

Today I come to Oslo as a trustee, inspired with renewed dedication to humanity. I accept this prize on behalf of all men who love peace and brotherhood. I say I come as a trustee, for in the depths of my heart 80 I am aware that this prize is much more than an honor to me personally.

Every time I take a flight I am always mindful of the many people who make a successful journey possible, the known pilots and the unknown ground crew.

So you honor the dedicated pilots of our struggle, who have sat at 85 the controls as the freedom movement soared into orbit. You honor, once again, Chief Albert Lithuli of South Africa, whose struggles with and for his people are still met with the most brutal expression of man's inhumanity to man.

You honor the ground crew without whose labor and sacrifices the 90 jetflights to freedom could never have left the earth. Most of these people will never make the headlines and their names will not appear in *Who's Who.* Yet the years have rolled past and when the blazing light of truth is focused on this marvelous age in which we live—men and women will know and children will be taught that we have a finer land, 95 a better people, a more noble civilization—because these humble children of God were willing to suffer for righteousness' sake.

I think Alfred Nobel would know what I mean when I say that I accept this award in the spirit of a curator of some precious heirloom which he holds in trust for its true owners—all those to whom beauty 100 is truth and truth beauty—and in whose eyes the beauty of genuine brotherhood and peace is more precious than diamonds or silver or gold.

Brendan Gill, "Misadventures in Verona"—from Brendan Gill, "Misadventures in Verona." Reprinted by permission. Copyright © 1977 The New Yorker Magazine, Inc.

Stephen Gould, "Left Holding the Bat"—first published in *Vanity Fair,* August 1983. Copyright © 1983 Stephen Jay Gould. Reprinted by permission of the author.

Donald T. Hall, "The Pervasive Set"—from *The Silent Language* by Edward T. Hall. Copyright © 1959 Edward T. Hall. Reprinted by permission of Doubleday & Company, Inc.

John E. Hankins, "Clues to Meaning"—from John E. Hankins, "Introduction" to William Shakespeare, *Romeo and Juliet,* edited by John E. Hankins, in "The Pelican Shakespeare," General Editor: Alfred Harbage (rev. ed.; New York: Penguin Books, 1970). Copyright © Penguin Books, Inc., 1960, 1970. Reprinted by permission of Penguin Books.

S. I. Hayakawa, "How Dictionaries Are Made"—from *Language in Thought and Action,* Fourth Edition by S. I. Hayakawa, copyright © 1978 by Harcourt Brace Jovanovich, Inc. Reprinted by permission of the publisher.

Ernest Hemingway, "The Flight of Refugees"—from Ernest Hemingway, *By-Line: Ernest Hemingway,* edited by William White. Copyright 1937, 1938 New York Times and North American Newspaper Alliance Inc.; copyright renewed. Reprinted by permission of Charles Scribner's Sons.

Fred Hiatt, "After Graduation, What Next?"—from Fred Hiatt, "Valediction to Complacency," first published in the *Boston Globe,* 1977. Reprinted by permission of the author.

Sir Edmund Hillary, "Epitaph to the Elusive Abominable Snowman"—first printed in *Life.* Copyright © 1961 Time, Inc. Reprinted by permission of the author.

Simon Hoggart, "The Prestige of PRAL"—from Simon Hoggart, "The Prestige of PRAL," *New Society,* 9th June 1983, copyright © *New Society,* London. Reprinted by permission.

Barbara Huttmann, "A Crime of Compassion."—Copyright 1983 by Newsweek, Inc. All rights reserved. Reprinted by permission.

Molly Ivins, "Why They Mourned for Elvis Presley"—copyright © 1977 by The New York Times Company. Reprinted by permission.

Jesse Jackson, "Challenge"—from Jesse Jackson, "Make a Decision," an address to the Eighth Annual Convention of Operation PUSH, July 12, 1979, Cleveland, Ohio. Reprinted by permission of the author.

Robert Jastrow, "Brains and Computers"—from Robert Jastrow, *The Enchanted Loom.* Copyright © 1981 by Reader's Library, Inc. Reprinted by permission of Simon & Schuster, Inc.

Carol Johmann, "Sex and the Split Brain"—OMNI, August 1983. Reprinted by permission.

E. J. Kahn, Jr. "The South Africans"—Selection is reprinted from *The Separated People, A Look at Contemporary South Africa,* by E. J. Kahn, Jr., by permission of W. W. Norton & Company, Inc. Copyright © 1966, 1968, by E. J. Kahn, Jr.

John F. Kennedy, "Inaugural Speech"—as quoted in *Kennedy* by Theodore C. Sorensen. Copyright © 1965 by Theodore C. Sorensen. Reprinted by permission of Harper & Row Publishers, Inc.

Richard M. Ketchum, "The Farmer—An Endangered Species." From *Second Cutting* by Richard M. Ketchum. Copyright © 1981 by Richard M. Ketchum. Reprinted by permission of Viking Penguin, Inc.

Martin Luther King, Jr., "The Decisive Arrest"—from pp. 43–44 in *Stride Toward Freedom* by Martin Luther King, Jr. Copyright © 1958 by Martin Luther King, Jr. Reprinted by permission of Harper & Row, Publishers, Inc. "The Nobel Prize Acceptance Speech." Reprinted by permission of Joan Daves. Copyright © 1964 by the Nobel Foundation.

Joseph Wood Krutch, "Killing for Sport"—from Joseph Wood Krutch, "If You Don't Mind My Saying So." Reprinted from *The American Scholar,* Vol. 25, No. 3, Summer 1956. Copyright © 1956 by the United Chapters of Phi Beta Kappa. By permission of the publishers.

Abba P. Lerner, "ACLU's Grievous Mistake"—copyright © 1978 by The New York Times Company. Reprinted by permission of The *New York Times* and the author.

M. M. Mahood, "Puns and Other Wordplay in Romeo and Juliet"—from M. M. Mahood, *Shakespeare's Wordplay.* Methuen & Co., Ltd., 1957. Reprinted by permission of the publishers.

Edwin McDowell, "When Is a Joke Not a Joke?"—printed as "Ethnic Jokebooks Flourish"—copyright © 1983 by The New York Times Company. Reprinted by permission.

Peter McGrath, "American Magazines and American Culture"—from Peter McGrath, "A Balkanized Business," *New Society,* 31st July 1980, copyright © *New Society,* London. Reprinted by permission.

H. L. Mencken, *"Le Contrat Social"*—from *Prejudices,* Third Series, by H. L. Mencken. Copyright 1922 by Alfred A. Knopf, Inc. and renewed 1954 by H. L. Mencken. Reprinted by permission of Alfred A. Knopf, Inc.

Ashley Montagu, "Parentage and Parenthood"—from Ashley Montagu, *The American Way of Life,* G. P. Putnam's Sons, Copyright © 1952, 1962, 1967 by Ashley Montagu.

Anne Moody, "The House"—from Anne Moody, *Coming of Age in Mississippi,* The Dial Press, Inc., New York, 1968. Copyright © 1968 by Anne Moody.

Lance Morrow, "Holding the Speaker Hostage" and "In Praise of Serious Hats"—copyright 1983 Time Inc. All rights reserved. Reprinted by permission from Time.

Negro History Bulletin, "The Meaning of 'Negro' "—Editorial, *Negro History Bulletin,* February 1971. Reprinted by permission of the Association for the Study of Afro-American Life and History, Inc.

Aryeh Neier, "Defending Free Speech for Those We Despise Most"—Editorial, *Civil Liberties,* November 1977. Reprinted by permission.

Enid Nemy, "Business Status—How Do You Rate"—copyright © 1980 by The New York Times Company.

New Society, "Social Control"—from "Social Control," *New Society,* 28th April 1983, copyright © New Society, London. Reprinted by permission.

The New Yorker, "The Bad and Worse Sides of Thanksgiving" and "Three Incidents"—from "The Talk of the Town," reprinted by permission; copyright © 1978, 1980, The New Yorker Magazine, Inc.

The *New York Times,* "Virtuous Sin" (Editorial)—copyright © 1977 by The New York Times Company. Reprinted by permission.

George Orwell, "A Hanging"—from *Shooting an Elephant and Other Essays* by George Orwell, copyright © 1945, 1946, 1949, 1950, by Sonia Brownell Orwell. Reprinted by permission of Harcourt Brace Jovanovich, Inc.

Louise Dickinson Rich, "Baking Beans"—from pp. 53, 113–114 in *We Took to the Woods* by Louise Dickinson Rich (J. B. Lippincott Company). Copyright © 1942 by Louise Dickinson Rich. Reprinted by permission of Harper & Row, Publishers, Inc.

Seymour St. John, "The Fifth Freedom"—in *Saturday Review,* October 10, 1955. Reprinted by permission of Saturday Review-World.

David Schoenbrun, "The Logical Cab Driver"—from David Schoenbrun, *As France Goes.* Copyright © 1957 by David Schoenbrun. Reprinted by permission of Harper & Row, Publishers, Inc.

Joan Smith, "One of Life's Simple Joys"—titled "Summer Time and the Livin' Is Easy" in the Bangor *Daily News,* 28 June 1983. Reprinted by permission.

Red Smith, "One-Man Show"—from "The Moving Finger Writes" by Red Smith. Copyright © 1977 by The New York Times Company. Reprinted by permission.

Theodore Sorensen, introductory note to President Kennedy's Inaugural Address. Abridged from pp. 240–248 in *Kennedy* by Theodore C. Sorensen. Copyright © 1965 by Theodore C. Sorensen. Reprinted by permission of Harper & Row, Publishers, Inc.

Walter Sullivan, "Cyclones"—copyright © 1977 by The New York Times Company. Reprinted by permission.

Lewis Thomas, "On Societies as Organisms"—from "The Lives of a Cell" by Lewis Thomas. Copyright © 1971 by Massachusetts Medical Society. Originally appeared in the *New England Journal of Medicine.* Reprinted by permission of Viking Penguin, Inc.

Frank Trippett, "A Red Light for Scofflaws"—Copyright 1983 Time Inc. All rights reserved. Reprinted by permission from *Time.*

Henri Troyat, "Tolstoy's Contradictions"—the *Literary Guild Magazine,* January 1968.

Lucian K. Truscott IV, "The Great Blue"—from "Two Fisherman" by Lucian K. Truscott IV, *Saturday Review,* November 25, 1972. Reprinted by permission of Saturday Review-World.

Maryon Tysoe, "And If We Hanged the Wrong Man"—from Maryon Tysoe, "And If We Hanged the Wrong Man?" *New Society,* 7th July 1983, Copyright © New Society, London. Reprinted by permission. "Do You Inherit Your Personality?"—from Maryon Tysoe, "Do You Inherit Your Personality?" *New Society,* 14th July 1983, copyright © New Society, London. Reprinted by permission.

Andrew Ward, "Yumbo"—copyright © 1978 by Andrew Ward. From the *Atlantic Monthly,* May 1977.

Webster's New World Dictionary, "Pleasure"—With permission. From *Webster's New World Dictionary,* Second College Edition. Copyright © 1982 by Simon & Schuster, Inc.

E. B. White, "Farewell My Lovely"—from "Farewell My Lovely" by Lee Strout White reprinted by permission; copyright © 1936, 1964 The New Yorker Magazine, Inc.

Samuel T. Williamson, "How to Write like a Social Scientist"—*Saturday Review,* 4 October 1947. Reprinted by permission of Saturday Review-World.

Virginia Woolf, "The Patron and the Crocus"—from *The Common Reader* by Virginia Woolf, copyright © 1925 by Harcourt Brace Jovanovich, Inc.; renewed 1953 by Leonard Woolf. Reprinted by permission of the publisher.

Richard Wright, "A Loaf of Bread and the Stars"—from pp. 201–204 in *Black Boy* by Richard Wright. Copyright © 1937, 1942, 1944, 1945 by Richard Wright. Reprinted by permission of Harper & Row, Publishers, Inc.

C. C. Wylie, "The Structure of a Comet"—from C. C. Wylie, Astronomy, Maps, and Weather, Harper & Row, Publishers, Inc., 1942.

William Zinsser, "Clutter"—from William Zinsser, *On Writing Well,* copyright © 1980 by William Zinsser. Reprinted by permission of the author. "Letter from Home"—copyright © 1977 by The New York Times Company. Reprinted by permission.

Thematic Table of Contents

This list gives only a few of the possibilities for grouping selections for similar or contrasting views on particular topics. Throughout the book cross-references suggest other groupings.

Varied Objects of Admiration or Love

Inner Conflicts

What Should Our Educational Goals Be?

Can Humor Make a Serious Point?

Note: Brief humorous touches, such as a little mild self-mockery or an amusing turn of phrase, lighten many other selections, for example, Schoenbrun's "The Logical Cab Driver" (3-D) and Thomas's "On Societies as Organisms" (5-B). Be on the lookout for them when you read.

How Do Our Minds Work?

How Independent Are Our Opinions?

Index

Asterisk (*) marks example with marginal notes
Dagger (†) marks rhetorical or logical term